T0360585

Economic Analyses Using the Overlapping Generations Model and General Equilibrium Growth Accounting for the Japanese Economy

Population, Agriculture and
Economic Development

Economic Analyses Using the Overlapping Generations Model and General Equilibrium Growth Accounting for the Japanese Economy

Population, Agriculture and Economic Development

Mitoshi Yamaguchi
Tomoko Kinugasa

World Scientific

NEW JERSEY • LONDON • SINGAPORE • BEIJING • SHANGHAI • HONG KONG • TAIPEI • CHENNAI

Published by

World Scientific Publishing Co. Pte. Ltd.

5 Toh Tuck Link, Singapore 596224

USA office: 27 Warren Street, Suite 401-402, Hackensack, NJ 07601

UK office: 57 Shelton Street, Covent Garden, London WC2H 9HE

Library of Congress Cataloging-in-Publication Data
Yamaguchi, Mitoshi, 1943–
  Economic analyses using the overlapping generations model and general equilibrium growth accounting for the Japanese economy : population, agriculture and economic development / Mitoshi Yamaguchi and Tomoko Kinugasa.
    pages cm
  Includes bibliographical references and index.
  ISBN 978-9814571487
  1. Economic development--Japan. 2. Endogenous growth (Economics) 3. Equilibrium (Economics) 4. Japan--Economic conditions--Econometric models. I. Kinugasa, Tomoko. II. Title.
  HC462.95.Y344 2014
  338.952--dc23

                                                                    2013050113

British Library Cataloguing-in-Publication Data
A catalogue record for this book is available from the British Library.

In-house Editor: Lum Pui Yee

Typeset by Stallion Press
Email: enquiries@stallionpress.com

Printed in Singapore

Preface

The relationships among population, agricultural technical change, and economic development are poorly understood. In this book, an attempt is made to see the interrelationships among these three items. In other words, this book contains novel and in-depth research regarding economic development. From both theoretical and empirical perspectives, we examine economic development in Japan in terms of population and agriculture. Using general equilibrium growth accounting and the overlapping generations model, we analyze the relationships between population, agriculture, and the economy. Our robust and unprecedented findings show the push-pull effects of technical change in agricultural and non-agricultural sectors; a quantitative demonstration of agricultural surplus labor and the positive effects of population on technical change and economic development; the effects of increased adult longevity on national savings; and the effects of demographic change on the industrial structure. This book consists of 10 chapters and mainly deals with economic development in Japan. The economic scenarios in Thailand, China, and Taiwan are addressed. We quantitatively analyze and graphically show economic development in Japan during its transition from a developing country to an advanced nation. The results are quite suggestive of the potential direction of other developing countries in the world.

The contents of this book are as follows: Chapter 1 — Basic Considerations in the Analysis of Economic Development, Chapter 2 — General Equilibrium Growth Accounting for the Japanese Economy, Chapter 3 — A Graphic Model of the Effects of Sectoral Technical Change, Chapter 4 — Factor Mobility and Surplus Labor in the Japanese Economy, Chapter 5 — Agricultural Surplus Labor and Growth Accounting for the Thai and Chinese Economies, Chapter 6 — Interrelationship between Population and Economy, Chapter 7 — A Consideration of the Positive Effects of Population, Chapter 8 — The Effects of Adult Longevity on the National

Saving Rate, Chapter 9 — Two Demographic Dividends, Saving and Economic Growth, and Chapter 10 — The Effect of Demographic Change on Industrial Structure.

This book is divided into two parts (1880–1970 and 1970–2010). The analyses in Chapters 2, 4, and 7 focus on the period 1880–1970. This is the period when the Japanese economy developed and became a matured economy. During the rapid economic growth after World War II, the real growth rate of per capita income was more than 10% (in the 1960s). However, the high growth rate stopped with the Food Shock of 1972 and the Oil Shock of 1973, which slowed the Japanese economy drastically and changed its trajectory completely. From the 1970s, the aging problem became an important issue. Chapters 8, 9, and 10 use the overlapping generations model to study the aging problem.

Then, we now highlight how our book stands out from existing publications and can be of value to readers. First, ordinary growth accounting (that is, partial equilibrium growth accounting) focuses on only one sector and does not consider the interrelationship between the agricultural and non-agricultural sectors. However, the growth accounting method employed in this book uses general equilibrium growth accounting to capture the interaction between the agricultural and non-agricultural sectors during economic development (Chapters 2, 3, 4, 5, and 7).

Second, we assess the factors influencing eight endogenous variables (per capita income, agricultural and non-agricultural outputs, agricultural and non-agricultural labors, agricultural and non-agricultural capitals, and relative price) in the process of transitioning from a developing to a developed country. This inquiry yields many suggestions and indications of the factors important for the economic development of the present developing countries (Chapters 2, 4, 5, and 7).

Third, further, because we consider the influence of each sector on the other, we can identify the asymmetrical effects of agricultural and non-agricultural technical changes (that is, agricultural technical change pushes the agricultural labor to the non-agricultural sector, but non-agricultural technical change pulls the agricultural labor to the non-agricultural sector). In addition, we show the numerical values for each 10-year period from 1880 to 1970 (we consider 1970 as the year when the Japanese economy finished its period of extremely high growth and matured). We gain useful insights into the important factors that affect the economic development of the present developing countries (Chapter 3).

Fourth, we measure the positive and negative numerical effects of population growth on economic development (that is, we showed the numerical amount of each 10-year period from 1880 to 1970). This inquiry also gives many suggestions and indications of the factors important for the economic development of the present developing countries (Chapter 7).

Fifth, we measure the increase or decrease in surplus labor in each 10-year period during the economic development of Japan (that is, from 1880 to 1970). We measure the impact of a decrease or increase in agricultural surplus labor on economic development of Japan (on eight endogenous variables). We also measure the impact of surplus labor on the economic development of China, Taiwan, and Thailand (Chapters 4 and 5).

Sixth, technical change, population, and agriculture are very important for economic development. Hence, we focus on these three items and show technical change, population, and agriculture in a systematic relationship. From this point of view, we provide each item's definition, characteristics and contribution, and empirical and theoretical background. In addition, the population and the economy interact with each other. Therefore, we observe the effect of population on the economy, the effect of the economy on population, and the interrelationship of the two variables. This analysis is very unique and of value for research in economic development (Chapters 1 and 6).

Seventh, adult longevity has received only modest attention from demographers, but we analyze in detail the effect of adult longevity on national savings. The overlapping generations model deals with the dynamic effects of adult longevity on the national savings rate in a small open economy and a closed economy. We analyze the effects of adult life expectancy on the national saving rate, using historical and empirical data. In the analysis, we establish an adult survival index that considers age-specific mortality. According to our results, gains in life expectancy are much more important than declines in child dependency. Population aging may not lead to lower saving rates in the future if life expectancy and the duration of retirement continue to increase. Our findings are significant for the research about a second demographic dividend, that is, the idea that longer adult longevity induces saving, capital accumulation, and economic growth (Chapter 8).

Eighth, we estimate the effects of the two demographic dividends on saving and economic growth. The first dividend derives from the fact that the share of the working-age population in the total population increases during the process of demographic transition. The second demographic dividend is related to an increase in adult longevity. As adult longevity increases, individuals tend to save more in order to prepare for old age. Higher savings induce an accumulation of wealth, which causes economic growth. Previous studies have not empirically analyzed the effects of two demographic dividends on the economy. In the analysis, we use the indices of two demographic dividends established by Mason [2005]. According to our empirical results, the first dividend seems to be less important than the second for saving and growth in Western and high-performing East Asian countries; this is not so for other countries (Chapter 9).

Ninth, it is novel that our research considers the effect of demographic change on industrial structure in terms of capital accumulation. Combining the overlapping generations model and general equilibrium growth accounting models and using Japanese data, we conduct simulation analysis. Our simulation results reveal that a rapid decline in the number of children and a rapid increase in adult longevity stimulated capital accumulation and increased the importance of non-agricultural constituents from the 1960s to the 1990s. Simulated capital growth not only increased non-agricultural output and capital more than it did the corresponding agricultural constituents, it also increased non-agricultural labor and decreased agricultural labor. In recent years, there has been a decrease in the working-age population, which comprises people whose savings are normally higher than that of the other generations, though the adult longevity in Japan has moderately increased. Hence, we cannot expect a rapid increase in aggregate capital in the future. Consequently, the advantages of the non-agricultural sector in Japan may disappear and agriculture may become increasingly important in the near future. Mitoshi Yamaguchi stresses that population aging will increase the importance of agriculture for a long time; our research clarifies this statement using, for the first time, economic models (Chapter 10).

This research is supported by JSPS KAKENHI Grant Numbers 20730181, 24310031 and 26292118. This research was assisted by a grant from the Abe Fellowship Program assisted by the Social Science Research Council and the American Council of Learned Societies in cooperation with funds provided by the Japan Foundation Center for Global Partnership. The authors are grateful to Professor Shigeyuki Hamori, Professor at the Kobe University and Professor Andrew Mason, Professor at the University of Hawaii for valuable comments. We also are grateful to Professors Chihiro Nakajima, Yoshihiro Maruyama, and Verrnon W. Ruttan. We are also grateful to Ms. Pui Yee Lum for her excellent editorial work.

By showing Keiseki (Mitoshi) Yamaguchi's work in Shodo (Japanese calligraphy) on the cover page, we wish to express the hope of a peaceful world. In 2011, Yamaguchi received the Asahi Newspaper Company's Award in Heian Shodo Tenrankai (Heian Japanese Calligraphy Association's Exhibition. This exhibition started 100 years ago, and is the oldest still-running Japanese calligraphy exhibition). Here, Heian means peace and calm, and we Japanese consider the period from 794 to 1183 in our history to be the Heian era. Keiseki is Mitoshi Yamaguchi's pseudonym in Shodo. We now state what the words on the cover mean: "When we look west in the direction of Lake Dòngtíng, we see that the Yangtze River is divided, and until the far south district, we cannot see any clouds. The sun has dropped and Changsha city is colored in autumn but we cannot know where Queen Xiang Jun (who married not the previous King's son but a wise and calm man who later became the King) are grieved."

Contents

About the Authors

Dr. Mitoshi YAMAGUCHI is an Emeritus Professor of Economics at Kobe University in Japan. He received his Ph.D. from University of Minnesota. He also received his Doctor of Economics from Kobe University. His research interests include the effects of technical change, population growth on economic development, econometric and theoretical analysis of economic development and aging problem. His works have been published in leading academic books, journals, including *Elsevier, American Journal of Agricultural Economics*. He also received the following four Economic Awards: Nikkei (Japanese Economic Newspaper) Economic Book Award, Japan Agricultural Economic Association Award, Japan Population Association Award, and The Best Paper Award of the World History Association.

Dr. Tomoko KINUGASA is an Associate Professor of Economics at Kobe University in Japan. She received her Ph.D. from University of Hawaii. Her research interests include the effects of demographic change on saving and economic development, determinants of technical change and efficiency of agriculture, and regional development by promoting agriculture. Her works have been published in leading academic journals, including *World Development* and *Journal of Asian Economics*.

Chapter 1

Basic Considerations in the Analysis
of Economic Development

Introduction

Considerable attention had been paid to the relationships between agriculture and population growth, since the time of Malthus; additionally, the "green revolution" and population growth was two prevalent research topics. Nonetheless, the relationships among technical change, population growth and economic development are poorly understood. This book attempts to construct a general equilibrium model (in order to obtain a general equilibrium growth accounting) that allows a simultaneous consideration of the effects of technical change on agricultural and non-agricultural sectors alike, and of population growth on economic development. This chapter first provides a brief overview of pre-World War II history as it relates to the Japanese economy. Second, it examines the theoretical considerations of agriculture, population and technical change. Third, it presents a critical review of the literature pertaining to Japanese agricultural and non-agricultural sectors.

1. Theoretical Considerations of Agriculture, Population and Technical Change

1.1. *Historical Growth Patterns in the Japanese Economy*

Figure 1-1 shows the annual growth rates of agricultural and non-agricultural outputs, inputs (the capital and labor in each sector), the relative price (agricultural price/non-agricultural price) and per capita income for the period 1880–1970. These are the endogenous variables in our model which has the matrix $Ax = b$ (see Chapter 2). The histogram in Fig. 1-1

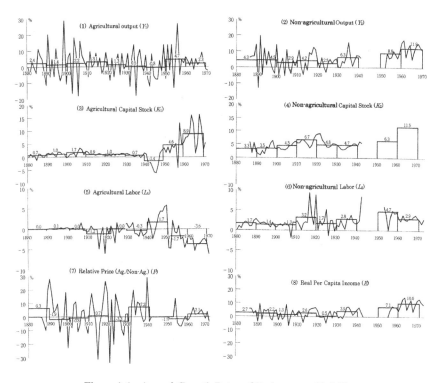

Figure 1-1   Annual Growth Rates of Endogenous Variables

also gives the historical average growth rate of each of the eight endogenous variables in each decade. For example, the value of the agricultural output in the 1880s shows 2.4. This means that real agricultural output grew at the rate of 2.4% between 1880 and 1890. Figure 1-1 also shows that the growth rate of per capita income (in real term) accelerated over time. This would indicate the phenomena of the trend acceleration of the Japanese economy, pointed out by Ohkawa and Rosovsky [1973] (see 3.2 in this chapter). Note that the trend acceleration is especially apparent after World War II. On the other hand, we find many numerous wave motions causing the long term wave motions in the moving average of the annual growth rate of each variable when we observe the annual growth rates for the variables.

Let us now consider the depression periods in the Japanese economy. Figure 1-1 shows that the growth rates of per capita income and non-agricultural output in the years 1890, 1898, 1900–1901, 1907–1908, the depression years, have zero or negative numerical values. However as a whole, Japanese economy experienced strong development until 1919. Economic difficulties came after the year 1920; Negative or zero growth rates of per capita income and non-agricultural output were experienced in the depression year of 1920, the Kanto earthquake of 1923, the monetary depression of 1927, the Great Depression of 1929, as Fig. 1-1 indicates. Especially after the heavy crops of rice harvested in 1930, which is indicated by a large positive growth rate of the agricultural output and a large negative growth rate of the relative price (agricultural price/non-agricultural price) in that year, there occurred an agricultural panic (stagnation) period which roughly corresponds to the period between the two World Wars.

If we compare the growth rates of each variable in the agricultural sector with those of the non-agricultural sector, the growth rates of output and inputs in the non-agricultural sector are much larger. Especially note that the growth rates of agricultural labor are zero or negative except during the depressions and between the two World War and become smaller after World War II, indicating the unequal development between agriculture and non-agriculture. The proportions of labor and capital employed in agriculture, and the share of income produced by agriculture which were 71, 43 and 50% respectively in 1880 decreased to 23, 7 and 6% respectively in 1965 (see Table 2-4 in Chapter 2. Also, this shows the agricultural and non-agricultural gap structure (Ohkawa–Rosovsky [1973]). For, agricultural labor's share in Japan was 23% in 1965, but it produced only 6% of total income).

Next observe the output growth in each sector. Among the variation in the output growth in each sector, the variation in the output of agriculture was very large in the beginning of the whole period (the period of Meiji era) and decreased trend-wise over time. This was due to the fact that agricultural technology was still in its infancy so that agricultural output was severely dependent on the weather and natural conditions. Note that the agricultural depression period which occurred in the 1930s rather than 1920s (the depression period of the Japanese economy as a whole) was characterized by very low growth rates of agricultural output and input. On the other hand, non-agricultural output shows a pattern similar to that of per capita income, and we can observe the trend acceleration (Ohkawa–Rosovsky [1973]) as a whole and the depression period in the 1920s similarly. The variation in the growth of non-agricultural output was fairly large in the beginning of the period. This stems from the fact that non-agricultural technology was still in a developing stage and was concentrated on fabrics, spinning and weaving which utilized the agricultural products as raw materials.

The agricultural sector shows a relatively smaller variation in the uses of factor inputs than the non-agricultural sector. However, agricultural labor decreased and agricultural capital increased (*i.e.*, capital was substituted for labor) in Japanese agriculture, especially after World War II. It is also seen that the uses of non-agricultural labor increased, and those of non-agricultural labor decreased and became negative in the depression periods and during the two World Wars. The relative price of agricultural output shows the largest variation owing to the low price elasticity of agricultural products and the large variation in variation of this agricultural output. However, the relative price decreased quite markedly after World War II, partly due to the agricultural price policy, the development of agricultural technology and the improvement of plant breeding. We can also observe in Fig. 1-1 that in the year of rice riot (1918) agricultural products had an extremely high relative price.

The annual and decadal growth rate of the five exogenous variables in our model are graphed in Fig. 1-2. These are population, land, total labor land and total capital. The growth rates of population and labor are around 1% and remain almost constant; note however that the growth rates of labor and population are different in the short run. Population has a relatively high growth rate in the periods between 1900–1930 but labor has a relatively high growth rate in the 1930s and the 1950s (this is related to the First Demographic Dividend. First Demographic Dividend means that the decrease of birth rate decreases the burden of children, and increases the production age's share. This contributes to the economic growth). Land increased until 1920 but decreased sharply in the 1940s and again after 1960. Population, labor and land increased at fairly constant rates of 1.2, 0.9 and 0.2% *etc.*, while total capital increased at much higher rates (about 5 or 6% on the average over the entire period). Especially, total capital stock increased extremely high after WWII as 11.3% in 1960–1970. This is the investment spurt (and export spurt) as Fujino [1965], Shinohara [1973] and Ohkawa–Rosovsky [1973] state (Sec. 3 of this chapter).

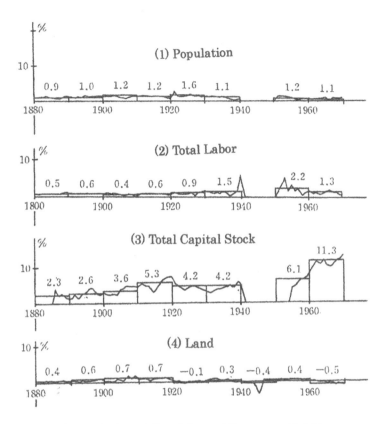

Figure 1-2   Annual Growth Rates of Exogeneous Variables

1.2. Theoretical Consideration of Agriculture

1.2.1 Definition of "agriculture"

This book focuses on population, technical change and agricultural and economic development; to that end, let us first describe the agricultural sector. "Agriculture" is defined as the order or system of objective human acts by which some organic living thing is economically obtained (Kashiwa [1962]). "Agriculture" is also an objective act that is developed as a means of life extension. Kashiwa shows that agriculture has developed in three stages. In the first stage, a pre-existing living thing is evaluated. In the second stage, work is undertaken on it, and in the third, a place is prepared for the production of the living thing. As such, agriculture is not an activity that takes place in a static world; rather, it occurs in a dynamic world and has a processive order (Table 1-1).

1.2.2 *Characteristics of agriculture*

We can list the many characteristics of agriculture and agricultural goods, which can be categorized in two ways: those on the demand side, and those on the supply or production side. Let us look at each of these in greater detail.

(1) Main characteristics of agricultural goods demand

(a) Small income elasticity: Almost all agricultural goods have small income elasticity values, as they constitute necessities of human life. If we look at Engel's law and the phenomenon of disproportional development between agriculture and non-agriculture, we can see that these phenomena derive from the small income elasticity of agricultural goods. (b) Small price elasticity: Almost all agricultural goods also have small price elasticity values. This creates instability of agricultural prices (see the large fluctuations of agricultural price in Fig. 1-3) and the strange phenomenon of poverty in the case of a good harvest.

(2) Characteristics of supply and production for agricultural goods

(a) Agriculture uses a great amount of land as an input. Therefore, it is easy to have a law of diminishing returns, given land limitations. (b) The production period and working process in agriculture necessarily adhere to the seasons, and they are restricted to a specific natural time. Therefore, it is impossible to rearrange the sequence of production time so as to promote simultaneous production. In other words, those who work in agriculture are compelled to follow the production process of the organic living thing (*e.g.*, plants, vegetables and livestock). Therefore, the demand for labor and agricultural machinery is seasonal, rather than constant. These factors and the law of diminishing returns have traditionally stated, in a straightforward manner, that large-scale production is unprofitable in agriculture. Most Japanese agricultural farms run on a small scale.

(c) The production of an agricultural good requires a considerable period of time. Usually, a period of several months or years is required to produce a long-term crop. Therefore, production very easily incurs climatic influences. As stated, agricultural prices fluctuate, largely owing to the low price

Table 1-1   Definition, Characteristics and Contribution of Agriculture

---

1. Definition of Agriculture:

Agriculture is defined as an order (or system) of human behavior with the objective of deriving an economically productive organic living. It is also objective behavior which is developed on the order of life extension.

2. Characteristics of Agriculture:

(1) Main characteristics of demand for agricultural goods: (a) Small income elasticity ($\because$ stomach size is finite)→Engel's law → The phenomenon of disproportional development between agriculture and non-agriculture. (b) Small price elasticity → Instability of agricultural prices and peculiar phenomena such as poverty during times of a good harvest.

(2) Characteristics of supply and production for agricultural goods: (a) Agriculture uses considerable land area as an input, but the limitation of land results in the law of diminishing returns. (b) The production period and working process in agriculture are restricted to a specific natural period → In agriculture, it is impossible to rearrange all sequences of production time to a simultaneous production (because of the organic living) as opposed to the industrial sector → The amount of demand for labor and capital changes from season to season. These factors and the law of diminishing returns mean that large-scale production is unprofitable in agriculture. For example, most of the Japanese farmers work on a small scale. (c) An agricultural good has a long lifecycle and is, hence, vulnerable to the changes of climate. As stated above, agricultural prices fluctuate largely owing to low price elasticity. In addition, as most agricultural goods are perishable, it is not easy to maintain their freshness. Therefore, the price elasticity of agricultural supply is also small. Owing to these supply and demand characteristics, the growth rate, and partial productivity of land, labor productivity, capital productivity, and total productivity in agriculture are lower than in non-agricultural sectors. Therefore, agricultural labor declines relatively and absolutely depending on the time. We can also observe the disproportional development between agriculture and industry.

3. Contribution of Agriculture to the Economy:

(a) Agriculture supplies food and raw materials. (b) Agriculture supplies the source of capital stock through land tax and other taxes which are absorbed from the agricultural sector. (c) Agriculture supplies labor to the non-agricultural sector. (d) Agriculture obtains foreign currencies. (e) Agriculture provides a domestic market for non-agricultural products. Recently, the following three contributions were evaluated in Japan. First is the contribution of agriculture to public wealth, given a large external economy connected with agriculture. Second is the contribution of agriculture in maintaining social balance. Agriculture is a basic industry in the rural areas of Japan→ Agriculture keeps people in rural areas and maintains a social balance between urban and rural areas. Third, is the contribution to the ethos of a community, society, and nation. Festivals, temples, and shrines have their origin in agriculture. These three contributions are especially important in the present world, judging from the prevalent environmental problem.

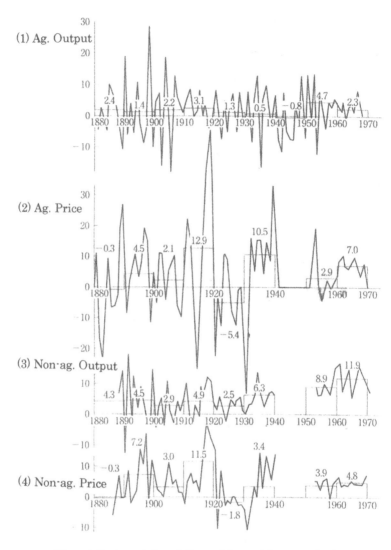

Figure 1-3   Annual Growth Rates of Sectoral Output and Price

elasticity of agricultural goods, and because so many agricultural goods are perishable. Even when it is possible to maintain the freshness of agricultural goods, it is never easy; as a result, the price elasticity of supply is also small with agricultural goods. Owing to these supply and demand aspects, the growth rate, partial productivity — such as land productivity, labor

Table 1-2   Definition, Characteristics and Contribution of Population

---

1. Definition of Population:
Population is defined as the total number of people who live in a certain place.

2. Characteristics of Population:
(a) Other than quantitative characteristics, population also has quality dimensions such as age, occupation, and gender. (b) Population shows a social, organic, and reproductive movement, and birth and death rates change the size and structure of population. (c) Population has a very gradual and long-term movement. For example, the gestation period for human beings is nine months, and the minimum age to enter the labor force is 15 years or more. (d) Population is closely related to the economy.

3. Contribution of Population to Production:
(1) Negative contribution of Population to the Economy: (a) Population could decrease per capita income (by definition), other things being equal. (b) Population could change the age structure and decrease the ratio of economically active members in the total population. Therefore, per capita income decreases. (c) Children increase the marginal utility of money and increase consumption. Therefore, household savings would decrease. (d) Per capita public service would decrease.

(2) Positive Contribution of Population to the Economy: (a) As labor is drawn from the population, it contributes to production. Moreover, several studies reveal that parents have a tendency to work harder when they have children. In addition, labor contributed by children is important in an agricultural society. (b) The benefits of economies of scale and division of labor appear when there is a large population. (c) Necessity is the mother of invention. (d) With a large population, diversity in knowledge and skill sets allow for the development of novel techniques in using resources. In case of a large population, the number of geniuses is also larger and contributes more to the economy.

(3) Contribution of Population to Consumption, Culture, Education, and Miscellaneous Fields: (a) Youths are more flexible and adapt to new occupations with more ease. This results in optimal allocation of labor. In addition, as they produce more than they consume, they save more. (b) Population growth and higher population density makes a positive contribution to the creation of infrastructure, such as roads, transportation, sanitation, and education. Overhead cost becomes relatively cheaper for a large population. A higher population growth rate leads to higher irrigation rates and higher investments in agricultural infrastructure as well.

---

productivity and capital productivity — and total productivity in agriculture are much smaller than those in non-agriculture. Therefore, the amount of agricultural labor declines relatively and absolutely, in a time-dependent manner. We also see a disproportionate development between agriculture and industry. (See the share of income produced by agriculture λ, the proportion of labor in agriculture l_1 and the proportion of capital in agriculture k_1, as seen later in Table 2-4 of Chapter 2; all these decrease over time.)

1.2.3 *Contribution of agriculture to the economy*

Most people would agree upon the various contributions that agriculture makes to the economy. First, agriculture supplies food and raw materials. Second, agriculture generates funds for capital accumulation, through land and other taxes that are absorbed from the agricultural sector. Third, agriculture supplies non-agricultural labor. Fourth, agriculture earns foreign currency through the export of agricultural products. Fifth, agriculture generates a domestic market for non-agricultural products. Most people would likely agree that the first role of agriculture is to supply the economy with food and raw materials. The demand for agricultural goods is influenced by the following two factors: the growth rate of the population, and the growth rate of income multiplied by income elasticity. As Jureen [1956] and Houthaker [1957] show, low-income countries have high income elasticity for agricultural goods; as a result, agricultural demand often exceeds the supply. "Population explosion" and "food crisis" was two well-known and well-used terms in the past.

In Japan, per capita agricultural output has increased steadily since the Meiji period. Although the contributions of raw materials to the Japanese economy may not be overly conspicuous, raw silk and tea are two typical examples that have allowed Japan access to foreign currency. Regarding the second contribution of agriculture, *i.e.*, capital accumulation, vast amounts of capital stock would be needed to drive the development of infrastructure, such as transportation, schools and roads. It is well known that the agricultural sector in Japan, through land taxes that it pays, contributes considerably in this respect. Indeed, both these taxes and land rent have played very important roles in Japan's economic development. These two factors, in addition to a high saving rate in the agricultural sector, have contributed considerably to capital accumulation in the Japanese economy.

The third contribution of the agricultural sector is its supply of labor force to the non-agricultural sector. At one time, there was a sizeable labor force in the Japanese agricultural sector, and so the Japanese economy experienced no shortage of labor for many years. The abundant labor supply from the agricultural sector, together with a traditionally low standard of living, lowered the wage rate and strengthened Japan's international competitive power. It also lowered the distribution share of laborers and raised the distribution share of capitalists, along with the saving rate. Furthermore, the agricultural sector has also funded the living and education fees of non-agricultural laborers migrating from the agricultural sector. It is widely admitted that unemployed laborers often returned to the agricultural sector when the economy becomes stagnant. In this way, the agricultural sector saved Japan's social security costs, and funds could be directed to other areas of the economy.

The other contributions are often considered smaller than the first three, but they have nonetheless been critical. The fourth contribution of agriculture has been to the acquisition of foreign currencies, through the export of surplus agricultural product. These foreign currencies enable the economy to buy many different kinds of raw materials. It is well known that the Japanese economy in the days of old obtained foreign currency through the export of raw silk and tea. The fifth contribution of agriculture has been its creation of a domestic market for non-agricultural products. This may not have been an extremely large contribution; however, the agricultural sector used to employ a large share of the population, especially during the early economic development of Japan (*i.e.*, during the Meiji period). Therefore, we cannot neglect this contribution. The agricultural population contributed by acting as buyers of not only fertilizer and agricultural machinery, but also, eventually, of cameras and cars.

Recently, three contributions of Japan's agriculture sector have become highly esteemed within the country. The first is its contribution to public wealth. Agriculture has large external economies, and many people in Japan recognize agriculture's function in this regard. The second is its contribution to social balance. Agriculture is a basic industry in rural areas of Japan, and helps keep people in rural areas; it therefore helps maintain a social balance between the urban and rural areas. The third is agriculture's cultural contributions. Festival, temples, shrines and the like have their origins in agriculture. These contributions are especially important in today's world, given the extent of today's environmental problems.

1.3. Theoretical Considerations of Population and Technical Change

1.3.1 Definition of "population"

Recently, the word "population" has been used not only with regard to humans, but also to cars, animals and other things. The English word "population" has Latin origins, and in that language, "population" connotes devastation, thus making a population increase highly undesirable. The words "population" (in English) and "bevőlkerung" (in German) in 17th and 18th centuries had another different meaning from that inferred today, referring instead to the increase in population itself. When this book speaks of "population", however, it is in reference to the total number of people who live in a certain place — or, it is defined as a group of humans restricted to a certain space. This is the definition widely used today (see Table 1-2).

1.3.2   *Characteristics of population*

We define "population" as the total number of people who live in a certain place; it therefore has a quantitative character, like a collective body. Second, besides its quantitative character, the population also has characteristics, such as age, gender, or occupation. Third, a population has the character of social, organic, and self-reproductive movement — in other words, a population always changes in terms of size and structure, as a result of births and deaths. Fourth, a population has the character of gradual and long-term movement: a birth, after all, requires several months of gestation. It also takes some time for the adaptive effect of a population to manifest. Fifth, a population has interrelationships with the economy: a population is influenced and regulated largely by the economy and society. Therefore, a population has a rather passive association with the economy; nonetheless, the association is a rather positive one. A population influences the economy and has repercussions that enlarge the life space. Therefore, population and economy have interrelationships with each other. We will describe this point in more detail.

Ryozaburo Minami [1963a, b; 1971] interprets Malthus's population principle as follows: population behaves like a living thing, in that it develops itself and improves its own mode of life. In other words, he considers population a living thing that has a principal power that supplants laws and rules. Minami notes that in the sixth edition of Malthus's book as follows. Malthus describes population as having the tendency to increase at a pace greater than that of subsistence materials. Therefore, he believes that Malthus pinpointed the dense relationships between the proliferate principal and the equilibrium principal. Malthusian theory can be summarized as follows: people cannot survive without food, and so the population is restricted by subsistence materials (first proposition). However, the human sex drive is so strong that it is easy for the population to exceed the available subsistence materials. In other words, the population has a persistent tendency to exceed its level of subsistence (*i.e.*, proliferate principal). The equilibrium between subsistence material and population is disturbed by the population's persistent tendency to exceed the level of subsistence; this reduces the living standard, and several kinds of misery appear.

At this point, the population undergoes a reversal and recovers equilibrium at a given subsistence level (*i.e.*, regulation principal). However, the equilibrium is recovered at a level higher than that seen at previous equilibrium points, thus resisting the pressure of population growth, which would otherwise force the members of the population into a lower standard of living. In other words, people try to enlarge the amount of subsistence material needed to support the increased numbers. Indeed, necessity is the mother of invention: subsistence materials would in some way increase, and this increase would cause the population to grow further, resulting in a net population that increases in size. Therefore, the population will increase whenever subsistence material increases, in the absence of any powerful and conspicuous check (second proposition) — that is, a forward movement of population occurs.

However, this forward movement again prepares for the next disturbance of equilibrium by virtue of the proliferate principal. Ryozaburo Minami [1963a, b; 1971] shows that Malthus considered these repeated forward and backward movements, *i.e.*, cyclical up and down movements. From this explanation, it is obvious that Malthus also considered aspects of the interrelationships between population and economic growth. In this way, population has two characteristic aspects. The first is the passive aspect of population, *i.e.*, a population is restricted by subsistence, and it increases as a function of the level of subsistence. The second is the aggressive aspect of population, *i.e.*, population has the power to create a new equilibrium by conquering inherent restrictions. Therefore, we can take two different views for the population: one is an optimistic view of population, and the other is a pessimistic one; we consider these views in Chapters 6 and 7, respectively.

1.3.3 *Contribution of population to the economy*

In terms of the positive and negative contributions of the population to the economy, it would be necessary to list labor's positive contribution and consumption's negative contribution. It is quite common today for the population to be considered to have a negative effect on the economy; such critics tend to note only negative consumption and distribution effects. It is true that, *ceteris paribus*, per capita income decreases as the population increases; population growth also changes the age structure and the ratio of the dependent population, and reduces per capita income. Furthermore, the marginal utility of money would increase, and time preferences would shift from the future to the present. As a result, consumption tends to increase, rather than saving. Per capita service — *i.e.*, that which is offered by public facilities — also decreases as the population increases. However, population growth would increase the demand for public goods and infrastructure.

Therefore, it is necessary to consider the positive contributions of the population. The first positive contribution is labor's contribution to output growth. Several empirical studies have shown that population growth would increase the total number of labor hours. Especially in developing countries, a mother with a newborn baby must reduce her number of labor hours for approximately two years, but the father of that child works harder in order to provide sustenance, and the total number of labor hours increases. It is also widely admitted that children's labor is very important in developing countries. Second, high population growth would increase competition and lead to a larger-scale economy; it also leads to a division of labor. As a third contribution, population growth would have a positive effect on infrastructure construction. High population growth would increase the population density and have a positive effect on the development of transportation, education and sanitation facilities.

A certain amount of overhead cost would be incurred for construction, and the per capita cost would decrease as the population increases. Some empirical findings show that population growth has a positive effect on irrigation and agricultural investment. In line with the proverb "Necessity is the mother of invention", some population pressures are needed to drive social progress. This would be the fourth contribution of population. Boserup [1965] says that population pressures would induce technological change; this relates, for example, to a large family that makes an effort to earn more income. Simon [1977] shows that it is often possible to produce an unbelievable increase in productivity during war time that would otherwise be almost impossible. Similarly, many firms undertake a considerably greater effort when they are facing difficult times.

As the population's fifth contribution to the economy, young people who occupy a large proportion of high population growth are sensitive to new products. They are vital and are highly adaptive to changes in society, and tend to take new and innovative occupations. They make efforts to change the economy and society, and accelerate modern economic growth. Young people also tend to have higher education levels and high saving rates, as well as high labor mobility; they also assist in resource allocation. The population's sixth contribution is in the accumulation of knowledge and the development of natural resources. As Kuznets [1960] points out, a large population group will contain many more intelligent people than a small population group, and these individuals will contribute more to society. It has been popular recently to list only some of the negative aspects of population growth; however, it is much more fair to evaluate also some of the positive aspects of population.

1.3.4 Definition of "technical change"

A "technique" is defined as a way of human behavior that is thought about and constructed; Kashiwa [1962] shows that a technique relates to human behavior. Of course, a technique is not a human behavior in itself, but a way of human behavior. A technique derives from a creative conception: a spider's web and a beehive are made very skillfully, but we cannot consider them techniques. Spider and bee behavior is not a behavior that is thought about and constructed, but rather something that is driven by instinct and scarcely changes. As per the definition, any technical change would derive from progression in the technique itself (see Table 1-3).

1.3.5 Characteristics of technical change

The first characteristics of technical change are that they shift the production function and increase the supply of goods. In most cases, this shift brings about improvements in quality and brand-making, which in turn ordinarily brings about increases in income. However, this chain of events depends upon the income elasticity of demand. In the case of agricultural goods — which have low income elasticity values — farmers can actually obtain lower revenues from a good harvest. This derives from the fact that demand will not increase to the same degree as the prices of agricultural goods decrease (because of the good harvest). A second characteristic of technical

Table 1-3   Definition, Characteristics and Contribution of Technical Change

---

1. Definition of Technical Change:

Technique is defined as the process or behavior to reach a purpose. Therefore, technical change is defined as the progress of the technique defined earlier.

2. Characteristics of Technical Change:

(a) Technical change shifts the production function and increases the supply of products. In several cases, technical change produces quality improvement, which creates a brand. In most cases, technical change increases the supplier's revenue. However, agricultural revenue decreases when agricultural technical change is produced given low price elasticities (*e.g.*, poverty during times of a good harvest). (b) Technical change decreases the number and type of inputs necessary to produce a certain quantity of products. In the case of a labor-saving technical change, the requirement of labor would decrease, possibly resulting in unemployment. (c) It takes about 20 or 30 years for an invention to be transformed into an innovation. In addition, time is required for extension. Therefore, people who adopt the invention first have an opportunity of making large profits. This then, opens up possibilities of enlarging income differences.

3. Contribution of Technical Change to the Economy:

(a) Technical change contributes to increases in supply. Therefore, it has the possibility to increase private income and exports. This makes a positive contribution to the economy. (b) Although technical change may produce large unemployment, it also presents possibilities to contribute positively by using unemployed labor in a more productive industry. (c) Technical change produces new products of a better quality and at cheap prices. Hence, it has the ability to create brands. Therefore, it gives the merits of employment to consumers. All of the above provide benefits to consumers.

---

change is that it reduces the input needed to produce a certain amount of product. Therefore, there is the possibility of sustaining an unemployment problem, especially in cases involving labor-saving technology. Everybody knows that automation has always fed fears concerning unemployment. A third characteristic is that there is a lag from the time of invention to when it is actually used — usually 10–20 years. Diffusion expands very slowly and takes time. People who adopted pertinent skills in an innovation's nascent stages will realize the bulk of the profits derived from that innovation's use; thus, there is the possibility of an income distribution problem.

1.3.6 *Contribution of technical change to the economy*

It is obvious that technical changes make enormous contributions to an economy. First, technical changes increase the supply of goods; therefore, they usually increase personal income, increase exports and contribute to the economy. Second, labor productivity would increase by virtue of using unemployed labor in sectors boasting higher levels of productivity. As with Japan and Taiwan, technical changes that reduce otherwise heavy demands for labor in the agricultural peak season — so that labor is instead used in areas that need it all year round — will increase the demand for agricultural labor. As a third contribution, technical changes bestow benefits upon the consumer by creating new products and brand products, and by lowering the prices of goods. There are many other contributions; however, technical change constitutes a very strong engine of the economy, and from it consumers and producers alike can derive benefits.

Summary and Conclusion

In this chapter, we addressed several theoretical studies that provide a general outline of Japanese economic development, agriculture, and technical change. These studies are not mere reviews; they must be considered together with those studies addressed in the following chapters. For example, the low income and price elasticities of agricultural products, and other characteristics have a strong influence on growth rate multipliers (*i.e.*, the impact of exogenous variables [*e.g.*, the growth rate of population] on endogenous variables [*e.g.*, the growth rate of per capita income]; see Chapter 2) and the estimated contribution values. We will summarize the content in terms of several points, as follows.

(1) In the Japanese economy, the growth rates of per capita income, agricultural output and non-agricultural output (all of which are measured in real terms) were 3.8, 2.0 and 5.7%, respectively, for the 1880–1970 period. For input, the growth rate of capital stock was high (5%); the growth rates of population and labor were each around 1%, but with a sharp contrast between agricultural labor (−0.6%) and non-agricultural labor (2.1%). The amount of agricultural land decreased substantially after World War II — and especially so, after 1960 — resulting in a reduction in land relative to 1920. Relative to the price of non-agricultural product, that of agricultural product has risen slightly more (0.4%), but varies very much over time. These figures point to a disparity in growth between agriculture and non-agriculture. Agricultural growth varied substantially in the Meiji period; however, the variation decreased markedly on account of technical changes

and improvements in plant-breeding and the like. Non-agricultural outputs also varied much during the Meiji period, but agricultural/non-agricultural relative price varied most, owing to the low price elasticity of agricultural product. Nonetheless, variation in the relative prices decreased greatly after World War II, as a result not only of the aforementioned technical changes and plant-breeding, but also because of changes in agricultural price policy.

(2) In this chapter, we outlined terminological definitions, as well as the characteristics and contributions of agriculture; this chapter also touched upon population and technical change. We adopted Kashiwa's definition of "agriculture" as an order or system of objective acts by humans in order to obtain some organic living things economically. However, Kashiwa's theory of agriculture rather stresses only the production side of things, although he does use the term in an economics sense in his definition. We think it necessary to consider the interrelationships between agriculture and the economy, even if we focus entirely on agriculture; for this reason, we consider not only the production (supply) side, but also the demand side. It would be impossible to explain the disparity in development between agriculture and non-agriculture — not to mention the fluctuation in relative price — if we were to omit considerations of the demand side. This tack is consistent with the research outlined in Chapters 2–7. In Chapter 2, we discuss general equilibrium growth accounting that contains ordinary growth accounting, as a special case of our general growth accounting. There, we show that it is necessary to consider not only the supply side, but also the demand and non-agricultural sides, even if we make growth accounting for agriculture. This approach is consistent with the aforementioned attitude.

(3) In this chapter, we discussed the five contributions that agriculture makes to an economy. In the next chapter, we discuss four theories of agricultural and economic development — especially, three theories that relate very closely to agriculture (*i.e.*, classic theory, stage theory and dualism). To consider Hayami and Ruttan's [1971] contribution of induced innovation, we incorporate into our macro model parameter values. For the 1880–1970 period, we changed the parameter values at five-year intervals and undertook growth accounting analysis at 10-year intervals (see Chapter 2).

(4) We found that a population has five characteristics, and that population and the economy have interrelationships (see Chapter 6). This finding derives from a consideration of Ryozaburo Minami's interpretation

of Malthus (Ryozaburo Minami [1963a, b; 1971]); related results of econometric analysis are shown in Chapter 6. We also consider, in Chapter 7, the more positive aspects of population growth.

(5) In this chapter, we defined "technical change", and outlined both its characteristics and its contributions to the economy. With respect to technical change and how it relates to the population, there is a duality of thought: one mode of thought is optimistic, while the other is more pessimistic. If the population is highly educated and is able to produce technical changes, it will be easy for the people to be more optimistic; on the other hand, the population has a relatively low level of education and does not produce technical changes, then it is more likely that the people therein will be pessimistic. In other words, technical change and the population can be seen as having a "tug of war", and outcomes of economic development will depend on the result of that "tug of war". In Chapter 7, we consider this point and devote some space to analysis.

2. Brief Overview of Pre-World War II History in Japanese Economy

In Chapter 2, we show a growth accounting for the Japanese economy that uses a general equilibrium growth accounting method. We unearthed several facts by embracing this methodology. Many people know of Japan's post-World War II history; not as many know of its pre-World War II history. We therefore provide a brief overview of that prewar history with respect to the Japanese economy, and provide a critical analysis of that country's agricultural and non-agricultural sectors. This analysis supplements and confirms the importance of the measurements outlined in subsequent chapters. We provide some critical analyses and comments for the work of Hayami [1973] with respect to the agricultural sector, and we also review some of the literature pertaining to the non-agricultural sector.

2.1. *Agricultural Development*

According to Kashiwa [1960], we can classify pre-World War II Japanese agricultural development under capitalism into three distinct periods. The first period is that of agricultural development at the beginning of Japanese capitalism. The second one is that during which Japanese capitalism prospered. The third one is a period of stagnation in Japanese capitalism. In the first period (from the beginning of the Meiji period in 1868 to the Russo–Japanese War in 1904), free movement with regard to residence, the free selection of occupation, and free land-owning were allowed. The authentication of land-owning, a land-certificate system for taxation and a registration system were all introduced; a perfect ownership system like that seen in Roman law was also established. A regulation for the land-tax revision was promulgated in 1873, and the land tax of a certain percentage of the land's price could be paid in cash. However, not all land was held by landlords, and it was not common to find many non-cultivating landlords who did not work on the farm.

However, the period of Matsukata deflation (from 1881) following inflation inflicted by the Seinan War (1877) had a strong economic influence on Japan's rural areas. An agricultural crisis occurred, wherein an estimated one-eighth of the land that had been mortgaged went into foreclosure. Commercial capitalists — e.g., fertilizer merchants and rice merchants — became prototypes of non-cultivating landlords who did not work on their own farm land, but nonetheless had an interest in land investments, as they earned profits from tenants' rice. (Land tax was paid at the rate of 3% [in 1874] or 2.5% [in 1878] of the land price, but the rent was free, and paid mostly in kind, and so the landlords realized high profits when rice prices were high.) These non-cultivating landlords did not contribute very much to agricultural development, but the change in land-owning made a remarkably large contribution. Self-sustaining landlords who still held a large percentage of the land had a dominant role in Japan's agricultural development.

In the 1877–1881 period, when the price of rice increased, the demand for agricultural products — and especially demand for rice — also increased, but the influence of neither the Japanese colony nor foreign agriculture was large. The high price of rice increased land revenues and induced a desire to clear wild land and to undertake landfill and drainage-based land reclamation efforts. As a result, Japan's total arable land area increased. The use of fertilizer increased, and fertilization methods improved; plant-breeding methods were also improved. These improvements increased both productivity and land-rent amounts; farm rents also increased. In this way, it is easy to see how agricultural productivity had been strongly influenced by cultivating landlords.

Typical agricultural policy of the Meiji period is demonstrated in the Kougyo-Iken (Opinion of Industrial Enterprise) of 1884, which promotes the development of various industries. Through it, various agricultural crops, farm tools and livestock were introduced and improved upon, as were the management methods later seen in the western prefectures. That policy also facilitated the creation of some agricultural experiment stations, model filature factories, and the Sapporo and Komaba agricultural schools. Kougyo-Iken had two purposes: to reform the aggravated state of public finance in the Matsukata deflation period, and to promote the development of various industries. That policy encouraged the pursuit of economic benefits and improvements in agricultural production methods. An industrial exhibition was held to promote the development of agriculture and other industries, country fairs, and itinerant teachers, in order to promote wider experiences and competitive minds among those involved. Farmers whose leaders were landlords also held a number of *Nodankai* (agricultural conversation meetings), through which information on technical changes could be exchanged, among other things. Finally, the *Dai-Nihon-Noukai* (Great Japanese Agricultural Association) meeting was held. This agricultural association system was organized and, as a result, farmers' organizational power became much stronger. In 1892, an agricultural association was organized systematically in Kyoto; these farmers' organization helped advance the government's efforts to promote the development of agriculture.

In the second period (from around 1905 to 1930), a big change occurred. Industrial development became conspicuous, and the shares of imported raw materials and exported homemade products increased. However, rice prices were kept low by the pressures of imported rice. Therefore, it was necessary to institute a protective tariff that kept the rice price at a certain level. Although the agricultural sector had very much developed, it had not sufficiently developed so as to keep pace with industrial development. The increased size of the rice sector was not an indication of the advantages of rice production, but rather the difficulties inherent in rice production. At the same time, the Japanese cotton and mulberry industries suffered a great blow from cheap imported products, and a great amount of agricultural labor flowed out from the agricultural sector. Nonetheless, the outflow of elder sons in rural exoduses of small landed peasants and tenant farmers were still very rare. Although the rice price was strongly depressed, the demand for agricultural land was still large, and the difficulties that agricultural economies were experiencing were becoming increasingly clear. Farm rents did not decrease, and landlords were starting to rent out their lands as much as possible.

Even small landowners with only 1–2 ha each became land-renters. However, these non-cultivating landlords allowed reductions in or even exemptions from farm rent in the case of natural disasters; therefore, they bore all the risk. They also had an entrepreneurial function in commercializing the harvested rice. For these reasons, the extension of land use and the development of agricultural production became stagnant, and the landlords' interests gradually shifted so as to more closely align with an open market. In 1900, the Industrial Association Law was established; it was closely related to the operation of an enterprise and business. This law played an important role in the operation of agricultural businesses (*e.g.*, finance without security) among small and medium landlords. In 1906, imported rice was levied a duty, with the intention of protecting landlords in Japan.

In these circumstances, many landlords became *Futokorote Jinushi* (non-farming landlords, or breast hand landowners), and agriculture itself also changed significantly. The sericulture industry also developed greatly, starting at around 1905. Quotations for cocoon from the sericulture industry fluctuated remarkably and forced farmers to adopt entrepreneurial minds and spirits. The sericulture industry demanded very intensive agricultural methods, the use of great volumes of fertilizers, and highly intensive fertilizer and cultivation management. Pomiculture and horticulture also developed conspicuously. Rice-planting also proliferated and developed rapidly in colder areas — *e.g.*, the Hokuriku and Tohoku districts — in clear contrast to the sericulture of the western and southern districts. The area under rice cultivation increased, and the cultivation technique was also developed further. Fertilization came to depend on soybean residuum (from fish fertilizer) that was imported cheaply and in large volumes from China.

The third period started with the agricultural depression period of the 1930s; however, we would like first to review development up to the 1930s. During World War I, the Japanese economy developed conspicuously, and the increased purchasing power of the Japanese economy increased the prices of agricultural products. The price of rice increased between 1916 and 1919; in 1918, price increases caused a Kome-Sodo (rice riot). However, after 1920, not only agricultural prices but also non-agricultural prices and the general price level fell to one-half of the previous levels. The lifting of the gold embargo, together with the occurrence of the world depression and the extremely good harvest year of rice in 1930 finally led to an agricultural panic recession period. The *Sanmai Zoushoku Keikaku* (Rice Production Development Program) in Taiwan and South Korea started to press the demand for Japanese domestic rice.

The expenditures of Japanese farmers remained almost the same throughout this period, even though agricultural incomes had decreased; therefore, the taxation burden increased. Several kinds of public works appeared in the prosperous days following World War I, and heavy taxation and donations were taken from small and medium landlords. Around 1930, labor migrated in a backward direction, *i.e.*, labor flowed from non-agricultural sectors and to the agricultural sector. Many tenancy troubles also arose from around 1917 and increased remarkably after 1920. In 1922, the first nationwide farmers associations — *e.g.*, *Nihon Nomin Kumiai* (Japanese Farmers' Association) and Nihon Nomin Soudoumei (Japanese Federation of Farmers Union) — were organized. Through these venues, tenants made their requests collectively and permanently (rather than personally and temporarily). Generally speaking, farm rents also decreased slightly. These circumstances greatly affected the existing landlord system. Farming areas showed tense and straitened circumstances.

Given these circumstances, it is not unusual to see the insolvency and the exchange of landholding that occurred in the rural areas. Some landlords ceased to work as farmers, dropping on the social-class ladder to become tenants. Even those who survived these situations made an effort to become landowner farmers; they demanded a return to their rented lands, rather than become renting-out farmers. Problems with tenancy also changed, fostering a new and more serious situation. From around 1928, the small and medium landlords tried to withdraw their rented-out lands in order to resolve their difficulties in earning a livelihood. The scale of the problem became smaller, although the number of tenancy problems had increased. The enactment of a tenancy bill became a large issue, and tenant farming was meant to protect the livelihoods of tenants. The Industrial Association, which worked closely with the landlords, passed away with the fall of the landlords.

This passage of events owed to the fact that neither business nor management thrived while the economy was depressed. Additionally, the Industrial Association was an association of unlimited liability and unsecured credit, and small and medium landlords had grown indebted to it; the Industrial Association had to close operations, simply because so many landlords had bolted without paying their debts. Therefore, both agricultural activity and productivity became rather stagnant during this period. In terms of hectares, the total arable land area reached a maximum of about 6.09 million ha in 1922; additionally, land productivity and total output became rather stagnant in this period. To mitigate a further fall in agricultural production and land productivity — and to promote efficiency in farm management — they introduced three new directions: the introduction of agricultural machinery and tools, the introduction of group works, and the growth in the scale of agricultural management.

First, the most prevalently used weeder changed from the traditional *gantsume* (trimming rake; literally "duck's nail") to the *tauchikuruma* (tilling machine); similarly, a rotary treadle threshing machine supplanted the *Sennba Inakoki* (thousand-tooth threshing machine). The oil engine and electric motor also gradually prevailed, increasing the efficiencies of threshing, hull removal, rice-refining, and milling; a great amount of labor that would otherwise have been needed in these processes were saved. Second, a group work recommended by the agricultural and commerce ministry became popular and helped improve labor efficiency. Third, growth in the scale of agricultural management was recommended, and it eventually increased — albeit extremely slowly and gradually. Although many efforts were made, both agricultural production and land productivity in Japan became stagnant.

Also, the Japanese government bestowed important roles upon certain agricultural policies, such as agricultural price policy and policy to increase the number of owner farmers; the most noteworthy agricultural price policy would be the stabilization policy for the price of rice. The Rice Law of April 1922 made it possible to buy, sell, exchange, process, and store rice to adjust the market situation. At first, quantity adjustments were made and the function of price adjustments was added in 1925. In 1933, the function was further strengthened and the criteria for selling and buying rice were set. The government set the maximum and minimum prices of rice and tried to sell or buy when the price was over the maximum or below the minimum price. The maximum price was set based on trends regarding price and the rice production cost.

The rice price control ordinance was established in 1933, allowing the free buying and selling of rice and facilitating price adjustments of rice, thus reducing rice price fluctuations. Figure 1-2 shows how agricultural prices — especially the price of rice — became more stable. A stability policy with regards to silk yarn was also crafted. Much fighting occurred between landlords and tenants during this period; therefore, one of the more remarkable policies instituted in this period was one by which the category of landed farmer was created and maintained. In 1920, an investigation commission for the tenant system was established; a board of investigation for the tenant system was organized and ultimately looked into tenant legislation. This landed farmer policy became very strong during this period.

2.2. *Non-agricultural Development*

K. Yamaguchi [1976] classifies the whole of prewar Japanese history into three distinct periods. The first period is called the creation period of Japanese capitalism, from the beginning of the Meiji period (1868) to 1885. The second period is called the development period of Japanese capitalism, from 1885 to around 1920. The third period is marked by the appearance of contradictory Japanese capitalism, from around 1920 to the end of World War II (1945). In the first period (1868–1885), a concentrated bureaucratic government system was established that considered the Japanese Emperor the top position in the land. To strengthen its modern military, the French army system and the English navy system were adopted; military transportation and communication systems were also established. Railroad, telegraph, telephone, and modern marine transportation infrastructure were supported by the Japanese government during this period.

The financial backing for these changes came from the *Hanseki-houkan* (the return of the land and people from the feudal lords to the emperor), *Haihan-chiken* (the establishment of prefectures in place of feudal domains, or the abolition of clans and the establishment of prefectures), and land tax reform (changes from in-kind to cash payments). Many feudal social and economic reforms — such as the abolition of a rank system, and the abolition of restrictions on commercial transportation, were instituted. Additionally, agricultural reforms — *e.g.*, *Chitsuroku-syobun* (hereditary stipend disposal, or disposal of *Chitsuroku*), land tax reform, and *Denbata-katte-saku* (free cultivation of fields) — were enacted. In embracing a modern industrial economic system and a systematic monetary system, the features of the banking system and modern communication and traffic systems became more evident, inducing the use of modern production styles. Foreign trade also increased, with silk yarn, tea, and aquatic products being exported, and woven cotton and wool, cotton thread, sugar, and iron being imported. During these periods, approximately 80–90% of all silk yarn and tea produced were ultimately exported.

The import of goods also increased. Japan's dependency on imports became large over time, and ultimately destroyed the domestic sugar and cotton industries. In Japan, the means of cotton-weaving and of cotton yarn and iron production were modernized. Fears of foreign capital invasion increased, and so the government prohibited foreigners from traveling in Japan without permission; the mining rights of foreigners and the infiltration of foreign capital were also prohibited. The Japanese government also prohibited feudal regulations, and a great amount of money was spent in transplanting modern systems and nurturing their growth. A great amount of funds used to cover expenditures was supplied by land tax reforms, borrowed money, money raised through the issuance of public bonds, and paper money issued by the government. However, this system did not work well, and eventually ruptured around 1878. At that point, a modern conversion system was established.

The liquidation of paper money and the disposal of government mining and government factories had important implications for the development of modern industry in Japan. In other words, the government's budget became very tight, because of the drop in value of paper money — owing in turn to its increased issuance — and because of increases in general price levels; therefore, the Japanese government disposed of its mining and factory facilities, albeit at prices lower than those at which they had been acquired. About 60% of Japan's industries in 1885 were involved in spinning or weaving; the percentages of heavy industries such as iron, shipbuilding, and machinery production were still very small. The silk-reeling industry represented an overwhelming share (about 90%) of all textile industries (*i.e.*, silk-reeling, and spinning and weaving [*e.g.*, textile and cotton-yarn spinning]) at that time; the textile and cotton-yarn spinning industries followed the scale of the silk-reeling industry. Especially, raw silk was adopted as the thread of choice among machine operators in Italy and French, and so that industry developed very rapidly.

Modern communication, business trade, and monetary banking also developed in Japan. Railroads had been originally operated by the government, but more private railroads were constructed in this period. The Japanese Railroad Company was established, and both the Tokyo–Aomori line and *Tohoku-sen* (Tohoku line) were created in 1891. In terms of national railroads, the Tokyo–Kobe Tokaido line was constructed in 1889. Modern shipping businesses also developed, and the Kyodo–Unyu Corporation — which was partially supported by the government — and the Mitsubishi Corporation competed with each other. However, in 1885, these two companies merged to form the Nihon–Yusen Corporation. This Nihon–Yusen Corporation and the Osaka Merchant Ship Corporation then went on to compete and develop together. As for communications, postal regulations were published in 1882, and the principle of "one price in any place" was practiced; provisions for *Yubin Kawase* (postal money order) and postal deposits were also made. The Bureau of Telegraph was established and initiated the use of a telegraph system in 1881; the telephone system was adopted in 1877. A national market of business trade was constructed at the end of the Meiji period; at this time, steamships started to carry goods to major ports, in preference to sailing ships carrying goods into local ports nationwide — the *modus operandi* (method of operation) that had prevailed previous to this period.

Inside the Japanese market, the use of carts was initiated after roads and railroads were constructed. Goods-based transactions increased in number, and many of them involved the use of credit. Business organizations were also developed. Foreign trade — such as that in the export of raw silk, tea, cotton fabrics, wool fabrics, and cotton yarn — increased. Three ports in Osaka, Kobe, and Niigata were constructed and added to the three existing ports of Yokohama, Nagasaki, and Hakodate. In the concession settlements of the new ports, many foreign dealers engaged in foreign trade. However, the Mitsui–Bussan Company, for example, could engage in the export and import of goods, without taking any foreigner's route. Many national banks were established following amendments to the National Bank Treaty (1876) and the publication of *Kinroku Kousai* (Kinroku salary public loan). In 1882, the government quit making use of national bank paper money, and the Bank of Japan was established. Some ordinary banks were also established after the birth of the Mitsui Bank in 1876; however, at that time, that bank was always in an overdraft situation (*i.e.*, loans to industry exceeded private savings).

In the second period (1885–1920), Japanese capitalism developed very rapidly; its development became very clear following the Sino–Japanese War (1894), the Russo–Japanese War (1904), and World War I (1914–1918). Although there were some crisis years — such as 1890, 1897–1898, 1900–1901, and 1907–1908 — Japanese capitalism as a whole developed very rapidly within this period. However, at the end of this period (1920), there was a great recession called Hando-kyoko (reactionary recession). In this second period, modern firms were established, and they then amalgamated in order to create some larger firms. The share of the spinning and weaving industry was still largest among Japan's manufacturing industries at that time (*i.e.*, 40–50%). Especially, the textile, cotton-yarn spinning and weaving, and silk-reeling industries were three particularly important ones. Many modern industries developed to a great extent, especially as the modern transportation and communication industries, trade, and Japan's monetary and financial systems developed.

More and more firms were amalgamating within the cotton-yarn spinning, mining, wool manufacturing, pulp, artificial fertilizer, and financial industries, creating some very large firms during this period. Especially, the amalgamation of cotton-yarn spinning firms was obvious, with Toyo-bo, Dainihon-bo, and Kanebuchi-bo accounting for about 50% of that industry; their individual shares were 18.6, 15.9, and 15.2%, respectively. In the wool manufacturing industry, Nihon-keori and Tokyo-keori occupied large shares; in mining, similarly, Mitsui-kozan and Mitsubishi-goushi-kougyoubu took a 34% share of the coal industry. Ashio, Besshi, Kosaka, Hitachi, and Saganoseki took a 60% share of the copper industry in 1917, and Nihon-sekiyu and Hoden-sekiyu together accounted for about 80% of the mining industry's oil business. Ohji, Fuji, Karahuto, and Osaka-iou were dominant firms. Tokyo-jinzo eventually took over Osaka-iou and had a ruling position in the artificial fertilizer industry.

Banks, too, were amalgamating at this time, and large banks such as Daiich, Mitsui, Mitsubishi, Sumitomo, and Yasuda were acquiring a great amount of power. The occurrence of *Zaibatsu* (financial mergers) became fairly prevalent in this period, and these Zaibatsu could be classified into three types. The first were aggregate Zaibatsu, which had power in the fields of mining, banking, and business; Mitsui, Mitsubishi, and Sumitomo were typical representatives of this type. The second type could be terms monetary Zaibatsu, and they had power in the field of banking; Yasuda is typical of this type. The third type could be called industrial Zaibatsu. In 1899, the gold standard was adopted completely in Japan, and foreign bonds were published as a result of success in the treaty revision process; at that point, in 1901, Japan imported foreign capital that bore low interest rates. This was a great change, as the Japanese government had previously adopted a stance that prohibited the import of foreign capital.

In September 1901, foreigners were allowed to own land in Japan and to hold mining rights; the government discussed opening itself to the import of foreign capital. The cost of the Russo–Japanese War was covered by foreign loans. As long-term debts, foreign bonds, local government debts, foreign corporate bonds, and foreign-borrowed money bonds were introduced, even after the war; many short-term debt instruments were also used. These changes came about as a result of three factors. First, Japanese capitalism had developed sufficiently, so as not to bear disadvantages. Second, the gold standard system reduced the fluctuations of exchange-rate. Third, Japan's credit capacity increased after its victory in the Russo–Japanese War. On the other hand, Japanese capital exports had developed large markets in South Korea and China, and Japan obtained the right to operate manufacturing businesses in China after victory in the Sino–Japanese War. In 1902, Japanese started to establish spinning factories in China.

After the Russo–Japanese War, Japan obtained the railroads of Changchun and Fushun by transfer, and the South Manchuria railroad was established. Mansyu-Seihun and Nissin-Kisen were established in Manchuria, and the Toyo-Takusyoku Joint Stock Corporation was established in South Korea. After the Russo–Japanese War, the Yokohama-Seikin Bank became an important bank in Manchuria. After World War I, Japan applied further pressure to China, very much increasing the size and number of the loans made, such as the Nishihara loan. Even for the export of capital and spinning-factory goods, business travel to China became very active, and more and more professional executive officers appeared. Mitsui and Sumitomo Zaibatsu had a clerk form system since the Edo period, and Hikojiro Nakamigawa of Mitsui, a graduate of ordinary school, became its professional executive officer. For Mitsubishi, Yasuda, Furukawa, Asano, and Ohkura, too, the scale of business became larger and complicated, and so they too made use of professional executive officers.

In the third period (1920–1945) according to K. Yamaguchi, Japanese capitalism started to show many problems and contradictions. As seen in Fig. 1-1, the Japanese economy had developed to such a great extent in the previous period, even though there had been some recessions (*e.g.*, in 1890, 1898, and 1907–1908). However, the Kanto earthquake (1923), a financial crisis (1927), and the world depression (1929) seriously assailed the Japanese economy, culminating in the Manchurian Incident in 1931. The conditions of overproduction and financial austerity after World War I changed suddenly, resulting in a recession. The Bank of Japan made some aggressive efforts to save the Japanese economy, but such inflationary efforts did not help much. The crisis of 1920 became moderate in the later months of that year, but many firms and shops fell into bankruptcy. The year 1921 was a moderate year for business, but it fell into stagnation by the fall. *Ishii shoten* (Ishii shop) fell into bankruptcy that year, and a monetary crisis occurred in late 1922. In 1923, the Kanto earthquake occurred, prompting the rescue and care of many refugees. The Japanese economy improved somewhat in 1924, but again fell into stagnation.

A great monetary crisis occurred in 1927, stemming from the fact that the government had tried to resolve this economic stagnation by undertaking some temporary inflationary means, but they were not sufficiently remedial. The world crisis in 1929 also assailed the Japanese economy; it had not yet recovered from the stagnant conditions of 1927, and so its great problems were merely made much more serious. In 1930, government lifted its embargo on the export of gold; however, the exchange rate fluctuated, and a great amount of gold flowed out of the country. The promotion of industry and the development of trade came to a standstill, and fell into a rather deep crisis. The general price level and the level of trade decreased remarkably, culminating in an agricultural crisis. During this period, the spinning industry was a leading industry, with the heavy, food, and chemical industries following. However, monopolistic firms formed as small and medium firms disappeared during the crisis and capital became more concentrated. Each industry organized a cartel and controlled its production, supply, sale, and price; it also prevented drops in output prices and the accumulation of goods. As such, *Zaibatsu* worked to increase the extent of control.

3. Critical Review of Japanese Agricultural and Non-agricultural Research

3.1. *Critical Study of Hayami's Agricultural Growth Process*

It would be very important for the developing countries to know the rapid growth process of Japanese agriculture even if her growth might not be applicable directly to their countries in the present situation. "Nihon Nougyo no Seicho Katei" (Growth Process of Japanese Agriculture) which was written by Hayami [1973] described the growth process of Japanese agriculture. The joint articles in his book, which were mostly written together with his associates were already published in many Journals of Japan and of foreign countries. Also, Hayami published another book with Hayami and Ruttan [1971]. However, these two books are independent to each other although some parts have a common content. Therefore, these two books compliment each other. The former book of Hayami [1973] is more related to our research than the latter book. Therefore, here we focus our attention on this former book (For the critics to Hayami's book [1973], see Yamaguchi [1975]). Hayami divided his book into three parts and each part had two chapters.

The first part focused on a quantitative measure of growth, the second part focused on the factors of growth, and the third part focused on some phases of growth. Chapter 1 ("Introduction") is an introductory part. In Chapter 2 ("Growth rate of Japanese agriculture"), the amount of agricultural output, input, productivity and the price change of agricultural products and production inputs were measured. Then Hayami concluded that Japanese agricultural output had grown at the rate of 1.6% on the average over the periods from 1880 to 1965. However, the whole period could be divided into three parts. Both World Wars (World War I and World War II) were a boundary line for this division. The first phase was the period which had a comparatively high growth rate, the second was the kinked and stagnated period, and the third was again the period of high growth rate. The growth of agricultural inputs such as agricultural labor, agricultural land and agricultural capital stock, except for the period after the World War II, was very slow.

The growth of current inputs purchased from the non-agricultural sector such as fertilizer, however, was very rapid. The relative price of current inputs purchased from non-agricultural sector to the price of the agricultural product became lower. Also, the distribution share of the factor whose price became lower increased. Then Hayami adopted a hypotheses of induced technical change from this fact. The total input indices which aggregated these factor inputs grew at the rate of 0.7% per year on average. Therefore, the growth rate of aggregate productivity was 0.9% which corresponded to about 50 to 60% of the growth rate of agricultural output. Also, labor productivity grew at the rate of 2% per year and 65% of the productivity came from the increase of land productivity and 35% of the productivity came from the increase of land–labor ratio. Hayami considered that the increase of land productivity was closely related to the increase of current inputs (such as fertilizer) purchased from the non-agricultural sector.

In Chapter 3 ("Does there exist the early growth phase in Japan?"), Hayami examined Nakamura's assertion [1966]. Nakamura suspected the statistics of representing a too high growth rate in the early stage of the Japanese economy. He thought that there was no kink in the growth rate from the first phase to the second phase. He thought that there were many underdeclarements of agricultural output to evade the land tax in the early stage of development. He also thought that the underdeclarements decreased over time; therefore, automatically showing a very high growth rate if we did not correct for the low bias during the early economic development. He insisted that the land productivity of rice in these days of Japan had already reached a high level of 1.6 koku (1 koku = 150 kg) per tan (1 tan = 0.1 ha) (although the Japanese formal statistics showed only 1.2 koku) which was much higher than the level of present Southeast Asia. Therefore, he thought that the growth rate of the early Meiji period of Japanese economy was not so high but was almost the same growth rate as Europe.

He also thought that the Japanese economy followed the preconditional hypothesis which was derived from the growth stage theory based on the European historical experience. He criticized the very unique concurrent growth hypotheses which was insisted on by Ohkawa and Rosovsky [1973]. This concurrent growth hypotheses presumed that the level of Japanese agricultural production was almost the same as in Southeast Asia, and that the industrialization started before the transformation of the agricultural structure and the improvement in agricultural productivity. However, Hayam and Yamada together realized that the level of 1.6 koku per tan in rice production of the early stage of the Japanese economy was higher than the level of present Korea and Taiwan. They thought that it would be impossible to accept it judging from their common sense. They suspected the data of Nakamura and found his data as inadequate. Then, they assumed that the underestimate disappeared after the year of 1890 and they corrected the data before 1890. They accepted the level of 1.3 koku per tan from the data of "Fuken betsu Chisokaisei Kiyou" (Bulletin of Land tax Reform by Prefecture). They also confirmed the value of 1.3 koku judging from the analysis of the production function and of food consumption.

In Chapter 4 ("Sources of agricultural technical change") of the second part, Hayami analyzed the factors which contributed to the agricultural growth. He applied the growth accounting approach made by Griliches [1964] to Japanese data. He measured several aggregate agricultural production functions. As an input he used both the conventional inputs (such as land, labor, capital and current input) and non-conventional inputs (such as the education level of farmers, and public investment in agricultural research and extension services). Also, he used cross sectional data (prefectural data) of pre-World War II (the years of 1930 and 1935) and after World War II (the years of 1960 and 1965). Then, he measured the level of contribution of each factor input to the output growth.

In this calculation he used the production elasticities which were obtained from the method mentioned above and the rate of factor shares which were obtained from the quantitative calculation. The residuals, which were obtained from the calculation based on the production elasticities were smaller than those based on the factor share. The unexplained residual was mainly explained by the following three factors: (1) Adoption of output elasticities; (2) Improvement of the educational level of farmers; and (3) Agricultural research and extension services. And only 3% of the unexplained residual still remained as a final unexplained residual. Although this analysis had succeeded in the long run (whole period) analysis, it was not enough to explain the growth of agricultural output in each phase. There was still a large positive residual in the early growing phase and the period after World War II which had very high growth rate. They also got a negative residual in the stagnation period between two World Wars.

The problem was that there was a great discrepancy between the calculated production elasticity and factor share. In the pre-World War II period, the production elasticity of fertilizer was larger than the factor share but the production elasticity of land was smaller than the factor share. In the period after World War II, the production elasticity of capital was larger than the factor share but the production elasticity of labor was smaller than the factor share. He interpreted these facts as follows: The decrease in the relative price of fertilizer to land, made farmers use land saving and fertilizer using technology in the Pre-World War II; and the decrease of the relative price of capital to labor made them use labor saving and capital using technology in the period after World War II. Therefore, the farmer used much fertilizer and capital but there existed a time lag to adjust the resources, and there occurred a discrepancy between production elasticities and factor shares. In other words, he thought that there was a disequilibrium in resource adjustment.

In Chapter 5 ("non-agricultural contribution to agricultural productivity"), Hayami tried to consider the relationships between agriculture and non-agriculture, especially to measure the contribution of the non-agricultural sector to agriculture. He showed that the contribution of conventional inputs to the growth of agricultural output was about 50% but the growth of agricultural inputs were very small except for fertilizer and agricultural machinery which were supplied from non-agricultural sector. The development of such production in the non-agricultural sector changed the supply condition and reduced their price relative to agricultural output. This induced the technology, which used the inputs, which became cheaper. In other words, he wanted to use an induced innovation hypothesis to show these facts. He considered the following two cases: Suppose there were no development in fertilizer industry (Case 1) and no development in chemical fertilizer industry (Case 2).

He measured the amount of fertilizer, which was used and agricultural land productivity in each case. Then, he compared each value with the Japanese historical value and evaluated the contribution of the fertilizer industry and chemical industry to agricultural productivity growth. He obtained the following conclusion: The relative price of nitrogen (which were included in the self-supplied or sold fertilizer) to the price of agricultural output decreased about 30% and the amount of nitrogen per tan (10 are) increased about 100%. Rice harvest per tan increased 43%. However, he did not interpret that these increases of fertilizer input and output per tan were brought by the movement along the static constant production function. Rather he considered that it was brought by canceling the effect of diminishing marginal product of fertilizer through seed improvement which was augmented by new technology for land improvement — deep cultivation and others. In other words, he considered a shift of the fertilizer productivity curve.

The calculated result showed that the rice product per tan would have been 1.86 koku (1 koku = 150 kg) and the growth rate would have been about 30% of the real historical value if we assumed Case 1. He also showed that the rice product per tan would have been 1.94 koku if we assumed Case 2. Therefore, he concluded that if the Japanese fertilizer industry had not increased so rapidly, the relative price of fertilizer input would not have decreased and the growth rate of purchased fertilizer input would have been about 1/20 of the real historical value. Therefore, the growth rate of Japanese total output and land productivity would have decreased significantly without the development of the Japanese fertilizer industry. Hayami also stated the following conclusion: "In the process of Japanese economic development, the agricultural sector supplied food, labor force and capital stock to the non-agricultural sector and supported the development of industrialization. The non-agricultural sector, however, also supplied the inputs such as fertilizer and machinery which were necessary for the modernization of agriculture. We should consider and grasp these interrelationships and divisions of labor between these two sectors."

In Chapter 6 ("Change of the phase of Japanese agriculture, and the accumulation and diffusion of rice technology") of part III, Hayami tried to understand the aspects of the change of the phase and the stagnation of growth in the period between the two World Wars which were not explained by the growth accounting analysis above. Once A. Tang [1963] showed that about 70% of the residual (*i.e.*, technical change) of Japanese economic growth was explained by government expenditure for agricultural education and research. However, his study still had several unclear points. For example, the growth rate of expenditure on education and research still increased rapidly even after 1915 (*i.e.*, even during the stagnation era). Therefore, it was not clear why the government expenditure for education and research would not help the growth of agricultural productivity during the later period.

Also, it was not clear what were the factors explaining the kinked growth. If we note that technical change appeared in two stages (*i.e.*, invention and diffusion), the government expenditure for research would correspond to invention, and the government expenditure for education would correspond to the diffusion. Therefore, he thought that it would be better to separate Tang's aggregate variable of research and education into a variable for each. Especially, it would be very important to grasp the role of Japanese rono (veteran farmer) who made a kind of extension work. Then, he thought that it would be very important to grasp the process of accumulation of agricultural technical change and the process of diffusion separately if we wanted to understand the change of the growth phase. Therefore, he considers that the growth of Stages I and II in the initial growth phase was brought by the extension and diffusion of the potential of traditional technology (rono technology accumulated, since the Tokugawa era).

The cause of the stagnation in the period between the two World Wars was considered (hypothesized) as follows: The potential of tradition technology gradually disappeared but it took a long time for the new potential derived from modern scientific research of the agricultural extension and research institutes of universities to be used widely. Therefore, Japanese agricultural output in this period stagnated. Although the cultivated acreage which used the seeds which were invented by the research institutes and extension services increased, the supplementary technology could not accompany the increase. Therefore, we could not enjoy the benefit of the increase of the productivity although government expenditure had increased. The period of sustained agricultural growth after the middle of the 1950s was regarded as resulting from the backlog of scientific knowledge which was accumulated during the war time.

He thought that the average land productivity of rice in each prefecture was an index of technical change, and the level of land productivity in advanced prefecture represented the accumulated potential of technological knowledge by the scientific research and farmer's effort. The coefficient of variation of land productivity is an index of extension and diffusion. Then, he separated the whole amount of technological progress into the following two elements, the accumulated potential of technological knowledge and its extension and diffusion. He measured the contribution of each to technical change in each phase. He made these calculations for the whole country, the eastern part of Japan and the western part of Japan. Judging from the calculated result, we could interpret the result as follows: The contribution of potential of technological knowledge was large in the Pre-World War II period (Stage I) and in the period after World War II (Stages V and VI); and the contribution of diffusion was large in the pre-World War II period (Stage II); but in the period between two World Wars the contribution of both potential and diffusion was small. Therefore, we can recognize that these results support the hypothesis.

In Chapter 7 ("Market condition and agricultural growth"), Hayami investigated the effects of Korean and Taiwan rice on Japanese agricultural stagnation. He considered that the decrease of food demand by the economic depression and the cheap imported rice from Korea and Taiwan deteriorated the market condition and led to the agricultural stagnation. This is another trial to explain the agricultural stagnation because the agricultural stagnation could not be explained completely by the development and extinction of the potential of traditional technology inherited from Tokugawa era or by the international market relationship. Sanmai Zoushoku Keikaku (Rice promotion program), which was advanced in Korea and Taiwan to help the Japanese after the bad experience of the Rice Riot in 1918, began to have a big influence and damaged Japanese agriculture. He constructed a demand and supply model of rice, and calculated a hypothetical value for the following two cases.

In Case 1, he assumed that the net import of Korean and Taiwan rice stayed at the average level of the period from 1913 to 1917. In Case 2, he assumed that the index of seed improvement after 1920 still grew at the growth rate of the period from 1890 to 1920. Then, he obtained the following conclusion in each case: In case of Case 2, all of the land productivity, total output and land acreage grew at the same rate as in the past after the year of 1920. However, we still obtained the kinked growth in the Case 1. Therefore, he concluded the following: "The import of rice from the colonies (Korea and Taiwan) had a secondary effect on the Japanese agricultural stagnation, but the main cause for the stagnation would be the extinction of the potential of traditional technology. However, the influence of rice imported from the colonies on the rice price and farmer's income was extremely large, and the rice income in the period between two World Wars would have risen very much if there were no import of rice from the colonies."

As we have seen above, Hayami's analytical method is very unique, clear and simple. Further, he had used a price element in his analysis of economic development. However, his analysis also contained many problems. Especially, his too simple and too clear analysis had many possibilities to hide a large number of complicated and important factors. Here, we confine ourselves to show only four criticisms of his method. The first criticism is that there was a big discrepancy between his critical mind and the analytical method. In all parts, especially in Chapter 5, he concluded that we had to grasp the economic development as a process of interrelationships between agriculture and non-agriculture (see page 128 of his book). However, almost all his methods omitted the interrelationships, using a very simple causal relationship. It would have been possible to construct an agricultural and non-agricultural two-sector model which could calculate both the contribution of the agricultural sector to non-agricultural output, which Hayami did not consider, and the contribution of non-agricultural sector to agricultural output (such as fertilizer and tractors), which Hayami did.

This method would be more suitable to his critical mind. In other words, his critical mind was constructed on a general equilibrium model but his actual analytical methods were constructed on a partial equilibrium model. This comment also relates to the following point. Probably, one of the major reasons why agriculture stagnated in the period between two World Wars would be that non-agricultural sector (or per capita income) stagnated and decreased the demand for agricultural goods in addition to two factors which were stated above (*i.e.*, extinction of the potential of technology and the pressure of colonial rice production on the Japanese rice production). In other words, it seems to me that the stagnation of per capita income through the stagnation of non-agricultural sector has led to the decrease of the demand for agricultural goods and affected on the agricultural sector (of course it is obvious that this is not an only reason).

Hayami also recognized that the stagnation of the demand for agricultural goods based on the economic stagnation deteriorated the market condition. However, only the price term was considered as an independent variable and the income term was treated as a shifter in his demand function. Even if the income term was included as an independent variable in his demand function, the income term in his model was not determined from the interrelationships of the endogenous mechanism between the agricultural and non-agricultural sectors. We always respect a simplest method. However, we cannot help but admit Hayami's defect and the discrepancy between his critical mind and his analytical method. Hayami's critical mind recognized the impact of fertilizer and of demand stagnation; his analytical tools could not. The second criticism relates to the studies made by other researchers.

Many people analyzed the causes of agricultural stagnation in the period between the two World Wars. We can summarize them into four causes or factors. As for the first factor, we should show the relationships of the rice price and the behavior of landlord versus tenant farmer as Kashiwa [1960] showed. As we had already seen, the landlord was a tezukuri jinushi (cultivated landlord) who lived in his village and cultivated his own land in the beginning of Meiji era (the period of rising rice price). In this period, the landlord was a profitable job and he gained a lot because the price of rice increased but the land tax was constant. Consequently, the earnings from land increased. The land acreage increased and technical improvements through the increase of fertilizer and seeds improvement were made and agricultural productivity increased. However, in the second period (after around the year of 1910), the decrease of the rice price and outmigration of agricultural labor through the development of the non-agricultural sector forced the farm management of landlord to face difficulties. Then the landlord did not try to make efforts to increase land utilization and land intensity as before. Therefore, the agricultural productivity did not increase so much as before but rather started to stagnate.

The second factor would be the pressure of colonial rice such as Korean and Taiwan rice to Japanese agriculture (as Hayami and Ruttan [1971] also showed). In Japan, this stagnation factor was already pointed out by many Japanese researchers before the work of Hayami. These two factors (behavioral change of landlords and the pressure of colonial rice) are well-known factors to explain Japanese agricultural stagnation in the period between the two World Wars. The third factor would be the disappearance of the potential of Rono technology, as Hayami stated above. This discussion relates to the assertion of Teranishi [1972] that land improvement, fertilizer index and seed improvement reached the level of diminishing return. The fourth factor would be the stagnation of the non-agricultural sector (same as occurred in the agricultural sector) and consequently the stagnation of the demand for agricultural products through the stagnation of per capita income.

Therefore, first it would be necessary for Hayami's agricultural demand function to have per capita income as an independent variable. Second, it would be necessary to have a non-agricultural sector (in addition to agricultural sector) for his model. In short, other factors besides the two factors (Rono technology and colonial rice) which Hayami studied would be necessary to add to his analysis. (our model can evaluate the effects such as colonial rice and others as we have already shown in previous papers). The third criticism relates to the problems of the ordinary estimation method of the production function. First, we have to describe the estimation problems of the Cobb–Douglas production function although it is a very strict criticism. Tsujimura and Watanabe [1966] showed the following problems for the ordinary estimation method of Cobb–Douglas production function. First, they were not sure whether the ordinarily estimated Cobb–Douglas production function would be a real production function or not.

There are at least two reasons, which are given below, for this problem. One, the estimation of the Cobb–Douglas production function would be usually made by a regression using the growth rate and data for output and capital in money terms. Therefore, the calculated values might be an elasticity of demand or supply for output and capital, rather than representing real input elasticity for output and capital. Also, the data is changed to logarithm value when it is calculated. Therefore, it is not easy to assure that the independent scatterness of the variables. Thus, it would not be so difficult to satisfy a statistical standard by choosing an appropriate data period. Consequently there are many possibilities for not setting a real production function. This argument also would be related to the criticism of Hara [1976] who commented that the production function of Hayami's work was not a real one but rather only an input–output relationship. Two, most of the Cobb–Douglas production functions which were estimated in the ordinary method were usually estimated by a single equation method. Therefore, there is a possibility to have estimation bias.

Tsujimura and Watanabe pointed out further problems for the estimation of the Cobb–Douglas production function. So far, many Cobb–Douglas production functions have been estimated. Therefore, it would be too strict to tell these problems to the researchers who estimated Cobb–Douglas production function. However, it would be at least necessary to realize that the estimation of Cobb–Douglas production function had these problems. The fourth criticism is related to the accounting identity. Hara [1976] criticized Hayami's work as follows: Hayami used the production elasticities which were obtained from the estimation of the Cobb–Douglas production function for his growth accounting. Therefore, it was natural for the estimated growth rate of the output from the aggregate of all factor inputs to be near the actual growth rate, leaving no residual. Although this might be a too strict criticism, Griliches [1964] also recognized this problem. Therefore, in our analysis we used a growth accounting method based on factor shares instead of elasticity (also, we made several sensitivity tests by changing those parameter values and obtained consistent results). In our model, we tried to improve these four problems and use a very different growth accounting method from the ordinary growth accounting method.

3.2. *Analytical Study of Non-agriculture and Economy*

Here, we show the research for non-agricultural sector or for the whole economy. In previous part, we have already shown the history of the non-agricultural sector. Shinohara [1973] showed two factors (*i.e.*, long-term factors and post-war factors) which enabled Japanese economy to succeed in her economic development. He listed four long-term factors and eleven post-war factors. However, here we want to systematize and classify the post-war factors into six factors. As the long-term factors, first, the objective condition of the industrial foundation was already in mature. In other words, there was a spontaneous power for growth in addition to the governmental policy for growth. As a subjective condition, Japanese educational level was very high and the Samurai was more public minded and worked for Japan. Further, many well-qualified entrepreneurs were very aggressive to take an initiative in private industry.

Second, exports increased very rapidly and the increase of exports enabled the Japanese economy to import raw materials from abroad. Also, there were many interactions and feedbacks between export and investment. 1t made Japan to develop through Gankou-teki Hatten (Development through the formation flight style of the wild-geese) which showed that first import wave developed the domestic demand, and the domestic demand developed the domestic output and export. Third, the traditional factor and modern factor combined well with each other. In other words, the Japanese economy had a dual structure of large and small traditional firms. Therefore, it was possible to have a combination of a high technology in large firms and a low wage rate in small and middle firms. Also, a whole life employment system and a seniority rule for wage determination enabled the Japanese economy to have a modern industrial labor force. Further, a demonstration effect of the introduction of technology and the high saving rate through the traditional consumption pattern led to have a high investment and saving rate.

Fourth, active competition among firms and active government intervention were also one of the very important factors in Japanese economic development. For example, the government produced some public model, firms in textiles, cement and war weapons, transferring them to private people later. Also, after World War II, inter-firm competition became very severe resulting in almost all industrial goods becoming exports. As the post-war factors, first we should mention that Japan had plenty of cheap, high-educated laborers who could use the new high technology. Second, the Japanese saving rate was very high as a result of the influence of Confucius. The profit rate of firms increased owing to the boom of equipment investment. Therefore, the weight of the bonus wage also increased. Further, the savings of farm households increased after 1960.

Also, active equipment investment through the over loan policy of the Japanese bank contributed to economic growth. Third, the long-term factors and the combination of export leading and investment leading development enabled Japanese economy to develop at an extremely high growth rate. Fourth, there were many government interventions and much inter-firm competition. Especially the inter-firm competition in the introduction of technology became very strong from around 1965. Also Japanese entrepreneurs had high quality transformation ability and had succeeded to transform the industrial structure toward heavy industrialization. Fifth, generally speaking, the world experience showed that the countries which were damaged heavily by the war developed much more rapidly than the countries which were not damaged. Sixth, there are still other factors. For example, the Japanese exchange rate was relatively cheap and Japanese military expenditure and defense expenditure were very small.

Research concerning the Japanese economy after 1950 was made by Ohkawa and Rosovsky [1973]. They used the following four concepts: (a) Long-term wave; (b) Investment spurt of the private firm in the non-agricultural sector; (c) Trend acceleration; and (d) Gap structure. This research had the following three themes: (1) Why the Japanese economy grew very fast for a long time? Also why the pace of the growth increased? (2) Why the growth rates of post-war Japan were so large as compared with those of the pre-war period? (3) Why the Japanese economy formed a special type of development; *i.e.*, an explicit spurt period (a rising wave-motion period) and a relatively slow growth period? Why the spurt continued for a long time? For these questions, Ohkawa and Rosovsky prepared the following four preparatory propositions: (a) There existed a gap between the actually operating technologies and the increase of the Japanese ability which enabled them to introduce and absorb the improving technological method.

(b) Independent investment depending on the imported technology was one of the main sources of the Japanese economic growth. (c) In order to explain a special pattern of Japanese economic growth, it would be necessary to construct a two-sector model which includes both a traditional and modern sector. (d) An unprecedented economic growth after the World War II had a connection with the forces which were already formed before the World War II. In this respect, the Japanese economic growth after the World War II was a one part of the trend acceleration growth which was developed before World War II. Therefore, it would be very significant to explain the growth of the post-World War II period as a part of the total historical experience. In other words, the technological gap of Japan formed a dual structure in industry and in the labor market.

The two sectors productivity and wage rate both showed large gaps. Also, owing to World War II and the period of the recovery, there existed a pool of the underemployed population. Therefore, the Japanese economy had an elastic labor supply resulting in a lag in wage increases. Also, the increase of the output owing to the increase of the capital was very large. Therefore, the profit and saving grew at a very rapid rate. The increase of savings was also supported by a low rate of military expenditure. As we mentioned above, the increase of output through the increase of investment was very large. This was brought not only by a technological gap which induced high investment, but also by rapid depreciation of the capital stock which required a further investment. Also, an extraordinary high growth rate in productivity and a high labor supply elasticity led to increased exports.

Ohkawa and Rosovsky gave the answers for question (1) Why the large, long term and increasing growth rate in post-war Japan and for (2) Why this rate was so much greater than the pre-World War II rate. First, to explain acceleration, they recognized that there was a normal or equilibrium growth path which passed through the period potential maximum growth and the period of adjustment (down wave-motion). The increase of capital formation raised the capital–labor ratio and, therefore, increased the total productivity (*i.e.*, residual). Also the increased capital–labor ratio and the residual supported the trend acceleration. This linkage was supported by an increase in the social capacity such as saving, learning effect, institutional change and others. Consider question (3) Why the Japanese economy formed a special type of development? In other words why there existed an explicit spurt period and a relatively slow growth period?

The following answer was given. Suppose that there was a hindrance to the growth of the Japanese economy. We can guess that there exists an unutilized pool of the modern technology. Therefore, new investment would produce an accelerated growth of output and productivity, and the velocity of growth would be very fast. The intensity of the labor utilization would decrease when the growth rate of demand decreased. Therefore, the return to the normal intensity of labor utilization would lead to a higher productivity growth. Also, an elastic labor response would lead to a lag in the wage increase. This would increase the rate of capital's profit and therefore increase the saving and investment very rapidly. Also, the process would continue for a long time because of the existence of a pool of redundant labor (this is similar to the Lewisian dualistic theory). In short, Japan who was a less developed country imported a new foreign technology and developed quite rapidly. Also, because of the duality of the

economy, labor was abundant. Thus, there was a lag in wage increases compared with the productivity increase. Therefore, the share of the profit was
quite large.

The high profit share led to expanded investment, and increased per
capita capital and therefore the productivity (*i.e.*, residual). Ohkawa and
Rosovsky also showed that the improvement of the social ability such as
the increase of the level of per capita income, saving, learning, and institutional ability worked to help this process. Although the method of our model
is quite different from their model, our conclusions support Ohkawa and
Rosovsky's work. In this book, we will show the importance of the agricultural and non-agricultural technical change to the Japanese economic
development, but these technical changes originated from investment activity using imported technology. We will also show the importance of the
two-sector model when considering the wage differential between the two
sectors. Also, we will show that technical change had a labor displacing
effect in agriculture because of the low income and price elasticities for
agricultural products. Therefore, we got the conclusion that the growth
of the non-agricultural sector would be necessary to accommodate the dis-
placed agricultural labor. These conclusions are consistent with the research
of Ohkawa and Rosovsky. Therefore, it would be very important to study
each other as a complementary works.

Next, we would shift our focus to the industrial sector. Teranishi [1972]
regarded the growth process of the manufacturing industry in Japan from
the Meiji era (1868) to 1940 to have had the following four characteristics.
First, the growth rate of manufacturing industry accelerated after 1900.
Second, the industries of food, textiles, non-ferrous metals, and printing
had a large growth rate in the first half of the period and the industries
of timber, wooden articles, chemistry, ceramics, iron and machinery had
a large growth rate in the later half of the period. Third, the industries of
food, textiles, and chemistry had a large share of industrial output (in value)
in the whole period but the industries of machinery, iron and others had a
large share of industrial output in the later part of the period. Fourth, for the
growth of industry, the food industry made a large contribution in the early
half of the period. But chemistry, metals and the machine industries made
a large contribution in the later half period. Also, the textile industry made
an overwhelmingly large contribution throughout the whole period.

Fujino [1965] used the words of Gankou Keitai teki Hatten (Development through the formation flight style of the wild-geese) for these innovative processes of Schumpeter through the borrowed technology. This meant that a new shift of the production function was occurred by an import of new foreign technology. It brought innovative investment which induced an increase in the demand and the utilization of industry and finally in induced investment. This brought an enlargement of the output, a decrease in prices, a selection of traditional firms and oligopolization of the modern firms. Also, the decrease in prices brought development through the formation flight style of the wild-geese of import, output and export. The increase of exports was connected to the wave of investment through the money supply system. Especially in the periods of the high growth, or kinked growth, the structure of a selection of the weak and small firm and oligopolization of the main firms advanced.

As we will show in this book, the rate of technical change in non-agriculture was 1.8% per annum in the whole period (1880–1970). The especially high rate of technical change in post-war period (4.1% in 1950th and 6.3% in 1960th) is noteworthy. These figures were consistent with the figures of other researchers (Watanabe [1965] obtained 1.1% for 1860–1933, Sato [1968a; 1968b] obtained 1.56% for 1930–1960). These high rates of technical change were possible through borrowed technology. There were two directions for this kind of study. The first one was the direction which examined the amount of technical change as a residual (*i.e.*, technical change of the Solow type). Judging from the comparative studies of technical change between the US and Japan, technical change of the Japanese economy was extremely large (see Watanabe and Egaitsu [1968]). Sato [1971] showed that the catching process of Japanese industry was made in the 1960s, instead of the 1950s.

The second one is the measurement of the technological bias of Japanese manufacturing industry [Watanabe, 1970]. Watanabe showed that the manufacturing industry from 1905 to 1933 had a type of labor saving technology. At that time, we had a very different type of factor endowments from the advanced countries. Therefore, this would be a kind of proof of the hypothesis that our economy developed through borrowed technology. Further, Watanabe [1970] analyzed the pattern of industrial development in Japan by using two methods. The first method was to apply the comparative study which was made by Chenery and others. The second method was to use an industrial linkage model and to find factors which changed the output and employment by decomposition into the influence of domestic demand, import, export and technological change.

In the first method, the output (or value added) was regressed on per capita income and population (he considered population to represent a scale of the national economy, market and demand factor). Then, he obtained the income and population elasticity. The income elasticities of agriculture, mining and food industry were less than 1 which were consistent with the Engel's law. Also, agriculture had a small population elasticity (less than 1). Next, Watanabe calculated the deviation of the Japanese industrialization pattern from the average pattern of industrialization of other countries. He calculated the deviation in the years of 1914, 1935, 1954, and 1959. He obtained the conclusion that Japanese industrialization was not so peculiar in the year of 1914. The pattern of 1935 was an extension of the pattern of 1914 and was not so different from the situation of 1914. However, a conspicuous change occurred in the years of 1953 and 1959. Therefore, Watanabe concluded that a rapid industrialization and a rapid movement of the focus to industrialization was made in these periods.

Then, he obtained the tentative conclusion that our economy had developed by putting much stress on the industrialization, especially on the heavy and chemical industries. This meant that sectorial unequal development occurred in our economy. The second method in Watanabe's research was using an industrial linkage model. He measured the deviation bias from the proportional growth pattern. Then, he tried to find the demand and technological factors which caused the deviation. For the demand factors, he concluded that the domestic demand and exports, especially the export of textiles were very large and occupied about 35% of the total demand factor. Import substitution, however, was still negligible over the 1914–1935 periods. However, many industries started to be based on import substitution over the 1935–1954 period.

Technological change was very large and the industrial structure became representative of a home production style. Further, over the periods 1955–1960, the position of the food and textile industries decreased but that of the final and intermediate products (especially machine industry) increased. Therefore, these changes in the pattern led to the transformation of Japanese industrial structure. The role of technological change was also far larger than the general expectation. About 30 or 40% of the deviation from the proportional growth pattern was brought from technological change. So far, we have seen the research of Japanese economic development very briefly. Here, we introduced only complementary research of the non-agricultural sector which had a close connection with our work. We had already constructed an agricultural and non-agricultural two-sector model to supplement Hayami's work and address problems with this work. Our research used a model which contained not only a supply side of one sector but also both demand and supply sides of the other sector. This non-agricultural section in this chapter can complement the results from our model.

Summary and Conclusion

(1) First, Hayami's analysis is a partial equilibrium analysis, although his thinking always considers the general equilibrium model. Nonetheless, a large gap exists between his thinking and the tools that he used. Hayami cites two reasons (*e.g.*, the pressure of South Korean and Taiwan rice, and the disappearance of potential growth) for the stagnation in the time between the two World Wars. There are some other reasons as to why the stagnation occurred during that period; we must also consider the demand side and non-agricultural sectors, in addition to the supply side. This point is developed in Chapter 2 of this book. More precisely, it is necessary for Hayami's agricultural demand function to have per capita income as an independent variable. Second, it is also necessary to include a non-agricultural sector (in addition to the agricultural sector) in his model. In short, other factors besides the two factors Hayami studied (*i.e.*, Rono technology and colonial rice) need to be added to his analysis. Our model can evaluate the effects of factors such as colonial rice, among others.

(2) Also, another criticism of Hayami's analysis relates to the problems inherent in the ordinary estimation method for the production function. First, we need to describe the estimation problems inherent in the Cobb–Douglas production function; this is part and parcel of a very strict criticism. Tsujimura and Watanabe [1966] highlight the following problems with the ordinary estimation method of the Cobb–Douglas production function. First, they are unsure whether or not the ordinarily estimated Cobb–Douglas production function is a real production function. Second, this argument also relates to the criticism of Hara [1976], who comments that the production

function of Hayami's work is only an input–output relationship; there also exists the possibility of estimation bias. Tsujimura and Watanabe point out further problems with the estimation of the Cobb–Douglas production function. In any case, at the very least, it is necessary to recognize that the estimation of the Cobb–Douglas production function has these problems. The fourth criticism relates to the accounting identity. Hara criticizes Hayami's work as follows: Hayami used production elasticities that had been obtained from the estimation of the Cobb–Douglas production function for his growth accounting. Therefore, it was natural for the estimated growth rate of the output from the aggregate of all factor inputs to approximate the actual growth rate, leaving no residual. Although this might be a too-strict criticism, Griliches [1964] also recognizes this problem. Therefore, in our analysis, we use a growth accounting method that is based on factor shares, rather than elasticity. In our model, we tried to overcome these four problems by using a growth accounting method that differed greatly from the ordinary growth accounting method.

(3) Shinohara [1973] discusses the two sets of factors (*i.e.*, long-term factors and post-war factors) that allowed the Japanese economy to succeed in terms of economic development. He lists four long-term factors and 11 post-war factors. However, we want to systematize and streamline the typology of the post-war factors into six types. As for the long-term factors, we can list them as follows: (a) a mature industrial foundation, (b) high export levels, (c) a dual structure, and (d) inter-firm competition and government intervention. As for post-war factors, these included: (a) cheap and educated labor, (b) a high saving rate, (c) high export and investment levels, (d) inter-firm competition and government intervention, (e) the countries damaged heavily by the war developed rapidly, and (f) the presence of a cheap exchange rate, a small military, and a small defense expenditure.

(4) Ohkawa and Rosovsky [1973], meanwhile, believe that the Japanese economy developed while bearing the following four characteristics: (a) long-term waves, (b) the investment spurts of private firms in the non-agricultural sector, (c) trend acceleration, and (d) a gap structure. The research within this book asks a number of key questions: (1) Why did the Japanese economy grow so quickly, over such a long period? Why did the pace of growth increase? (2) Why were the growth rates of post-war Japan so large, compared to those of the pre-war period? (3) Why did the Japanese economy take a special type of development, *i.e.*, an explicit

growth-spurt period (*i.e.*, a rising wave-motion period) and a relatively slow growth period? Why did that growth spurt continue over a protracted period? Fujino's *Gankou-teki Hatten* (Development through the formation flight style of the wild-geese) states that Japan developed by embracing Gankou-teki Hatten, that the first wave of imports helped develop domestic demand, that this domestic demand helped enhance domestic output, and that exports then increased.

(5) As shown in Chapter 2, the rate of technical change in non-agriculture was 1.8% per annum during the whole of the 1880–1970 period. The high rate of technical change in the post-war period (*e.g.*, 4.1% in the 1950s and 6.3% in the 1960s) is noteworthy. Watanabe [1970] found that the Japanese economy was marked by extremely high rates of technological change and the appearance of labor-saving technology; these changes were derived from the use of borrowed technology. He also studied patterns of industrial development in Japan by using comparative study and an industrial linkage model. Through comparative study, he found that the income elasticities of the agricultural, mining, and food industries were very small, and that agriculture also had a small population elasticity. Rapid industrialization occurred, especially in the heavy and chemical industries in 1953 and 1959.

In examining the results of Watanabe's industrial linkage model analyses, we found the following: in terms of demand factors, the export of textiles used to be very large, occupying approximately 35% of the total demand factor. During the 1935–1954 period, more and more industries were becoming based on import substitution; furthermore, during the 1955–1960 period, the stature of the food and textile industries diminished, but that of final and intermediate products (*e.g.*, machinery) increased. These changes in pattern led to a transformation in the Japanese industrial structure. The role of technological change was also far larger than had been generally expected: an estimated 30–40% of the deviation from the proportional growth pattern derived solely from technological change.

Conclusion

We offered within this chapter various definitions and characteristics of agriculture, population, and technical change, along with their contributions to a given economy; we also supplied overviews of the history of agricultural and non-agricultural sectors in Japan. We reviewed and summarized a subsection of the agricultural and non-agricultural research, while highlighting the several important points therein. Hayami's analysis is a partial equilibrium analysis, although his thinking always considers the general equilibrium model. Hayami also offered two reasons for the stagnation in Japan's economy in the time between the two World Wars (*i.e.*, the pressure of colonial rice, and the disappearance of potential growth). However, there are some other reasons. The Kanto earthquake (1923), financial crisis (1927), and the world depression (1929), for example, heavily assailed the Japanese economy. Second, there was an attitude change among the Japanese landlords, who used to work in agriculture and were very aggressive about improving Japanese agriculture by generating technical change. However, as discussed, they became Futokorote landlords (*i.e.*, nonfarming landlords, or breast–hand landowners) who did not work in agriculture. This change reduced the number of agricultural technical changes that occurred. As a result, it is clear that we need to consider non-agricultural sectors and the demand side, besides the supply side.

These points are included in our model. To be precise, it is necessary that Hayami's agricultural demand function contain per capita income as an independent variable. Second, it needs to contain a non-agricultural sector for his model. Additionally, factors other than the two that Hayami studied (*i.e.*, Rono technology and colonial rice) need to be considered within his analysis. Our model can evaluate the effects of colonial rice and the other three factors. By examining the results of Japanese non-agricultural research by Shinohara [1973], Ohkawa and Rosovsky [1973], Fujino [1965], and Watanabe [1965], we have come to understand that the following factors led to a high rate of growth within the Japanese economy: cheap educated labor, inter-firm competition and government intervention, high levels of technical change via borrowed technologies, high rates of saving and investment (and therefore high export levels), a cheap exchange rate, and not-burdensome military expenses. Our research, here, can reflect all these aspects, in terms of the parameter, endogenous, and exogenous variables of our model.

Chapter 2

General Equilibrium Growth Accounting
for the Japanese Economy

Introduction

The experience of the Green Revolution focused the attention of economists on the role of agricultural technical changes as a powerful engine of growth. Increased allocation of resource to agricultural research at national and international levels highlights this changing emphasis. At the same time, this emphasis also causes worries about a possible adverse employment of capital and labor needed to produce a given level of output. Offsetting increases in labor use requires either increase in rates of growth of agricultural output, a lowering of agricultural wage rates which is highly unattractive or a transfer of labor to non-agricultural activities. Since technical change in agriculture increases per capita income in the economy and tends to reduce agricultural prices, we can expect positive effects on agricultural and non-agricultural demands to occur as a result of the technical change.

But how big these effects will be is largely a guess. It is also likely that the increased demand alone generated by the technical change will be insufficient to prevent downward pressure on the wage rate. If this should be the case, what then are most attractive policy alternatives to generate demand for the labor released by the agricultural technical change? In order to answer these questions and to get some feel for the magnitudes of income generating and labor displacement effects, a relatively simple general equilibrium model with an agricultural and a non-agricultural sector was constructed along neoclassical lines. The economy is closed, but it is not too difficult to evaluate how the opening of the economy would affect the conclusions. In this chapter, we consider first, theoretical foundations for building model.

Second, theoretical explanation of the model. Third, empirical results from the model.

1. Theoretical Foundations for Building the Model

1.1. *Some Basic Foundations for General Equilibrium Growth Accounting*

1.1.1 *Income Distribution, Rybczynski's Theorem, the Hecksher–Ohlin Theorem, and the Production Possibility Curve*

First, in this book, it is assumed that there exists a production function in each sector; we also intend to make use of the Cobb–Douglas production function. However, there are many kinds of production function, such as the Leontief, CES, and VES types, among others. In Japan, Kamiya [1941] used the Cobb–Douglas production function; Ohkawa [1945] also undertook many analyses based on it. In Japanese agriculture, most people use a Cobb–Douglas-type production function and obtain far better results than they would with other types. This derives from the fact that agriculture makes use of land, besides labor and capital; therefore, it is difficult to use a CES-type production function in such considerations. Additionally, most research has obtained results with a constant return to scale; Ohkawa thinks that this is why most Japanese farms at that time were very small. Upon surveying multiple studies, Ohyabu [1969] states that the Cobb–Douglas production function is also useful with respect to the non-agricultural sector. Therefore, the Cobb–Douglas production function is used in this book.

Second, in our model the existence of an aggregate production function, the theory of marginal productivity (*i.e.*, neoclassical theory) are assumed. Factor movement from one sector to another sector is due to the difference of factor prices. As a consequence, vertical income distribution, which is the income distribution between the capitalist and laborer, and horizontal income distribution, which is the one between agricultural and non-agricultural sectors, are important for our model. In fact, a farmer is a mixture of a capitalist and laborer. This fact adds interest to our analysis. Therefore, income distribution theories are investigated here. We can classify income distribution theories into three schools: (1) The classical theory of Ricardo and Marx, (2) The neoclassical theory, and (3) The Keynesian theory. Keynesian and Neoclassical theories are the two main branches at the present time. Neoclassical theory approaches income distribution problems from the production side, *i.e.*, by using the production function. On the other hand, Keynesian theory approaches it from the demand side.

As is well known, neoclassical distribution theory is based on the marginal productivity theory. Traces of the neoclassical theory can be found in Von Thünen in 1826 and Jevons, Menger, and Walras in the 1870s. However, in the 1880s, Walras, Wicksteed, Marshall, Wicksell and Clark independently developed the marginal productivity theory. In 1894, Flux combined the Wicksteed work with Euler's theory. Cobb and Douglas [1928] used the Cobb–Douglas function and further tried to test the marginal productivity theory in practice. However, the greatest contribution was by Hicks [1966]. In his "The Theory of Wage", he insists on three propositions:

(1) An increase in the supply of any factor of production will increase the absolute share, *i.e.*, absolute income, accruing to that factor if the elasticity of demand for that factor is greater than unity. If we take labor for instance, this is expressed mathematically as follows:

$$d(wL)/dL = w(1 - 1/E_L),$$

where $E_L = -(w/L) \times dL/dw$, and $E_L =$ elasticity of demand for labor. If $E_L > 1$, then $d(wL)/dL > 0$. This means that an increase of labor increases the absolute share accruing to labor.

(2) An increase in the supply of any factor will always increase the absolute share, *i.e.*, absolute income, of all other factors taken together.

(3) An increase in the supply of any factor will increase its relative share (*i.e.*, its proportion of the National Dividend) if its elasticity of substitution is greater than unity. The most important concept "the elasticity of substitution" is defined as follows:

$$E_s = -[d(K/L)/(K/L)]/[d(r/w)/(r/w)].$$

Since the main purpose of this chapter is to consider economic development by assuming the existence of aggregate production functions in agriculture and non-agriculture, the neoclassical income distribution theory is assumed in this model.

Third, Rybczynski's theorem shows that if the relative price is being held constant and one input is increased, the output of an industry that does not use the increased input more intensively would experience an absolute decrease in output. Here, we consider the case of an increase in labor: an increase in labor leads to a decrease in any capital-intensive sector's output (*i.e.*, agricultural output, in our case). Rybczynski's theorem assumes two inputs, rather than three; therefore, here we include agricultural land as agricultural capital. For this reason, the agricultural sector is more capital-intensive. To sidestep this situation and increase the agricultural output, the relative price should be favored when considering the agricultural sector. Therefore, in most cases, $PL \geq 0$ (where, $PL = (\partial \dot{P}/\partial \dot{L})$). Additionally, an increase in total labor would have a negative effect on agricultural capital ($K_1 L \leq 0$) and a positive effect on non-agricultural capital ($K_2 L \geq 0$). This means that agriculture releases capital to the non-agricultural sector. In Rybczynski's theorem — which focuses only on the output side — the output of a capital-intensive sector decreases under conditions of a constant relative price. However, the Hecksher–Ohlin theorem tells us that a labor-intensive sector has a relative advantage, and that the relative price will increase ($PL \geq 0$). As a result, we have the positive effect of sector-based output and per capita income ($Y_i L \geq 0$ and $EL \geq 0$, respectively).

Fourth, the model makes use of the Cobb–Douglas production function, and of thinking that imperfect competition will affect the form of the transformation curve between the two sectors. Johnson [1966] shows that if one combines two Cobb–Douglas production functions into a transformation curve, the result will be a transformation curve with very little curvature, unless one chooses output elasticities that differ radically between the two sectors. Furthermore, if one adds a market imperfection between the two sectors, the transformation curve can easily lose its curvature — which it has, in the present case — and it may indeed become convex, rather than concave, relative to the origin. In the Japanese example considered here, the transformation curve would be almost a straight line, which implies that changes in consumption patterns have had little influence on the sector-based terms of trade. It is important to keep this finding in mind when interpreting the results.

1.1.2 *Agricultural and Economic Development Theories*

There are four types of economic development theory: classic economic theory, growth stage theory, neoclassical theory, and dual economic models.

Among these four theories, classic economic theory, growth stage theory, and dual economic models treat the problems of agricultural and economic development in greater detail than does neoclassical theory. Smith, Ricardo, and Malthus in classic economic theory devoted their efforts to the study of agricultural and industrial problems. We take up Malthusian theory later in this book, and here focus our attention on Smith, as well as on Ricardo, who further developed Smith's theory. Both considered the growth of national wealth and the stationary state. However, Smith's theory is considered a prototype work of the dual economic model. Both Smith and Ricardo admitted to a law of diminishing returns in agriculture, and a law of constant returns (or increasing returns, in Mill) in the industrial sector. Therefore, both industry and agriculture — the latter of which is a fundamentally important sector — are crucially important to economic development.

Both Smith and Ricardo admitted that the rate of capital accumulation in increasing national wealth dictated economic progress. Smith stressed the advantages of the division of labor, and Ricardo clarified and corrected the difference between the ideas of fixed and variable capitals, and between gross and net incomes. Smith implicitly includes the possibilities relating to the stationary state, but Ricardo has a very pessimistic view of economic development in the future; the latter has an unstable view of future society, given the stagnant rate of capital accumulation stemming from a decrease in the profit rate. Therefore, Smith recommends the export of capital and the expansion of the economy to less-developed countries and colonial countries, while Ricardo suggests an increase in productivity by undertaking agricultural and industrial technical changes, importing cheap food, and exporting industrial products through free trade. There are three kinds of growth stage theory; we can classify stage theory into three different categories: the German tradition, typified by List [1841]; structural transformation, embodied by Fisher [1945] and Clark [1940]; and the leading sector of Rostow [1960] (see Hayami and Ruttan [1971]).

List's type of stage theory, furthermore, has five subcategories: savage, pastoral, agricultural, agricultural–manufacturing, and agricultural–manufacturing-commercial. Agriculture develops through export, or by stimulating the development of domestic industry; therefore, the development of domestic industry is very important to the development of agriculture. List intended to protect the German economy from England, which at that time was much further advanced. The second type of stage theory, structural transformation, was developed by Clark and Fisher, but originally developed by Petty; this formulation is similar to the final subcategory of List. Clark and Fisher believe that economic progress occurs as a result of shifts in employment and investment from primary activities to secondary and tertiary activities. Fisher thinks that this chain of events derives from scientific progress; however, there have been some criticisms of his work. For Clark, the criticisms are that Fisher's work is too empirical, lacks an adequate theoretical foundation, and has no significant policy guidance. Ruttan [1965; 1968] thinks that there is a lack of uniformity for the income elasticities of demand among products classified within each of the three categories; he also says that the amounts of time spent in secondary and tertiary activities are too easily concealed.

In terms of agricultural development theory, Ruttan [1965; 1968] and Hayami and Ruttan [1971] offer six theoretical models: the resource exploitation model, the conservation model, the location model, the diffusion model, the high-payoff model, and the induced innovation model. In this book — which treats the issues of population and agriculture — we should address the work of Boserup [1965], as another model. As another conservation model, we should also consider the work of Thaer [1798], the first builder of agricultural science who created his own system of agricultural science based on the following four streams: cameralistics, *hausvater-literatur* (house–father–literature), the empirical research of experimental economists, and agriculture and agricultural science based on the business economics of England. Thaer considers humus, or decomposing organic matter, essential to crops; therefore, barnyard manure and the like, which compensate for nutrients absorbed by crops from the soil as they grow, is needed to supplement the soil.

Thaer's theory highlights five important agricultural issues: humus theory, a compensation theorem, animal-breeding in sheds, crop-rotation systems, and the Norfork rotation system. This theory was developed in the direction of inorganic nutritive substance theory by Liebig, and further reworked by Thünen, in 1826; Aereboe, in 1905; and Brinkman, in 1922. The third theory, from Boserup [1965], insists that population growth is a rather important factor in producing technical change in agriculture (see Chapter 7). Relatedly, we should also consider the location model of Schulz

[1953]. In Thaer's model, environmental differences stem from regional differences, but he does not consider the influence of non-agricultural sectors. However, Thünen considers how a large city influences agricultural and forestry methods as the distance from the city increases. He thinks that the best agricultural method in the vicinity of a city is the free crops method, followed by forestry, the crop-rotation system, the granary system, the three-field system, and the animal husbandry system, in that order.

In the United States, Schulz [1953] states that (1) economic development occurs in a specific locational matrix, (2) these locational matrices are primarily industrial and urban in composition, and (3) an existing economic organization works best at or near the center of a particular matrix of economic development; it can also work optimally in those areas of agriculture that are situated favorably in relation to such a center. These studies look to consider the influence of non-agricultural sectors on agricultural development; however, this research was applied only in advanced countries that have fully developed industrial sectors; it would be difficult to generalize the findings of that research to agriculture in a developing country. The fourth of the six aforementioned theories is that pertaining to the diffusion model. This theory shows that better husbandry practices and the use of better crop and livestock varieties are the major sources productivity growth in agriculture. The high-payoff input model — which assumes some level of international technical diffusion — and the induced innovation model of Hayami and Ruttan are discussed in what follows.

The induced innovation model examines how technical change is induced in the process of conserving a scarce resource. Ruttan stresses the importance of the microeconomic method (*i.e.*, a model that incorporates the importance of the role of price in agricultural development), but he does not deny the importance of the macroeconomic method. In other words, he suspects that the macroeconomic approach neglects the influence of price change on agricultural development, but he nonetheless considers it important. It is certain that the influence of price change is not incorporated into this theoretical and empirical research; it is likely that he did not observe the influence of the induced innovation process, at least empirically. For this reason, here, we change the parameter every five years between 1880 and 1970 — a period for which we have empirical data for the Japanese economy — and include the induced results in terms of price change (see Chapters 2–7).

In other words, we are anxious to bridge the microeconomic and macroeconomic methods, and we are keen to bridge abstract economic theory and real-life history. Finally, the bridge between the population and the economy are also made in this book.

1.2. *Agricultural and Non-agricultural Two-Sector Model*

1.2.1 *Capital and Consumption Two-Sector Models*

Harrod [1939] and Domar [1946] assumed the Leontief production function (fixed coefficient production function) and argued that the X/L ratio is rigid; and if the growth rate of capital K and labor L is different for some reason, the difference will become larger and larger (X means output. However, neoclassical economists insisted that if there is the possibility of being able to substitute between capital and labor as the price changes, the economy is rather stable. Solow [1956] argued that in the equilibrium growth path of a neoclassical growth model, the capital–labor ratio (K/L) has been stable. Uzawa [1961; 1963] extended Solow's contribution to a two-sector model and derived sufficient conditions for convergence of the K/L ratio in the consumption sector over time. Takayama [1963] discussed that the whole K/L ratio is stable to a certain limit when the elasticity of substitution of either the capital or consumption sector is one or more than one. In these models, the consumption and capital sector include the whole economy. Therefore, if we assume that the consumption sector consists of only agriculture, and the non-agricultural sector consists of only the capital goods industry, we can apply this model to our analysis. Such a situation may be found in underdeveloped countries where the agricultural sector dominates the economy and only a few capital sectors exist. Capital–Consumption two-sector models is applicable to the advanced matured economies such as present day Japan and the United States. However, this is not such a useful model for early economic development which is also included in our study.

1.2.2 *Critical Study of the Dualistic Model*

There are many types of dualistic models. In a typical dualistic model, the whole of an economy is divided into two sectors: *i.e.*, the traditional and modern sectors. Most dualistic models are also classified into one of two categories: those that hinge on static dualistic theory, as embodied in the work of Boeke [1953] and Higgins [1956], and those that hinge on the dynamic dualistic theory of Lewis [1954], Ranis and Fei [1961; 1964 (Fei and Ranis)], and Jorgenson [1961], *inter alia*. The static dualistic theory can be further divided into two subcategories: the social dualism of Boeke and the technical dualism of Higgins. The dynamic dualistic theory, meanwhile, can be divided into the classical dualism of Lewis and of Ranis and Fei, and the neoclassical dualism of Jorgenson. Of course, these divisions are too simplistic to represent the real world, which is better expressed by the differential structure in the work of Ohkawa [1972]. Static dualism also contains a dynamic aspect, and there are also mixed classical and neoclassical dualism models.

This dualism was probably first recognized by Smith; since then, there have been many discussions with respect to neoclassical and classical dualism. Classical Lewisian dualistic theory was developed rigorously by Ranis and Fei and by Jorgenson; within that theory, the whole of an economy is divided into the agricultural and the industrial sectors, compared to the Lewisian division between traditional and modern sectors. However, in the Ranis and Fei model, and in that of Jorgenson, a more dynamic element was added; those models, however, neglected the problem of unemployment in a city — a problem taken very seriously in the Lewisian model. There may be many problems inherent in these dualistic theories. We think that they have so many criticisms precisely because their contributions are so clear, and that they stem from the following facts. Both analyses are, in a sense, too eccentric graphically (Ranis and Fei) or mathematically (Jorgenson), and lack the somewhat naive contribution of Lewis. Some critics of theory may feel that their analyses resemble intellectual games, but we cannot neglect the significance and contribution of these theories from the policy perspective. In other words, while we should not discount the merits of these dualistic theories, we must remain mindful of their limitations. Especially, we need to evaluate the merits of their assertions that the agricultural and non-agricultural sectors should develop together, while maintaining a good balance.[1]

---

[1]One of the criticisms of the dualistic model would be its neglect of unemployment. Harris and Todaro [1970] offer the following equation for rural to urban migration, which they say takes place if $w_r < (l_e/l_{us})w_u$ where, w_r and w_u are the wage rates in the rural (r) and urban (u) sectors, respectively; l_e is the total number of jobs available in the urban sector; and l_{us} is the total number of jobs-seekers. Their model considers the possibility of

This assertion is applicable to the Japanese economy, because the con- current growth theory of Ohkawa is applicable to the Japanese economy. Additionally, the policy implication that we should adopt labor-saving technology in the period of early economic development is consistent with the historical Japanese experience. Therefore, we would like to examine the classical and neoclassical dualistic theories in greater detail, while bearing in mind their many criticisms. In the model of Lewis, who was a representative of the classical dualistic theory, the whole economy was divided into two sectors (*i.e.*, subsistence and capitalistic sectors). He noted the increase of the savings rate during modern economic development and, realized that it came from the increase of profit. Therefore, he separated the whole economy into a capitalistic sector and a subsistence sector. Two of the most important ideas in Lewisian theory would be unlimited labor supply and minimum subsistence wage rate which bring a large profit to the capitalistic sector.

This unlimited labor is supplied from subsistence agriculture, casual labor, petty trade, domestic service, wives and daughters in the household and others. Their marginal product in the subsistence sector is very small or zero and sometimes could be negative. Also, the subsistence wage rate which the surplus labor would obtain is assumed to be equal to the average product of the subsistence agriculture plus margin. Thus, for the capitalistic sector, unlimited labor is supplied at a very low subsistence wage rate from the subsistence sector. Therefore, the capitalistic sector has a large profit rate which would be reinvested and lead to high capital accumulation. This high capital accumulation and technical change shifts the marginal productivity curve of labor (*i.e.*, the demand curve for labor) to the right. In other words, the demand for labor would increase. But there is an unlimited labor supply from the subsistence sector. Therefore, rapid acceleration of

---

unemployment within the context of the migration of rural people. Fortunately, Japanese unemployment used to be very low — only 1–2% during the time of non-crisis. For example, the unemployment rates within the post-war economy were as follows: for 1958–1960, it was about 2.5%, and for 1960–1973, it was about 1% (Ministry of Internal Affairs and Communications Statistics Bureau [1958–1973]). Even during the Great Depression, the unemployment rate within the Japanese economy was only 2.24% in the urban areas. These low unemployment rates stem from the fact that Japanese agriculture absorbed unemployed labor during times of recession, as discussed in Chapter 1. In this way, Japanese agriculture made use of a considerable amount of surplus labor.

capital accumulation enables the economy to have a high rate of economic development.

This Lewisian model was developed and made more sophisticated by Ranis and Fei [1961] and Fei and Ranis [1964]. In their model they also divided the whole economy into two sectors, one is a stagnant but large subsistence agricultural sector whose wage rate is fixed institutionally and the other is a small industrial sector whose wage is determined competitively. They used this agricultural and industrial two-sector model and obtained several policy implications. Each agricultural and industrial sector has a production and household sector. Therefore, the whole economy has four sectors in total. They considered the accounting relationships between these four sectors. The agricultural household sector has a large pool of disguised unemployment and they supply their labor and land to the agricultural production sector. Some of the agricultural products (L_a) are consumed by agricultural labor (A_a) and the rest of the agricultural products which are called "total agricultural surplus (TAS)" are consumed by landlords (A'_a) and the residual is sold to the industrial sector. This residual is consumed by the labor in the industrial sector (A_i) and is also used for the raw materials (R).

The industrial household sector supplies its labor and capital to the industrial production sector. The industrial products are used for consumption by the industrial household (Q_i), for consumption by the agricultural sector (Q_a) and for investment (I). Therefore, the income in the agricultural household sector is equal to the food consumption by agricultural labor using the entire institutionally determined wage for food (A_a) plus food consumption by landlords (A'_a) plus the industrial goods consumption by landlords (Q_a) plus the saving (S_a). The income of industrial household sector is equal to the industrial goods consumption by industrial labor (Q_i) plus the food consumption by industrial labor (A_i) plus the savings (S_i). Therefore, the net contribution of the agricultural sector to industrial sector, S_a, would have the following relation: $S_a = R + A_i - Q_a = \text{TAS} - A'_a - Q_a$.

The agricultural goods which are sold to the industrial sector from TAS have a very important role to industrial development. In other words, it helps industrial development as the wage fund or investment fund. The surplus labor in the agricultural sector migrates to the industrial sector and gradually the center of the gravity moves from agriculture to industry.

Therefore, it would be very important for the industrial sector to have a large labor absorption ability. They found that a necessary condition in order to develop economically is for industrial labor to have a larger growth rate (η_L) than the growth rate of population (η_p). They considered this condition as essential for successful economic development and called the condition as a criterion of critical minimum effort. They also concluded that the larger the growth rate of the industrial capital (η_K), the strength of the industrial technical change (J) and the labor intensive bias (B_L) were, then the larger the industrial labor absorption was.

Having an effect in the opposite direction, the less the elasticity of the marginal productivity of industrial labor (ε_{LL}) and the lesser the rate of change in the wage rate (η_w) were, then the larger the industrial labor absorption in the economy was. When one has industrial capital growth, strong technical change, a labor intensive bias along with inelastic marginal labor productivity and stable wage rate, it would be very easy to satisfy the criterion of critical minimum effort. In short, the labor absorption ability of the industrial sector would increase when capital stock and industrial technical change increase. Therefore, we can conclude that one of the best policies for the economy would be to increase the profit rate of the industrial sector, the saving rate of the agricultural sector and technical change, along with using labor intensive technology.

In the first stage there is an unlimited labor supply in the agricultural sector. However, the wage elasticity of the labor supply would decrease when the economy proceeds from the Stage 1 to 2 and 3. Therefore, it would be necessary to increase the agricultural productivity and agricultural surplus in order not to change the relative price of agricultural goods. Otherwise, the industrial wage rate would increase relatively, and consequently the labor absorption ability of the industrial sector would decrease significantly. Therefore, we can conclude that both agricultural and non-agricultural sectors should grow proportionately (*i.e.*, balanced growth is necessary). The Ranis and Fei analyzed the balanced growth path in detail. Their analysis showed that their classical theory became the same as the neoclassical theory after the turning point.

Jorgenson [1961; 1966; 1967; 1969], who is a representative of the neoclassical dualistic theory, denies the concept of unlimited labor supply, especially the assumption of zero marginal productivity of agricultural labor in the classical dualistic theory. He applied the neoclassical marginal theory for labor in both sectors. First, he used and analyzed a model which had only one traditional backward sector (actually an agricultural sector). In this model, he assumes that the amount of land is constant and only one consumption good is produced. The agricultural goods (Y_1) are produced by using agricultural labor (L_1) and fixed land (B). Current inputs and agricultural capital (K_1) are treated as an exogenous variable and are included into agricultural technical change. The agricultural production function is assumed to be the following Cobb–Douglas type with homogeneity of degree of one.

$$Y_1 = e^{at} L_1^{1-\beta} \overline{B}^{\beta}.$$

From this equation, we can obtain the growth rate of agricultural production $[\dot{Y}_1 = (dY_1/dt)/Y_1]$ as follows: $\dot{Y}_1 = \alpha + (1-\beta)\dot{L}_1$. Therefore, the growth rate of per capita food production $y_1(= Y_1/L_1)$ is $\dot{y}_1 = \alpha - \beta \dot{L}_1$. Also the growth rate of population (population L equals L_1 because there exists only an agricultural sector) is assumed to have a linear relationship with per capita food consumption whose positive slope is γ and negative intercept is δ (death rate). The positive relationship between per capita food consumption and growth in the labor force holds until the level of a constant per capita food consumption y_1^* (the minimum level of income needed to attain the physiological maximum growth rate of population). Therefore, $\dot{y}_1 > 0$ is necessary to get a sustained growth of the agricultural sector and obtain an agricultural surplus. Therefore, it would be necessary to have a relationship $\alpha - \beta v > 0$ to get this situation.

On the other hand, the production function of the industrial sector (Y_2) is as follows:

$$Y_2 = e^{\lambda t} K_2^{\sigma} L_2^{1-\sigma}.$$

The industrial goods are produced using two inputs: industrial capital (K_2) and labor (L_2). By using the four equations above — i.e., production function, growth equation of population, equation of sectoral allocation of population, equation of per capita consumption — we can obtain the following equations for the agricultural and industrial labors:

$$L_1(t) = L(0)e^{\{(v-\alpha)/(1-\beta)\}t},$$
$$L_2(t) = L(0)(e^{vt} - e^{\{(v-\alpha)/(1-\beta)\}t}).$$

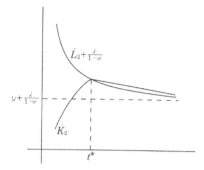

Figure 2-1   Growth Rates of Labor and Capital in the Jorgenson Model

The necessary condition for sustained growth and agricultural surplus, $\alpha - \beta \nu > 0$, can be transformed into the following condition: $\nu > (\nu - \alpha)/(1 - \beta)$. Therefore, the condition $\dot{L}_2(t) > 0$ is obtained from this necessary condition; finally, now we have industrial labor in our model. We can understand that the growth rate of labor $(\dot{L}_2)$ would approach the level of ν in the long run. The growth rate of industrial goods $(\dot{Y}_2)$ and the growth rate of capital $(\dot{K})$ are approaching the level of $\dot{Y}_2 = \dot{K} = [\lambda/(1 - \sigma)] + \nu$ in the long run. Therefore, the growth rates of capital and industrial goods would become larger when population growth (ν) and technical change in the industrial sector are larger and the distributive share of industrial labor $(1 - \lambda)$ is smaller.

Following to the work of Dixit [1970], we can also obtain the following relationships for the growth rate of capital $(\dot{K} = \dot{K}_2)$ and the industrial labor $(\dot{L}_2)$:

$$G(\dot{K}) = (1 - \sigma)[\dot{L}_2 + \lambda/(1 - \sigma) - \dot{K}].$$

Figure 2-1 shows this relationship. From Fig. 2-1, we can see that the growth rate of capital $\dot{K}_2$ would increase until the point of t*, but it is always smaller than the value of $\dot{L}_2 + \lambda/(1 - \sigma)$. Also, $\dot{K}_2$ would have a maximum point at t* and decrease and then approach to the point of $\nu + \lambda/(1 - \sigma)$. Therefore, we can see the capital shallowing phenomena until the point of t* and capital deepening phenomena after the point of t*. However, both $\dot{K}_2$ and $\dot{L}_2 + \lambda/(1 - \sigma)$ approach the balanced growth path $\nu + \lambda/(1 - \sigma)$. From the analysis and conclusion of Ranis and Fei model, we can get the policy implication that it would be better to use a labor-intensive technology in the early economic development.

We can give the following three comments for the Ranis and Fei, and the Jorgenson models. The first point is a comment as to the peculiarity of Jorgenson model. One of the problems of his model would be the peculiarity of consumption function, which affects the operation of his model. His model neglects Engel's law. This would be one of the reasons why he got the peculiar conclusion. The second point is concerned with the relative prices. The constant wage rate of the industrial sector in the surplus stage of Ranis and Fei model is made based on the assumption that an institutionally determined wage rate and constant relative prices are prevailing in the economy. Also, the relative prices of the Jorgenson model are determined at a level which has a constant wage gap. It means that it would not be easy to consider the price effect in the agricultural demand.

As we showed it in Chapter 3, this would make it impossible to analyze the income and price effect of technical change in each sector and of population. The third point is that agricultural capital is not included explicitly in the agricultural production function as Ruttan [1969] also has criticized. The early model of Kelley and Williamson considered this point and included agricultural capital and labor in the agricultural production function. However, it would be necessary to include three inputs (1 and, capital, and labor) at least in the agricultural production function as the later model of Kelley and Williamson showed. Therefore, we made a growth accounting analysis which considered Engel's law, agricultural capital and the price and income effect of technical change and of population.

1.3. *Some Model Analyses for Japanese Economic Development*

We can classify the research on Japanese economic development that is relevant to our purpose into three categories (see Table 2-1.). The first category of research estimates the data and simulates results by using estimated parameters. The work of Ogawa and Suits [1982], Ogawa [1982], and Minami and Ono [1971; 1972; 1975a; 1975b] are found within this category. The research within the second category uses an appropriate parameter that is borrowed from other research, and it compares the simulated results to actual data; the work of Kelley and Williamson [1971; 1973; 1974] and

Table 2-1   Historical Development of the Dualistic Model, and Econometric Analysis of the Japanese Economy

---

(1) Theoretical Research of Dualistic Models

○ Static dualism: Boeke, Higgins and others.

○ Dynamic dualism:

(1) Classical Dualism

*Lewis model: Two sectors (subsistence and capitalist sectors) + Unlimited labor supply in the subsistence sector + Lowest wage rate in the subsistent sector + High profit rate in the capitalist sector → Investments in new capital machines *etc.* → Greater accumulation of capital → Shifts in the demand curve for labor → Increase in the demand for labor → Unlimited labor supply in the subsistence sector → Accelerations in capital stock → High rates of economic development.

*Fei–Ranis model: Yamaguchi evaluates the model positively, but admits their graphical eccentricity. Two sectors (agricultural and industrial sectors) + Redundant labor (labor whose $MPL = 0$) and surplus labor (labor whose $MPL <$ real wage rate) in the agricultural sector + Industrial sector develops from hiring cheap labor → (a) Critical minimum effort criterion ("the condition where the growth rate of industrial labor > Growth rate of total labor" is necessary for development). (b) To satisfy the critical minimum effort criterion, high growth rate of industrial capital, high technical change in the industrial sector, and labor intensive technical change are necessary. Labor elasticity of supply decreases as surplus labor decreases.

(2) Neoclassical Dualism

*Jorgenson model: (Yamaguchi evaluates the model as robust, but admits their mathematical eccentricity.) Two sectors: agricultural and industrial sectors. Denies the existence of $MPL = 0$.

(2) Empirical Research of Dualistic Models

(1) Classical Dualism

*Minami–Ono model: Classical two-sector model (capitalist and non-capitalist sectors). The model is estimated utilizing the usual econometric methods. High population growth, high technical change, and flexible labor markets reduce surplus labor and increase economic growth. Slow increases in the wage rate in the non-capitalist sector and high technical change in the capitalist sector increase the wage gap between the two sectors. Population growth, technical change in the non-capitalist sector, and increase in labor mobility decrease the wage gap.

(2) Neoclassical Dualism

(*Continued*)

Table 2-1   (*Continued*)

---

*Kelley–Williamson–Cheetham model: Neoclassical two-sector model (agricultural, and industrial sectors). Method: Kelley–Williamson–Cheetham utilize appropriate parameters and compare the predicted values from their model with real historical data, and make use of predicted values closest to the real historical values. Problems: (1) Empirical background presented in the demand side is weak. (2) Argument pertaining to biases in the production side was still not clear. (3) Technical change in both sectors is not independent. (4) The authors adopt the Japanese structure of 1885 for 30 years. (5) Kelley–Williamson, and Kelley *et al.* treated population and labor as identical. Yamaguchi has already criticized this in his Ph.D. Thesis [1973]. Williamson developed this point in Bloom and Williamson [1998], after which they developed the "First Demographic Dividend" concept. However, Yamaguchi had already realized this phenomenon in 1973, that is, the growth rate of labor in the 1950s was 2.2%, although the growth rate of population was 1.2% during the same period (see Table 2-5). Therefore, the contribution of labor to per capita income in the 1950s was the second highest; following the contribution of non-agricultural technical change (see panel 8 in Fig. 2-3). (6) Desired conclusions can be reached by employing certain appropriate parameters.

(3) Growth Accounting: Combination of Classical and Neoclassical Dualism (general equilibrium growth accounting is a type of extension of ordinary growth accounting). Two sectors: agricultural and non-agricultural sectors.

*Yamaguchi, Yamaguchi–Binswanger, Yamaguchi–Kennedy model (which includes the imperfect competition of labor market). We extend the ordinary growth accounting (partial growth accounting) model, which includes only the supply side of one sector, into the general equilibrium growth accounting model which includes both demand and supply sides of both sectors.

Our method: This study makes use of suitable parameters drawn from similar studies. As is the case with the growth accounting model, the model values and real values are identical (100%). In short, the Yamaguchi model has the following characteristics: (1) Effects of both the supply and demand side and the other sector can be seen. (2) Adequate attention has been paid to mathematical and graphical representation. (3) In the Ranis–Fei and Jorgenson model, relative price is treated as constant. Therefore, the price effects on demand cannot be observed. The Yamaguchi model can measure both price and income effects of both sectors. Given low income and price elasticities of agricultural goods, the asymmetric effect of technical change (*i.e.*, push effect of agricultural technical change and pull effect of non-agricultural technical change, see Chapter 3) can be found. (4) We introduce the agricultural capital variable into the agricultural production function. This is different from the Fei–Ranis, Jorgenson, and Kelley–Williamson–Cheetham models. (5) The notion of imperfect competition in both sectors is included in order to evade the controversy of redundant labor.

(*Continued*)

Table 2-1   (*Continued*)

---

(3) Empirical Research of Demographic Models

(1) Ogawa–Suit model: This is a primary and secondary two-sector model, and presents more advanced research as compared with several previous development models. Capital and labor are treated as endogenous variables. On the population side, new estimation methods such as the Brass fertility function and Coale–Demeny model are used, and the methodology uses the spline function. My six criticisms for their model are as follows: (1') Two-sector model for the output side, but a one-sector model for the demand side denoted as C, I, G, X, M. (2') No explicit price aspect. Therefore, it is impossible to see the effects of population on demand and income. (3') Capital is treated as an endogenous variable. However, population is treated to affect only savings and not investments. (4') The ratio of primary labor to total labor is derived from the ratio of primary income to total income and primary labor to total labor of the prior period. Therefore, the authors did not consider input market side. (5') Only non-agricultural exports are considered. However, tea and cocoons were very important export products at that time in Japan. (6') Information on data sources is desired.

(2) Ogawa model: This is not a two-sector but a one-sector model. The author estimates four aspects: population, labor participation rate, investment function, and growth rate function of GNP. On the population side, Ogawa uses the modified Brass fertility function and Coale–Demeny model. Literacy rate (*LT*), primary school enrollment rate (*EN*), and total fertility rate (*TFR*) create a loop, that is, $TFR \rightarrow EN \rightarrow LT \rightarrow TFR$. However, important estimations such as the growth rate of I and GNP are adopted from the Suits–Mason model. Note that there is no demand side, which is very important to population estimation. Several t values and R^2 are not significant. Generally, a one-time estimation result affects simulation analysis. However, the estimated result is affected by technical assumptions, data, estimation period and so on. Therefore, the author's method is a good way to estimate and provide policy implications. However, we have to be careful whether the estimates are affected by factors such as technical assumption, data, and estimation period.

Kelley *et al.* [1972a; 1972b] are found within this category. The third category is work that makes use of the method of growth accounting analysis. Yamaguchi model in this book belongs to this category.

1.3.1   *The Ogawa and Ogawa–Suits Models*

(1) The Ogawa and Suits model: This model, as well as the primary and secondary two-sector models, is much more advanced than those found in previous research. Capital and labor are treated as endogenous variables. On the population side, Ogawa and Suits use new estimation methods, like the Brass fertility function and the Coale–Demeny model; their method also

uses the spline function. However, their model contains the following six problems. (a) Their model is a two-sector model on the output side, but only one sector is considered on the demand side (*e.g.*, *C*, *I*, *G*, *X*, and *M*). (b) The model has no explicit price aspect; therefore, it is impossible to see the effects of the population side on demand and income. (c) In their model, capital is treated as an endogenous variable; however, population is treated as affecting only the saving side, and not the investment side. (d) In their model, the primary labor–total labor ratio is determined from the primary income–total income ratio, and from the primary labor–total labor ratio of one period previous. As such, they do not consider the input market side. (e) In their model, exports are determined from non-agricultural output; however, tea and silk cocoons were very important export products at that time. (f) The model's data source is not written.

(2) The Ogawa model: Ogawa's model contains one sector, not two. He estimates four aspects: population, labor participation rate, investment function, and growth rate function of gross national product (*GNP*). On the population side, he uses a modified Brass fertility function and the Coale–Demeny model. The literacy rate (*LT*), primary school enrollment rate (*EN*), and total fertility rate (*TFR*) create a loop such as *TFR* → *EN* → *LT* → *TFR*. However, important estimations — such as the growth rate of *I*, *GNP* — are adopted from the Suits–Mason model. There is no demand side, despite the fact that it is important in relation to population. Several *t* values and R^2 are not very good. Generally speaking, a single time estimation result can have too great of an effect for use in simulation analysis, because the estimated result is affected by technical assumptions, data, and the estimation period, among other things. Therefore, while his model is a good tool by which to estimate and derive policy implications, we must be careful to ensure that estimates are affected by (and therefore reflect) technical assumptions, data, and the estimation period.

1.3.2   The Minami–Ono Model

As we have already seen, the unlimited labor supply model of classical dualism was presented by Lewis [1954] and Ohkawa [1955]. Ranis and Fei [1961] extended the Lewisian model, especially for the agricultural sector, in more detail (Also, see Kao and *et al.* [1964] too). They considered the relationships between agricultural and industrial sectors and also observed

Table 2-2   Hayami's Factor Share, and Output Elasticity in Agriculture

	Distribution Share of Labor (Yamada and Hayami)	Labor Elasticity of Output (Akino and Hayami)
1930	0.542	0.465
1935	0.477	0.344
1955	0.558	—
1960	0.483	0.287
1965	0.494	0.250

the influence of technical change more explicitly. Also, Minami [1970] considered that the Japanese economy could be described by the Lewisian model until the decade of the 1950s. Minami and Ono [1971; 1972; 1975a; 1975b] constructed a two-sector model for the Japanese economy. Then, they obtained the following conclusions: (1) A high growth rate of population, a low rate of increase in the wage rate, a high rate of technical change, a more mobile labor market and a low distribution share of labor would raise the growth rate of the economy. (2) A high growth rate of the population, a low growth rate of the wage rate in the non-capitalistic sector, a high rate of technical change, a more mobile labor market, a high growth rate of economy would decrease the share of surplus labor.

(3) A low growth rate of wages in the non-capitalistic sector, a high rate of technical change in the capitalistic sector would increase the wage differential between the two sectors. Also, the increase of the growth rate of gainfully employed workers, a high rate of technical change in the non-capitalistic sector and a more mobile labor market would decrease the wage differential. Minami and Ono model was published in many Japanese Journals and books. However, Jorgenson [1973] and Ichimura [1973], who were the commentators of Minami and Ono's articles at the Japanese Conference in 1973, gave many critical comments whose essence was summarized as follows. Jorgenson [1973] summarized the Minami and Ono model. Then, he agreed with their stress on the importance of a two-sector model, but he pointed that their model had a serious defect. Especially, he stressed that their model neglected the supply side of labor completely.

He showed that the idea of disguised unemployment had been contradicted by the research of Akino and Hayami [1973] and of Yamada and Hayami [1972]. In other words, he showed Table 2-2 summarizing their research (see Table 2-2), from which he concluded that the hypothesis of the disguised unemployment meant that the distributive share of labor exceeded the labor elasticities of output. Judging from the results measured by Akino and Hayami, and Hayami and Yamada, the proportion of the surplus labor in the sense of Minami and Ono was greater in 1960 and 1965 than those in 1930 and 1935. This would be really a contradictory result and would cause a serious doubt on the idea of the disguised unemployment. Although it might be natural for their classical dualistic model to be criticized by Jorgenson who is a neoclassical dualistic theorist, he criticized that their model was too ambitious. Also, Ichimura [1973] gave a following comment: He believed that a neoclassical hypothesis seemed to be more appropriate to the Japanese economy because the growth rate of the real wage rate in the primary sector was 0.72% and the growth rate of labor productivity was 0.74% over their calculated period (*i.e.*, almost same growth rates).

1.3.3   *The Kelley et al. Model*

Jorgenson, who gave a comment to the model of Minami and Ono published a neoclassical duality theory in 1961. However, Kelley and Williamson [1971; 1973; 1974], Kelley *et al.* [1972a; 1972b] used a more neoclassical duality theory by using an agricultural and non-agricultural two-sector model (whose wage was assumed to be equal to the marginal product of labor in each sector in their basic model). They tried to combine theoretical work with empirical work. The basic model of Kelley and Williamson was based on the Jorgenson's two-sector model instead of the Ranis and Fei model. But they generalized the Jorgenson model in a more applicable way for empirical work. They constructed a model of the Japanese economic structure of 1885 and adopted the parameters for the model from other research and simulated the model until the beginning of the World War I. They chose the Japanese economy because of the following reasons: (1) Many data were available; (2) Japan had a steady economic growth; and (3) Japan was a typical labor surplus country.

Their model had sectoral demand functions, and sectoral production functions, factor demand equations, employment conditions and an equation to balance the market. In their model, they used a Stone and Geary demand system and stressed sectoral differences in the demand. However, we are able to identify seven problems with their research: (1) We would evaluate their work further, if they were to treat population and labor as non-identical: the majority of children and the elderly do not contribute to the production side, for example, but they nonetheless demand agricultural and non-agricultural products. In other words, the Kelley–Williamson model treats population and labor as though they were identical. The experiences of Japan and the United States show that the growth rates of population and labor are very different in the short term, and that the labor–population ratio changes considerably over time. Therefore, in this book, we treat population and labor independently, and also consider the imperfect competition of the input market in the following two ways. First, the value of the marginal product of labor (*VMPL*) differs from the nominal wage rate (*i.e.*, imperfect competition is considered). Second, a wage differential exists between the agricultural and non-agricultural sectors.

The method of Kelley and Williamson is similar to that inherent in typical growth models, which treat labor as identical to population. Because population growth thus increases the labor force automatically, such a treatment leads to an optimistic, overestimated evaluation of population effects on per capita income. Only to the extent that diminishing returns to labor exist will there be a detrimental impact on growth. If, however, an economy is experiencing unemployment problems, an increase in population may be accompanied by a decrease in the labor participation rate: there would be an addition to the ranks of consumers, but not to the ranks of labor. As stated above, Kelley and Williamson [1971; 1973; 1974], and Kelley *et al.* [1972a; 1972b] treat population and labor as identical—something I criticized in my Ph.D. dissertation back in 1973 (Yamaguchi, 1973). Later, this point is developed by Bloom and Williamson [1998], who later pinpointed the First Demographic Dividend (*i.e.*, if the birth rate decreases, then the percentage of children would decrease, but the percentage of production age would increase, therefore bringing about economic growth). I had already recognized this phenomenon, in 1973: Japan's growth rate of labor in the 1950s was 2.2%, despite its growth rate of population being 1.2% in that decade (see Table 2-5 in Sec. 3). Therefore, as we discuss in the next section, the contribution of labor to per capita income in the 1950s was second largest, following the contribution of non-agricultural technical change (see panel 8 of Fig. 2-3, in Sec. 3).

(2) It would still not be enough to support the sectoral differences of the demand system empirically. For example, they adopted the parameters of their model from many Japanese researchers. However, the parameters which they adopted were obtained from a variety of quite different data sources and obtained by different methods by many researchers. Therefore, it would not be so attractive to use them together as if they had a homogeneous quality.

(3) They used a biased technology in their production function. In their early articles, they adopted Watanabe's work [1970] which showed a labor-saving technology for the non-agricultural sector and adopted Hayami and Ruttan's work [1971] which showed a labor using technology for the agricultural sector. However, later works showed that even the agricultural sector used a labor-saving technology.

(4) They assumed that the factor augmenting rates in both agricultural and non-agricultural sectors were the same. This meant that they did not treat the sectoral technical change independently. However, generally speaking technical change is not transferable between sectors with the exception of some advances in basic sciences and increases in general education. For examples: plant breeding has no effect on industrial productivity; new pesticides, even though developed in the industrial sector, only affect agricultural factor productivity; and basic mechanical advances will pay off in terms of industrial productivity. Further, the institutions and environment in the two sectors of research and development are quite different. Much research in agriculture was made by agricultural experiment stations, an investment of the government. But most of the research in the non-agricultural sector was made by private people and extended through private channels. Therefore, it would be more important to measure how sectoral technical change would contribute to the economic growth.

(5) They applied a general equilibrium analysis to the Japanese economic history, 1885–1915, and the initial conditions for 1885 were estimated. Therefore, they used the basic structure of 1885 to simulate the model for a period of 30 years. Also they intended to apply their model to present Southeast Asia. However, the structures of the present Southeast Asia and Japanese economy in 1885 are quite different. (6) For simulation work, it would be possible to grasp the benefit of technical change. However, they did not consider the cost aspect. Therefore, even if they could understand the

benefit by simulation work, the cost varies very much among the Southeast Asian countries. In other words, there would be many possibilities to lead to a mistake if we claim policy implications based on the consideration only of the benefits without consideration of the costs.

(7) In their early papers, they stated that the low growth rate of population had a very important role in Japanese economic development. They compared the growth rate of population between Southeast Asian countries (2.7%) and Japan (about 0.9%) and concluded that about 60% of the extraordinary high growth rate of the Japanese economy was explained by this low growth rate of population. Therefore, they concluded that the low growth rate of population made a very important role to the Japanese economic growth. However, in their later researches they changed their view of population growth completely. In other words, they began to have a relatively optimistic view with respect to the impact of population growth. It seems to me that they could manipulate their simulation values by choosing a fairly arbitrary combination of parameters and thus their results contradict each other.

As stated above, Lewis, Ranis and Fei versus Jorgenson theoretically, and Minami and Ono versus Kelley and Williamson (basic model) empirically are opposed to each other as a classical dualistic economist versus neoclassical dualistic economist. The concept of the disguised unemployment was first used by Robinson in 1936. And many researchers have been developing this field empirically. In Japan, Kamiya and others worked in this field. The theory of unlimited labor supply by Lewis and Ohkawa were developed under these circumstances. However, Schulz [1953], for example, changed his opinion from the belief of zero marginal product of labor, discarding the concept after he studied the situation of Latin America and India. Some other studies also showed a positive marginal product of labor in the agricultural sector. There are also many theoretical studies by Sen [1966], and Zarembka [1972], and others. Taira [1970] denied the unlimited labor supply theory of Minami [1970]. He showed that the real wage rate of unskilled labor increased and the wage differences decreased at the rising periods of the business cycle and increased at the falling periods of the business cycles.

Also, Ito [1978] showed that the wage differentials between skilled and unskilled labors increased as a trend. He concluded that the Japanese economy was not in a state of the unlimited labor supply after the latter half of the 1910s. He also concluded that there was no reason to confirm the unlimited labor supply even before the latter half of the 1910s although there remained some ambiguous points in this period. Further, Yasuba [1980] showed that the Japanese economy passed the turning point in the beginning of the 20th century and entered a labor shortage economy. But she turned back to the labor surplus economy again by World War II and again passed the turning point after World War II. On the contrary, Ohkawa [1975] denied the empirical background of the neoclassical theory (*i.e.*, in neoclassical theory, they assume that even in the traditional sector it is possible to use the marginal principle). But his book contained an article which adopted the marginal principle and admitted that this controversy had not been settled even at the international conference.

In this way, the controversy has not been settled yet. Therefore, we use a model which includes the imperfect competition between factor prices and its marginal product, and also have the wage differentials between two sectors too (in Chapter 4, we examine the surplus labor of Japanese agriculture in detail). Therefore, the Yamaguchi model [1969; 1972; 1973; 1982a; 1982b; 1984a; 1984b] was, first, characterized as a mixture of the classical dualistic theory by Minami and Ono and the neoclassical dualistic theory by Kelley *et al.* [1972b]. In other words, our model contained an aspect of the labor surplus economy such as imperfect competition between factor prices and its marginal product and the wage differentials between two sectors, although we adopted the neoclassical theory basically. Second, our method also had an empirical characteristic. The empirical study of Minami and Ono used an ordinary method. They estimated their parameter values by using ordinary least squares or a conditional least square method.

On the other hand, the method of Kelley *et al.* [1972b] was a simulation technique. They gave an initial condition for 1885 and parameter values and simulated the model. They compared the simulated values and the actual historical values. However, we tried to simplify our model as much as possible and calculated the influence and contribution of the exogenous variables (such as technical change in each sector and population and others) to the eight endogenous variables (such as per capita income, sectoral output and input and relative prices) for each five year interval (or decade) over the 1880–1970 period. This was growth accounting and we called it as a general equilibrium growth accounting model (we may call the ordinary growth accounting as partial equilibrium growth accounting.). We also tried to see the structural change of the Japanese economy through a growth rate multiplier (see Sec. 2 in this chapter) which was obtained as a by-product. In other words, we calculated the average growth rates of the exogenous and endogenous variables for each decade over the period 1880–1970, and used each decadal average value as a representative value of the decade. Then, we made a general equilibrium growth accounting analysis and also saw the structural change. Thus, our method was quite different from previous studies.

1.3.4 *The Growth Accounting Model*

The most popular and simple method of growth accounting analysis would be to explain the growth of output by the contribution of production factor inputs and technical change. This method has been used by many people after Solow [1957] showed the method to provide technical change as a residual, and provide a measure of the contribution of technical change to output growth. One of the problems for this method would be that it is easy to make a too low estimate of the contribution of capital and estimate the contribution of technical change too high. Solow also recognized this problem and developed the research method of using a vintage-type production function. However, another new direction which was started by Schulz and developed by Griliches [1964] was to add some additional explanatory variables and lessen the residual in the production function. Actually, Griliches introduced seven explanatory variables such as education (average years of schooling of farmers), research and extension (state government expenditure) and others (expenditure for feed and livestock) besides the conventional inputs such as labor, capital (machine), land and building, and fertilizer.

In Japan, some of the research of Akino and Hayami [1973] used this method. Denison [1962] also developed this kind of research. He noted the change of the quality of labor. He considered that time reduction effect, education, improvement of the status of woman, age and sex composition and other factors would affect the quality of labor. As a contrast to this labor study of Denison, the research of the quality change and utilization rate of capital were started by Schmookler, Kendrick and Solow, and developed by Christensen and Jorgenson [1970]. In Japan, Ohkawa [1968] also adopted this method. This research contributed a lot to the understanding of the content of technical change. However, it also included several problems as Yasuba [1980] pointed out: "Aggregate factor productivity is a kind of residual and it contains not only technical change in narrow sense but also the improvement of labor quality, improvement of management, the development of the division of labor, scale economies, the effect of the external economies, policy improvement and institutional reform *etc.* Therefore, this research has a great significance in the sense that it tries to study the factors which are neglected. However, these analyses are made by making many arbitrary assumptions."

Yasuba also stated as follows: "Sometimes a private effect of education may be evaluated too much and a social effect is often neglected. Also, the formation of human capital could be made not only by school but also in the home and working place. However, it is impossible to capture these aspects in their model." Yasuba further continued: "We are not sure whether the total amounts of technical change through the improvement of the quality of capital are brought only by the research and development. Some accidental private inventions and findings by individuals and firms would also contribute to technical change. Conversely, the supply price of capital may be too high because of the shortage of capital. These elements would also affect the result of their model. In short, these studies are made by making many arbitrary assumptions. However, an important thing would be that growth accounting analysis, especially a simple growth accounting analysis, is very useful in describing the economic growth by a social accounting method.

An important finding is that the largest contributor to economic growth is the improvement of total factor productivity (*i.e.*, technical change or residual)." Therefore, we also followed Yasuba's comment and investigated the role of the total factor productivity (*i.e.*, technical change in wide sense) in our paper and made a few extensions in Yamaguchi and Kennedy [1984a; 1984b]. Tolley and Smidt [1964] produced a research to measure how much agricultural technical change contributed to the US economy from 1930 to 1960. However, per capita income was treated as an exogenous variable in their model. Also, they measured only the contribution of agricultural technical change to non-agricultural output. They also divided all variables by population. However, we rather wanted to measure the effect of population more explicitly. Therefore, we extended their model to incorporate these aspects for our purpose.

1.3.5 *Recent Development of a Model Related to Japanese Economic Development*

The computable general equilibrium (CGE) model has prevailed since around 1975. However, Ezaki [1984] evaluated that Yamaguchi [1969; 1972; 1973; 1982a; 1982b] — the first person ever to apply the theoretical general equilibrium growth model to the CGE model — had made the bridge to the present-day CGE model. More accurately, Kelley *et al.* [1972a; 1972b], Kelley and Williamson [1971; 1974], and Yamaguchi began in the early 1970s to build the bridge to the present-day CGE model. Kelley and Williamson [1971] published a CGE model similar to the present-day CGE model. However, the Yamaguchi model is a CGE model, and also a general equilibrium growth accounting model whose endogenous variables precisely coincide with actual values. In this sense, the Yamaguchi models are also growth accounting models, and they are completely different from those of Kelley and Williamson and other present-day CGE models.

The recent research on economic development, which must be considered in our study, tends to focus on the following four areas: (1) The problem of agricultural and non-agricultural distortion. Hayashi and Prescott [2008] consider that Japan's labor barrier existed because among farming households, the pre-war patriarchy forced the son designated as the heir to remain in agriculture. Moreover, Temple [2005] points out the problem of distortion, *i.e.*, output losses associated with factor misallocation and aggregate growth in the presence of factor market distortion. Therefore, we consider the problem of distortion and assume in our model the existence of imperfect competition in both the labor and capital markets (m_1, m_2, m_3, m_4, N_w, and N_r), as described in Sec. 2. (2) The second area is the reconfirmation that agriculture is the center of development (Gollin *et al.* [2002]), although this conclusion may be reversed when we consider the international situation (Matsuyama [1992]).

In other words, two diametrically opposed opinions of agriculture exist. Gollin *et al.* [2002] believe that agriculture is very important and must occupy the center of development, while on the other hand, Matsuyama, for example, opposes this thinking with respect to international trade. (3) In the third research area, Temple [2005] evaluates the two-sector model as being still important to research on development; therefore, in this study, we use a two-sector model that contains the agricultural sector. (4) Laitner [2000] (p. 546) suggests that while an unusual level of thrift may lead to a high income level (as shown in Solow's framework), the causality can run the other way: a higher standard of living can lead to a higher measured savings rate. In our study, we calculate how population, labor, and capital stock influence income levels and sector-based outputs through savings.

2. Theoretical Explanation of the Model

The model relates technical change in two sectors, capital accumulation and labor and population growth, to per capita income. sectoral outputs, allocation of resources, and terms of trade. We use it to measure the impact of the exogenous variables on the endogenous ones at different states of the development of Japan, *i.e.*, we trace structural changes in that economy. In addition, the model is used to measure the contributions of the exogenous variables to per capita income for each decade from 1880 to 1970. The focus of the study, therefore, is on growth accounting in a general equilibrium context. In this model, technical changes is treated as sector specific, *i.e.*, productivity advances in the agricultural production process have no impact on the efficiency of the non-agricultural production process. This strongly differentiates the mode from apparently similar work of Kelley and Williamson [1971; 1973; 1974], and Kelley *et al.* [1972a; 1972b]. Technical change is also viewed as the result of an investment activity in basic and applied research. It is therefore quite similar to physical capital accumulation. These two investment categories compete for the aggregate savings of the economy (as does investment in human capital, which is not considered in the model).

To prevent asymmetric treatment of those that are considered in the model, the investment activities, saving and investment are not treated endogenously in the model. Rather, capital accumulation rates and rates of technical change are treated exogenously. This is appropriate because these variables can be viewed as policy targets and because the goal of this study is to find out what the effect of changes in these rates are on per capita income and other endogenous variables. The disadvantage of not modeling both investment categories endogenously is that no way exists in the model to tell whether the economy allocated its overall investment resources efficiently to physical capital accumulation and to generating technical changes in the two sectors. For example, one finding of this study is that a 1% increase in non-agricultural technical change has a higher effect of per capita income growth than a similar increase in the rate of agricultural technical change.

Does this mean that the economy should allocate more resources to non-agricultural technical change? This question cannot be answered without data on how much it costs to achieve a 1% increase in each of these rates of change. If non-agricultural technical change is more expensive than agricultural technical change, it may still be better to concentrate on the latter. The model, therefore, can only assess benefits of alternative courses of action. This is a deficiency, which it shares with other growth accounting frameworks.

2.1. Static Relationships

The total Demand for agricultural products is as Eq. (2.1) in Table 2-3, with the notations summarized. In this study, the demand for agricultural products (Y_1) is assumed to be a function of real per capita income (E), the price of agricultural products relative to non-agricultural products (P), population (Q), and a demand shifter (a). A log–log linear demand function is assumed. The agricultural production function can be expressed as Eq. (2.2) in Table 2-3: where $L_1 = $ agricultural labor, $K_1 = $ agricultural capital and $T_1 = $ technical change in agriculture. Non-agricultural products are produced by using non-agricultural capital (K_2) and non-agricultural labor (L_2) as Eq. (2.3) in Table 2-3: where $T_2 = $ technical change in non-agriculture. The adding up constraint for labor is as Eq. (2.4) in Table 2-3: where $Q = $ population and $N = $ non-labor. The adding up constraint for capital is as Eq. (2.5) in Table 2-3: The demand for factors in each sector depends on the price of the output, the rate of return paid for the factor, and the marginal productivity of the factors. To allow for market imperfections (m_i) the wage rate is equal to a fraction of the value of the marginal product.

The labor demands in each sector are as Eqs. (2.6) and (2.7) in Table 2-3: The capital demands in each sector are as Eqs. (2.8) and (2.9)

Table 2-3   Static and Dynamic Versions of the Mathematical Model

(2.1)	$Y_1 = a Q P^\eta E^\varepsilon$	Agricultural demand function
(2.2)	$Y_1 = T_1 L_1^\alpha K_1^\beta B^{1-\alpha-\beta}$	Agricultural production function
(2.3)	$Y_2 = T_2 L_2^\gamma K_2^\delta$	Non-agricultural production function
(2.4)	$L = L_1 + L_2$	
(2.5)	$K = K_1 + K_2$	Adding up constraint Value of marginal product equals factor price
(2.6)	$w_1 = m_1 \alpha P_1 (Y_1 / L_1)$	
(2.7)	$w_2 = m_2 \gamma \, P_2 (Y_2 / L_2)$	
(2.8)	$r_1 = m_3 \beta \, P_1 (Y_1 / K_1)$	
(2.9)	$r_2 = m_4 \delta \, P_2 (Y_2 / K_2)$	
(2.10)	$w_1 = m_w w_2$	
(2.11)	$r_1 = m_r r_2$	Factor mobility condition
(2.12)	$P' Q E = P_1 Y_1 + P_2 Y_2$	Income identity

Dynamic model

Equation No.	Coefficients of the A matrix of structural parameters								Vector x of endogenous variables	Vector b of exogenous variables
(2.13)	1	0	0	0	0	0	$-\eta$	$-\varepsilon$	$\dot{Y}_1$	$\dot{a} + \dot{Q}$
(2.14)	1	0	$-\beta$	0	$-\alpha$	0	0	0	$\dot{Y}_2$	$\dot{T}_1 + (1 - \alpha - \beta)\,\dot{B}$
(2.15)	0	1	0	$-\delta$	0	$-\gamma$	0	0	$\dot{K}_1$	$\dot{T}_2$
(2.16)	0	0	0	0	l_1	l_2	0	0	$\dot{K}_2$	$\dot{L}$
(2.17)	0	0	k_1	k_2	0	0	0	0	$\dot{L}_1$	$\dot{K}$
(2.18)	0	0	1	-1	-1	1	0	0	$\dot{L}_2$	$\dot{N}_w - \dot{N}_r$
(2.19)	0	0	$\beta - \delta$	0	$\alpha - \gamma$	0	1	0	$\dot{P}$	$\dot{T}_2 - \dot{T}_1 - (1 - \alpha - \beta)\dot{B}$ $+ \gamma \, \dot{N}_w + \delta \dot{N}_r$
(2.20)	λ	$1 - \lambda$	0	0	0	0	0	-1	$\dot{E}$	$\dot{Q}$

$i = 1,2$	= agricultural and non-agricultural sector, respectively
Y_1, L_1, K_1, B	= sectoral outputs, labor inputs, capital inputs, and agricultural land
P_1	= sectoral output prices
P	= P_1 / P_2 = terms of trade
P'	= general price level
w_1, r_1	= sectoral wage and capital rental rates
T_1	= sectoral level of technical efficiency
Q	= population

(*Continued*)

←

Table 2-3   (*Continued*)

E = per capita income
m_i = degree of imperfect competition
m_w = agricultural wage rate as a proportion of non-agricultural wage rate
a = agricultural demand shifter
η, ε = agricultural price and income elasticity
α, β = output elasticity of agricultural labor and capital
γ, δ = output elasticity of non-agricultural labor and capital
λ = proportion of income generated in agriculture

---

in Table 2-3: In the intersector mobility condition for wage rate, labor is assumed to migrate to the non-agricultural sector only if the wage rate there exceeds the agricultural wage rate by Eq. (2.10), given proportion (m_w). This leads to the equilibrium condition. The intersectoral mobility condition for interest rate is as Eq. (2.11): In other words, capital flows from agriculture to the non-agricultural sector only if the interest rate there exceeds the agricultural interest rate by Eq. (2.11), given proportion (m_r). Finally, total nominal income ($P'QE$) is the sum of the agricultural nominal income (P_1Y_1) plus the non-agricultural nominal income (P_2Y_2) as Eq. (2.12) shows: where P' is the general price level. Equation (2.12) is needed because real per capita income (E) must be an endogenous in the model, and enters the demand relationship. If this aspect were to be neglected, as in the Tolley–Smidt model [1964], simulation would lead to erroneous results. Table 2-3 shows a summary of the static relationships.

The six equations from Eq. (2.6) to Eq. (2.11) can be reduced to two equations as follows:

$$N_w = P\alpha(Y_1L_2)/\gamma\,(Y_2L_1) \qquad (2.21)$$

and

$$N_r = P\beta(Y_1K_2)/\delta(Y_2K_1), \qquad (2.22)$$

where N_w is the degree of imperfection of the labor markets.

$$N_w = m_w m_2/m_1. \qquad (2.23)$$

N_r is the degree of imperfection of the capital market.

$$N_r = m_r m_4/m_3. \qquad (2.24)$$

From these two equations, we can obtain the following two equations.

$$N_w/N_r = (\alpha \delta K_1 L_2)/(\gamma \beta L_1 K_2), \tag{2.25}$$

$$P = (\alpha \delta)^\delta (\gamma T_2 N_w^\gamma N_r^\delta)/(\beta \gamma)^\delta (\alpha T_1 L_1^{(\alpha-\gamma)} K_1^{(\beta-\delta)} B^\xi). \tag{2.26}$$

2.2. Dynamic Relationships

$\dot{X}$ is defined as a proportional change of variable X over time. Differentiating Eq. (2.1) totally and converting in proportional rates of changes, the dynamic equivalent of the demand relation is

$$\dot{Y}_1 = \dot{a} + \dot{Q} + \eta \dot{P} + \varepsilon \dot{E}, \tag{2.13}$$

where η is the price elasticity of demand for agricultural products, and ε is the income elasticity and this is the Eq. (2.13) in matrix form of dynamic model in Table 2-3. If T_1 is defined as the percentage rate of change of output per unit of input in the agricultural sector, α as the share of product accruing to labor in agriculture, and β as the share of product accruing to the capital inputs, then the dynamic relations corresponding to the production functions (2.2) becomes Eq. (2.14) in Table 2-3: If γ is defined as the share of product accruing to labor in the non-agricultural sector and δ as the share of product accruing to the capital input, and production function (2.3) becomes Eq. (2.15) in Table 2-3:

The adding up constraints (2.4) and (2.5) lead to the Eqs. (2.16) and (2.17): The factor mobility conditions (2.21) and (2.22) can be converted into the Eq. (2.18) which comes from the condition (2.25). Equations (2.21) and (2.22) also lead to the Eq. (2.19) *i.e.* Eq. (2.19) which comes from the condition (2.26). Equation (2.19) relates the terms of trade, technical change, sectoral allocation of resources, *etc.* Assuming for simplicity, that the degree of imperfection remains constant (*i.e.*, $\dot{N}_w$ and $\dot{N}_r$ equal zero) and two inputs (*i.e.*, only labor and capital, and no land), then this equation shows that the rate of change of the terms of trade depends on: (1) the difference in the rate of technical change in the two sectors, (2) the difference in the labor shares in the two sectors, and (3) the change in the labor–capital ratio in the agricultural sector. Finally, Eq. (2.12) would be changed as Eq. (2.20):

$$\dot{Q} = \lambda \dot{Y}_1 + (1 - \lambda) \dot{Y}_2 - \dot{E}. \tag{2.20}$$

As stated above, Table 2-3 gives a summary of the dynamic relationships too. The equations are exhibited in matrix form with eight endogenous variables $(\dot{Y}_1, \dot{Y}_2, \dot{K}_1, \dot{K}_2, \dot{L}_1, \dot{L}_2, \dot{P}, \dot{E})$ on the left-hand side and nine exogenous variables $(\dot{a}, \dot{Q}, \dot{T}_1, \dot{T}_2, \dot{K}, \dot{L}, \dot{N}_w, \dot{N}_r, \dot{B})$ on the right-hand side. In other words, our model is expressed in matrix form as follows: $Ax = b (A = 8 \times 8, x = 8 \times 1,$ and $b = 8 \times 1)$ or $x = A^{-1}b$ where, x is a vector of endogenous variables, b is a vector of exogenous variables, and the elements of the A^{-1} matrix are growth rate multipliers (Table 2-3). Therefore, a growth rate multiplier shows how an exogenous variable affects an endogenous variable. As an example, the $(A^{-1})_{2,4}$ element is $Y_2 L$, which indicates by how much the rate of change of non-agricultural output $(\dot{Y}_2)$ increases due to an increase in labor growth $(\dot{L})$ (the multipliers of those exogenous variables which appear twice in the vector b, such as technical change in both sectors, are the sum of the two corresponding elements of A).

All functional forms are of the Cobb–Douglas type. The agricultural demand function includes an autonomous demand-shifter that picks up changes in tastes and consumption that are not reflected in the demand elasticities (which include exports and imports). Technical change is assumed to be neutral in both sectors as stated above; the rate of technical change is treated separately for the agricultural and non-agricultural sectors because, with the exception of some advances in the basic sciences and increases in general education, technical change is not transferable among sectors: advancements in machinery, soil science, and the skills of the labor force, for example, are sector-specific. Furthermore, the institutional environments of research in the two sectors differ widely. Research in the agricultural sector is carried out primarily in government-financed experiment stations, and the research results are disseminated with the help of government-operated extension services. In the non-agricultural sector, almost all applied research is carried out privately, and its results are disseminated through private channels. Therefore, an important question to ask is: to what extent has technical change in each sector contributed to growth in the economy at large?

Again, here, population and labor are treated independently, to permit separate evaluations of their effects on per capita income. A special feature of our model is the inclusion of market imperfection in the form of differentials between *VMPL* and the factor price, and exogenous differentials in factor prices between the sectors. As can be seen from Table 2-4,

Table 2-4 Parameter Values Used in the Model

Year	(1) Labor's Share in Agric. Output $\alpha = \frac{w_1 L_1}{P_1 Y_1}$	(2) Capital's Share in Agric. output $\beta = \frac{r_1 L_1}{P_1 Y_1}$	(3) Labor's Share in Non-agric. Output $\gamma = \frac{w_2 L_2}{P_2 Y_2}$	(4) Capital's Share in Non-agric. Output $\delta = \frac{r_2 K_2}{P_2 Y_2}$	(5) Price Elast. of Agric. Goods η	(6) Income Elast. of Agric. Goods ε	(7) Prop. of Labor in Agric. $l_1 = \frac{L_1}{L}$	(8) Prop. of Capital in Agric. $k_1 = \frac{K_1}{K}$	(9) Share of Income Produced by Agric. $\lambda = \frac{P_1 Y_1}{P'QE}$
1880	0.58	0.12	0.80	0.20	-0.60	0.80	0.71	0.43	0.50
1885	0.57	0.12	0.80	0.20	-0.60	0.80	0.70	0.42	0.35
1890	0.54	0.12	0.74	0.26	-0.60	0.80	0.68	0.39	0.39
1895	0.54	0.11	0.70	0.30	-0.60	0.80	0.66	0.37	0.33
1900	0.56	0.10	0.65	0.35	-0.60	0.80	0.65	0.33	0.29
1905	0.55	0.11	0.63	0.37	-0.60	0.71	0.63	0.31	0.25
1910	0.56	0.11	0.62	0.38	-0.60	0.71	0.62	0.27	0.24
1915	0.55	0.12	0.52	0.48	-0.60	0.71	0.57	0.23	0.22
1920	0.55	0.12	0.62	0.38	-0.60	0.71	0.51	0.18	0.22
1925	0.59	0.11	0.62	0.38	-0.60	0.71	0.48	0.15	0.22
1930	0.61	0.12	0.55	0.45	-0.60	0.71	0.47	0.13	0.13
1935	0.55	0.13	0.50	0.50	-0.60	0.71	0.44	0.11	0.14
1940	0.55	0.10	0.46	0.54	-0.60	0.71	0.40	0.09	0.13
1945	0.55	0.10	0.46	0.54	-0.60	0.80	0.44	0.10	0.14
1950	0.55	0.10	0.46	0.54	-0.60	0.71	0.44	0.09	0.14
1955	0.65	0.12	0.72	0.28	-0.60	0.61	0.37	0.09	0.16
1960	0.57	0.13	0.65	0.35	-0.60	0.61	0.30	0.08	0.09
1965	0.60	0.16	0.69	0.31	-0.60	0.61	0.23	0.07	0.06

Sources: Columns (1) and (2), from the data of Yamada and Hayami [1972]; Columns (3) and (4), from Minami and Ono [1978]; Column (5), from Yamaguchi [1982]; Column (6), from Ohkawa [1972]; Columns (7), (8), and (9), from Ohkawa and Shinohara [1979].

the proportion of labor in agriculture (l_1) far exceeds the proportion of agriculture in output (λ). This large difference cannot be explained by the factor intensity differences in the two sectors. On the basis of the labor coefficients α and γ of the production functions, agriculture should be less labor-intensive than non-agriculture. The high value of l_1 is explained by the lower factor rewards in agriculture; this is consistent with the generally observed lower wage rate in agriculture. This feature of the model means that resources are more productive in the non-agricultural sector, and this strongly affects our conclusions. As shown above, the imperfections also affect the form of the transformation curve between the two sectors.

As stated above, Johnson [1966] showed that if one combines two Cobb–Douglas production functions into a transformation curve, the result will be a transformation curve with very little curvature, unless one chooses output elasticities that differ radically between the sectors at hand. Furthermore, if one adds a market imperfection between the two sectors, the transformation curve can easily lose its curvature; it may indeed become convex to the origin, rather than concave. In the Japanese example considered here, the transformation "curve" would be almost a straight line, and this implies that changes in consumption patterns have had little influence on the sector-based terms of trade. This is important to the interpretation of the results. As stated previously, the behavior of these growth rate multipliers tells us how each exogenous variable influences each endogenous variable in the general equilibrium context. Since the parameters of the A matrix change over time, we can see how these growth rate multipliers have changed over time. Growth rate multipliers were obtained for each five-year interval from 1880 to 1970, by using the parameters shown in Table 2-4.

Multiplying the growth rate multipliers of each decade by the corresponding decade's rates of change of the exogenous variables as they occurred in Japan (see Table 2-5 and Appendix Table 2 for detail) derives a measurement of the contribution of the exogenous variables to the observed rates of change of the endogenous variables: $(\partial \dot{Y}_1/\partial \dot{L})\dot{L}_t = (A^{-1})_{1,4}\dot{L}_t = (Y_1 L)\dot{L}_t = CY_1 L$ where $CY_1 L$ (Y_1 for agricultural output, L for labor, C for contribution) is the measured contribution of the growth rate of labor to agricultural output growth at time t. As such, this book focuses on the measurement of growth accounting and structural change in the Japanese economy. The parameters of the model are not assumed to be constant and

Table 2-5   Average Annual Growth Rates of Endogenous and Exogenous Variables

	1880 ¿ 1890	1890 ¿ 1900	1900 ¿ 1910	1910 ¿ 1920	1920 ¿ 1930	1930 ¿ 1940	1940 ¿ 1950	1950 ¿ 1960	1960 ¿ 1970	Average
<Endogenous Variables>										
$\dot{Y}_1$	2.4	1.4	2.2	3.1	1.3	0.5	−0.3	4.7	2.3	2.0
$\dot{Y}_2$	4.3	4.5	2.9	4.2	2.5	6.3	—	8.9	11.9	5.7
$\dot{K}_1$	0.7	1.0	1.7	0.9	1.0	0.7	−1.4	4.6	8.9	2.0
$\dot{K}_2$	3.3	3.5	4.5	6.7	4.8	4.7	—	6.3	11.5	5.7
$\dot{L}_1$	0.0	0.1	0.0	−1.2	0.0	−0.3	1.7	−1.7	−3.6	−0.6
$\dot{L}_2$	1.7	1.4	1.3	3.2	1.7	2.8	−1.0	4.7	2.9	2.1
$\dot{P}$	6.3	−1.9	−0.8	0.7	−3.3	7.2	—	−1.5	2.1	0.4
$\dot{E}$	2.7	2.2	1.3	2.6	0.5	3.9	—	7.1	10.0	3.8
<Exogenous Variables>										
$\dot{K}$	2.3	2.6	3.6	5.3	4.2	4.2	—	6.1	11.3	5.0
$\dot{L}$	0.5	0.6	0.4	0.6	0.9	1.5	0.2	2.2	1.3	0.9
$\dot{Q}$	0.9	1.0	1.2	1.2	1.6	1.1	1.6	1.2	1.1	1.2
$\dot{B}$	0.4	0.6	0.7	0.7	−0.1	0.3	−0.4	0.4	−0.5	0.2
$\dot{F}$	0.8	2.8	5.3	4.5	3.7	2.1	8.1	10.2	9.2	5.2
$\dot{T}_1$	2.1	0.9	1.4	2.9	0.8	0.2	−2.1	3.7	1.4	1.2
$\dot{T}_2$	2.3	2.6	0.5	−0.5	−0.2	2.8	—	3.8	6.5	1.4
$\dot{a}$	3.2	−2.5	−0.4	0.5	−2.6	1.0	—	−1.7	−3.6	−0.8
$\dot{Y}_1$	3.4	1.7	2.2	3.2	1.1	0.4	−0.5	3.6	2.1	1.9
$\dot{Y}_2$	3.7	3.9	2.6	4.0	2.4	5.7	—	9.2	11.9	5.4
$\dot{T}_1$	3.2	1.3	1.8	3.5	1.0	0.4	−1.2	4.1	3.0	1.9
$\dot{T}_2$	1.7	1.9	0.1	−0.9	−0.5	2.0	—	4.1	6.3	1.8
$\dot{a}$	4.2	−2.2	−0.4	0.6	−2.8	0.9	—	−4.7	−4.1	−1.1

Note: Y_1, Y_2, T_1, T_2, and a of the upper half are output values and those of the lower half are value added values. Suffix 1 represents agriculture, while Suffix 2 is for non-agriculture. Y_i denotes output in each sector, K_i, capital stock, L_i labor, P relative price (ag. price/non-ag. price), E per capita income, Q population, B land, F current inputs produced from non-agriculture (such as fertilizers), T_i technical change in each sector, and a is the demand shifter. Further, dot ($\cdot$) represents growth rate, as in $\dot{Y}_1 = \Delta Y_1 / Y_1$.

were obtained for each decade, as shown in Table 2-4. This allows us to trace structural changes within Japan's economy and measure how the effects of the exogenous variables have changed over time for growth accounting, by using the structural changes in each decade. In a small model like ours, it would also not be wise to assume that the structural parameters of the model have remained unchanged over the entire 90-year period.

3. Empirical Results from the Model

The structural parameters used and the observed growth rates of the endogenous and exogenous variables are given in Tables 2-4 and 2-5. The sources of these parameters and data are shown in Appendix Tables 1 and 2 of this book. On the basis of the labor coefficients α and γ of the production function, the non-agricultural sector is more labor intensive than the agricultural sector throughout the whole period in Japan as stated before. This small labor share in agriculture results from the fact that the agricultural sector uses land, capital and labor as factor inputs while the non-agricultural sector uses only capital and labor. The price and income elasticities used are from Ohkawa's data [1972], which is markedly different from the old data reported by Kaneda [1968]. The differences obtained in the results from using these two data series and a sensitivity test involving changes in parameter values have been analyzed by Yamaguchi [1982a; 1982b]. The rates of technical change were measured using Eqs. (2.14) and (2.15). This is the familiar Solow approach.

Note in particular that the average rate of non-agricultural technical change, particularly after World War II, exceeded the agricultural rate of technical change, but the former fluctuated much more than the latter (Table 2-5). Figure 2-2 shows the growth rate multipliers (GRM) with respect to the eight endogenous variables. The calculated results of the GRM have been analyzed in other papers (Yamaguchi [1982a; 1982b]). Here, we focus only on the aspect of the competition between technical change and population growth. The GRM of T_1, T_2 and Q with respect to per capita income (*i.e.*, ET_1, ET_2 and EQ) have the following relationship: $|ET_1 + ET_2| = |EQ|$. From the theoretical value (see Appendix Table 3), $ET_1 = [(\eta+1-\lambda)(\gamma l_1+\delta k_1) - \eta\lambda]/|A|$, $ET_2 = [(\eta+1-\lambda)(\alpha l_2+\beta k_2) + \eta(\lambda-1)]/|A|$ and $EQ = [(\eta+1-\lambda)\{(\gamma-\alpha)l_2+(\delta-\beta)k_2\}+\lambda-1]/|A|$, where $|A| = (\alpha+\beta)(1+\eta-\lambda\varepsilon) - \eta + [-\alpha - \eta(\alpha-\gamma) + \varepsilon\{\gamma + (\alpha-\gamma)\lambda\}]l_1 + [-\beta - \eta(\beta-\delta) + \varepsilon\{\delta + (\beta-\delta)\lambda\}k_1]$.

From the numerical values of Fig. 2-2 and Appendix Table 4, we can also confirm the relationship $|ET_1 + ET_2| = |EQ|$.

This comes from the fact that technical change and population are included in both the supply and demand sides of the model. Thus the model is constructed so as to enable us to analyze whether population growth or technical change was more influential in the economic development of

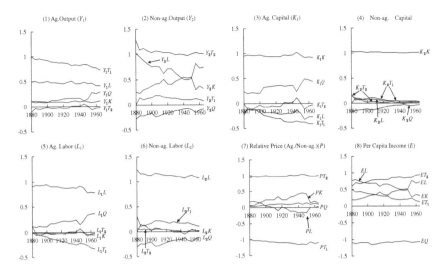

Figure 2-2   The Effects of Population, Technical Change and Others on Eight Endogenous Variables

Japan. Appendix Table 3 shows the theoretical values of GRM for five principal exogenous variables. Figure 2-3 and Table 2-5 show that the growth rates of per capita income (in real terms) are always positive, ranging from 0.5% in the 1920s to 10% in the 1960s, *i.e.*, Japanese per capita income grew continuously through the period. This implies that technical change compensated the downward effect of population growth on per capita income growth. As stated above, multiplying the growth rate multipliers of each decade by the corresponding decadal rates of change of the exogenous variables as they occurred in Japan gives us measurements of the contribution of the exogenous variables to the observed rate of changes of the endogenous variables.

The histogram of Fig. 2-3 shows the historical average growth rates (shown by the height of histograms) of the eight endogenous variables as the sum of all the contributions of nine exogenous variables in each decade. We have nine exogenous variables but only seven principal exogenous variables (sectoral technical change T_i, total capital K, total labor L, population Q, and two imperfect competition variables m_1 and m_w) are shown in Fig. 2-3 to avoid complicating the picture. Appendix Table 6 also shows the contribution of these exogenous variables (eight variables, $N = m_1 + m_w$) on the eight endogenous variables and the percentage of each contribution. First

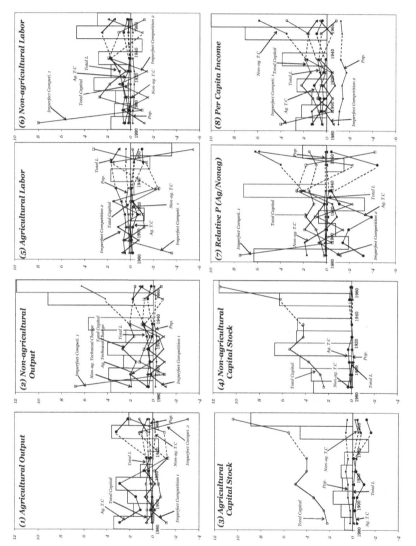

Figure 2-3   Contributions of Seven Exogenous Variables to Eight Endogenous Variables

observe the calculated results of Fig. 2-3 and Appendix Table 6 very briefly. It is seen that with respect to agricultural output, the largest contribution is agricultural technical change with total labor, total capital and population following in importance. This is almost the same order as the GRM's. The order of total capital and total labor are reverse from the order of the GRM in Fig. 2-2, since the historical growth rate of total capital is larger than the growth rate of total labor as shown in Table 2-5 and Fig. 2-3. The contribution of non-agricultural technical change has a zero or negative value in each decade.

For non-agricultural output, non-agricultural technical change makes the largest contribution, but the contribution varies widely. Total capital, total labor and agricultural technical change follow in importance with the order of the contribution of total capital and total labor are reversed from the order of the GRM in Fig. 2-2. This comes from the same reasons as with agricultural output. Population growth makes a small negative contribution. Agricultural technical change tends to push resources out of agriculture ($L_1 T_1 < 0$ and $L_2 T_1 > 0$), while non-agricultural technical change tends to pull resources into non-agriculture ($L_1 T_2 < 0$ and $L_2 T_2 > 0$). The asymmetrical effect of technical change is due to the low price and income elasticities for agricultural goods (see Chapter 3 in detail). Therefore, agricultural technical change makes a positive contribution to the growth of non-agricultural output, especially in the 1910s and 1920s when agricultural technical change makes a larger contribution than non-agricultural technical change, this in contrast to the negative contribution of non-agricultural technical change to the agricultural output. For agricultural capital stock, the largest contributor is, of course, total capital. Other contributions are fairly small. The effect (GRM) and the contributions of technical change in both sectors are negative. As stated above, technical change pushes and pulls agricultural factor inputs to the non-agricultural sector (see Chapter 3 in detail).

For non-agricultural capital stock, the largest effect and contributor is, of course, total capital. Agricultural technical change, non-agricultural technical change and total labor follow in markedly smaller contributions. Finally, population has a negative effect making an opposite contribution as compared with technical change. For agricultural labor, total labor makes the largest contribution (and effect) with population following. The rest of the variables have a negative effect and push and pull agricultural labor to the non-agricultural sector. For non-agricultural labor, total labor again has the largest effect and contribution. Agricultural technical change, total capital and non-agricultural technical change follow in importance. This also corresponds to the pushing and pulling effect of technical change. Population obviously has a positive effect and contribution for agricultural inputs as stated above. For relative price (ag. price/non-ag. price), non-agricultural technical change makes the largest positive effect and contribution. Agricultural technical change makes the largest negative effect and contribution. The contributions of the other variables are very small except for the fairly large contribution of total capital (see Johnson [1966]).

For per capita income, non-agricultural technical change has the largest effect and contribution as a whole, due to the fact that the GRM of non-agricultural technical change has the largest value and the historical rate of technical change in non-agriculture is fairly large, especially after World War II. However, its contribution depends on the decade and shows large variation. On the other hand, the contribution of agricultural technical change is fairly stable and almost the same size as the contribution of total labor on average. Also the contribution of agricultural technical change is relatively larger in the early stage of economic development in Japan. This is because the GRM of agricultural technical change is larger in this period. The contribution of capital is somewhat larger than that of labor. Note that the GRM of labor was larger than the GRM of capital since the historical growth rate of capital was very large indicated in Fig. 2-3. Population has, of course, a negative effect on per capita income. However, the net contribution of population which is the sum of the contributions of population and of labor has a much smaller negative value. In the ordinary model which treats labor and population together, we can only obtain the net contribution of population. However, this model allows us to evaluate the contributions of population and labor independently and see the effect of the labor participation rate as well.

Conclusion

The main conclusions can briefly be summarized as follows:

(1) Technical change in forces determine the output mix. Agricultural technical change tends to push resources out of agriculture, while

non-agricultural technical change tends to pull resources into non-agriculture. The asymmetrical effect of technical change is due to the low price and income elasticities for agricultural products in a closed economy.

(2) Technical change in Japan has contributed more to growth than traditional factors, because the rates of technical change exceeded the rates of accumulation of the traditional factors.

(3) Non-agricultural technical change has contributed more to per capita income growth than agricultural technical change, primarily because the agricultural technical change multiplier has been smaller than the non-agricultural one and because it has been steadily declining through time as the importance of that sector declined in the economy. However, non-agricultural technical change varies very much and has negative contribution to per capita income in the decades of 1910 and 1920.

(4) Population growth has a more detrimental effect on per capita income in the early economic development.

(5) Terms of trade are primarily determined by sectoral technical change and not by demand forces because the transformation curve has very little curvature, but demand forces determine the output mix.

How much do these conclusions reflect the restrictive assumptions of the approach used in this paper? The growth accounting conclusions (2), (3), and (4) are probably fairly robust with respect to changes in basic assumptions or parameters used in the model. Conclusion (5) on the flatness of the transformation curve deserves more caution because it derives quite directly from the assumption of Cobb–Douglas functions and of a labor market imperfection. It is probably unlikely that a transformation curve would be flat throughout its range and for very wide shifts in commodity mix. However, it may be quite realistic as a local approximation of the transformation curve in the neighborhood of the production point. Conclusion (1) is the most controversial, it is due primarily to the low demand elasticities for agricultural commodities, but these low elasticities of demand are well documented empirically. However, if the model was opened to international trade, the relevant price elasticity of agricultural demand would increase substantially. With such high demand elasticities, technical change in agriculture would not necessarily tend to push resources out of that sector.

The additional international demand generated by a reduction in agricultural prices due to the technical change may be sufficient to offset the reduced resource use at any given level of output and hence lead to expanding employment opportunities in agriculture. In the current era, many less developed countries have agricultural sectors comparitively large or larger than Japanese agricultural sector during 1880s. In addition, they have larger population growth rates than Japan had at that time, which makes employment problems more difficult. And most of these countries now attempt to achieve growth via agricultural technical change. Clearly these countries cannot expect an agricultural sector which experiences rapid technical change to absorb vast amounts of additional labor, unless the agricultural sector is heavily export oriented. By recognizing this problem, we emphasize that the non-agricultural sector cannot be neglected. Unless this sector experiences growth and technical change, labor has nowhere to go and will only depress wage rates.

What emerges out of the conclusions of this paper is a difficult balancing act between the sectors because it is more difficult the higher the population growth rates and the earlier the development stage. Agriculture could, of course, absorb more labor if technical change was labor using rather than neutral. However, in 1880, technical change in Japanese agriculture was not based on usage of labor with respect to its own factor proportions. It is therefore unlikely that other less developed countries will be able to develop technology which is based on usage of labor with respect to their own present position. On the other hand, if they should decide on a course of borrowing technology from countries with highly capital-intensive technological paths, such as the United States, then agricultural technical change will result in even more labor displacement than predicted by our model. Therefore, there is a strong necessity to guide agricultural technical change according to factor endowments of each country as suggested by Hayami and Ruttan [1971].

This research also brings back earlier concerns of the development based literature with the transfer of resources from agriculture to the non-agricultural sector. Growth is due to technical change in either sector and to capital accumulation. The resulting increases are spent primarily on non-agricultural goods. This permits the non-agricultural wage rate to rise sufficiently above the minimum differential to draw additional labor out of agriculture and capital as well. Probably, higher maintenance cost of a person in non-agriculture is reflected in the differential needed to induce him to migrate and stay in the non-agricultural sector. The economy pays for such conditions in equilibrium by wage differential. The system does not move primarily through capital accumulation in non-agriculture alone but through technical change in both sectors and through capital accumulation in both sectors. The framework is closer to Clark's framework [1940] which recognizes two sources of benefit: growth of output per worker in both sectors and transfer of labor to higher productivity sectors. Development policy in the 1950s chose to emphasize the transfer of labor rather than the growth of output per worker in both sectors, which was probably not intended initially in that kind of framework.[2]

---

[2]The introduction and conclusion of this chapter were developed and rewritten from Yamaguchi and Binswanger [1975] to meet the purpose of the book. We appreciate *American Journal of Agricultural Economics* and Dr. Binswanger for permitting the use of this paper for this book.

Chapter 3

A Graphic Model of the Effects of Sectoral Technical Change*

Introduction

The effects of technical change in Japan are of interest to other countries that seek to use technical change to accelerate their growth. The role of technical change in Japan's development from 1880 to 1970 was analyzed in Chapter 2. However, we did not focus on the process by which agricultural resources are pushed and pulled by sectoral technical change. A brief analysis of the contributions of seven exogenous variables to eight endogenous variables in Japan was also conducted in Chapter 2. The main objectives of this chapter are to provide a graphic version of the two-sector growth accounting model to explain the process by which technical change exerts push and pull effects and modulates demand for agricultural resources. Unlike previous investigations, in this study, we explain the push and pull effects of technical change graphically. Further, we provide some policy implications of the results. As shown in Chapter 2, the agricultural production function contains variables representing agricultural technical change (T_1), agricultural labor (L_1), agricultural capital (K_1), and land (B). The growth rates of the model's endogenous and exogenous variables are given in Table 2-5, and the parameter values used in the model are given in Table 2-4. In the next section, we present a very brief graphic explanation of the push and pull effects of technical change; the following section gives the full graphic model and policy implications of the results.

*The content of this chapter was developed and rewritten from Yamaguchi and Kennedy [1984a] to meet the purpose of the book. We appreciate *Canadian Journal of Agricultural Economics* and Dr. Kennedy for permitting the use of this paper for this book.

1. Push and Pull Effects of Sectoral Technical Change

The growth accounting results of Chapter 2 can be summarized as follows. Regarding the growth of agricultural output in Japan, the contribution of agricultural technical change ranged from a high of 105% in the last decade studied (1960–1970) to a low of 50% in the sixth decade studied (1930–1940; see Fig. 2-3 and Appendix Table 6 for details). These estimates are lower than those of conventional growth accounting (as $Y_1 T_1$ is smaller than 1 because of the push effect of agricultural technical change), as shown in Fig. 2-2. Although it was small, the contribution of non-agricultural technical change was negative, given that it pulls resources from the agricultural to the non-agricultural sector. Regarding non-agricultural output growth, the contribution of non-agricultural technical change ranged from −21% (1920–1930) to 53% (1960–1970; see Appendix Table 6).

These estimates are higher than those of conventional growth accounting (as $Y_2 T_2$ is greater than 1 because of the pull effect of non-agricultural technical change). The contribution of agricultural technology was small, but unlike the contribution of non-agricultural technical change to agricultural output growth, it was positive, given that it pushes resources from the agricultural to the non-agricultural sector. Therefore, we focus on the push and pull effects of technical change in this chapter. First, we show the push and pull effects of technical change very simply. As the upper part of Fig. 3-1 shows, agricultural technical change would shift the production possibility curve, as shown by the panel containing the production possibility curve. The agricultural production curve also shifts, as the panel shows.

Then, agricultural labor decreases from L_1^0 to L_1^1 (*i.e.*, agricultural labor is pushed), and non-agricultural labor increases from L_2^0 to L_2^1. This would be the simplest expression of the push effect of agricultural technical change, although we performed detailed analysis that includes the demand side in Sec. 2. On the other hand, non-agricultural technical change would shift the production possibility curve, as the panel containing the production possibility curve in the lower part of Fig. 3-1 shows. The non-agricultural production curve also shifts, as the panel shows. Then, non-agricultural labor increases from L_2^0 to L_2^1, and agricultural labor decreases from L_1^0 to L_1^1 (*i.e.*, agricultural labor is pulled). This would be the simplest expression of the pull effect of non-agricultural technical change, although we will also

Push Effect of Agricultural Technical Change

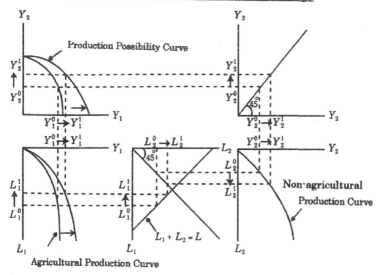

Pull Effect of Non-Agricultural Technical Change

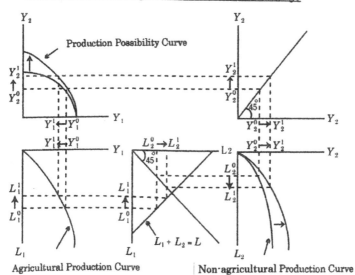

Figure 3-1   Push and Pull Effects of Sectoral Technical Change

perform such analysis in more detail later. This shows that technical change has asymmetric effects in both sectors.

2. Graphic Model of the Effects of Sectoral Technical Change

As pointed out before, the general equilibrium approach used here differs from conventional growth accounting, which is typically partial equilibrium. In this model, the contribution of technical change to output growth in each sector is calculated by multiplying the relevant GRMs by the sectoral rate of technical change (*i.e.*, $CY_1T_1 = Y_1T_1 \times \dot{T}_1$ and $CY_2T_2 = Y_2T_2 \times \dot{T}_2$). In conventional growth accounting, however, the contribution of technical change to output growth is calculated simply by equating it to the rate of technical change in that sector. Thus, under conventional growth accounting, the contribution of agricultural technical change to agricultural output growth equals $\dot{T}_1$ and the contribution of non-agricultural technical change to non-agricultural output growth equals $\dot{T}_2$. This implies that the estimated contributions of technical change from the model will differ from those of conventional growth accounting, where this model's estimates of the Y_1T_1 and Y_2T_2 (GRMs) differ from one.

Referring back to Fig. 2-2 and Appendix Table 4, one can see that these GRM estimates do differ from one. Y_1T_1 begins at a value of 1.00 in 1880 and becomes less over time, reaching 0.73 in 1965. Y_1T_1 declines over time due to an increase in the push of capital and labor from the agricultural to non-agricultural sector caused by agricultural technical change. Y_2T_2 on the other hand, begins at a value of 1.28 in 1880 and almost converges to 1.01 in 1965. Y_2T_2 decreases over time due to a decrease in the pull of capital and labor from the agricultural to non-agricultural sector caused by non-agricultural technical change.[1] The above implies that the contributions of technical change estimated by the model and by conventional growth

---

[1] In 1965, for example, each 1% increase in T_1 increases Y_1T_1 by 0.72% (Appendix Table 4). It does not increase 1% as it would in conventional growth accounting because T_1 pushes agricultural capital and labor to the non-agricultural sector. A 1% increase in T_1 pushes 0.41% of K_1 and 0.34% of L_1 to the non-agricultural sector, causing an increase in K_2, equal to 0.03% and an increase in L_2, equal to 0.10%. These increases in K_2 and L_2 cause Y_2, to increase to 0.08%. These measures of the push (or pull) of agricultural capital and labor to the non-agricultural sector by T_1 (or T_2) are not obtainable from one-sector models.

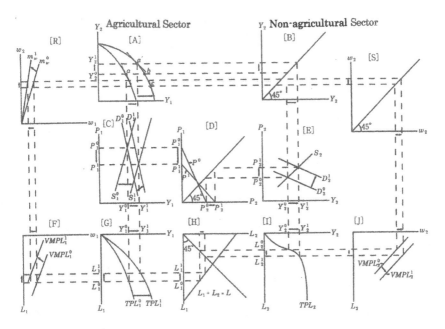

Figure 3-2   Push Effect of Agricultural Technical Change

accounting will differ. Since $Y_1 T_1$ is less than one, the model's estimates of the contribution of agricultural technical change are less than those of conventional growth accounting. Similarly, since $Y_2 T_2$ exceeds one, the model's estimates of the contribution of non-agricultural technical change exceed those of conventional growth accounting.

These differences are largely due to demand factors and intersectoral resource flows which the model's general equilibrium approach is able to capture. To help explain how these demand effects and resource flows arise, a graphic model of the effects of agricultural and non-agricultural technical change is provided above. Figure 3-2 describes the effects of agricultural technical change (T_1) and Fig. 3-3 describes the effects of non-agricultural technical change (T_2) on both the agricultural and non-agricultural sectors. To simplify the graphic models, it is assumed that labor is the only resource, as the treatment of capital would be analogous. T_1 increases the productivity of agricultural labor, shown in Fig. 3-2 as an upward movement of the total productivity curve of agricultural labor, from TPL_1^0 to TPL_1^1. In panel G, T_1 is assumed to have no effect on the total productivity curve of

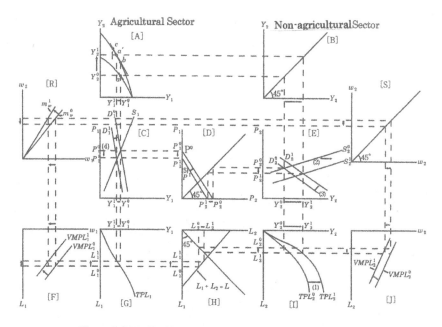

Figure 3-3   Pull Effect of Non-Agricultural Technical Change

non-agricultural labor, TPL_2 in panel I. The increased productivity of agricultural labor supplies an outward shift in the production possibility curve, depicted in panel A. This means that more Y_1 and Y_2 can be produced given the total amount of labor available (L).

The supply and demand effects of T_1 on the agricultural and non-agricultural sectors are shown in panels C and E.[2] When T_1 occurs, the agricultural supply curve shifts to the right, from S_1^0 to S_1^1 (panel C). Agricultural demand is also affected. T_1 increases per capita income and increased per capita income results in increased demand for agricultural and non-agricultural products. For agricultural products, this is shown as a shift in the demand curve from D_1^0 to D_1^1 (panel C). The amount of Y_1 produced

---

[2]The demand and supply curves for the agricultural sector (panel C) are drawn steeper than those for the non-agricultural sector (panel E) to reflect the lower price elasticities in agriculture. The agricultural relative price elasticity is given in column 5, Table 2-4. Agricultural and non-agricultural price elasticities can be calculated from columns 5, 6 and 9 in Table 2-4 using microeconomic theory. For example, in the 1880, 1925 and 1970, the agricultural price elasticity was −0.28, −0.26 and −0.24 while the non-agricultural price elasticity was −0.48, −0.85 and −0.96.

increases from Y_1^0 to Y_1^1 and the price falls from P_1^0 to P_1^1. T_1 results in two cross effects on the non-agricultural sector, both on the demand side: a decrease in demand because the fall in the price of agricultural goods has increased the relative price of non-agricultural goods (the price effect) and an increase in demand due to the increase in per capita income noted above (the income effect).

Given the relatively high income elasticity for non-agricultural products, the positive income effect outweighs the negative price effect (This finding comes from our calculation), resulting in a rightward shift in demand, from D_2^0 to D_2^1 (panel E). This increase in demand results in an increase of Y_2 produced (from Y_2^0 to Y_2^1) and an increase in its price (from P_2^0 to P_2^1). The decreased price of Y_1 and increased price of Y_2 cause the relative (agricultural/non-agricultural) price (P) to decline. This is shown in panel D where the relative price line becomes less steep, from P^0 to P^1. The optimal combination of Y_1 and Y_2 moves from point a to a' in panel A, where the new production possibility curve is tangent to the new price line. More of both Y_1 and Y_2 are produced. The increased productivity of agricultural labor (L_1) means the increase in Y_1 can be produced with less labor, shown by a decrease in L_1 from L_1^0 to L_1^1 in panel G. Since the productivity of non-agricultural labor (L_2) has not increased, the increase in Y_2 produced requires an increase in L_2, from L_2^0 to L_2^1 in panel I.

These changes in sectoral requirements of labor simultaneously change sectoral demand for labor. The value of marginal productivity of L_1 declines relative to that of L_2. This is shown in Fig. 3-2, assuming $VMPL_1$ shifts downward (from $VMPL_1^0$ to $VMPL_1^1$ in panel F) and $VMPL_2$ shifts upward (from $VMPL_2^0$ to $VMPL_2^1$ in panel J).[3] The increased demand for L_2 relative to L_1 leads to increased wages for the former relative to the latter, shown as a decline in the relative wage rate from m_w^0 to m_w^1 in panel R. The new wage rates and new values of marginal productivity for L_1 and L_2 are equated in panels F and J respectively. The result is a shift in agricultural labor ($L_1^0 - L_1^1$ in panel G) to the non-agricultural sector. Panel H ensures that the sum of labor used in each sector equals the total amount available (L).

---

[3]For L_1, this assumes that the fall in the price of Y_2 offsets the decrease in its marginal product. For L_2, this assumes that the increase in the price of Y_2 offset the decrease in its marginal product.

As for the effects of non-agricultural technical change (T_2), a similar graphic model is given in Fig. 3-3, again assuming labor to be the only resource. T_2 increases the productivity of non-agricultural labor, shown as an upward shift of its total productivity curve, from TPL_2^0 to TPL_2^1 in panel I. T_2 is assumed to have no effect on the total productivity curve of agricultural labor, TPL_1 in panel G. T_2 causes the non-agricultural supply curve to shift to the right, from S_2^0 to S_2^1 (panel E). T_2 increases profits in the non-agricultural sector leading to increased per capita income and increased demand for agricultural and non-agricultural products. For non-agricultural products, this is shown as a shift in the demand curve from D_2^0 to D_2^1 (panel E). The amount of Y_2 produced increases from Y_2^0 to Y_2^1 and the price falls from P_2^0 to P_2^1. Regarding T_2's effects on the agricultural sector, the same two cross effects on demand (as T_1 exerted on the non-agricultural sector) occur. Agricultural demand is affected negatively by the price effect, since agricultural goods are now priced higher relative to non-agricultural goods. It is affected positively by the income effect, given increased per capita income resulting from T_2.

Due to the relatively low income elasticity of agricultural products, the positive income effect is outweighed by the negative price effect, resulting in a leftward shift of the demand curve, from D_1^0 to D_1^1 in panel C. The decrease in demand results in a decrease of Y_1 produced (from Y_1^0 to Y_1^1) and a fall in price (from P_1^0 to P_1^1). The fall in price of agricultural products is less than that of non-agricultural products causing P to increase. This is shown in panel D, where the relative price line becomes steeper (from P^0 to P^1). The decreased amount of Y_1 produced requires less L_1, shown as a decrease of L_1 from L_1^0 to L_1^1 in panel G. Despite the increased productivity of L_2, the large increase in Y_2 produced requires more L_2, shown as an increase from L_2^0 to L_2^1 in panel I. These changes in sectoral requirements of labor simultaneously change sectoral labor demand. The value of the marginal productivity of L_1 again declines relative to that of L_2.

This is shown in Fig. 3-3 (panels F and J), assuming both VMPL$_1$ and VMPL$_2$ shift downwards, the former shifting relatively more.[4] The lowered

---

[4]The marginal productivity of L_1 increases due to the reduction of L_1 used, whereas the marginal productivity of L_2, increase due to T_2, even though more L_2 is used. In both cases, the decline in product price is assumed to offset the increase in marginal productivity. The

demand for L_1 relative to L_2 leads to a decline in the relative wage rate, from m_w^0 to m_w^1 in panel R. The new wage rates and new values of marginal productivity for L_1 and L_2 are equated in panels F and J, causing a shift in agricultural labor to the non-agricultural sector ($L_1^0 - L_1^1$ in panel G). In summary, one can compare and contrast the effects of T_1 and T_2. Their effects on labor also apply to capital. The direct effects of T_1 and T_2 are similar in that they lower product price (increased supply exceeding increased demand) and increase the marginal productivity of labor in their respective sectors. With respect to cross effects, T_1 and T_2 affect demand in the other sector in similar ways but different directions. T_1 leads to increases in non-agricultural demand and hence increased output in the non-agricultural sector. T_2 on the other hand, results in decreases in agricultural demand, causing a decline in agricultural output. Both T_1 and T_2 lead to increases in the VMP of L_2 relative to that of L_1.

3. Policy Implications Derived from the Analysis

The purpose of this paper has been to estimate and clarify the process of the effects of technical change on economic development in Japan, not the effects of policy on development. However, the results suggest the following policy implications. As pointed out in the previous section, the GRMs of technical change, with respect to output in the same sector, differ from 1.00, due to the push and pull effects of technical change. $Y_1 T_1$ has a maximum value of 1.00 in 1880, while $Y_2 T_2$ has a minimum value of 1.01 in 1965. Thus, at any point in the period 1880–1970, a policy which increases T_2 will produce a greater percentage output response in the non-agricultural sector than a policy which increases Y_1 would produce in the agricultural sector. This is particularly important given the large size of the non-agricultural sector relative to the agricultural sector.[5]

The cultural, social, institutional and policy environment in Japan during this period influenced the parameters of the model and hence the results of

---

greater decline in $VMPL_1$ implies MP_1 has increased less than MP_2, since P_2 has declined more than P_1.

[5] Share of income produced by agriculture, λ, decreases from 0.50 in 1880 to 0.06 in 1970 (Table 2-4).

this study. The influence of these factors tended to increase the movement of capital and labor from the agricultural to the non-agricultural sector. For example, the policy of land (and other) taxes in the agricultural sector caused an outflow of agricultural capital to the non-agricultural sector, thus decreasing the value of k_1.[6] Differentiating $Y_1 T_1$ and $Y_2 T_2$ in Appendix Table 3 with respect to k_1 shows that the decreased value of k_1 lowers $Y_1 T_1$ and raise $Y_2 T_2$ (you can also refer to Table 3-1). In 1885, for example, one can note that if not for agricultural taxes, the value of the GRM $Y_1 T_1$ would be greater than 0.95 (Table 3-1) and $Y_2 T_2$ would be less than 1.09.[7] However, the value of $Y_2 T_2$ is still larger than 1 and the value of $Y_2 T_2$ minus $Y_1 T_1$ becomes larger over time except the period of 1880s.

Regarding the impact of agricultural taxes on the contribution of T_1 to Y_1 ($C Y_1 T_1$) and T_2 to Y_2 ($C Y_2 T_2$), one needs to consider the influence of agricultural taxes on the rates of technical change ($\dot{T}_1$ and $\dot{T}_2$), in addition to their influence on GRM values.[8] A capital outflow from the agricultural to the non-agricultural sector tends to increase $\dot{T}_2$ at the expense of $\dot{T}_1$. The increased capital available to the non-agricultural sector allowed the government to increase $\dot{T}_2$ through such activities as building model factories and importing new technology and scientific expertise.[9] The tendency of agricultural taxes to decrease $\dot{T}_1$ as well as $Y_1 T_1$ implies a large decrease in the contribution of T_1 to Y_1. Similarly, their tendency to increase $\dot{T}_2$ (keeping $Y_2 T_2$ larger than 1 and $Y_2 T_2 - Y_1 T_1$ increases over time except the beginning of economic development like 1880s) implies a still large increase in the contribution of T_2 to Y_2.

---

[6]The movement of capital from the agricultural to the non-agricultural sector was also increased by the tendency of landlords to change their investments to the more quickly developing non-agricultural sector.

[7]The year 1885 is used as an example because it occurs in one of the periods (1881–1890) in which Johnston and Mellor [1961] point out that agricultural taxes played an important role in financing Japan's development.

[8]In this chapter, the rates of technical change are taken as given and then they are measured and their effects explained. How policy affects the rates of sectoral technical change is an important question, but it is beyond the scope of this chapter. Thus, it is only touched on here.

[9]A well-known example of a government-built factory is the Tomioka silk mill in Gumma Prefecture.

Table 3-1   Effect of Parameter Change on GRM

GRM	Parameters which increase GRM	Parameters which decrease GRM
Y_1T_1	$\varepsilon, |\eta|, \lambda, l_1, k_1, \gamma, \delta$	α, β
Y_1T_2	$\varepsilon, l_1, k_1, \gamma, \delta$	$|\eta|, \lambda, \alpha, \beta$
Y_1K	$\varepsilon, l_1, k_1, \beta, \gamma$	$|\eta|, \lambda, \alpha, \delta$
Y_1Q	λ, α, β	$\varepsilon, |\eta|, l_1, k_1, \gamma, \delta$
Y_1L	$\varepsilon, l_1, k_1, \alpha, \gamma, \delta$	$|\eta|, \lambda, \beta$
Y_2T_1	l_1, k_1, γ	$\varepsilon, |\eta|, \lambda, \alpha, \beta, \delta$
Y_2T_2	$|\eta|, \lambda, l_1, k_1, \gamma$	$\varepsilon, \alpha, \beta, \delta$
Y_2K	$|\eta|, \lambda, l_1, k_1, \beta, \gamma, \delta$	ε, α
Y_2Q	$\varepsilon, |\eta|, \alpha, \beta, \delta,$	$\lambda, l_1, k_1, \gamma$
Y_2L	$|\eta|, \lambda, l_1, k_1, \alpha, \gamma$	$\varepsilon, \beta, \delta$
K_1T_1	$\varepsilon, |\eta|, \lambda, k_1, \alpha, \beta, \gamma, \delta$	l_1
K_1T_2	$\varepsilon, k_1, \alpha, \beta, \gamma, \delta$	$|\eta|, \lambda, l_1$
K_1K	$\varepsilon, k_1, \alpha, \gamma$	$|\eta|, \lambda, l_1, \beta, \delta$
K_1Q	λ_1, l_1	$\varepsilon, |\eta|, k_1, \alpha, \beta, \gamma, \delta$
K_1L	$\varepsilon, k_1, \beta, \gamma, \delta$	$|\eta|, \delta, l_1, \alpha$
K_2T_1	l_1, k_1	$\varepsilon, |\eta|, \delta, \alpha, \beta, \gamma, \delta$
K_2T_2	$|\eta|, \delta, l_1, k_1$	$\varepsilon, \alpha, \beta, \gamma, \delta$
K_2K	$|\eta|, \lambda, l_1, k_1, \beta, \delta$	$\varepsilon, \alpha, \gamma$
K_2Q	$\varepsilon, |\eta|, \alpha, \beta, \gamma, \delta$	λ, l_1, k_1
K_2L	$|\eta|, \lambda, l_1, k_1, \alpha$	$\varepsilon, \beta, \gamma, \delta$
L_1T_1	$\varepsilon, |\eta|, \lambda, l_1, \alpha, \beta, \gamma, \delta$	k_1
L_1T_2	$\varepsilon, l_1, \alpha, \beta, \gamma, \delta$	$|\eta|, \lambda, k_1$
L_1K	$\varepsilon, l_1, \alpha, \gamma$	$|\eta|, \lambda, k_1, \beta, \delta$
L_1Q	λ, k_1	$\varepsilon, |\eta|, l_1, \alpha, \beta, \gamma, \delta$
L_1L	$\varepsilon, l_1, \beta, \gamma, \delta$	$|\eta|, \lambda, k_1, \alpha$
L_2T_1	$l_1 k_1$	$\varepsilon, |\eta|, \lambda, \alpha, \beta, \gamma, \delta$
L_2T_2	$|\eta|, l_1, k_1$	$\varepsilon, \lambda, \alpha, \beta, \gamma, \delta$
L_2K	$|\eta|, \lambda, l_1, k_1, \beta, \delta$	$\varepsilon, \alpha, \gamma$
L_2Q	$\varepsilon, |\eta|, \alpha, \beta, \gamma, \delta$	λ, l_1, k_1
L_2L	$|\eta|, \lambda, l_1, k_1, \alpha$	$\varepsilon, \beta, \gamma, \delta$
PT_1	$\varepsilon, |\eta|, \lambda, l_1, k_1, \alpha, \beta$	γ, δ
PT_2	$\varepsilon, l_1, k_1, \alpha, \beta$	$|\eta|, \lambda, \gamma, \delta$
PK	$\varepsilon, l_1, k_1, \alpha, \delta$	$|\eta|, \lambda, \beta, \gamma$
PQ	λ, γ, δ	$\varepsilon, |\eta|, l_1, k_1, \alpha, \beta$
PL	$\varepsilon, l_1, k_1, \beta$	$|\eta|, \lambda, \alpha, \gamma, \delta$
ET_1	$\lambda, l_1, k_1, \gamma$	$\varepsilon, |\eta|, \alpha, \beta, \delta$
ET_2	$|\eta|, l_1, k_1, \gamma$	$\varepsilon, \lambda, \alpha, \beta, \delta$
EK	$|\eta|, l_1, k_1, \beta, \gamma, \delta,$	$\varepsilon, \lambda, \alpha$
EQ	$\varepsilon, |\eta|, \lambda, \alpha, \beta, \delta$	l_1, k_1, γ
EL	$|\eta|, l_1, k_1, \alpha, \gamma$	$\varepsilon, \lambda, \beta, \delta$

With respect to labor, its movement from the agricultural to the non-agricultural sector was increased by many factors, including primogeniture (whereby the oldest son inherits the land), combined with a limited land base in Japan. Such factors decrease the value of l_1. Differentiating $Y_1 T_1$ and $Y_2 T_2$ with respect to l_1 shows that the decreased value of l_1 lowers $Y_1 T_1$ and $Y_2 T_2$ (see Table 3-1). But $Y_2 T_2$ is still larger than 1 and $Y_2 T_2 - Y_1 T_1$ increases over time. Therefore, this coupled with policies (like those mentioned above), which tended to increase T_2, also imply an effective contribution to Japanese economic development. The reason both $Y_1 T_1$ and $Y_2 T_2$ decrease as economic development proceeds is due to changes in the push and pull effects of technical change. $Y_1 T_1$ decreases because the push of agricultural capital and labor by T_1 ($K_1 T_1$, $L_1 T_1$) becomes stronger over time (*i.e.*, more negative). $Y_2 T_2$ decreases because the pull of agricultural capital and labor by T_2 ($K_1 T_2$, $L_1 T_2$) becomes smaller over time (*i.e.*, less negative).

These trends in the push and pull effects of technical change drive from the decreasing size of the agricultural sector and the increasing size of the non-agricultural sector. This can be seen theoretically by examining the parameters which have decreased with the relative decline of the agricultural sector [*i.e.*, k_1(the proportion of capital in agriculture), l_1(the proportion of labor in agriculture), λ (the share of income produced by agriculture) and ε (the agricultural income elasticity)]. By partially differentiating $K_1 T_1$, $K_1 T_2$, $L_1 T_1$ and $L_1 T_2$ with respect to k_1, l_1, λ and ε, one can determine how these parameters influence the push and pull effects of technical change. Differentiating $K_1 T_1$ shows that $K_1 T_1$ decreases as k_1, λ and ε decrease but increases as l_1 decreases (see Table 3-1). $K_1 T_1$ becomes more negative over time because the decreasing effects of k_1, λ and ε outweigh the increasing effect of l_1. Differentiating $L_1 T_1$ shows that $L_1 T_1$ decreases as l_1, λ and ε decrease, but increases as k_1 decreases (see Table 3-1).

$L_1 T_1$ becomes more negative because the decreasing effects of l_1, λ and ε outweigh the increasing effect of k_1. Similarly, it can be shown that the tendency of $K_1 T_2$ to become less negative over time is due to decreases in k_1 and λ, while the tendency for $L_1 T_2$ to become less negative is due to decreases in l_1 and λ. The changes in the push and pull effects of technical change explained above suggest an interesting policy implication. If a shift in agricultural capital and labor to the non-agricultural sector is desired, then an efficient way to effect this shift is to deemphasize non-agricultural technical change in favor of agricultural technical change as economic development proceeds (because $K_1 T_1$ and $L_1 T_1$ become increasingly strong relative to $K_1 T_2$ and $L_1 T_2$ after 1885 as Fig. 2-2 shows). Conversely, if a shift in agricultural capital and labor to the non-agricultural sector is desired, then an efficient way to effect this shift is to emphasize non-agricultural technical change in the beginning of the economic development.

Here, we change the topic and mention trade in Japan. The decadal growth rates of agricultural demand shifter a are as follows (see Appendix Table 1): 1880s (4.2%), 1890s (−2.2%), 1900s (−0.4%), 1910s (0.6%), 1920s (−2.8%), 1930s (0.9%), 1940s (—), 1950s (−3.1%), and 1960s (−4.1%). From these values, we can understand that the values for many periods (except the 1880s, 1910s, and 1930s) have a negative sign. Demand shifter a is an adjustment item that contains export X, import M, taste, preference, and other factors. Equation (2.13) in Chapter 2 was as follows:

$$\dot{Y}_1 = \dot{a} + \dot{Q} + \eta \dot{P} + \varepsilon \dot{E}. \tag{2.13}$$

From this equation,

$$\dot{a} = \dot{Y}_1 - \dot{Q} - \eta \dot{P} - \varepsilon \dot{E}.$$

Therefore, the export X is expressed as

$$\dot{X} = \dot{Y}_1 - (\dot{a}' - \dot{Q} - \eta \dot{P} - \varepsilon \dot{E}),$$

where $\dot{a}'$ is the ordinary demand shifter of taste and preference. Then export $\dot{X}$ becomes positive when agricultural output $\dot{Y}_1$ is larger than the domestic demand $(\dot{a}' - \dot{Q} - \eta \dot{P} - \varepsilon \dot{E})$.

Therefore, in decades with more importation of agricultural goods, the growth rate of demand shifter $\dot{a}$ has a significant possibility of being negative; conversely, in decades with more exportation of agricultural goods, the growth rate of demand shifter $\dot{a}$ has a greater possibility of having a positive sign. The reason for the large, negative values for the post-World War II period (*i.e.*, the 1950s and 1960s) was significant importation of meat and dairy products. Therefore, our model looks like a closed model, but we can grasp aspects of import and export through demand shifter a. Table 3-2 shows that the 1880s, 1910s, and 1930s were periods of significant exportation of agricultural products. This fact is consistent with the sign of demand

Table 3-2   Agricultural Exports and Imports of Japan, and Totals Thereof

	Agricultural Export		Agricultural Import			
	%		%		Export, total	Import, total
1880s	11,765	(32)	6,368	(22)	37,143	29,357
1890s	21,971	(16)	22,116	(17)	136,112	129,261
1900s	43,198	(13)	97,059	(20)	321,534	488,538
1910s	80,177	(11)	38,141	(7)	708,307	532,450
1920s	143,315	(6)	392,012	(15)	2,305,590	2,572,658
1930s	197,110	(8)	192,065	(8)	2,449,073	2,472,236
1940s	75,000	(19)	231,000	(24)	388,000	957,000
1950s	45,436,000	(6)	225,027,000	(25)	723,816,000	889,715,000
1960s	1,163,000,000	(5)	4,991,000,000	(17)	24,023,000,000	28,575,000,000

Table 3-3   Growth Rate Multipliers of Demand Shifter a

	Y_1a	Y_2a	K_1a	K_2a	L_1a	L_2a	Pa	Ea
1880	0.57	−1.77	1.52	−1.14	0.77	−1.89	0.32	−0.30
1885	0.43	−1.28	1.14	−0.82	0.59	−1.37	0.24	−0.53
1890	0.48	−1.29	1.28	−0.82	0.67	−1.43	0.32	−0.40
1895	0.42	−1.04	1.12	−0.66	0.61	−1.17	0.32	−0.49
1900	0.42	−0.94	1.14	−0.56	0.60	−1.11	0.35	−0.46
1905	0.43	−0.87	1.16	−0.52	0.62	−1.06	0.38	−0.48
1910	0.45	−0.83	1.22	−0.45	0.63	−1.04	0.39	−0.45
1915	0.46	−0.69	1.24	−0.37	0.69	−0.92	0.45	−0.38
1920	0.50	−0.62	1.27	−0.28	0.76	−0.79	0.43	−0.34
1925	0.56	−0.57	1.31	−0.23	0.80	−0.74	0.40	−0.28
1930	0.54	−0.49	1.23	−0.18	0.75	−0.66	0.38	−0.33
1935	0.52	−0.45	1.26	−0.16	0.80	−0.63	0.45	−0.29
1940	0.60	−0.37	1.26	−0.12	0.83	−0.55	0.41	−0.22
1945	0.56	−0.41	1.23	−0.14	0.76	−0.60	0.40	−0.25
1950	0.58	−0.41	1.27	−0.13	0.78	−0.61	0.41	−0.25
1955	0.64	−0.43	1.30	−0.13	0.90	−0.53	0.37	−0.24
1960	0.61	−0.33	1.28	−0.11	0.97	−0.42	0.46	−0.19
1965	0.65	−0.24	1.22	−0.09	1.01	−0.30	0.42	−0.16

shifter a. The GRM of demand shifter a is shown in Table 3-3. In addition, the contributions of demand shifter a (*i.e.*, CY_1a, CY_2a, CK_1a, CK_2a, CL_1a, CL_2a, CPa, CEa) are shown in Appendix Table 6. Appendix Table 6 infers that the demand shifter a (and therefore, exportation) contributes significantly to agricultural output Y_1 for the decades of 1880 (50% of agricultural output) and 1930 (125% of agricultural output).

Conclusion

As shown before, this book combines growth accounting with a two-sector model to measure the effects of agricultural and non-agricultural technical changes on sectoral resource use and output growth in Japan over the period 1880–1970. In this chapter, we focused on the push and pull effects of technical change. Here, we summarize the content as follows:

(1) The growth accounting results of the model can be summarized as follows. Regarding agricultural output growth in Japan, the contribution of agricultural technical change ranged from a high of 105% in the last decade studied (1960–1970) to a low of 50% in the sixth decade studied (1930–1940; see Appendix Table 6 for details). As shown in Chapter 2, these estimates are lower than those of conventional growth accounting; $Y_1 T_1$ is smaller than 1 because of the push effect of agricultural technical change. The contribution of non-agricultural technical change, although small, was negative, given that it pulls resources from the agricultural to the non-agricultural sector. Regarding non-agricultural output growth, the contribution of non-agricultural technical change ranged from -21% (1920–1930) to 53% (1960–1970; see Appendix Table 6). These estimates are higher than those of conventional growth accounting (as $Y_2 T_2$ is greater than 1 due to the pull effect of non-agricultural technical change). The contribution of agricultural technology was small, but unlike the contribution of non-agricultural technical change to agricultural output growth, it was positive, given that it pushes resources from the agricultural to the non-agricultural sector.

(2) Very simple explanations of the push and pull effects of agricultural and non-agricultural technical change are given in Fig. 3-1. For simplicity, we did not include the demand side in the simple Fig. 3-1. However, it is much easier to understand the most important core aspects of the push and pull effects of agricultural and non-agricultural technical change. A graphic version of the two-sector growth accounting

model was provided to explain the process by which sectoral technical change affects demand and supply factors and causes intersectoral resource flows. Agricultural technical change increased demand and output in the non-agricultural sector, while non-agricultural technical change decreased demand and output in the agricultural sector. This asymmetry in the cross effects of agricultural and non-agricultural technical changes arose from the relatively low price and income elasticities of agricultural products. The result was a shift in labor and capital from the agricultural to the non-agricultural sector. Figure 3-2 shows the push effect of agricultural technical change in more detail.

(3) In the same way, technical change in the non-agricultural sector shifts agricultural labor and capital to the non-agricultural sector. In other words, non-agricultural technical change pulls agricultural labor and capital to the non-agricultural sector. We call this the pull effect of non-agricultural technical change. Figure 3-3 shows the pull effect of non-agricultural technical change in more detail.

(4) Next, we noted some policy implications suggested by the results. We showed how efficiently the agricultural tax and the movement of labor from the agricultural to the non-agricultural sector aided the economic development of Japan. We also suggest an interesting policy implication. If a shift in agricultural capital and labor to the non-agricultural sector is desired, then an efficient way to effect this shift is to deemphasize non-agricultural sector in favor of agricultural technical change as economic development proceeds (because $K_1 T_1$ and $L_1 T_1$ become increasingly strong relative to $K_1 T_2$ and $L_1 T_2$). Conversely, if a shift in agricultural capital and labor to the non-agricultural sector is desired, then non-agricultural technical change should be emphasized in the beginning stages of economic development.

(5) Finally, demand shifter a is an adjustment item that contains export X, import M, taste, preference, and other factors. In decades with more importation of agricultural goods, the growth rate of demand shifter a has a much stronger possibility of being negative, and conversely, in decades with more exportation of agricultural goods, the growth rate of demand shifter a has a greater possibility of being positive. In fact, the large, negative values of the post-World War II period (*i.e.*, the 1950s and 1960s) were due to significant importation of meat and

dairy products. Therefore, our model looks a closed model, but we can grasp aspects of importation and exportation through a. Further, the contributions of demand shifter a (*i.e.*, CY_1a, CY_2a, CK_1a, CK_2a, CL_1a, CL_2a, CPa, CEa) are shown in Appendix Table 6. Appendix Table 6 demonstrates that demand shifter a (and therefore, exportation) contributed significantly to agricultural output Y_1 in the 1880s (50% of agricultural output) and 1930s (125% of agricultural output). Then, we showed that our model looked closed, but through demand shifter a, we could also see the impact of agricultural importation and exportation.

Summaries (2) and (3) of the push and pull effects of technical change are very important and clear. However, especially, the following three contributions of the above conspicuous findings would be very important: First, agricultural technical change contributes positively to non-agricultural output, whereas non-agricultural technical change contributes negatively to agricultural output. This asymmetric phenomenon gives the impression that agricultural technical change looks very sincere but non-agricultural technical change looks very selfish. Second, agriculture contributes significantly to economic development. The same thing happened in Japan: there were agricultural contributions through the land tax, supplies of capital and labor, and other means. In this way, the agricultural sector reduced the position and share of agriculture within the economy. However, this reduction of the agricultural share in itself increased the whole economy's capacity, signified by increased values of $Y_2T_2 - Y_1T_1$. Third, we could see that agricultural technical change is the most efficient method in the later stage of economic development to reduce the agricultural surplus labor. This would be a very important policy implication for a mature economy that cannot remove agricultural surplus labor.

Chapter 4

Factor Mobility and Surplus Labor
in the Japanese Economy

Introduction

Much controversy has surrounded the nature of the relationships between
business cycles and movements in the agricultural labor force. Namiki
[1956] started by saying that there was no relationship between these two
phenomena; he thought that the agricultural sector always released a certain amount of agricultural labor, without adhering to business cycles. This
claim was based on analyses of Takagi's data (*i.e.*, statistical data submitted
to the 40th workshop on the rural population problem), which shows that
the numerical values of the average migrant agricultural population in each
five-year period (*i.e.*, 1920–1925, 1925–1930, and 1930–1935) were almost
constant. Namiki's thinking was based on the background thinking that the
Japanese employment market was flexible enough to absorb at any time the
outflows of farmers' second and third sons.

Hatai [1963] doubts Namiki's assertion and thinks it is impossible that
the agricultural population — which contains second and third sons and
new graduated individuals — could remain constant, even during the Great
Depression. Therefore, he thinks that there is a tendency for labor outflows to cease. Minami and Ono [1962] criticizes the method of Namiki,
who used only data pertaining to the outflows of the farm population every
five years, and provide a new estimation of the number of migrant farm
workers. They then found there to be in Japan strong relationships between
the number of net migrants and the economy's growth rate. In this chapter, we consider first the movement of inputs between the agricultural and
non-agricultural sectors. Second, we consider agricultural surplus labor and

economic development. Third, we undertake analysis of agricultural surplus labor and growth accounting.

1. Movement of Inputs between the Agricultural and Non-agricultural Sectors

Here, we show our calculated results of the relationships between the movement of factor inputs and the business cycle. In our model, we observe the relationships $|L_1T_1 + L_2T_2| = |L_1Q|$, $|L_2T_1 + L_2T_2| = |L_2Q|$, $|K_1T_1 + K_1T_2| = |K_1Q|$, and $|K_2T_1 + K_2T_2| = |K_2Q|$, from Appendix Table 3. What we next want to know is which element between population growth and technical change has a stronger effect on the movement of factor inputs in each period. This is closely related to the discussion of the relationships between the business cycle and the movement of factor inputs, undertaken by Duesenberry [1960], Kirk [1960], Silver [1965] in general terms, and by Namiki [1962] versus Minami and Ono [1962; 1963] in terms of labor, and by Ishikawa [1966] and Ruttan [1966] versus Lee [1968], Kato [1963, 1970], Fujino [1965], and Teranishi [1972] in terms of capital stock. In our model, factor inputs flow out from the agricultural sector when technical change exceeds population growth and the economy is in good condition. On the other hand, factor inputs flow into the agricultural sector when the population growth exceeds technical change. Here, we can see which of population growth or technical change had a large influence on the factor input movements in each decade since the Meiji period.

Figure 2-3 and Appendix Table 6 show the calculated results. Judging from the results for capital stock, the periods in which $|CK_1T_1 + CK_1T_2| \le |CK_1Q|$ are the 1900s, 1920s, and 1930s. The periods in which $|CK_2T_1 + CK_2T_2| \le |CK_2Q|$ are the 1920s, 1930s, and 1960s. Therefore, these results suggest that when population growth exceeds technical change, it has had a ratcheting effect on the outflow of capital from the agricultural sector. On the other hand, the periods in which $|CK_1T_1 + CK_1T_2| > |CK_1Q|$ are the 1880s, 1890s, 1900s, 1910s, 1950s, and 1960s. Especially, in the periods of early economic development and post-war economic boom (*e.g.*, the 1880s, 1890s, 1950s, and 1960s), technical change had a great influence on the outflow of agricultural capital movement. Additionally, the periods in which $|CK_2T_1 + CK_2T_2| > |CK_2Q|$ are the 1880s, 1890s, 1900s, 1910s, and 1950s. Especially, the 1880s, 1890s, and 1910s saw large increases in non-agricultural capital, on account of technical change. These findings are consistent with those of Teranishi [1972].

Next, we would like to turn our attention from the movement of capital, to labor. The periods in which $|CL_1T_1 + CL_1T_2| \leq |CL_1Q|$ are the 1900s, 1920s, and 1930s, and the periods in which $|CL_2T_1 + CL_2T_2| \leq |CL_2Q|$ are the 1920s and 1930s. Therefore, in the economically stagnant periods of the 1920s and 1930s, whenever population growth exceeded technical change, it had a ratcheting effect on the outflow of labor from the agricultural sector. On the other hand, the periods in which $|CL_1T_1 + CL_1T_2| > |CL_1Q|$ are the 1880s, 1890s, 1910s, 1950s, and 1960s. Especially, in the periods of early economic development and post-war boom (*e.g.*, the 1880s, 1890s, and 1950s), technical change had a much stronger influence on the outflow of agricultural labor. Additionally, the periods in which $|CL_2T_1 + CL_2T_2| \geq |CL_2Q|$ are the 1880s, 1890s, 1900s, 1910s, 1950s, and 1960s.

Especially in the 1950s, technical change had a much stronger influence on increases in non-agricultural labor. These results, too, are consistent with those of Teranishi. Panel 3 in Fig. 2-3 shows that the contribution values of total capital stock exceed the growth rates of agricultural capital in all periods prior to World War II. However, the differences decreased drastically. Additionally, panel 4 in Fig. 2-3 shows that before 1940, there are fairly large differences between the contribution values of total capital stock and the growth rates of non-agricultural capital stock. We can also understand that the differences derive from the contributions of technical change and population. This means that the growth rates of capital stock in both sectors are influenced more in the beginning of economic development by technical change, total labor, and population.

Next, we would like to turn our attention to the labor force. Compared to the growth rates of non-agricultural labor, the values of the contribution of total labor are far smaller. This means that non-agricultural labor is influenced considerably by technical change, total capital, and population. This assertion becomes more clear when we see the contribution of these factors to the growth rates of agricultural labor. Panel 6 in Fig. 2-3 shows that technical change in each sector, total capital, and population contribute greatly (compared to the growth rates of non-agricultural labor) to the growth rates of agricultural labor. There are still large differences between the contribution values of total labor and the growth rates of non-agricultural labor. This is very different from the case of capital stock. In other words, even in the 1960s, non-agricultural labor still contributed, by virtue of agricultural labor that had flowed out as a result of technical change and total capital stock. On the other hand, the capital market remained almost unaffected by those factors. In this sense, we can see that the labor market and the capital market now behave in quite different ways.

2. Agricultural Surplus Labor and Economic Development[1]

Denote m_1 as the difference between the value of marginal product of agricultural labor ($VMPL_1$) and the wage rate in agriculture (w_1). If we express this in an equation, it is expressed as $m_1 = w_1/VMPL_1$. Define m_w as the ratio between wage rates in agriculture and non-agriculture (w_2). If we express this in an equation, $m_w = w_1/w_2$. Table 4-1 shows the calculated values of $\dot{m}_1$ ($= \Delta m_1/m_1$) and $\dot{m}_w$ ($= \Delta m_w/m_w$). Judging from the previous studies, the value of marginal product of agricultural labor is smaller than the wage rate in agriculture. Therefore, m$_1$ is larger than 1 (*i.e.*, $m_1 > 1$). From the equation $m_w = w_1/w_2$, the wage differential between w_1 and w_2 becomes larger when the value of $\dot{m}_w$ is negative because w_1 is usually smaller than w_2. Table 4-1 and Fig. 4-1 show that in the 1880s, 1900s, 1920s and 1950s, the wage differentials are widening. On the other hand, the differentials between w_1 and $VMPL_1$, *i.e.*, m_1, decrease when $\dot{m}_1$ is negative. In other words, the $VMPL_1$ approaches to the wage rate in agriculture and the surplus labor defined in this way decreases when $\dot{m}_1$ is negative.

Table 4-1 and Fig. 4-1 show that the periods except the 1890s, 1920s, 1960s correspond with this category. Especially, the surplus labor decreased at a high speed in the 1880s and 1930s. Both the 1890s and 1960s were periods with an enlarging gap between $VMPL_1$ and wage rate in agriculture. However, the difference of the calculated value is clear between the two periods. From the above discussion, we can see that the 1920s is a period which has increased surplus labor in agriculture in both senses (*i.e.*, the

---

[1]The contents of Secs. 2 and 3 of this chapter were developed and rewritten from Yamaguchi and Tanaka [2006] to meet the purpose of the book. We appreciate *Kobe University Economic Review* and Mr. Tanaka for permitting the use of this paper for this book.

Table 4-1   Degree of Surplus Labor in Agriculture

	(1) $\dot{w}_1$	(2) $\dot{w}_2$	(3) = (1) − (2) $\dot{m}_w$	(4) $VM\dot{P}L_1$					(5) = (1) − (4) $\dot{m}_1$				
				(A)	(B)	(C)	(D)	(E)	(A)	(B)	(C)	(D)	(E)
1880–1890	−6.4	−4.4	−2.0	4.8	—	3.1	2.4	5.3	−11.2	—	−9.5	−8.8	−11.7
1890–1900	8.3	7.4	0.9	7.0	—	6.1	6.5	6.9	1.3	—	2.2	1.8	1.4
1900–1910	2.0	4.8	−2.8	5.1	—	4.3	4.3	10.0	−3.1	—	−2.3	−2.3	−8.0
1910–1920	15.9	14.1	1.8	18.3	17.3	17.3	17.1	19.2	−2.4	−1.4	−1.4	−1.2	−3.3
1920–1930	−3.2	0.2	−3.4	−2.9	−3.5	−4.3	−3.2	−4.1	−0.3	0.3	1.1	0	0.9
1930–1940	6.8	2.2	4.6	11.9	18.8	11.2	10.2	13.0	−5.1	−12.0	−4.4	−3.4	−6.2
1940–1950	77.6	—	—	—	—	—	—	—	—	—	—	—	—
1950–1960	6.1	9.2	−3.1	8.6	—	8.2	8.6	6.9	−2.5	—	−2.1	−2.5	−0.8
1960–1970	19.8	11.1	8.7	13.8	—	12.7	13.8	10.6	6.0	—	7.1	6.0	9.2

Note: Columns (4) and (5): (A): Shintani [1983], (B): Minami [1970], (C): Akino and Hayami [1973], (D): Yamada and Hayami [1972]. (E): Yamaguchi [1987] $\dot{w}_1$, for example, means $\Delta w_1/w_1$.

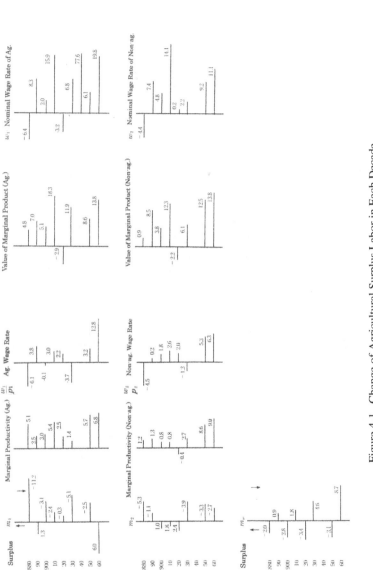

Figure 4-1   Change of Agricultural Surplus Labor in Each Decade

The panel m_1 shows the change of surplus labor (population) by first definition. The panel m_w shows the change of surplus labor (population) by second definition. m_1 is obtained subtracting MPL_1 from w_1/p_1 (*e.g.*, in 1880, the growth rate of MPL_1 is 5.1%, and w_1/p_1 is −6.1%. Therefore, we can obtain −11.2% (−6.1 − 5.1 = −11.2)). m_w is obtained subtracting w_2 from w_1 (*e.g.*, in 1880, the growth rate of w_1 is −6.4%, and the growth rate of w_2 is −4.4%. Therefore, we can obtain −2.0% (−6.4 − (−4.4) = −2.0)).

period of enlarged wage differentials, and the period of enlarged differences between $VMPL_1$ and w_1). As is well known, the serious Japanese economic depression and the great Kanto earthquake occurred in this period. We can understand that the growth rates of $VMPL_1$ are negative in this period. In addition, the growth rate of the wage rate in agriculture was negative in this period. On the contrary, the periods which decreased both the wage differentials and the gaps between $VMPL_1$ and w_1 are in the 1910s and 1930s.

In short, the agricultural surplus labor increased in the 1920s, but decreased in the periods before (*i.e.*, 1910s) and after 1920s (*i.e.*, 1930s). Also, the gap between $VMPL_1$ and w_1 (or the amounts of surplus labor) decreased at a high speed in the 1880s, but increased in the 1890s. However, the gap (the surplus labor) decreased again in the 1900s and continued until the 1920s. In the 1920s, the gap (the surplus labor) stayed at almost the same level or increased very slightly, but decreased at a fairly high speed in the 1930s. For the post-World War II periods, the gap or surplus labor decreased in the 1950s. In the 1960s, the gap increased at fairly large rates. However, this comes from the fact that the wage rate in agriculture increased more than the growth rate of $VMPL_1$. This means that the Japanese economy passed the turning point and the labor became a scarce factor (therefore, w_1 increased) as Minami [1970] pointed out.

Figure 4-1 graphically shows the change in agricultural surplus labor, in terms of two definitions. As shown above, m_1 is agricultural surplus labor in terms of the first definition; m_w shows the agricultural surplus labor in terms of the second definition. If we examine the periods (1890s, 1920s, 1930s, and 1960s) in which wage differentials decreased in terms of the second definition m_w, the decrease rate accelerates from 0.9 to 1.8, 4.6, and 8.7. This is very different from the periods in which the wage differentials increased, where the increase rate is almost constant at 2–3%. Except the period of the 1940s (the period of World War II), the wage differentials repeated cyclically: increase (–2.0), decrease (0.9), increase (–2.8), decrease (1.8), increase (–3.4), decrease (4.6), increase (–3.1), and decrease (8.7). In these cyclical movements, the values of the wage-differential increase periods are about 2–3%; however, the values of the decrease periods accelerated to a larger degree over time. Figure 4-1 shows that the decrease of surplus labor in terms of the first definition was largest in 1880, and trended smaller over time. Conversely, the decrease in the degree of surplus labor in terms

Table 4-2   Degree of Imperfect Competition of Capital and Non-agricultural Labor Markets

	$(VM\dot{P}L_2)$	$\dot{m}_2$	$\dot{r}$	$(VM\dot{P}K_1)$	$(VM\dot{P}K_2)$	$\dot{m}_3$	$\dot{m}_4$
1880–1890	0.9	−5.3	−1.3	1.2	3.1	−2.5	−4.4
				(2.4)	(0.1)	(−3.7)	(−1.4)
1890–1900	8.5	−1.1	3.9	3.8	11.1	0.1	−7.2
				(5.2)	(7.6)	(−1.3)	(−3.7)
1900–1910	3.8	1.0	−4.2	1.0	2.0	−5.2	−6.2
				(2.6)	(1.1)	(−6.8)	(−5.3)
1910–1920	12.3	1.8	7.8	13.9	8.8	−6.1	−1.0
				(15.2)	(8.8)	(−7.4)	(−1.0)
1920–1930	−2.2	2.4	−9.6	−6.7	−2.3	−2.9	−7.3
				(−5.3)	(−4.2)	(−4.3)	(−5.4)
1930–1940	6.1	−3.9	−6.9	8.7	6.4	−15.6	−13.3
				(10.2)	(4.4)	(−17.1)	(−11.3)
1940–1950	—	—	—	—	—	—	—
1950–1960	12.5	−3.3	−1.0	4.9	2.8	−5.9	−3.8
				(1.9)	(6.8)	(−2.9)	(−7.8)
1960–1970	13.8	−2.7	−3.1	5.2	5.2	−8.3	−8.3
				(0.2)	(5.2)	(−3.3)	(−8.3)

Note: The figures of parenthesis are the values which assume that production elasticity is constant in each period.

of the second definition became larger over time. Therefore, it seems that the decrease in agricultural surplus labor starts from inside the agricultural sector and later reduces the wage gap between the two sectors.

Here, we would switch our topics to the capital market and calculate the gap between the interest rate and the value of marginal product of capital $VMPK_1$. Note that m_3 was the gap between the growth rates of $VMPK_1$ and agricultural interest rate r_1, and m_4 was the gap between the growth rates of $VMPK_2$ and non-agricultural interest rate r_2. Judging from the calculated values of m_3 and m_4 in Table 4-2, m_3 has negative signs in most of the periods except the 1890s, which has a very small positive value (0.1%). m_4 takes negative signs in whole periods. (As it is hard to obtain the sectoral interest rates for almost 100 years, we adopt the same interest rates in both sectors. However, it would be possible to assume that the interest rates in both sectors would move in a parallel way, because of the difficulties of gathering data

Table 4-3   Growth Rates of Marginal Product of Labor and Capital

	$(\dot{M}PL_1)$	$\left(\frac{\dot{w}_1}{\hat{P}_1}\right)$	$(\dot{M}PL_2)$	$\left(\frac{\dot{w}_2}{\hat{P}_2}\right)$	$(\dot{M}PK_1)$	$\left(\frac{\dot{r}}{\hat{P}_1}\right)$	$(\dot{M}PK_2)$	$\left(\frac{\dot{r}}{\hat{P}_2}\right)$	$\dot{P}_1$	$\dot{P}_2$
1880–1890	5.1	−6.1	1.2	−4.7	1.5	−1.0	3.4	−1.0	−0.3	−0.3
1890–1900	2.5	3.8	1.3	0.2	−0.7	−0.6	3.9	−3.3	4.5	7.2
1900–1910	3.0	−0.1	0.8	1.8	−1.1	−6.3	−1.0	−7.2	2.1	3.0
1910–1920	5.4	3.0	0.8	2.6	1.0	−5.1	−2.7	−3.7	12.9	11.5
1920–1930	2.5	2.2	−0.4	2.0	−1.3	−4.2	−0.5	−7.8	−5.4	−1.8
1930–1940	1.4	−3.7	2.7	−1.2	−1.8	−17.4	3.0	−10.3	10.5	3.4
1940–1950	—	—	—	—	—	—	—	—	—	—
1950–1960	5.7	3.2	8.6	5.3	2.0	−3.9	−1.1	−4.9	2.9	3.9
1960–1970	6.8	12.8	9.0	6.3	−1.8	−10.1	0.4	−7.9	7.0	4.8

for these long periods) m_3 and m_4 are the differences between the growth rates of the interest rate and the value of marginal product of capital. What does the growth rates of m_3 and m_4 are negative mean? We can interpret this phenomenon as follows: Interest rates go up only in periods with extremely high growth rates in the value of marginal product of capital. In other words, interest rates usually stay the same or decrease even in periods with a positive growth rate in the value of marginal product.

Therefore, in such a period like the 1920s, which had a negative growth rate in the value of marginal product of capital, the growth rate of the interest rate took a negative value. In short, interest rates seem to follow the movements of *VMPK* and drop their level whenever the growth rates of VMPK become negative. This is very different from the case of labor. If we rearrange the numerical values of the growth rates of *VMPL*$_1$ in each period from the largest to the smallest, the result would be as follows: 1910s (18.3%), 1960s (13.8%), 1930s (11.9%), 1950s (8.6%), 1890s (7.0%), 1900s (5.1%), 1880s (4.8%), and 1920s (−2.9%). Subtracting the growth rates of agricultural price (p_1) from these growth rates, we can obtain the growth rates of the marginal product of labor in agriculture (MPL_1). If we also rearrange these values from the largest to the smallest, we can obtain the result as follows (see Table 4-3): 1960s (6.8%), 1950s (5.7%), 1910s (5.4%), 1880s (5.1%), 1900s (3.0%), 1890s (2.5%), 1920s (2.5%), and 1930s (1.4%).

From these results, we can say that the growth rates of the marginal product of labor in agriculture (MPL_1) are large in the post-war periods like the 1950s and the 1960s, and small in the depression periods like the 1930s (agricultural depression) and the 1920s (economic depression). Similarly, we can rearrange for the growth rates of the value of marginal product of labor in non-agricultural sector ($VMPL_2$) as follows: 1960s (13.8%), 1950s (12.5%), 1910s (12.3.%), 1890s (8.5%), 1930s (6.1%), 1900s (3.8%), 1880s (0.9%), and 1920s (-2.2%). Subtracting the growth rates of non-agricultural price (p_2) from these growth rates, we can obtain the growth rates of the marginal product of labor in non-agriculture (MPL_2). The result is as follows (see Table 4-3): 1960s (9.0%), 1950s (8.6%), 1930s (2.7%), 1890s (1.3%), 1880s (1.2%), 1910s (0.8%), 1900s (0.8%), and 1920s (-0.4%). Therefore, the non-agricultural sector is similar to the agricultural sector in a sense that the growth rates of the marginal product of labor in non-agriculture (MPL_2) are large in post-war periods like the 1950s and the 1960s and small in economic depression periods like the 1920s.

The difference is that non-agricultural values in 1930s are rather large and this means that the non-agricultural sector is in rather good condition in this period. On the other hand, the growth rates of $VMPK_1$ are as follows: 1910s (13.9%), 1930s (8.7%), 1960s (5.2%), 1950s (4.9%), 1980s (3.8%), 1880s (1.2%), 1900s (1.0%), and 1920s (-6.7%). Subtracting the growth rates of agricultural price (p_1) from these growth rates, we can obtain the growth rates of marginal product of capital in agriculture (MPK_1). The growth rates of marginal product of capital in agriculture is as follows: 1950s (2.0%), 1880s (1.5%), 1910s (1.0%), 1890s (-0.7%), 1900s (-1.1%), 1920s (-1.3%), 1930s (-1.8%) and 1960s (-1.8%). We can see how small they are as compared with the result of the case of labor. In other words, they have much smaller positive or in most cases rather negative growth rates. The growth rates of $VMPK_2$ are as follows: 1890s (11.1%), 1910s (8.8%), 1930s (6.4%), 1960s (5.2%), 1880s (3.1%), 1950s (2.8%), 1900s (2.0%) and 1920s (-2.3%).

Subtracting the growth rates of non-agricultural price (p_2) from these growth rates, we can obtain the growth rates of the marginal product of capital in non-agriculture (MPK_2) as follows (see Table 4-3): 1890s (3.9%), 1880s (3.4%), 1930s (3.0%), 1960s (0.4%), 1920s (-0.5%), 1900s (-1.0%), 1950s (-1.1%) and 1910s (-2.7%). This result is similar to the case of agricultural capital and has fairly small positive or negative values. This result shows that there is a clear difference between the labor and capital market. First, the growth rates of the marginal product of labor in both sectors have positive values. The only one exception is the 1920s (-0.4%). However, the growth rates of the marginal product of capital in both sectors have smaller positive or mostly negative values. Second, the growth rates of the marginal product of labor in both sectors in the post-war periods have large positive values (*e.g.*, 6.8% in the 1960s, 5.7% in the 1950s for the agricultural sector and 9.0% in the 1960s, 8.6% in the 1950s for non-agricultural sector) but the growth rates of the marginal product of capital in both sectors have negative or near zero values.

From the equation of marginal product of labor = output elasticity of labor multiplied by labor productivity, the marginal product of labor would increase when labor productivity increases. The surplus labor in agriculture decreased with the exception of the 1890s (the 1960s which experienced the turning point of the Japanese economy, was different from the point of the 1890s although $\dot{m}_1$ was positive in the 1960s), therefore this brought an increase in agricultural productivity. Also, the growth rates of agricultural capital were very large in the post-war periods. This also brought an increase in agricultural productivity. In the non-agricultural sector, the growth rates of capital were very large from the beginning and led to productivity increases. These factors increased the marginal productivity of labor in both sectors. On the other hand, capital productivity did not change so much. This comes from the well-known fact that the capital coefficient which is the reciprocal value of capital productivity is usually almost constant over time.

Therefore, the growth rates of the marginal productivity of capital had zero or negative values. The values of $\dot{m}_3$ and $\dot{m}_4$ (which are defined as the growth rate of interest minus that of *VMPK*) were negative with the exception of the value of $\dot{m}_3$ in the 1890s. This was in sharp contrast to the case of labor. This comes from the following two reasons. First, the growth rates of the interest rate were negative except for the 1890s and 1910s as Table 4-2 shows. Second, the growth rates of the value of marginal product of capital were negative but had smaller absolute values than the interest rate in the 1920s. For these two reasons, the values of $\dot{m}_3$ and $\dot{m}_4$ were negative. In any case, real interest rates were large in the beginning of the Meiji period and the period immediately after World War II and they decreased over time.

3. Agricultural Surplus Labor and Growth Accounting Analysis

Table 4-4 shows the calculated values of the growth accounting for the Japanese economy using our model. In our calculation, first we calculated the contribution values of total imperfect competition N using the value of m_1, m_w, m_r, m_2, m_3 and m_4 in Table 4-1 and 4-2, and the growth rate multiplier of Appendix Table 5. They show that the contribution values are very large; therefore we need to analyze the contribution factors in more detail. The result is shown in the lower part of Table 4-4. Total imperfect competition N can be divided into six items from our model, *i.e.*, the contribution of wage differentials in both sectors $CY_1 m_w$, the contribution of the difference between the agricultural wage rate and the value of marginal product of labor in agriculture $CY_1 m_1$, the contribution of the difference between the non-agricultural wage rate and the value of marginal product of labor in non-agriculture $CY_1 m_2$, the contribution of the difference between the agricultural interest rate and the value of marginal product of capital in agriculture $CY_1 m_3$, the contribution of the difference between the non-agricultural interest rate and the value of marginal product of capital in non-agriculture $CY_1 m_4$, the contribution of the interest rate differentials in both sectors $CY_1 m_r$.

From these calculations, we can see how wage differentials, interest rate differentials, the differences between factor price and the value of marginal product of factor inputs contribute to the growth rates of agricultural output. From Table 4-4, we can see that the contributions of wage differentials $CY_1 m_w$, the difference between the agricultural wage rate and the value of marginal product of labor in agriculture $CY_1 m_1$, the difference between the agricultural interest rate and the value of marginal product of capital in agriculture $CY_1 m_3$ are fairly large contributors to the growth rates of agricultural output. Especially in the 1930s, the contribution of total imperfect competition N had four times the numerical values of the growth rate of agricultural output. Judging from the calculated values, the contributions of the differences between wage rates and the value of marginal product of labor in both sectors $CY_1 m_3$ and $CY_1 m_1$ and the contributions of the differences between the interest rate and the value of marginal product of capital in non-agriculture $CY_1 m_4$, and the contribution of wage differentials $CY_1 m_w$ are very large in the 1930s.

Table 4-4   Growth Accounting for Japanese Agricultural Output

	$\Delta Y_1/Y_1$	CY_1T_1	CY_1T_2	CY_1K	CY_1L	CY_1Q	CY_1B	CY_1a	CY_1N
1880–1890	3.4 (100)	2.9 (85)	−0.1 (−3)	0.5 (15)	0.1 (3)	0.1 (3)	0.1 (3)	1.7 (50)	−1.9 (−56)
1890–1900	1.7 (100)	1.1 (65)	−0.1 (−6)	0.5 (29)	0.2 (12)	0.1 (6)	0.2 (12)	−0.9 (−53)	0.6 (35)
1900–1910	2.2 (100)	1.5 (68)	−0.0 (0)	0.5 (23)	0.1 (5)	0.1 (5)	0.2 (9)	−0.2 (−9)	0 (0)
1910–1920	3.2 (100)	2.9 (91)	0.0 (0)	0.6 (19)	0.2 (6)	0.2 (6)	0.2 (6)	0.3 (9)	−1.2 (−38)
1920–1930	1.1 (100)	0.8 (73)	0.0 (0)	0.4 (36)	0.4 (36)	0.3 (27)	−0.0 (0)	−1.5 (−136)	0.7 (64)
1930–1940	0.4 (100)	0.2 (50)	0.0 (0)	0.4 (100)	0.6 (150)	0.2 (50)	0.1 (25)	0.5 (125)	−1.6 (−400)
1940–1950	−0.5 (100)	−1.0			0.1	0.2	−0.1		
1950–1960	3.6 (100)	3.2 (89)	−0.2 (−6)	0.5 (14)	1.0 (28)	0.3 (8)	0.1 (3)	−3.3 (−92)	2.0 (56)
1960–1970	2.1 (100)	2.2 (105)	−0.1 (−5)	1.2 (57)	0.5 (24)	0.3 (14)	−0.1 (−5)	−3.1 (−148)	1.2 (57)

	CY_1N	CY_1m_w	CY_1m_1	CY_1m_2	CY_1m_3	CY_1m_4	CY_1m_r
1880–1890	−1.9 (−56)	0.2 (6)	−1.2 (−35)	0.6 (18)	−0.3 (−9)	0.6 (18)	−1.8 (−53)
1890–1900	0.6 (35)	−0.1 (−6)	0.2 (12)	0.1 (6)	0.0 (0)	0.9 (53)	−0.5 (−29)
1900–1910	0.0 (0)	0.4 (18)	−0.5 (−23)	−0.2 (−9)	−0.6 (−27)	0.7 (32)	0.2 (9)
1910–1920	−1.2 (−38)	−0.3 (−9)	−0.4 (−13)	−0.3 (−9)	−0.6 (−19)	0.1 (3)	0.3 (9)
1920–1930	0.7 (64)	0.7 (64)	−0.1 (−9)	−0.5 (−45)	−0.5 (−45)	1.2 (109)	−0.1 (−9)
1930–1940	−1.6 (−400)	−1.2 (300)	−1.3 (−325)	1.0 (250)	−1.6 (−400)	1.3 (325)	0.2 (50)
1940–1950							
1950–1960	2.0 (56)	1.1 (31)	−0.9 (−25)	1.1 (31)	−0.5 (−14)	0.3 (8)	0.9 (25)
1960–1970	1.2 (57)	−3.0 (−143)	2.0 (95)	0.9 (43)	−0.9 (−43)	0.9 (43)	1.3 (62)

Note: CY_1T_1, for example, means the contribution of technical change in agriculture T_1 to agricultural output Y_1.

Table 4-5 shows the calculated contribution values of the wage differentials m_w and of the differences between agricultural wage rates and the value of marginal products of labor m_1, to the growth rates of eight endogenous variables such as agricultural output Y_1, non-agricultural output Y_2, agricultural capital K_1, non-agricultural capital K_2, agricultural labor L_1, non-agricultural labor L_2, relative price P, and real per capita income E. For example, CY_1m_w shows the contribution of wage differentials m_w to the growth rates of agricultural output. Table 4-5 shows that the wage differentials m_w and the difference between the agricultural wage rates and the value of marginal product of labor in agriculture m_1 have a large contribution. In this way, this chapter showed the calculated values of imperfect competitions, and saw how this imperfect competition affected and contributed to the economic development of Japan.

Next, let us look at the growth accounting results in Fig. 2-3, in Chapter 2. As panel 5 of that figure shows, the contributions of imperfect competition to agricultural labor growth were fairly large; (see the *GRM* of imperfect competition in Appendix Table 5) similarly, panel 6 shows that its contributions to non-agricultural labor growth were also fairly large. Here, we consider the labor absorption ability of the non-agricultural sector. We showed in Chapter 3 the push and pull effects of technical changes on agricultural labor; conversely, population growth was found here, in Chapter 4, to hamper the outflow of agricultural labor to the non-agricultural sector. As Fei and Ranis [1964] show, the absorption ability of the non-agricultural sector (in their words, the industrial sector) from the agricultural sector depends on the factors of capital stock and non-agricultural technical change.

Therefore, Fei and Ranis assert that agricultural saving and the profits of the industrial sector are important. Additionally, they say that it is necessary to increase technical change and use labor-intensive technology. These assertions were obtained solely from differentiation in the industrial sector's production function; our results, on the other hand, are obtained through the use of general equilibrium growth accounting. Therefore, we were able to measure the factors of both the agricultural and non-agricultural sectors; we were also able to measure the demand and supply factors of both sectors. As shown in Fig. 2-3, the labor absorption ability of industry (in our case, non-agriculture) depends on capital stock and non-agricultural technical change; this finding aligns with that of Fei and Ranis. Additionally, agricultural technical change and labor contributed positively, while

Table 4-5   Contribution of Imperfect Competition to Eight Endogenous Variables

	CY_1m_w	CY_2m_w	CK_1m_w	CK_2m_w	CL_1m_w	CL_2m_w	CPm_w	CEm_w
1880–1890	0.2 (6)	−1.2 (−32)	0.1 (14)	−0.0 (0)	−0.6 ()	−1.5 (−88)	−1.3 (−21)	−0.7 (−26)
1890–1900	−0.1 (−6)	0.4 (10)	−0.0 (0)	0.0 (0)	0.3 (300)	0.8 (57)	0.5 (−26)	0.2 (9)
1900–1910	0.4 (18)	−1.1 (−42)	−0.0 (0)	0.0 (0)	1.0 ()	2.4 (185)	−1.5 (188)	−0.7 (−54)
1910–1920	−0.3 (−9)	0.5 (13)	0.1 (11)	−0.0 (0)	−0.7 (58)	1.4 (44)	0.9 (129)	0.3 (12)
1920–1930	0.7 (64)	−0.9 (−38)	−0.2 (−20)	0.0 (0)	1.6 ()	−2.1 (−124)	−1.9 (58)	−0.5 (−100)
1930–1940	−1.2 (−300)	0.8 (14)	0.6 (86)	−0.0 (0)	−2.3 (767)	1.7 (61)	2.6 (36)	0.6 (15)
1940–1950								
1950–1960	1.1 (31)	−0.7 (−8)	−0.4 (−9)	0.2 (3)	1.7 (−100)	−1.0 (−21)	−2.2 (147)	−0.4 (−6)
1960–1970	−3.0 (143)	1.0 (8)	1.7 (19)	−0.1 (−1)	−5.4 (150)	1.6 (55)	5.7 (271)	1.0 (10)

	CY_1m_1	CY_2m_1	CK_1m_1	CK_2m_1	CL_1m_1	CL_2m_1	CPm_1	CEm_1
1880–1890	−1.2 (−35)	6.7 (181)	−0.3 (−43)	0.2 (6)	−3.6 ()	8.3 (488)	7.3 (116)	3.9 (144)
1890–1900	0.2 (12)	−0.6 (−15)	0.0 (0)	−0.0 (0)	0.5 (500)	−1.1 (−79)	−0.8 (42)	−0.4 (−18)
1900–1910	−0.5 (−23)	1.2 (46)	0.0 (0)	0.0 (0)	−1.1 ()	2.6 (200)	1.7 (−213)	0.8 (62)
1910–1920	−0.4 (−13)	0.7 (18)	0.1 (11)	−0.0 (0)	−1.0 (83)	1.9 (59)	1.2 (171)	0.4 (15)
1920–1930	−0.1 (−9)	0.1 (4)	0.0 (0)	−0.0 (0)	−0.1 ()	0.2 (12)	0.2 (−6)	0.0 (0)
1930–1940	−1.3 (−325)	0.9 (16)	0.6 (86)	−0.1 (−2)	−2.5 (838)	1.9 (68)	2.9 (40)	0.6 (15)
1940–1950								
1950–1960	−0.9 (−25)	0.6 (7)	0.3 (7)	−0.1 (−2)	−1.4 (82)	0.8 (17)	1.8 (−120)	0.4 (6)
1960–1970	2.0 (95)	−0.7 (−6)	−1.1 (−12)	0.1 (1)	3.7 (−103)	−1.1 (−38)	−4.0 (−190)	−0.7 (−7)

Note: Y_1: Agricultural Output, Y_2: Non-agricultural Output, K_1: Agricultural Capital Stock, K_2: Non-agricultural Capital Stock, L_1: Agricultural Labor, L_2: Non-agricultural Labor, P: Relative Price (Ag./Non-ag.), E: Per Capita Income.

Table 4-6   Estimated Results of Affecting Surplus Labor in Agriculture

Dependent variable	Agricultural surplus m_1		Agricultural surplus m_w
	(1)	(2)	(1)
Ag. Tech. Change (T_1)	−1.023	−1.022	0.002
	(−64.09)	(−58.80)	(0.708)
Non-ag. Tec. Change (T_2)	−0.032	−0.024	0.010
	(−2.128)	(−1.480)	(3.082)
Population (ΔQ)	0.804	0.963	−0.095
	(2.784)	(3.113)	(−1.837)
Dummy 1 (Year of 1918)	−1.129		
	(−3.326)		
Dummy 2 (1886–1905)	0.258		
	(3.120)		
Constant	−0.238	−0.146	−0.013
	(−3.847)	(−2.464)	(−1.158)
Adjusted R^2	0.989	0.987	0.191

population contributed negatively. However, the contribution of imperfect competition was far larger than those of non-agricultural technical change or capital stock. In conclusion, owing to our use of general equilibrium growth accounting, our analysis was able to gather an understanding of factors on both the demand and supply sides, and those of both the agricultural and non-agricultural sectors; as such, this methodology differs greatly from that of Fei and Ranis.

Next, we would like to demonstrate our econometric analysis of m_1 and m_w, to show that our result is consistent with that derived through regression analysis. As we showed above, technical change pushes agricultural labor to the non-agricultural sector but non-agricultural technical change does not push non-agricultural labor to the agricultural sector, but pulls agricultural labor to the non-agricultural sector. This came from the low agricultural income and price elasticity. As a result, technical change in both sectors reduces agricultural labor and increases the value of marginal product of labor in agriculture ($VMPL_1$). Therefore, m_1 ($=w_1/VMPL_1$) decreases. On the other hand, population growth has the opposite effect on agricultural labor. Table 4-6 shows the regression analysis for this. The result shows good support to this view. In the same way, technical change in both sectors reduces agricultural labor and increases non-agricultural labor. Then, the wage rate of non-agricultural labor (w_2) decreases. Therefore, m_w ($=w_1/w_2$) increases. On the other hand, population growth has the opposite effect on agricultural labor. Table 4-6 shows the regression analysis for these. The result also shows good support to these views.

Conclusion

(1) Technical change and population were set symmetrically in our model. For that reason, we were able to see which of technical change or population drove agricultural labor and capital to the non-agricultural sector. Judging from our calculations, population growth obstructed outflows of agricultural labor and capital in Japan's economically stagnant periods (*e.g.*, the 1920s and 1930s). Conversely, in periods of early-stage economic development or with good economic conditions (*e.g.*, the 1880s, 1890s, 1910s, 1950s, and 1960s), technical change had stronger effects than population growth; therefore, during those periods, agricultural labor and capital moved from the agricultural sector to the non-agricultural sector. We calculated the change in the degree of imperfection in each decade from 1880 to 1970. Judging from the sense of the widening of wage differentials, we found that the imperfection increased in the 1880s, 1900s, 1920s, and 1950s. For the sense of a widening value between the agricultural wage rate and the value of marginal product in agricultural labor, we found that the imperfection increased in the 1890s, 1920s, and 1960s. Therefore, we can understand that the decade of the 1920s is the period which increased the agricultural surplus in both senses. Only in the 1920s, the growth rate of the value of marginal product of labor in agriculture had a minus sign. Also, the growth of wage rate in agriculture had a minus sign too.

(2) Judging from the ordinary calculation method which is the method to check the gap between the wage rate and the marginal product of labor, surplus labor in agriculture decreased greatly in the 1880s but increased in the 1890s. Again, surplus labor in agriculture decreased greatly from the 1900s to the 1920s. However, the degree of decrease became smaller over time. And the 1920s is an almost stagnant period or rather the increase was very small. The 1930s was the period of large decrease

of agricultural surplus. We do not have data for the 1940s but we can guess that the surplus labor in agriculture increased greatly in the 1940s. However, surplus labor in agriculture again decreased fairly much in 1950s. In the beginning of the 1960s, the Japanese economy experienced a turning point for labor and both the values of marginal product of labor in agriculture and the agricultural wage rate increased. Therefore, we should interpret the 1960s as it is a decreasing period of agricultural surplus labor although the calculation result shows positive. In other words, the decrease in surplus labor in terms of the first definition was largest in 1880, and trended smaller over time. Conversely, the degree of decrease in surplus labor in terms of the second definition became larger over time. Therefore, it seems that the decrease in agricultural surplus labor starts from inside the agricultural sector and later reduces the wage gap between the two sectors.

(3) The gap between the interest rate and the marginal product of capital decreased over time except for the agricultural sector in the 1890s. The growth rates of the interest rate had minus signs except for the 1890s and the 1910s which showed a large increase in the value of marginal product of capital. The interest rate decreased greatly in the 1920s which had a large decrease in the value of marginal product of capital in both sectors. In other words, the interest rate looks likely to follow the movement of the value of marginal product of capital very slowly and decrease immediately when the growth of the value of marginal product of capital decreases. Therefore, the growth rates of the real interest rate always had negative signs. The Japanese interest rate was very large in the beginning of the Meiji period and after World War II and decreased over time. Also, the growth rates of the marginal product of capital were zero or negative, although those of the marginal product of labor had very high positive values.

(4) Growth accounting for agriculture shows that the contribution of imperfect competition is very large. Therefore, it would be necessary to analyze the content of imperfection. This imperfect competition is classified into six items, $CY_1 m_w$ (contribution of the growth of the wage differential to agricultural output growth), $CY_1 m_1$ (contribution of the difference between the growth rate of the wage rate in agriculture and that of the marginal product of labor to agricultural output

growth), CY_1m_2 (contribution of the difference between the growth rate of the wage rate in non-agriculture and that of the marginal product of labor to agricultural output growth), CY_1m_r (contribution of the growth of the interest rate differential to agricultural output growth), CY_1m_3 (contribution of the difference between the growth rate of the wage rate in non-agriculture and that of the marginal product of labor to agricultural output growth), CY_1m_4 (contribution of the difference between the growth rate of the wage rate in non-agriculture and that of the marginal product of labor to agricultural output growth). For the growth of agricultural output, CY_1m_w, CY_1m_1, CY_1m_2 and CY_1m_3 have large values. Especially, six contributions of imperfections total amounted to about four times the growth of agricultural output in the 1930s. For the growth of labor in agricultural and non-agricultural sectors, and relative price, the contribution of m_1 and m_w have very large values.

(5) Technical change in both sectors reduces agricultural labor and increases the *VMPL* in agriculture $(VMPL_1)$. Therefore, m_1 $(=w_1/VMPL_1)$ decreases. On the other hand, population growth has the opposite effect on agricultural labor; Table 4-6 shows the results of the related regression analysis, which seem to support this view. In the same way, technical change in both sectors reduces agricultural labor and increases non-agricultural labor; then, the wage rate of non-agricultural labor (w_2) decreases, and m_w $(=w_1/w_2)$ therefore increases. On the other hand, population growth has the opposite effect on agricultural labor; Table 4-6 shows the results of the related regression analysis, and they too seem to support these views.

Summaries (1)–(5) are clear. Among them, there are four especially noteworthy points. First, the historic depression period in Japan — *i.e.*, the 1920s — was the worst period from the viewpoint of agricultural surplus labor, as decreasing trend of agricultural surplus labor disappeared or again increased in this period. Second, the decrease in agricultural surplus labor in terms of the first definition was largest in the 1880s, but trended smaller over time. Conversely, the lower degree of agricultural surplus labor in terms of the second definition increased over time. Therefore, it seems that agricultural surplus labor decreases from inside the agricultural sector and later reduces agricultural surplus labor by decreasing the wage gap between the two sectors. Third, many agricultural contributions in the early stage of economic development are well known; here, through the use of growth accounting analysis, we found newly that the reduction of agricultural surplus labor contributed far more than was previously thought to per capita income growth, especially in that early stage of economic development (Fig. 2-3). Fourth, from our general equilibrium growth accounting analysis, we found that the contribution of non-agricultural technical change to reductions in agricultural surplus labor was very important in Japan's early stage of economic development.

Chapter 5

Agricultural Surplus Labor and Growth Accounting for the Thai and Chinese Economies*

Introduction

The recent growth of the Thai economy has been associated with certain problems. However, their growth was very rapid, and many people throughout the world have been observing the country's development. The purpose of this chapter is to examine Thailand's economic development since 1950, especially the conflict between technical change and population growth in terms of their respective influences on economic growth. We conduct growth accounting for the Thai economy, especially to measure the changes in surplus labor in the agricultural sector and calculate the contribution of this change in the surplus labor to the economic development of Thailand. We also compare the results for the Thai economy with those of Japan, Taiwan, and China. Owing to the restriction in available data (we need consistent data on 17 variables [eight endogenous and nine exogenous] from each year), we measure the general equilibrium growth accounting of Thai economy from 1950 to 1995 using the data from the study by Shintani [1993] and Thai's Statistical Data Bank and Information Dissemination Division [Various years]. In this chapter, we first consider the general outline of the economic development of Thailand. Second, we address the planning of economic and social development in Thailand. Third, we discuss surplus labor in the agricultural sector in Japan, Taiwan, China, and Thailand.

---

*The content of this chapter was developed and rewritten from Yamaguchi [1997] to meet the purpose of the book. We appreciate *Kobe University Economic Review* for permitting the use of this paper for this book.

1. General Outline of the Economic Development of Thailand

Typically, there is a lot of surplus labor in the beginning phase of economic development. In this chapter, an attempt is made to conduct growth accounting for the Thai economy, especially to measure the change in the surplus labor in the agricultural sector in Thailand and to calculate the contribution of this change (a decrease or increase) in the surplus labor to economic development [*i.e.*, to the eight endogenous variables: agricultural output Y_1, non-agricultural output Y_2, agricultural labor L_1, non-agricultural labor L_2, agricultural capital K_1, non-agricultural capital K_2, relative price of the agricultural goods to non-agricultural goods (agriculture/non-agriculture) P, real per capita income E, where suffix 1 denotes the agricultural sector and 2 denotes the non-agricultural sector] of Thailand (see the model of these variables in Chapter 2).

Figure 5-1 shows how Thailand achieved its economic development during the period from 1950 to the present, by showing the growth rate[1] of eight endogenous variables [sectoral output Y_i, sectoral inputs (labor and capital) L_i, K_i, the relative price P and per capita income E] as stated above. Panel 1 in Fig. 5-1 shows the historical growth rates of agricultural output Y_1 and agricultural price P_1. From this panel, we can see how the size of the fluctuations in the growth rate in agricultural output have decreased over time. Also, the fluctuations in agricultural price are much larger than those in agricultural output. Agricultural price still had a large degree of fluctuation even around 1990. Especially, we can see that growth rate of agricultural price from 1972 to 1973 was 33.9%. The growth rate from 1971 to 1972 was also large and was −20.3%. These extremely high growth rates in agricultural price were the result of the world food crisis in 1973 (which started in 1972).

However, the fluctuations in non-agricultural output are much smaller than those of agricultural output. The fluctuations in non-agricultural price are also small compared with those in agricultural price. We can observe that agricultural output and agricultural price are negatively correlated, as Fig. 5-1 shows. Non-agricultural output and price are also negatively correlated, but not so clearly as in the case of agriculture. Agricultural prices

---

[1]Growth rate from the previous year, based on the data of Appendix Table 5-1.

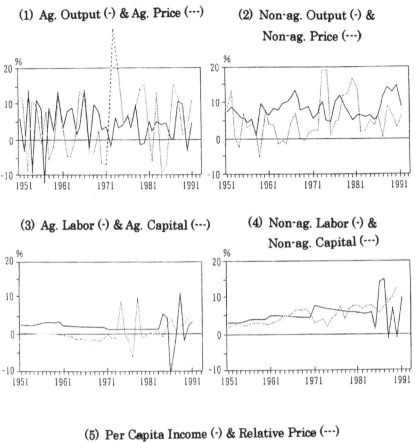

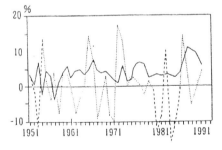

Figure 5-1   Growth Rates of Eight Endogenous Variables in Thailand

were clearly negatively correlated with agricultural output until around 1960 (In this point, Thailand economy is similar to Japanese economy), but the degree of correlation gradually decreased over time in Thailand. This is due to the fact that the agricultural price in Thailand came to be influenced by the world situation or that of foreign countries (*e.g.*, the food crises in 1972 and 1973) rather than by her own output. Figure 5-1 also displays the fluctuations in the growth of inputs in Thailand. However, we can see that the fluctuations in inputs are far smaller than those in outputs.

We can divide the economic development of Thailand since 1960 into three periods. The first period starts from 1960, which was the time of the beginning of industrialization by import substitution. The second period starts from 1970 and continues until the beginning of the 1980s. This was a time of adjustment and change from industrialization through import substitution to export-oriented industrialization. The third period, which was the time of export-oriented industrialization started from the late years of the 1980s. The height of the bar graphs in Fig. 5-2 depend heavily on the situations resulting from the planning policies discussed in Sec. 2. The height of the bar graphs in Fig. 5-2 shows the average growth rates during five year periods.[2] Panel 1 in Fig. 5-2 shows the average growth rates (during five-year periods) of agricultural and non-agricultural output. These figures show that the Thai economy grew at an accelerating rate in the 1950s and 1960s. For example, the agricultural output of the Thai economy grew at the rates of 3.6, 4.1, 5.0 and 6.3% in 1950–1955, 1955–1960, 1960–1965, and 1965–1970 respectively. Similarly, non-agricultural output grew at the rates of 6.9, 5.3, 8.2 and 9.4% in 1950–1955, 1955–1960, 1960–1965 and 1965–1970 respectively. However, the growth rate of agricultural output decreased to about 3% in 1970–1975, and 1980–1985.

The growth rate of non-agricultural output also decreased to the rate of 5 or 6% but then increased to the rate of 12% in 1985–1990. Therefore, unequal development between agriculture and the non-agricultural sector became clear after 1970. On the input side, the growth rate of agricultural

---

[2]1950–1955 in Fig. 5-2 means the average of 5 years of the growth rates of 1951 (the growth rate from 1950 to 1951), 1952 (the growth rate from 1951 to 1952), 1953 (the growth rate from 1952 to 1953), 1954 (the growth rate from 1953 to 1954) and 1955 (the growth rate from 1954 to 1955).

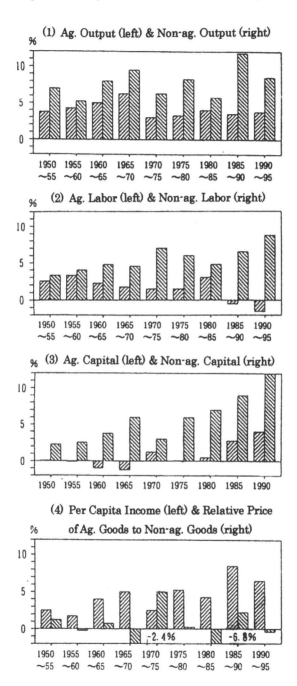

Figure 5-2   Average Growth Rates of Eight Endogenous Variables in Thailand

labor had a tendency to decline. However, the growth of non-agricultural labor increased at an accelerating rate and maintained a level of 6 to 8%. Also, the growth rate of agricultural labor finally became negative in 1985–1990 and then reached a large negative value. For capital stock, the growth of the non-agricultural capital stock increased at an accelerating rate but the growth of the agricultural capital stock had a zero or negative rate until 1970. However, the agricultural capital stock has had a positive growth rate since 1970. The growth rate of real per capita income increased at an accelerating rate except during the periods from 1970–1975, and from 1980–1985.

2. Economic and Social Development Planning in Thailand

Thailand had seven economic and social development plans from 1950 to 1995. Also, the foreign investment policy of the Board of Investment (BOI) has played an important role in the economic development of Thailand. Thailand did not have any economic and social development plans until the World Bank advised her to formulate such a plan in 1957. The first economic and social development plan started in 1961 and ended in 1966. The second one started in 1967 and ended in 1971. The National Economic and Social Development Board (NESDB) which produced these plans planned to increase Thailand's infrastructure during these two periods. The third economic and social development plan started from 1972 and ended in 1976 and the fourth started from 1977 and ended in 1981. These two plans were intended to strengthen social fairness and social equity in Thailand. In these periods, there were many unpredictable worldwide event such as the "Nixson shock", two oil shocks and a food crisis.

Therefore, these two of Thailand's plans were also intended to seek political, economic and social stability. The import substitution policy almost reached a satiation point and the economic growth rate was low in these periods (see the low growth rate of real per capita income in 1970). The plan was intended to foster heavy industry, agribusiness, labor-intensive industry and export-oriented industrialization. However, foreign investment decreased very drastically due to the instability of the world economic situation. Therefore, Thailand had many problems including inflation, unemployment, and deficits in its internal and external balances during this period. The fifth plan (1982 to 1986) was introduced to push industrialization and increase the share in exports of industrial goods. However, the international price of agricultural goods decreased and the deficits in internal and external balances did not improve.

The sixth plan started in 1987 and ended in 1991. However, the policy goal of its economic growth rate was not so high. Moreover, the plan was rather intended to improve the state of the economy such as the goals of decreasing unemployment and improving the international balance. The seventh plan started in 1992 and ended in 1996. The sixth plan succeeded but increased the imbalances and inequality. Therefore, the goal of the seventh plan had the following three aspects. The first was to obtain sustainable and moderate development, the second to promote income redistribution and local development and the third was to develop human resources and improve the quality of life and the environment.

3. Surplus Labor in the Agricultural Sector of Japan, Taiwan, China and Thailand

3.1. *Surplus Labor in the Agricultural Sector in Thailand*

Table 5-1 shows the values of the change in the surplus labor in the agricultural sector as calculated by the first of two methods used.[3] This first method of calculating the increase or decrease in surplus labor calculates the change in the indices of m_1 [which is defined as $m_1 = MPL_1/(w_1/p_1)$] as shown in Chapter 4. Here, MPL_1 is the marginal productivity of labor in agriculture, w_1 is the nominal wage rate and P_1 is the price of agricultural goods. If the growth rate of MPL_1 is larger than the growth rate of (w_1/p_1) in a period, then we believe that agricultural surplus labor decreased in this period. [Usually, MPL_1 is smaller than the real wage rate (w_1/p_1) if there is surplus labor in the economy. According to Ranis and Fei [1961] and Fei and Ranis [1964] definition, redundant labor is labor whose MPL is zero, and surplus labor is labor whose MPL is less than the real wage rate.]

Indices 1 of the growth rate of surplus labor in Thailand (*i.e.*, $\dot{m}_1$ in Table 5-1) have negative values in the period from 1973 to 1977 (the value

---

[3]The growth rate of five-year moving averages. For example, the value of 1973 means the five-year average of the growth rates of 1971, 1972, 1973, 1974 and 1975.

Table 5-1 Growth Rates of Agricultural Surplus Labor in Thailand

%

Y_1	L_1	w_1/p_1	m_1	w_1	w_2	m_w	N
(1)	(2)	(3)	(4)	(5)	(6)	(7)	(8)
		= (3) − (1) + (2)				= (5) − (6)	= (4) − (7)
1973 3.0	1.4	−1.8	−3.4	10.7	11.6	−0.9	−2.6
1974 3.5	1.4	−3.5	−5.6	12.0	10.5	1.5	−7.1
1975 4.5	1.4	0.5	−2.6	13.5	10.9	2.7	−5.3
1976 5.3	1.4	2.4	−1.5	11.3	11.5	−0.2	−1.2
1977 4.3	1.4	2.4	−0.5	10.2	11.4	−1.2	0.7
1978 3.2	1.4	2.2	0.4	12.4	12.1	0.3	0.1
1979 3.0	1.4	2.0	0.4	10.9	14.0	−3.1	3.5
1980 2.9	1.4	1.5	0.0	8.0	12.0	−4.0	4.0
1981 1.9	1.4	0.8	0.3	8.0	8.0	0.0	0.4
1982 3.1	2.2	0.5	−0.4	2.8	6.1	−3.2	2.8
1983 4.3	2.8	−0.4	−1.8	−2.8	4.1	−6.9	5.0
1984 3.3	0.2	−3.9	−7.0	−5.4	1.0	−6.4	−0.6
1985 2.8	−0.5	−6.7	−10.0	−4.1	0.4	−4.4	−5.6
1986 4.0	1.4	−5.8	−8.4	−3.4	3.5	−6.9	−1.5
1987 5.0	−0.1	−3.2	−8.4	1.5	2.1	−0.6	−7.7
1988 3.4	−0.5	−2.9	−6.8	4.1	2.5	1.6	−8.4
1989 4.2	2.4	1.0	−0.8	9.1	6.7	2.5	−3.2
1990 5.2	3.6	3.2	1.6	9.9	9.2	0.7	0.9
1991 3.5	1.2	5.4	3.1	10.6	7.1	3.5	−0.4
1992 0.4	2.8	1.3	−1.1	8.5	11.9	−3.4	2.3
1993 4.4	3.2	2.6	1.4	13.2	16.1	−2.9	4.3

Note: The growth rate of five-year moving averages. For example, the value of 1973 means the five-year average of the growth rates of 1971 [*i.e.*, the growth rate from 1970 to 1971], 1972, 1973, 1974 and 1975.

of 1975 in Tables 5-1, for example, is the value of the five-year moving average growth rate of 1973, 1974, 1975, 1976 and 1977). This means that the agricultural surplus labor decreased in this period. However, agricultural surplus labor increased in the next period (from 1978 to 1981). In the following period (from 1982 to 1989), agricultural surplus labor decreased again. In particular, the speed of decrease was very large in the years from around 1983 to 1988. The second method of calculating the increase or decrease in surplus labor calculates the change in indices of m_w [which is defined as $m_w = (w_1/w_2)$]. Here, w_1 is the nominal wage rate in agriculture, w_2

is the nominal wage rate in the non-agricultural sector. If the growth rate of w_1 is larger than that of w_2 in a period, then we believe that agricultural surplus labor decreased in the period. Usually, the wage rate in agriculture (w_1) is lower than the wage rate in the non-agricultural sector (w_2) if there is surplus labor in the agricultural sector.

Therefore, we interpret this to that surplus labor, in terms of the second definition, would decrease if the growth rate of m_w had a positive sign. The result of the calculated value of m is shown in Table 5-1. Indices 2 that measure the surplus labor in Thailand (m_w in Table 5-1) have negative values in 1973, in the period from 1976 to 1980 (except for 1978), the period from 1982 to 1987, and the period from 1992 to 1993. This would be interpreted as indicating that the agricultural surplus labor, according to the second definition increased in these periods. Conversely, agricultural surplus labor decreased in the periods from 1974 to 1976, and from 1988 to 1991. In order to see the net increase or decrease in the surplus labor, we calculated the net increase or decrease in surplus labor N (see N in Table 5-1). In other words, N is defined as $N = m_1 + m_w$. This shows that the surplus labor decreased in the period from 1973 to 1976, but increased from 1977 to 1983. The surplus labor again decreased in the period from 1984 to 1991. However, the surplus labor then increased in 1992 and 1993.

3.2. Contribution of Surplus Labor in the Agricultural Sector to the Economic Development of Thailand

In Thailand, the share of agricultural income Y_1/Y was 39.9% and the share of agricultural capital in total capital stock K_1/K was 36.6% in 1950. In 1990, the share of agricultural income Y_1/Y declined to 13.6% and the share of agricultural capital K_1/K fell to 8.5%. These figures are shown[4] in Table 5-2. If we compare these figures with those of Japan, we can understand that the year 1950 in Thailand corresponds to 1880 in Japan. We can also understand that 1990 in Thailand corresponds to 1950 in Japan.

---

[4]Same as Table 5-1, *i.e.*, the growth rate of five-year moving averages. For example, the value of 1953 means the five-year average of the growth rates of 1951, 1952, 1953, 1954 and 1955. However, the values of Y_1/Y, L_1/L and K_1/K are the values of 3 years before the year shown in Table 5-2. For example, Y_1/Y in 1953 in Table 5-2 shows 39.9. This means that the agricultural share of income in 1950 (instead of 1953) was 39.9%.

Table 5-2   Technical Change and Population Growth in Thailand

	E	T_1	T_2	T	Q	$T-Q$	Y_1/Y	L_1/L	K_1/K
1953	2.5	2.3	4.0	6.3	3.0	3.3	39.9	84.6	36.6
1954	2.3	2.2	3.3	5.5	3.0	2.5	39.6	84.5	36.2
1955	1.4	0.6	2.6	3.2	3.0	0.2	36.9	84.4	35.7
1956	0.1	−0.7	1.0	0.4	3.0	−2.6	38.3	84.3	35.2
1957	1.4	1.5	1.6	3.0	3.0	0.0	34.6	84.2	34.6
1958	1.7	1.8	1.8	3.6	3.0	0.6	35.8	84.1	34.1
1959	1.6	1.0	2.0	3.0	3.0	0.0	36.6	84.0	33.5
1960	3.3	4.6	2.4	7.0	3.0	3.9	32.6	84.0	32.9
1961	4.2	4.6	3.6	8.2	3.1	5.1	34.3	83.9	32.2
1962	4.2	4.4	3.4	7.9	3.1	4.8	32.8	83.8	31.6
1963	3.9	2.4	3.7	6.1	3.1	3.0	34.1	83.7	31.0
1964	5.1	4.7	4.4	9.2	3.1	6.1	33.5	83.3	30.4
1965	5.2	2.7	5.3	8.0	3.1	4.9	33.4	83.0	29.6
1966	5.0	2.9	5.2	8.1	3.3	4.7	33.7	82.6	28.7
1967	5.2	4.1	4.9	8.9	3.3	5.6	32.0	82.3	27.5
1968	4.9	3.9	4.5	8.4	3.4	5.0	30.8	81.9	26.4
1969	3.6	1.7	3.3	5.0	3.4	1.6	31.5	81.5	25.1
1970	2.9	1.8	1.8	3.5	3.4	0.2	28.4	81.2	23.7
1971	3.3	0.9	2.1	3.0	3.1	−0.1	28.8	80.8	22.3
1972	2.7	0.1	1.4	1.5	3.0	−1.5	28.7	80.4	21.0
1973	2.5	0.8	0.5	1.3	2.9	−1.6	27.7	80.0	19.9
1974	3.4	1.6	1.4	3.1	2.8	0.3	27.4	79.0	19.5
1975	4.5	3.0	2.4	5.4	2.7	2.8	25.7	78.1	18.8
1976	4.7	3.8	2.3	6.2	2.6	3.6	25.0	77.2	18.1
1977	4.9	3.1	2.6	5.7	2.5	3.2	24.7	76.3	19.1
1978	5.1	1.9	2.6	4.5	2.1	2.4	24.6	75.4	18.4
1979	4.6	1.6	1.8	3.4	2.0	1.3	24.0	74.6	17.4
1980	3.8	1.4	0.7	2.1	1.9	0.2	22.5	73.7	15.6
1981	3.2	0.7	0.0	0.6	1.9	−1.2	22.6	72.8	16.3
1982	3.3	1.4	−0.3	1.1	1.9	−0.7	21.2	72.0	15.3
1983	3.3	2.1	0.4	2.5	2.1	0.4	20.2	71.1	14.4
1984	3.3	2.6	−0.5	2.1	2.0	0.0	20.0	70.3	13.6
1985	4.2	2.5	−0.8	1.7	2.0	−0.3	19.5	69.5	12.8
1986	5.7	2.3	1.7	4.0	1.9	2.1	19.4	68.7	12.2
1987	7.2	4.1	2.8	6.9	1.7	5.2	19.1	68.6	11.4
1988	8.6	2.7	4.7	7.4	1.7	5.7	19.1	69.3	11.0
1989	9.1	3.2	5.9	9.1	1.6	7.5	18.2	59.8	10.8
1990	8.8	4.4	6.3	10.7	1.5	9.2	16.6	62.7	10.2
1991	7.9	3.5	4.0	7.5	1.4	6.1	16.2	60.7	9.7
1992	7.3	2.5	3.5	6.0	1.3	4.7	15.8	61.6	9.1
1993	6.7	3.6	0.2	3.8	1.3	2.5	13.6	60.3	8.5

Note: Same as Table 5-1. The growth rates of five-year moving averages, *i.e.*, the value of 1953 means the five-year average of the growth rates of 1951, 1952, 1953, 1954 and 1955.

Therefore, we can see that Thailand took only 40 years to transform her economy into its present situation although Japan took 70 years to transform her economy in the same way. Table 5-2 also shows the rates of technical change in agriculture (T_1), the non-agricultural sector (T_2) and the growth rate of population (Q) in Thailand. The notation T is the sum of technical change in agriculture (T_1) and technical change in the non-agricultural sector (T_2). In equation form, this means that $T = T_1 + T_2$. Technical change increases per capita income and has a tendency to move agricultural inputs to the non-agricultural sector.

Conversely, population growth decreases per capita income and has a tendency to move non-agricultural inputs to the agricultural sector. These two factors (technical change and population growth) have a completely opposite influence on economic development (see the push and pull effects of technical change in Chapter 3, Yamaguchi and Binswanger [1975], and Yamaguchi and Kennedy [1984a], and also see the population effect in Yamaguchi and Kennedy [1984b]). So, population growth and technical change have a tug of war for influence over economic development. If the rate of technical change is larger than the growth rate of population, per capita income increases. On the other hand, if the rate of technical change is smaller than the growth rate of population, per capita income decreases. Table 5-2 shows that the rate of technical change was usually larger than the growth rate of population in Thailand except for a few periods like 1971–1973 and 1981–1985. Therefore, the economic development of Thailand was very rapid in most periods as Fig. 5-2 shows.

Growth accounting for the Thai economy (for per capita income) is indicated in Table 5-3. This shows that the growth of the total labor supply made the largest contribution to the growth of per capita income (see *CEL* in Table 5-3. Here, *CEL* refers to how the growth of the total labor supply L contributed to the growth of per capita income E). Non-agricultural technical change also made a fairly large contribution to the growth of per capita income though there were many fluctuations in its contribution (see CET_2). In the case of Japan (1880–1970), the growth of the total capital stock made the largest contribution to the growth of per capita income (see *CEK* in the Japanese case at the bottom of Table 5-3). Agricultural technical change also made a fairly large contribution to the growth of per capita income (see CET_1 in the Japanese case) but non-agricultural technical change made a very small contribution to the growth of per capita income (see CET_2 in the

Table 5-3 Growth Accounting for the Thai Economy

<Per capita income>

	$\Delta E/E$	CET_1	CET_2	CEK	CEL	CEQ	CEm_1	CEm_w
1950–1955	2.5	1.05	2.73	0.38	1.82	−3.41	—	—
	(100)	(42)	(109)	(15)	(73)	(−136)		
1955–1960	1.7	0.79	1.26	0.47	2.41	−3.41	—	—
	(100)	(47)	(74)	(28)	(142)	(−201)		
1960–1965	3.9	1.03	2.63	0.62	1.90	−3.53	—	—
	(100)	(26)	(67)	(16)	(49)	(−91)		
1965–1970	4.9	1.60	3.25	1.13	1.68	−3.85	—	—
	(100)	(33)	(66)	(23)	(34)	(−79)		
1970–1975	2.5	0.31	0.37	0.74	1.90	−3.27	0.62	−0.16
	(100)	(12)	(15)	(30)	(76)	(−131)	(25)	(−6)
1975–1980	5.1	0.70	1.95	1.33	1.90	−2.35	−0.07	0.05
	(100)	(14)	(38)	(26)	(37)	(−46)	(−1)	(1)
1980–1985	3.3	0.72	0.32	1.72	2.47	−2.40	0.31	−1.19
	(100)	(22)	(10)	(52)	(75)	(−73)	(9)	(−36)
1985–1990	8.6	1.23	3.21	2.09	1.24	−1.93	1.11	0.26
	(100)	(14)	(37)	(24)	(14)	(−22)	(13)	(3)
1990–1995	6.7	1.06	0.17	2.93	4.12	−1.50	—	—
	(100)	(16)	(3)	(44)	(65)	(−22)		
Average	(100)	(26)	(52)	(27)	(63)	(−95)		
Japan	(100)	(37)	(8)	(92)	(35)	(−103)		

Japanese case). Therefore, on the whole, we can say that the contribution of the total labor supply to the growth of the Thai economy (1950–1995) was large and that the contribution of the total capital stock to the growth of the Japanese economy (1880–1970) was also large.

In terms of the growth of agricultural output, the contribution of agricultural technical change ($CY_1 T_1$) has the largest value (see $CY_1 T_1$ in Appendix Table 5-2 of the appendix of this chapter, which was found to be 51% on average over the whole period) and the growth of the total labor supply made the second largest contribution (see $CY_1 L$ in Appendix Table 5-2 found to be 37% over the whole period). The contribution of total capital stock ($CY_1 K$) was 11% and that of population was 4% over the whole period. However, the contribution of agricultural technical change ($CY_1 T_1$) was extremely large (81%) and the contribution of total capital stock ($CY_1 K$) was fairly large (35%) in the Japanese case. In terms of the growth of non-agricultural output, the contribution of non-agricultural technical change (CY_2T_2) has the largest value (see CY_2T_2 in the lower part of Appendix Table 5-2, which was found to be 37% on average over the whole period) and the growth of the total labor supply also made a very large contribution (see CY_2L in the same Appendix Table 5-2, found to be 32%). However, the contribution of non-agricultural technical change (CY_2T_2) was not so large in the case of Japan (see CY_2T_2 in the same Appendix Table 5-2, found to be 20% over the whole period), but the change in total capital made a very large contribution (see CY_2K in the same Appendix Table 5-2, found to be 45%) in the Japanese case.

The upper part of Table 5-4 shows the contribution of surplus labor calculated by the first method, to the economic development of Thailand[5] [in terms of agricultural output Y_1, non-agricultural output Y_2, agricultural labor L_1, non-agricultural labor L_2, agricultural capital K_1, non-agricultural capital K_2, relative price (agricultural price/non-agricultural price) P, real per capita income E]. As shown in the top row of Table 5-4, the values in the parentheses after the year show the growth rates of m_1. The values in the parentheses in row CEm_1 ($\Delta E/E$) show the growth rates of real per capita income E (Δ shows the amount of increase of the corresponding variable). The growth rates of m_1 ($\Delta m_1/m_1$) in 1970 (1970–1975 as stated in Foot-note 5. Please interpret all the years hereafter in the same way), 1980 and 1985 have negative values, meaning that agricultural surplus labor decreased in these periods. These decreases in surplus labor contributed positively to the non-agricultural sector (see the positive values of CY_2m_1, CK_2m_1, and CL_2m_1. Here, CY_2m_1, for example, refer to the way in which the growth of m_1 contributed to the growth of non-agricultural output Y_2) and nega-tively to the agricultural sector (shown by the fact that CY_1m_1, CK_1m_1, and CL_1m_1 have negative values). As a result, these decreases in surplus labor contributed positively to the growth of real per capita income E ($CEm_1 > 0$).

The lower part of Table 5-4 shows the contribution of surplus labor (m_w), calculated by the second method, to economic development [in terms of agricultural output Y_1, non-agricultural output Y_2, agricultural labor L_1,

---

[5]For example, the numerical values shown for 1970 in Table 5-4 are average values from the five years 1970–1975.

Table 5-4   Contribution of Changes in Agricultural Surplus Labor to Eight Endogenous Variables

%

( ) = $\Delta m_1/m_1$	1970 (−3.4%)	1975 (0.4%)	1980 (−1.8%)	1985 (−6.8%)
CY_1m_1	−0.58	0.07	−0.36	−1.47
CY_2m_1	1.09	−0.11	0.48	1.72
CK_1m_1	−3.86	0.41	−2.19	−8.79
CK_2m_1	0.97	−0.10	0.36	0.98
CL_1m_1	−0.29	0.04	−0.22	−0.92
CL_2m_1	1.14	−0.12	0.53	2.04
CPm_1	−1.80	0.21	−0.99	−3.85
CEm_1 ($\Delta E/E$)	0.62 (2.5%)	−0.07 (5.1%)	0.31 (3.3%)	1.11 (8.6%)

( ) = $\Delta m_w/m_w$	1970 (−0.9%)	1975 (0.3%)	1980 (−6.9%)	1985 (1.6%)
CY_1m_w	0.15	−0.05	1.38	−0.35
CY_2m_w	−0.29	0.09	−1.83	0.41
CK_1m_w	1.02	−0.35	8.40	−2.07
CK_2m_w	−0.26	0.08	−1.36	0.23
CL_1m_w	0.08	−0.03	0.83	−0.22
CL_2m_w	−0.30	0.09	−2.03	0.48
CPm_w	0.48	−0.16	3.79	−0.91
CEm_w	−0.16	0.05	−1.19	0.26

Note: The values in the parentheses after the years in the top row show the growth rates of m_1 and m_w. The values in the parentheses in row CEm_1 show the growth rates of real per capita income E. The numerical values for 1970, for example, are the 5-year average values of 1970–1975.

non-agricultural labor L_2, agricultural capital K_1, non-agricultural capital K_2, relative price (agricultural price/non-agricultural price) P, and real per capita income E]. The value in the parentheses after the years in the top row shows the growth rates of m_w. The growth rates of m_w ($\Delta m_w/m_w$) were negative in 1970 and 1980. This meant that agricultural surplus labor, calculated by the second method, increased in these periods. These increases in the surplus labor contributed negatively to the non-agricultural sector (all the signs of CY_2m_w, CK_2m_w, and CL_2m_w are negative) and positively to the agricultural sector (all the signs of CY_1m_w, CK_1m_w and CL_1m_w are positive). As a result, these increases of the surplus labor contributed negatively to real per capita income as the negative signs of CEm_w show.

If we calculate the contribution of the net increase or decrease in agricultural surplus labor to real per capita income, *i.e.*, $CEN(= CEm_1 + CEm_{w})$ from Table 5-3, we get the following values. The calculated values are 0.46 (18.2%) in 1970, -0.02 (-0.3%) in 1975, -0.88 (-26.8%) in 1980, and 1.37 (16.0%) in 1985. The values in the parentheses are the percentages of the contribution of the decrease or increase in agricultural surplus labor to the growth of real per capita income. From these values, we can understand that the decrease in agricultural surplus labor was significant in 1970 and 1985 and contributed about 16 to 18% to the growth of real per capita income. However, the economy of Thailand in 1980 (remember that the value for 1980 is the average value of 5 years from 1980 to 1985) was in some difficulties and could not produce a decrease in agricultural surplus labor. Table 5-2 showed that the rates of technical change were almost same or smaller than the growth rates of population in the periods from 1980 to 1985. This fact is consistent with the negative contribution of the increase in agricultural surplus labor to the growth of real per capita income in 1980.

3.3. Surplus Labor in Agricultural Sector and Growth Accounting for Japan, Taiwan, China and Thailand

In Fig. 5-3, we show the changes in agricultural surplus labor in Taiwan, China, and Thailand, and later, we discuss how the change in agricultural surplus labor contributed to their countries' economies (by growth accounting). Thus, we demonstrate what types of factors (besides population and labor growth) are important for their economic development by using the general equilibrium growth accounting method. First, in Japan (where the turning point was the beginning of 1960s), according to our analysis in Chapter 4: (1) The agricultural surplus labor decreased continuously for a long period. (2) Wage differentials between the agricultural and non-agricultural sectors tended to decrease but changed cyclically. (3) Agricultural labor decreased continuously after the middle of the 1950s (Fig. 1-1). (4) The real agricultural wage growth rate after the turning point of 1960s was 12.8%, an extremely high value.

Second, in Taiwan (where the turning point was around 1968): (1) Surplus labor decreased continuously for a fairly long period. (2) Wage differentials also tended to decrease cyclically. (3) Agricultural surplus labor decreased continuously after the turning point (Fig. 5-4). (4) The real wage

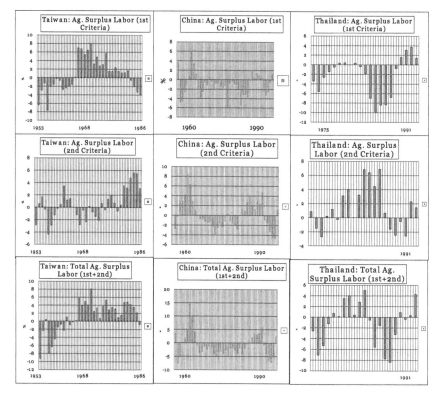

Figure 5-3   Agricultural Surplus Labor of Taiwan, China and Thailand

growth rate around the turning point was about 10%. Third, in China, the results contrasted with the previous ones: (1) Agricultural labor decreased for several years in the 1980s and 1990s; however, such decrease was not continuous (Fig. 5-4). (2) The real wage growth rate was still around only 5%. (3) The agricultural surplus labor tended to decrease for a fairly long period, but there were also some periods of increase. (4) Wage differentials changed cyclically; however, they had no tendency to decrease overall. Fourth, in Thailand: (1) The growth rate of agricultural labor stayed positive even near the year of 1990 (Fig. 5-4). (2) The real wage growth rate was around 5% or less. (3) The agricultural surplus labor decreased, but there were some periods of increase in recent years. (4) Wage differentials changed cyclically; however, there was no general tendency toward decrease. Further, China and Thailand are much larger countries and still have many more regional differences than Japan has. The above analysis

Growth Rates of Agricultural Labor in Taiwan

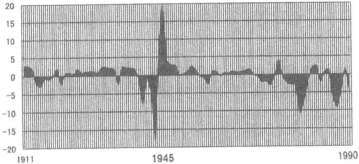

Growth Rates of Agricultural Labor in China

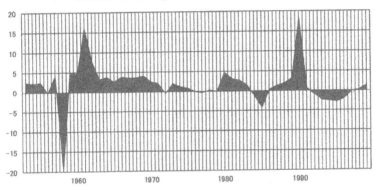

Growth Rates of Agricultural Labor in Thailand

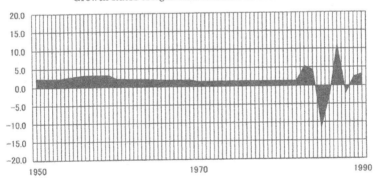

Figure 5-4   Growth Rates of Agricultural Labor in Taiwan, China and Thailand

indicates that China and Thailand still have yet to reach the turning point of labor (as of 2013).[6]

Next, as we stated above, we would see the results of general equilibrium growth accounting results about four countries. Table 5-5 is the

Table 5-5   Growth Accounting for the Chinese Economy

Agricultural output   %

	$\Delta Y_1/Y_1$	CY_1T_1	CY_1T_2	CY_1K	CY_1L	CY_1Q	CY_1m_1	CY_1m_w
1955	0.8	−1.29	−3.48	0.85	1.45	0.26	0.86	0
(1953–1957)	(100)	(−161)	(−435)	(106)	(181)	(33)	(108)	(0)
1960	−9.5	−8.35	−0.11	0.09	1.02	0.08	0.15	0.91
(1958–1962)	(−100)	(−88)	(−1)	(1)	(11)	(1)	(2)	(10)
1965	9.3	5.67	−0.59	1.56	0.89	0.23	−0.67	−0.07
(1963–1967)	(100)	(61)	(−6)	(17)	(10)	(2)	(−7)	(−1)
1970	2.0	0.19	−0.26	1.37	1.70	0.22	−0.00	−0.21
(1968–1972)	(100)	(10)	(−13)	(69)	(85)	(11)	(0)	(−11)
1975	3.4	2.25	−0.04	0.75	1.04	0.14	−0.27	−0.36
(1973–1977)	(100)	(66)	(−1)	(22)	(31)	(4)	(−8)	(−11)
1980	3.3	1.58	−0.08	1.05	1.47	0.12	−0.16	−0.33
(1978–1982)	(100)	(48)	(−2)	(32)	(45)	(4)	(−5)	(−10)
1985	7.6	2.00	−0.06	1.78	1.66	0.16	−0.70	0.59
(1983–1987)	(100)	(26)	(−1)	(23)	(22)	(2)	(−9)	(8)
1990	5.7	3.15	−0.05	1.16	1.28	0.15	−0.27	0.54
(1988–1992)	(100)	(55)	(−1)	(20)	(22)	(3)	(−5)	(9)
1995	5.4	5.22	−0.04	1.33	0.64	0.12	−0.62	−1.04
(1993–1997)	(100)	(97)	(−1)	(25)	(12)	(2)	(−11)	(19)
Av. of China	(100)	(52)	(−4)	(30)	(32)	(4)	(−6)	(0)
Av. of Thai	(100)	(51)	(−0)	(11)	(37)	(4)		
Av. of Japan	(100)	(81)	(−2)	(35)	(43)	(17)		

(2) Non-agricultural Output   %

	$\Delta Y_2/Y_2$	CY_2T_1	CY_2T_2	CY_2K	CY_2L	CY_2Q	CY_2m_1	CY_2m_w
1955	32.1	−0.42	34.66	3.98	3.01	−1.17	−3.95	0
(1953–1957)	(100)	(−1)	(108)	(124)	(9)	(−4)	(−12)	(0)
1960	18.5	−1.22	5.18	0.23	1.53	−1.53	−0.30	−1.84
(1958–1962)	(100)	(−7)	(28)	(1)	(8)	(−8)	(−2)	(−10)

(*Continued*)

Table 5-5 *(Continued)*

	$\Delta Y_2/Y_2$	CY_2T_1	CY_2T_2	CY_2K	CY_2L	CY_2Q	CY_2m_1	CY_2m_w
1965	14.0	0.08	8.97	4.88	3.17	−0.77	2.66	0.27
(1963–1967)	(100)	(1)	(64)	(35)	(23)	(−6)	(19)	(2)
1970	16.4	0.02	8.42	3.65	2.64	−0.62	0.18	0.82
(1968–1972)	(100)	(0)	(51)	(22)	(16)	(−5)	(11)	(41)
1975	7.6	0.36	1.79	1.89	1.57	−0.34	0.89	1.20
(1973–1977)	(100)	(5)	(24)	(25)	(21)	(−4)	(12)	(16)
1980	9.6	0.26	4.15	2.61	2.20	−0.24	0.44	0.92
(1978–1982)	(100)	(3)	(43)	(27)	(23)	(−3)	(5)	(10)
1985	15.7	0.30	4.08	4.41	2.47	−0.24	0.84	−0.71
(1983–1987)	(100)	(2)	(26)	(28)	(16)	(−2)	(5)	(−5)
1990	9.8	0.48	4.86	2.85	1.90	−0.21	0.30	−0.59
(1988–1992)	(100)	(5)	(50)	(29)	(19)	(−2)	(3)	(−6)
1995	11.9	0.81	4.85	3.23	0.94	−0.13	0.59	0.99
(1993–1997)	(100)	(7)	(41)	(27)	(8)	(−1)	(5)	(8)
Av. of China	(100)	(3)	(43)	(28)	(18)	(−3)	(9)	(8)
Av. of Thai	(100)	(5)	(37)	(17)	(32)	(−8)		
Av. of Japan	(100)	(8)	(20)	(45)	(15)	(−7)		

(3) Per Capita Income   %

	$\Delta E/E$	CET_1	CET_2	CEK	CEL	CEQ	CEm_1	CEm_w
1955	5.6	−0.74	8.75	1.86	1.94	−2.60	−0.68	0
(1953–1957)	(100)	(−13)	(156)	(33)	(35)	(−46)	(−12)	(0)
1960	−0.1	−3.38	3.58	0.19	1.38	−0.87	−0.16	−1.01
(1958–1962)	(−100)	(−3380)	(3580)	(19)	(1380)	(−870)	(−160)	(−1010)
1965	10.0	2.81	4.31	3.26	2.54	−2.88	1.04	0.10
(1963–1967)	(100)	(28)	(43)	(33)	(25)	(−29)	(10.4)	(1)
1970	7.7	0.09	5.29	2.82	2.29	−3.01	0.09	0.44
(1968–1972)	(100)	(1)	(69)	(37)	(30)	(−39)	(1)	(6)
1975	3.9	0.96	1.21	1.53	1.40	−1.89	0.52	0.71
(1973–1977)	(100)	(25)	(31)	(39)	(36)	(−48)	(13)	(18)
1980	6.5	0.65	2.88	2.13	1.98	−1.44	0.26	0.55
(1978–1982)	(100)	(10)	(44)	(33)	(30)	(−22)	(4)	(8)
1985	10.4	0.78	2.91	3.67	2.24	−1.63	0.73	−0.61
(1983–1987)	(100)	(8)	(28)	(35)	(22)	(−16)	(7)	(−6)
1990	6.4	1.20	3.53	2.39	1.73	−1.51	0.26	−0.52
(1988–1992)	(100)	(19)	(55)	(37)	(27)	(−24)	(4)	(−8)
1995	9.0	1.97	3.58	2.75	0.86	−1.19	0.57	0.95
(1993–1997)	(100)	(22)	(40)	(31)	(10)	(−13)	(6)	(11)
Av. of China	(100)	(16)	(44)	(35)	(26)	(−27)	(6)	(4)
Av. of Thai	(100)	(26)	(52)	(27)	(63)	(−95)		
Av. of Japan	(100)	(37)	(8)	(92)	(35)	(−103)		

general equilibrium growth accounting result for the Chinese economy, which also includes the results for the Japanese and Thai economies. We summarize the calculated general equilibrium growth accounting results for each country as follows. First, for the agricultural output growth of China, the contribution of agricultural technical change was largest (*i.e.*, 52%; 51% in Thailand), the contribution of total labor was second largest (*i.e.*, 32%; 37% in Thailand), the contribution of total capital was 30% (11% in Thailand), and the contribution of population was only 4% (4% in Thailand). As shown in Chapter 2, in Japan, the contributions of agricultural technical change (81%) and population (17%) were very large. Second, for non-agricultural output growth, the contribution of non-agricultural technical change (43%) was the largest in China. The contribution of non-agricultural technical change to Japanese non-agricultural output growth was very small, because its contributions in the 1910s and 1920s were especially small (20%). Although the contributions of total capital in Japan (45%) and total labor in Thailand (32%) to non-agricultural output growth were very large, the contribution of total capital was also fairly large (28%) in China.

Third, in China, the contribution of non-agricultural technical change to per capita income growth was the largest (44%), and that of total capital was also fairly large (35%). However, in Thailand, the contribution of total labor was the largest (63%), and that of non-agricultural technical change was second (52%). However, the contribution of total capital to per capita income growth in Japan was extremely large (92%), and that of agricultural technical change was also fairly large (37%); however, the corresponding contribution of non-agricultural technical change was fairly small (8%). The reasons for this are the same as those stated above (*i.e.*, non-agricultural technical change in the 1920s and 1910s was almost zero or negative in these periods; the contribution of non-agricultural technical change becomes 39% if we exclude these periods). Further, China took only 30 years to generate the same degree of economic development as Japan took almost 90 years to create, and Thailand took only 40 years to experience the same degree of economic development that took 70 years to realize in Japan. Japan used to be regarded as the fastest-growing country in the world, but China and Thailand exceed the Japanese growth rate drastically. This is consistent with Gerschenkron's conclusion (*i.e.*, that later comers can develop faster; see Gerschenkron [1962; 1968]).

Conclusion

We can summarize the discussion as follows:

(1) We can divide the economic development of Thailand since 1960 into three periods. The first period starts from 1960, the beginning of industrialization by import substitution. The second period starts from 1970 and continues until the early 1980s. This was a time of adjustment and change, from industrialization through import substitution to export-oriented industrialization. The third period (*i.e.*, the time of export-oriented industrialization) started from the late 1980s. The growth rate of the Thai economy accelerated in the 1950s and 1960s: however, the agricultural output growth rate decreased to about 3% in 1970–1975 and 1980–1985. The non-agricultural growth rate also decreased to 5–6% but then increased to 12% in 1985–1990. Therefore, unequal development between agricultural and non-agricultural sectors became clear after 1970.

(2) Thailand has had seven economic and social development plans from 1950 to 1995. We are restricted to these periods, because we could not use all 17 consistent data series for other periods in our growth accounting. The first economic and social development plan started in 1961 and ended in 1966, and the second started in 1967 and ended in 1971; Thailand's infrastructure increased during these two periods. The third plan started in 1972 and ended in 1976, and the fourth started in 1977 and ended in 1981; the latter two plans tried to strengthen social fairness and social equity. The import substitution policy almost reached a satiation point, and the economic growth rate slowed. The fifth plan (1982–1986) was introduced to push industrialization and increase the share of exports among industrial goods. However, international prices of agricultural goods decreased, and internal and external budget deficits did not improve. The sixth plan started in 1987 and ended in 1991; however, it did not set high economic growth-rate goals. Rather, the plan was intended to improve the state of the economy, with goals of decreasing unemployment and improving the international trade balance. The seventh plan started in 1992 and ended in 1996.

(3) Index 1 of surplus labor in Thailand (*i.e.*, m_1 in Table 5-1) had negative values in the period from 1973 to 1977. This means that the agricultural

surplus labor decreased in this period. However, agricultural surplus labor increased in the next period (1978–1981), whereas in 1982–1989, agricultural surplus labor decreased again. Index 2, which measures surplus labor in Thailand (m_w in Table 5-1) had negative values in 1973 and the periods from 1976 to 1980 (except for 1978), from 1982 to 1987, and from 1992 to 1993. This might indicate that the agricultural surplus labor, according to the second definition, increased in these periods. Conversely, agricultural surplus labor decreased in the periods from 1974 to 1976 and from 1988 to 1991. In order to see the net increase or decrease in surplus labor, we calculated the net increase or decrease in surplus labor N (see N in Table 5-1). In other words, N is defined as $N = m_1 + m_w$. This shows that surplus labor decreased in the period from 1973 to 1976 but increased from 1977 to 1983, then decreased again in the period from 1984 to 1991. However, the surplus labor then increased in 1992 and 1993.

(4) Growth accounting for the Thai economy shows that growth of the total labor supply made the largest contribution to the growth of per capita income. Non-agricultural technical change also made a fairly large contribution to the growth of per capita income, though there were many fluctuations in that contribution. The growth rates of $\dot{m}_w$ ($= \Delta m_w / m_w$) were negative in 1970 and 1980; this signifies that agricultural surplus labor, as calculated by the second method, increased in these periods. As a result, these increases in surplus labor contributed negatively to real per capita income. Calculation of the contribution of the net change in agricultural surplus labor to real per capita income, that is, $CEN(= CEm_1 + CEm_w)$ from Table 5-3 yields the following values. The calculated values are 0.46 (18.2%), −0.02 (−0.3%), −0.88 (−26.8%), and 1.37 (16.0%) in 1970, 1975, 1980, and 1985, respectively. From these values, we can understand that the decrease in agricultural surplus labor was significant in 1970 and 1985 and contributed about 16–18% to the growth of real per capita income. However, Thailand's economy was experiencing difficulties in 1980 and could not produce a decrease in agricultural surplus labor.

(5) The data analyses of Japan, Taiwan, China, and Thailand yielded the following results. First, in Japan (where the turning point was the beginning of the 1960s): (1) The agricultural surplus labor decreased

almost continuously. (2) Wage differentials between the agricultural and non-agricultural sectors tended to decrease but changed cyclically. (3) Agricultural labor decreased continuously after the mid-1950s. (4) The growth rate of real agricultural wages after the turning point of the 1960s was 12.8%. Second, in Taiwan (where the turning point was around 1968): (1) Surplus labor decreased continuously for a fairly long period. (2) Wage differentials also tended to decrease but changed cyclically. (3) Agricultural labor decreased continuously after the turning point. (4) The real wage growth rate around the turning point was about 10%. However, China and Thailand still have yet to reach the turning point of labor (as of 2013). Second, the results of our general equilibrium growth accounting for per capita income growth in China show that the contribution of non-agricultural technical change was the largest (44%), while that of total capital was also fairly large (35%). However, the contribution of total labor was the largest (63%), and that of non-agricultural technical change was second largest (52%) in Thailand. The contribution of total capital to per capita income growth in Japan was extremely large (92%), and that of agricultural technical change was also fairly large (37%). However, the contribution of non-agricultural technical change was fairly small.

Summaries (1)–(5) are very clear. They have the following noteworthy points: For per capita income growth in China, the contribution of non-agricultural technical change was the largest (44%), and that of total capital was also fairly large (35%). However, the contribution of total labor was the largest (63%), and that of non-agricultural technical change was second largest (52%) in Thailand. The contribution of total capital in Japan was extremely large (92%), and that of agricultural technical change was also fairly large (37%) for per capita income growth in Japan. However, the contribution of non-agricultural technical change was fairly small. These results share the same causes as stated above (*i.e.*, non-agricultural technical change in the 1910s and 1920s was almost zero or negative in these periods). Further, Japan used to be regarded as the fastest-growing country in the world, but China and Thailand have exceeded its growth rate drastically. This is consistent with Gerschenkron's conclusion (*i.e.*, that later comers can develop faster).

Appendix Table 5-1   Growth Rates in Each Year and of Five-Year Moving Averages

<Growth rate in each year>   %

	Y_1	Y_2	L_1	L_2	K_1	K_2	P	E	K	L	Q	B
1950	6.1	7.2	2.4	3.1	0.0	1.7	3.6	3.7	1.1	2.5	3.0	−1.5
1951	−3.5	8.3	2.4	3.0	0.2	2.4	−1.8	0.6	1.6	2.5	3.0	−0.9
1952	14.1	7.5	2.3	3.0	0.1	2.5	−10.4	6.7	1.7	2.4	3.0	−0.5
1953	−9.7	6.1	2.4	3.1	0.1	2.6	13.7	−2.9	1.7	2.5	3.0	−0.1
1954	11.1	5.5	2.7	3.4	0.0	2.4	1.6	4.3	1.6	2.8	3.0	0.3
1955	8.1	4.3	3.0	3.7	0.0	2.5	−3.9	2.6	1.6	3.1	3.0	6.9
1956	−12.0	5.2	3.2	3.9	−0.2	2.8	3.9	−4.0	1.8	3.3	3.0	−4.8
1957	8.8	0.6	3.2	3.9	0.0	2.9	−7.9	0.3	1.9	3.3	3.0	1.5
1958	2.2	9.3	3.2	3.9	0.0	2.8	3.5	3.7	1.9	3.3	3.0	2.5
1959	13.6	7.1	3.3	3.9	−0.2	2.6	3.5	6.1	1.7	3.4	3.0	1.2
1960	3.2	6.3	2.2	4.8	−0.4	2.7	0.0	2.0	1.7	2.6	3.1	7.0
1961	7.5	7.9	2.2	4.8	−0.6	3.2	−8.0	4.6	2.1	2.7	3.1	3.1
1962	8.9	7.6	2.1	4.8	−0.6	3.7	−3.3	4.8	2.4	2.6	3.1	4.0
1963	1.5	9.3	2.1	4.7	−1.3	4.7	1.0	3.5	3.0	2.5	3.1	5.1
1964	3.8	9.7	2.0	4.6	−1.2	4.6	14.6	4.6	3.0	2.5	3.1	6.5
1965	13.8	10.5	1.9	4.5	−1.4	5.6	6.5	8.2	3.7	2.4	3.1	3.3
1966	−2.5	13.0	1.8	4.4	−1.4	6.4	−9.8	4.9	4.5	2.3	3.1	4.5
1967	9.7	7.5	1.8	4.4	−1.4	6.3	−3.5	3.8	4.5	2.3	4.2	5.2
1968	7.6	8.0	1.8	4.4	−1.7	6.5	3.0	4.6	4.7	2.3	3.1	5.9
1969	2.8	8.2	1.9	4.4	−1.1	5.3	−8.3	3.0	4.0	2.4	3.6	6.6
1970	3.8	5.4	1.4	7.4	−0.2	2.9	−9.2	1.8	2.3	2.6	3.1	7.3
1971	−2.3	6.6	1.4	7.1	−1.1	3.4	17.8	1.2	2.5	2.6	2.9	5.5
1972	6.2	10.1	1.4	6.9	−0.8	3.8	12.5	6.1	3.0	2.6	2.9	8.5
1973	3.1	4.8	1.4	6.6	8.7	1.8	0.2	1.6	3.0	2.6	2.7	0.8
1974	4.2	4.6	1.4	6.5	−0.2	4.1	2.9	1.8	3.3	2.6	2.7	−0.3
1975	6.3	10.0	1.4	6.3	−1.8	5.1	2.0	6.3	3.8	2.6	2.6	1.3
1976	2.9	11.8	1.4	6.1	−6.4	7.1	0.6	7.0	4.8	2.6	2.5	1.8
1977	9.8	9.0	1.4	5.9	9.8	3.8	−2.6	6.6	4.7	2.6	2.4	2.4
1978	−1.5	7.0	1.4	5.8	−1.1	6.6	1.6	2.7	5.4	2.6	2.3	1.5
1979	−1.3	4.9	1.4	5.7	−0.3	7.4	−0.9	2.9	6.2	2.6	0.6	1.2
1980	5.1	6.1	1.4	5.5	0.4	7.5	−11.7	3.5	6.5	2.6	2.3	1.7
1981	2.5	6.1	1.4	5.4	−0.1	6.5	−7.6	3.2	5.6	2.6	2.1	1.9
1982	4.8	5.8	1.4	5.3	1.0	7.3	10.6	3.5	6.5	2.6	2.0	0.5
1983	4.4	6.1	5.4	5.7	−0.6	7.6	−13.9	3.3	6.6	5.5	2.4	1.0
1984	4.5	4.7	4.3	0.9	2.3	6.5	−11.3	2.7	6.0	3.3	1.9	2.6
1985	0.4	6.7	−11.3	14.1	4.0	5.5	−0.5	3.7	5.4	−3.5	1.8	1.1
1986	0.1	11.6	−2.6	14.9	0.8	7.1	14.6	7.6	6.4	3.8	1.7	3.9
1987	10.5	13.8	11.0	−1.6	2.3	8.5	3.0	11.4	7.9	5.9	1.7	3.8
1988	9.7	12.8	−2.1	6.7	2.4	10.1	−4.9	10.5	9.4	1.2	1.6	0.6
1989	−3.7	14.4	2.4	−1.4	4.2	12.6	0.2	9.8	11.9	0.9	1.6	1.9
1990	4.4	8.4	3.2	9.0	—	—	4.1	6.3	—	5.4	1.5	1.9

(Continued)

Appendix Table 5-1 (*Continued*)

<Growth rate of five-year moving averages> %

	Y_1	Y_2	L_1	L_2	K_1	K_2	P	E	K	L	Q	B
1953	3.6	6.9	2.4	3.1	0.1	2.3	1.3	2.5	1.5	2.5	3.0	−0.6
1954	4.0	6.3	2.6	3.2	0.1	2.5	−0.2	2.3	1.6	2.7	3.0	1.1
1955	2.3	5.7	2.7	3.4	0.0	2.6	1.0	1.4	1.7	2.8	3.0	0.4
1956	1.3	4.3	2.9	3.6	0.0	2.6	1.5	0.1	1.7	3.0	3.0	0.7
1957	3.6	5.0	3.1	3.7	0.0	2.7	−0.6	1.4	1.8	3.2	3.0	1.3
1958	4.1	5.3	3.2	3.8	−0.1	2.7	−0.2	1.7	1.8	3.3	3.0	1.4
1959	3.2	5.7	3.0	4.1	−0.2	2.8	0.6	1.6	1.8	3.2	3.0	1.5
1960	7.1	6.2	2.8	4.3	−0.2	2.8	−1.7	3.3	1.9	3.1	3.0	3.0
1961	7.1	7.6	2.6	4.4	−0.4	3.0	−0.8	4.2	2.0	2.9	3.1	3.5
1962	6.9	7.6	2.4	4.6	−0.6	3.4	−1.3	4.2	2.2	2.8	3.1	4.1
1963	5.0	8.2	2.1	4.7	−0.8	3.8	0.9	3.9	2.4	2.6	3.1	5.1
1964	7.1	9.0	2.1	4.7	−1.0	4.4	2.2	5.1	2.8	2.5	3.1	4.4
1965	5.1	10.0	2.0	4.6	−1.2	5.0	1.8	5.2	3.3	2.5	3.1	4.7
1966	5.2	10.0	1.9	4.5	−1.4	5.5	1.7	5.0	3.7	2.4	3.3	4.9
1967	6.5	9.7	1.9	4.5	−1.4	5.9	2.2	5.2	4.1	2.3	3.3	5.1
1968	6.3	9.4	1.8	4.4	−1.4	6.0	−2.4	4.9	4.3	2.3	3.4	5.1
1969	4.3	8.4	1.7	5.0	−1.2	5.5	−5.6	3.6	4.0	2.4	3.4	5.9
1970	4.3	7.1	1.7	5.5	−1.1	4.9	0.0	2.9	3.6	2.4	3.4	6.1
1971	3.6	7.7	1.6	6.0	−1.0	4.4	3.2	3.3	3.3	2.5	3.1	6.8
1972	2.7	7.0	1.5	6.5	1.1	3.4	2.6	2.7	3.0	2.6	3.0	5.8
1973	3.0	6.3	1.4	6.9	1.3	3.2	4.9	2.5	2.8	2.6	2.9	4.4
1974	3.5	7.2	1.4	6.7	1.0	3.6	7.1	3.4	3.1	2.6	2.8	3.2
1975	4.5	8.3	1.4	6.5	−0.1	4.4	3.7	4.5	3.6	2.6	2.7	2.4
1976	5.3	8.0	1.4	6.3	2.0	4.4	0.6	4.7	3.9	2.6	2.6	1.2
1977	4.3	8.5	1.4	6.1	0.1	5.4	0.9	4.9	4.4	2.6	2.5	1.4
1978	3.2	8.6	1.4	6.0	0.1	6.0	0.1	5.1	5.0	2.6	2.1	1.7
1979	3.0	7.8	1.4	5.8	0.5	6.5	−2.6	4.6	5.5	2.6	2.0	1.7
1980	2.9	6.6	1.4	5.7	1.8	6.4	−4.3	3.8	5.7	2.6	1.9	1.7
1981	1.9	6.0	1.4	5.6	0.0	7.1	−1.6	3.2	6.0	2.6	1.9	1.4
1982	3.1	5.8	2.2	5.5	0.1	7.3	−4.7	3.3	6.3	3.2	1.9	1.2
1983	4.3	5.7	2.8	4.6	0.6	7.1	−6.8	3.3	6.2	3.3	2.1	1.5
1984	3.3	5.9	0.2	6.3	1.3	6.7	−4.5	3.3	6.0	2.1	2.0	1.4
1985	2.8	7.0	−0.5	8.2	1.5	6.8	−0.1	4.2	6.2	2.3	2.0	1.8
1986	4.0	8.6	1.4	6.8	1.8	7.0	−1.6	5.7	6.5	3.0	1.9	2.5
1987	5.0	9.9	−0.1	7.0	2.3	7.6	0.2	7.2	7.0	2.1	1.7	2.4
1988	3.4	11.9	−0.5	6.6	2.7	8.8	2.5	8.6	8.2	1.7	1.7	2.3
1989	4.2	12.2	2.4	5.5	−18.1	−12.3	3.4	9.1	8.9	3.5	1.6	2.4
1990	5.2	12.4	3.6	3.2	3.0	10.4	0.6	9.5	9.7	3.4	1.6	2.1
1991	3.5	11.9	1.2	4.8	3.3	11.4	−0.2	8.9	10.7	2.5	1.6	1.5
1992	0.4	11.4	2.8	3.8	4.2	12.6	2.2	8.1	11.9	3.2	1.6	1.9
1993	4.4	8.4	3.2	9.0	—	—	4.1	6.3	—	5.4	1.5	1.9

Appendix Table 5-2   Growth Accounting for the Thai Economy

<Agricultural output>

	$\Delta Y_1/Y_1^*$	CY_1T_1	CY_1T_2	CY_1K	CY_1L	CY_1Q	CY_1m_1	CY_1m_w
1950–1955	3.6	2.24	−0.14	0.15	1.28	0.17	—	—
	(100)	(62)	(−4)	(4)	(36)	(5)		
1955–1960	4.1	1.74	−0.05	0.18	1.70	0.17	—	—
	(100)	(42)	(−1)	(4)	(42)	(4)		
1960–1965	5.0	2.31	−0.08	0.24	1.34	0.18	—	—
	(100)	(46)	(−2)	(5)	(27)	(4)		
1965–1970	6.3	3.72	−0.07	0.43	1.18	0.21	—	—
	(100)	(59)	(−1)	(7)	(19)	(3)		
1970–1975	3.0	0.76	−0.00	0.29	1.34	0.19	−0.58	0.15
	(100)	(25)	(0)	(10)	(45)	(6)	(−19)	(5)
1975–1980	3.2	1.77	0	0.51	1.33	0.15	0.07	−0.05
	(100)	(55)	(0)	(16)	(42)	(5)	(2)	(−2)
1980–1985	4.3	1.90	0	0.61	1.64	0.20	−0.36	1.38
	(100)	(44)	(0)	(14)	(38)	(5)	(−8)	(32)
1985–1990	3.4	2.64	−0.16	0.80	0.87	0.10	−1.47	−0.35
	(100)	(78)	(−5)	(24)	(26)	(3)	(−43)	(−10)
1990–1995	3.8	3.12	0	1.12	2.58	0.17	—	—
	(100)	(82)	(0)	(29)	(68)	(5)		
Average	(100)	(51)	(−0)	(11)	(37)	(4)		
Japan	(100)	(81)	(−2)	(35)	(43)	(17)		

<Non-agricultural output>

	$\Delta Y_2/Y_2$	CY_2T_1	CY_2T_2	CY_2K	CY_2L	CY_2Q	CY_2m_1	CY_2m_w
1950–1955	6.9	0.25	4.64	0.54	2.18	−0.84	—	—
	(100)	(4)	(67)	(8)	(32)	(−12)		
1955–1960	5.3	0.25	2.00	0.63	2.81	−0.74	—	—
	(100)	(5)	(38)	(12)	(41)	(−14)		
1960–1965	8.2	0.39	4.02	0.82	1.94	−0.74	—	—
	(100)	(5)	(49)	(10)	(24)	(−9)		
1965–1970	9.4	0.64	4.73	1.44	1.90	−0.74	—	—
	(100)	(7)	(50)	(15)	(20)	(−8)		
1970–1975	6.3	0.14	0.51	0.92	2.12	−0.58	1.09	−0.29
	(100)	(2)	(8)	(15)	(34)	(−9)	(17)	(−5)

(Continued)

Appendix Table 5-2 (*Continued*)

	$\Delta Y_2/Y_2$	CY_2T_1	CY_2T_2	CY_2K	CY_2L	CY_2Q	CY_2m_1	CY_2m_w
1975–1980	8.6	0.34	2.60	1.60	2.08	−0.38	−0.11	0.09
	(100)	(4)	(30)	(19)	(24)	(−4)	(−1) .	(1)
1980–1985	5.7	0.43	0.40	2.00	2.68	−0.43	0.48	−1.83
	(100)	(8)	(7)	(35)	(47)	(−8)	(8)	(−32)
1985–1990	11.9	0.29	5.46	2.95	1.48	−0.46	1.72	0.41
	(100)	(2)	(46)	(25)	(12)	(−4)	(14)	(3)
1990–1995	9.0	0.73	0.20	4.13	4.37	−0.30	—	—
	(100)	(8)	(2)	(46)	(49)	(−3)		
Average	(100)	(5)	(37)	(17)	(32)	(−8)		
Japan	(100)	(8)	(20)	(45)	(15)	(−7)		

* Δ shows the amount of increase of the corresponding variable.

Chapter 6

Interrelationship between Population and Economy*

Introduction

Research into interrelationships between population and economic growth have been made very energetically. In this chapter, an attempt is made to study and evaluate this research into population and economic growth. The chapter is divided into three parts. The first observes the effect of population growth on the economy. The second looks at the effect of economy on the population growth. The third looks at the interrelationships between population and economic growth. Although we have many studies on the effect of population growth on the economy, we still need more research on the other two fields. In 1970s, many people have discussed the arguments concerning the relationships between population growth and per capita income growth by using the data of the World Bank Atlas. For example, Guillaumont [1976] at the population conference in France in 1973 divided the whole world into advanced and less developed countries and came to the conclusion that countries with a middle rate of population growth in each section had the largest economic growth rate. However, there are also a fairly large number of people who assert that there is no relationship between population and economic growth. In fact, we have to consider many factors such as sociological, economical, natural and medical factors when we consider the relationships between population and economic growth.

---

*The content of this chapter was developed and rewritten from Yamaguchi [1985] to meet the purpose of the book. We appreciate *Kobe University Economic Review* for permitting the use of this paper for this book.

Therefore, it would not be wise to conclude that there is no relationship between population and economic growth just by observing the correlation which appears in a figure. A more positive way would be to make a factor analysis and to consider both positive and negative effects of population growth. Fortunately, we can see many articles recently which observe the interrelationship between population and economic growth. However the causality of interrelationships is not simple as P. Mombelt who states that population and economic growth have a loose and not tight relationship. In this way, a problem of population and economic growth is very complicated in character and we cannot consider a too simple causality for them. However, it is our duty to make a further research and solve these complicated causalities. We economists have to use more energies for studying these problems, as Hazledine and Moreland [1977] state. In this chapter, we first consider the effects of population growth on the economy. Second, we consider the effects of the economy on population. Third, we consider the interrelationships between population and economy.

1. Effect of Population Growth on Economy

In order to observe the effect of population growth on the economy, Coale and Hoover [1958] considered the items of population, the growth rate of population and age distribution. Yasuba [1969] also made the same kind of analysis. However, a better way would be to see how population growth was brought about to see the factors which contributed to population growth. For population growth, we have the following equation:

$$P(t + N) = P(t) + B(t, t + N) - D(t, t + N)$$
$$+ IM(t, t + N) - OM(t, t + N), \qquad (6.1)$$

where P denotes population, B birth, D death, IM and OM immigration and emigration. Therefore, it would be enough to see the effect of the right-hand side items in Eq. (6.1) in order to see the population growth's effect on the economy. $P(t)$ items on the right hand side of Eq. (6.1) would be divided into such as male and female, age, occupation, religion, and institutional and social classes. The people who immigrate or emigrate usually have a variety of ages and occupations.

Therefore, it would not be so easy to observe the effect of these migrations on the economy. Also we would be allowed to neglect these migrations if they are small in number. Therefore, first we would like to see the effect of *P* on the economy, that is how population itself has an effect on the economy. As Coale and Hoover showed, the theory of optimum population would be classified in this class. We should list the name of Mill [1848] as father of the optimum population theory. Cannan [1888] amended two unclear points of Mill's theory (first, Mill stressed that the law of diminishing return prevails in agriculture but the law of increasing return prevails in non-agriculture. However, Cannan showed that the law of diminishing return prevails in both sectors. Second, Mill also treated the theory as if it worked just a dynamic and historical law). He also defined an optimum population as the population which would maximize per capita output. Meade [1955] introduced the concept of maximization of social welfare.

However, there is still great criticism of this concept. Hicks [1960] criticized that yesterday's optimum point was not today's optimum, therefore the concept of optimum population was not useful. Therefore, many efforts have been made in order to develop this optimum population theory into more dynamic theory. In the population conference of Valescure in 1973, Ohlin [1976], Guillaumont [1976] and Sauvy [1976] made a presentation and the papers were published. However, the articles of Ohlin and Sauvy did not seem very attractive. Hicks criticized Guillaumont's article fiercely even though Guillaumont's article was more attractive. Next, we would like to go further and analyze in a more specific way. First, we would like to see the effect of male and female population on the economy. There is not much difference with respect to the influence of sex difference (male and female) of the development population (*i.e.*, young people under 15 years old and old people over 60 years old) on the economy. However, there is a great difference between both sexes as regards the productive population. Female labor force participation rate is usually smaller than male and it varies a lot over time. Also, the male sex ratio is about 1.06 at birth but decreases over time approaching 1.00 as the babies grow. Simon [1977] showed that the labor supply by the mother decreased but the labor supply by the father increased when a birth occurred.

In order to observe the effect of age specific population growth on the economy, it is necessary to distinguish whether the population is at a productive age or not. The increase in the proportion of the aged population is a very important topic in present-day Japan. For example, the problem of the ageing population started to be discussed in our Japanese population conference in 1977. Next, we would like to observe the effect of occupational population on the economy. It is true that a productivity difference does exist between primary and secondary sectors. Therefore, the influence on the economy should be different between these two sectors. However, it would be more natural to say that the causality is rather in the opposite direction. In other words, it would be more natural to say that the economy influences the sectoral allocation of population judging from the opinion of Clark [1967].

It is also very important to investigate the influence of religion, institution and social classes on the economy, especially for the developing countries. This area is rather close to sociology but a further study is expected in the future. Next, we would like to shift our focus to the effect of birth rate, death rate and migration on the economy. Birth rate is one of the most important factors which affect population growth. For, in the present situation we cannot use the method which increases the death rate in order to decrease population growth. According to the theory of Coale and Hoover [1958], a high population growth has a negative effect on the economy. Yasuba [1969] also connected this view with Nelson's theory [1956]. Here, let us look back on views of the effect of population growth on the economy. We find that there are two opinions in sharp contrast: one is the view of an optimistic demographer, the other the view of a pessimistic demographer.

As a typical pessimistic demographer, most people would point to Malthus [1798]. Malthus assumed that an appetite for food and sexual desire were two essential needs of human life. And he was in sharp opposition to Goodwin [1796] who denied human sexual desire in the future. Then Malthus showed the following three propositions: (1) Population cannot increase without the means of subsistence (first: proposition of regulation principal). (2) Population does invariably increase, where there are the means of subsistence (second: proposition of proliferate principal). (3) The superior power of population cannot be checked, without producing misery or vice (third: proposition of equilibrium principal). On the other hand, Adam Smith [1776], who had showed the advantages of the scale of economy and the division of labor, was very famous as an optimistic demographer.

Table 6-1   Optimistic and Pessimistic Views for Population, Classified by Overbeek

Optimistic View		Pessimistic View
⟨1800～1914⟩	⟨1930～1940⟩	⟨1798⟩
Senior	Keynes	Malthus
Carley	Hansen	⟨1918～1940⟩
Marx	Harrod	Keynes
Dumont	Myrdal	East
Leroy–Beauliew	⟨1945～⟩	Ross
⟨1918～1940⟩	De Castro	Mukerzee
Carr–Saunders	De Lestapis	⟨1945～⟩
Dupreel	Clark	Darwin
Gini	⟨Present⟩	Coale
Landry	Kuznets	Spengler
Charles	Hirshman	⟨Present⟩
	Boserup	Meade
		Reddaway
		Davis

Overbeek [1974] classified economic, sociological, and biological demographers into two classes, *i.e.*, the group which supports the view of Malthus and the group which denies that view. He also showed that there were many historical waves in these two differing opinions. Table 6-1 shows a classification of these contrasting demographers based on his book. In this table, Malthus is classified as a pessimistic demographer. A noteworthy point is that Keynes has changed from a pessimistic demographer to an optimistic one. In other words, Keynes before the Keynesian revolution was a faithful classical economist. In Japan, there are several works that attempt to account for this change of Keynes' view. For example, Nakayama and Minami [1959] described Keynes' view as follows: In sum, Keynes was a very faithful Malthusian who believed in the law of diminishing returns and the theory of overpopulation. However, after the controversy with Beveridge [1923] around the year of 1930, Keynes changed his way of thinking and argued that population would instead increase the demand for capital stock (Keynes [1937]).

Also Ryozaburo Minami [1963a, b; 1971] classified population studies into three fields, *i.e.*, economic population studies, sociological population studies and biological population studies. He also classified the anti-Malthusian theories into three theory types, *i.e.*, the population pre-dominance theory, population capacity theory and historical population law theory. As for the agricultural development theory, we should not forget Boserup [1965] and Clark [1967] as optimistic demographers. Both Boserup and Clark opposed the Malthusian theory and showed that population growth could instead induce technical change. They showed that population growth would lead to clearing of uncultivated land, land reclamation by draining ponds and swamps and improvement in crops and green manure. They also asserted that many agricultural revolutions were caused by population pressure.

They showed the development process as follows: Although people tried to increase their labor when population increased, there was a limit to this increase of labor. Therefore, they developed several different means of improving productivity. In the first stage, only a hatchet was used without any kind of capital stock. Population growth required their farming to develop into a new system called a forest fallow system. They burned and dried a well-conditioned forest and planted some crops with digging sticks in those burned lands. However, the fertility decreased after a few years and they were forced to move out of these lands into new forests. However, the number of good forests decreased over time. More population growth finally required a change from the forest fallow system to a new different system (*i.e.*, a bush fallow system). In this stage, a digging stick is not useful and finally they started to use a hoe. Also, they tried to increase productivity by using some fertilizers such as animal manure and pond mud. Further population growth required changing their agricultural method into a three-field system. Even further population growth forced them to use more intensive farming methods such as short fallow systems and multi-crops systems.

In this way, Boserup [1965] opposed Malthusian theory and insisted that population would rather induce technical change. This controversy was called the controversy between population preceding theory and economic growth preceding theory by Umemura [1969]. However, recently Simon [1977] termed them the invention pull hypothesis and the population push hypothesis. The invention pull hypothesis is the theory which asserts that an invention which is an independent variable of population growth would increase productivity and population growth. In most cases, these inventions are characterized as labor saving. On the other hand, the productivity

Invention pull hypothesis is described as follows:

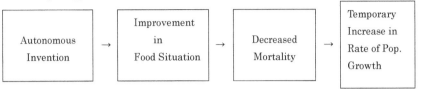

Population push hypothesis is described as follows:

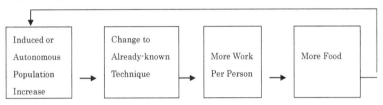

Figure 6-1 Invention Pull vs. Population Push Hypotheses

have been already invented independently of population growth. However, population growth is necessary for this invention to become widely used. Therefore, it is clear that two conditions (one the invention which is already invented, the other population growth) are necessary for this population push hypothesis. Therefore, invention pull hypothesis and population push hypothesis are described as Fig. 6-1.

In conclusion, Simon showed that both Malthus and Boserup were not contradictory but rather complimentary to each other. Although I had also showed that Malthus considered some of the elements of Boserup's points even though maybe not enough, Simon came to the same conclusion. On this point, we should not forget the contribution of Ryozaburo Minami [1963a, b; 1971] who clarified that Malthus also admitted the positive aspects of population. Then, what is a positive contribution for population growth to economic growth? Ryozaburo Minami [1963a, b; 1971] described these points as follows: If we look back on our history, we can see that people in Greek and Roman eras, Mercantilists in 17th and 18th centuries and populationists who regarded population growth as a powerful engine for economic growth tried to consider these positive aspects of population growth although they considered them in a very simple form. However, the optimistic view disappeared in the beginning of the 19th century when Malthus appeared. Wagner [1893] tried to evaluate both negative distributive (consumption) and positive productive (production) aspects of population. However, the positive effect of population growth on the economy was made only through the production aspect (through the labor supply).

However, after 1930 they succeeded in evaluating a positive consumption aspect of population growth which was regarded as only having a negative effect before. The Keynesian economists who feared the threat of a declining population made an effort to develop these positive consumption aspects. Hansen [1941] advised us to return to the view of Smith [1776] who evaluated the positive aspects of population growth. Hansen measured the contribution of population growth to the economic growth in the US and Europe. He estimated that about half of annual output (*i.e.*, 3%) was contributed by population growth in Europe. He also measured the contribution of population growth to capital stock growth in Europe (USA) and estimated that about 40% (60%) of capital stock growth was contributed by population growth. And he concluded that we could see how a low rate of population growth decreased investment opportunities.

Although Hicks [1960] also evaluated the positive aspects of population growth, a more comprehensive understanding of the positive aspects of population growth was made by Kuznets [1960]. Although he mentioned that the following arguments were based on his inference, he described more comprehensive positive production, saving, and consumption aspects of population growth. Before describing positive production aspects of population growth, he made the following assumptions: (1) Population would grow at the same rate as the labor force. (2) The same percentage of capital stock is supplied for this increase of the labor force. However, he asserts that there are following reasons for population growth increasing per capita income even if they keep the same amount of per capita capital stock for labor (or population). First, an increase in the labor force facilitates labor's specialization and makes for a more effective utilization of various undeveloped natural resources. Therefore, he concludes that these facts lead to increases in the per capita production. Second, the proportion of young people in the population would increase when there was a rapid increase in the labor force. Generally speaking, young people have a tendency to move from rural areas to urban areas without much trouble, which contributes to economic growth. Third, the absolute number of geniuses would increase when the population increases.

For a positive saving aspect of population growth, he suspects that population growth actually hinders capital accumulation. First, he admits that a family which has 10 children cannot spend the same amount of money on education and training costs for each child as the family which has only two children. Therefore, population would contribute negatively to capital accumulation. However, a private shortage of investment for education and other costs is easily amended by some public policies in advanced countries. Therefore, population growth has many more possibilities to increase economic growth in advanced countries. He asserts that there are not firm foundations to support the view that an increase of expenditure due to population growth would sacrifice all saving. In other words, it is not obvious whether expenditure for children is a substitute for saving or not. He thinks that expenditure for children is rather a substitute for consumption and amusement costs. Also children help their parents by supplying labor. It is very important especially for an agrarian society. Also children stimulate their parents to increase their saving. The government expenditure for education does not necessarily decrease the government capital accumulation and the saving through tax which is used for public education.

Second, total saving would rather have a tendency to increase when population increases. This stems from the fact that high population growth would increase the non-old-age classes which save money. Third, children are a substitute for luxurious consumption and amusements in advanced countries. Therefore, per capita consumption would be smaller for a high population growth. Also, people in the lower classes would decrease their per capita consumption when population grows very rapidly. Therefore, generally speaking high population growth would have the possibility to lead to high saving. Fourth, although population growth might depress capital accumulation, it would be also possible to find capital saving invention and an administration. For a positive consumption aspect of population growth, first we should mention that rapid population growth would enlarge the domestic market and give the merit of economy of scale to industry. In other words, a country which has a small population and small home market would not easily develop its economy. Second, a country which has a high rate of population growth has a large share of young people who are very adaptable to new products. Therefore, it would accelerate modern economic growth and contribute to the growth of per capita production.

Sauvy [1976] made a cost and benefit analysis of population growth to economic growth. As benefit aspects of population growth he listed the following items: (1) An overhead cost is not strictly proportional but rather unrelated to the size of population, therefore it needs a certain amount of minimum cost for any society. Therefore, a country which has a large population has a smaller burden for each member. (2) A high rate of population growth would increase the general productivity through the merit of scale of economy and competition. (3) Technical change requires a division of labor which is easily facilitated in a country with a large population. (4) A high growth rate leads to high population density which has advantages for transportation, education and sanitation. (5) As the proverb says, necessity is the mother of invention. Therefore, a high growth rate benefits both mental and social elements. Also, a low growth rate leads to a high share of old people and it tends to lead to a conservative way of thinking which lacks initiative and vitality.

Simon [1977] showed that a high growth rate of population had a detrimental effect on per capita income in the short run for advanced countries. However, he also showed that a high growth rate would lead to a high per capita income growth in the long run (about 30–80 years) if we consider the elements of development and accumulation of knowledge, economies of scale from population growth, and the development of natural resources. Minami and Ono [1972a, b] used a classic two-sector model which covered the period from 1886 to 1940 in order to observe the influence of population growth on the economy. They obtained the following conclusion: A high growth rate of population, a low growth rate of wages in the traditional sector, a high rate of technical change, a high mobility in the labor market, and a low distribution share of labor would lead to a high economic growth.

As stated before, Kelley *et al.* [1972b] and Kelley and Williamson [1971; 1974] used a more neoclassical two-sector model which measured the effect of population growth on the economic development of Japan. In their earlier papers [1971; 1972b], they concluded that the low population growth rate had an important role in the economic development of Japan. In other words, they showed that about 60% of Japanese economic growth (since 1885 to 1900) came from the low growth rate of population. However, in their later paper [1974], they changed their attitude to asset that population growth was not so important factor in the economic development of

Japan. In other words, they changed to a more optimistic view point about population growth although they were not as optimistic as Simon [1977], and Minami and Ono [1972]. We considered the concept of surplus labor because we assumed our model to include the imperfect competition in factor market (to include the surplus labor aspect) and also to have a wage differential between two sectors.

Therefore, our model is a mixture between the Kelley *et al.* [1972b] model and Minami and Ono [1972a, b] model. Furthermore, our estimation method is completely different from these two models. Although we adopted the Kelley *et al.* method which observes not only the influence of simple population growth on the economy but also the influence of population (labor) growth on technical change, we came to the conclusion that our model instead supports Minami and Ono's conclusions with certain restrictions. The Simon model has a more challenging view which considers the positive aspects of population more than these three models (Kelley *et al.*, Minami and Ono, and Yamaguchi). The Simon model is very instructive for us but some conclusions have to be waited for in further works.

2. Effect of the Economy on Population

So far it has not been popular to analyze the effect of economy on population growth and the interrelationships between population and economic growth as compared with the analysis of the effect of population growth on the economy. However, many works have been made in this field. Among them, one of the first noteworthy works is the first and second propositions of the theory of Malthus [1798] . As stated above his first and second propositions are as follows: (1) Population cannot increase without the means of subsistence; and (2) Population does invariably increase, where there are the means of subsistence. In our solitary islands, we found many mysterious waves of population growth. In fact, population growth was influenced by food which was produced on the islands. The population increased when there was a chance to increase food production. Therefore, the introduction of sweet potatoes substantially increased the island's capacity to carry population. Also there is much research which observes how the business cycle affects the rate of marriage and the birth rate. There are also several sociological analyses, which are in opposition to the Malthusian theory.

However, the greatest contribution of this field (*i.e.*, the field which studies the effect of economy on population growth) is the theory of demographic transition. Here, we do not intend to introduce all kinds of works on the theory of demographic transition. However, we should describe it at least briefly because it is one of the most important theories which analyses the effect of economy on population growth. There are several varieties of the theory of demographic transition, such as the three stages of Thompson [1929], the five stages of Blacker [1968], the corrected three stages of Notestein [1950] and the peculiar classification of Petersen [1969]. In short, the main essence of this theory is that at first a high level of birth rate and death rate prevail, but the death rate starts to decrease thereby keeping the birth rate high. However, after a certain interval, the birth rate also decreases. Therefore, the rate of population growth becomes very high in periods when the death rate decreases but the birth rate remains high. The growth rate would decrease when the birth rate decreases after a certain interval. By checking the studies of historical demography and statistical materials many exceptions were found to this theory of demographic transition. And there is also merit and demerit in this theory, which is very similar to the stage theory of Rostow [1960]. The biggest problem is that it does not show the reasons why some countries develop and why some do not.

Leibenstein [1957], who developed a theory of critical minimum effort, drew a connection to the household consumption theory developed by Becker [1960]. The theory was explained as follows: He investigated how the utility of the population would change when per capita income increased over time. He did not think that it would be as easy to see population utility as a consumption good. However, population utility as a consumption good does not seem to change much, even if per capita income increases. He also admitted that the utility obtained from children would be very large if other goods were restricted. Next, the utility of the population as a production good (especially the utility of children who earn income) would decrease over time. Further, it becomes increasingly difficult for parents to use children as income earners, because much more time is necessary to train, educate, and develop their children. The utility of children's support for the older adult population tends to decrease over time. It becomes easier to provide for one's old-age period when per capita income increases and the social security system becomes more comprehensive. Leibenstein divided population costs into direct and indirect costs. Direct population cost was defined as the ordinary expenditure necessary for a baby to become an adult, whereas indirect population cost was defined as an opportunity cost sacrificed to raise children. The way children are raised depends on income.

Further, opportunities to engage in productive activities and consumption activities increase over time. Therefore, Leibenstein admitted that both direct and indirect costs would increase over time. Becker [1960] regarded children as a consumption durable good and applied that consumption theory to his fertility analysis. He believed that parents would decide whether or not to have a baby by comparing the utility with the cost of the baby. Therefore, people can decide whether to have children or other goods. Further, he produced the following equation: net cost of children = value of expected expenditure by parents + evaluated service by parents − present value of expected money revenue − evaluated service by children. From this equation, he concluded that children would constitute a durable consumption good if the result of the equation had a positive sign. He also considered that parents could determine both the quality and quantity of their children. Therefore, he wrote that parents would increase both the quantity and quality of their children when their income increased; thus, the costs of children increase as income grows. In such a case, parents would choose a smaller number of children than in the previously discussed case.

Although many people applauded the Becker model, it received much criticism. Some of the more important criticisms by economists and sociologists are as follows: (1) There is a shortage of data on income and fertility. (2) The statistics on marriage and birth are decided by institutional conditions rather than economic variables (*e.g.*, income). (3) There is also an argument about whether or not children are regarded as a consumer durable good. Some people assert that children are not treated like ordinary goods explicitly in the market; therefore, it would be a problem to use consumption theory excessively in this fertility analysis. (4) Choice of quantity and quality of children would be restricted by institutional and social factors. (5) It is necessary to consider indirect costs, as Leibenstein [1957] has shown. It is necessary to consider these points. However, Becker's analysis significantly contributed to the development of fertility theory, even though we admit the limits of the theory. Many works followed Becker's work, and Volume 81

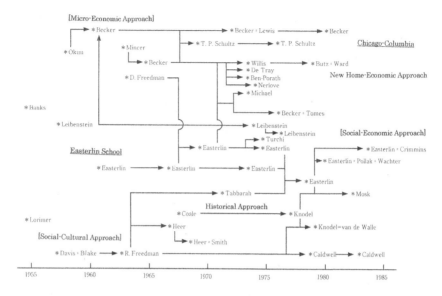

Figure 6-2   Historical Stream of Fertility Analysis after World War II

of JPE was a collection of these works (*e.g.*, Sanderson [1976]; Fig. 6-2 comes from Ohbuchi [1988]).

Although Okun [1958] and then Becker [1960; 1965] analyzed similar topics, Becker thought that there was also production activity within households and developed a new idea of full income. The work of Willis [1973] is regarded as almost perfect. De Tray [1973] adopts a model in which both wife and husband participate to perform service for children. Michael [1973] considers the supply side of fertility; however, many are against the ideas of the Chicago School, especially those of Becker. Sanderson [1976], Simmons [1985] and Srikantan [1982] wrote very clear reviews on this point. Figure 6-2, from Ohbuchi [1988], is also well written and describes the flow of these researchers. As this figure shows, many researchers (not only in sociology but also in economics) are against the Chicago school.

They adopted the social economic approach (social relative hypothesis) of Leibenstein [1974; 1975], the historic approach of Coale [1967; 1976], the social–cultural approach of Davis and Blake [1956], and Mosk's Patriarchy approach [1983]. Further, there are two streams (*i.e.*, the microeconomic approach and new home economics) in the Chicago school. The most prominent opponent of the Chicago approach is Easterlin [1961; 1966;

1969; 1973; 1976; 1978], [Easterlin *et al.* 1980] and the Easterlin School. He does not make as many assumptions as does the Chicago School. Especially, he criticizes consumer choice theory's assumption of unchanged or constant taste. He thinks that social factors are very important and takes the sociological approach. He presented the framework of the Easterlin hypothesis. His famous hypothesis is that potential earning ability, the desirable living level, and the relative economic condition between parents and their children determines the birth rate. Further, Easterlin and Crimmins [1985] also consider both the supply and demand sides.

We should not forget the econometric research, which analyze the economic factors affecting birth and death rates. The first econometric analysis was made by Weintraub [1962], and Adelman [1963] and other researchers developed this analysis. Weintraub obtained the following simple estimation equation.

$$\mathrm{BR} = 6.6 + 0.06y + 5.98L_a/L + 0.25M,$$
$$(0.0045)(7.68)(0.06)R^2 = 0.67,$$

where BR = birth rate, y = per capita income, L_a/L = the share of agricultural labor, M = infant mortality rate and the numbers in the parenthesis are standard error. Adelman [1963] made an econometric analysis in which the age-specific birth rate and death rate are dependent variables and per capita income, the share of non-agriculture, education level and population density are independent variables. She obtained the following conclusions: Income has a positive and the other three variables a negative effect on birth rate. On the other hand, per capita income, the growth rate of per capita income, non-agricultural share and medical level have are negative effect on death rate. Friedlander and Silver [1967] made a fertility analysis by using much more independent variables and Adelman and Morris [1966] used a factor analysis method in order to analyze the factor which affects the birth rate.

T. Paul Schulz [1976] made a survey of econometric analysis of fertility behavior, *i.e.*, the effect of family income, infant mortality rate, education levels of men and women, and wage rates on the fertility behavior in developed and developing countries. The following is the summary which he provided: (1) In low income countries, female education elasticities of birth rate range from -0.17 to -0.66, male education elasticities of birth rate range from -0.98 to $+0.55$, female wage elasticities of birth rate range from -0.35 to -0.16, the male wage elasticity of birth rate is about 0.05, infant mortality elasticities of birth rate range from 0.05 to 0.28. (2) In high income countries, family income elasticities of birth rate range from 0.09 to 0.38, female education elasticities of birth rate range from -1.1 to -0.19, male education of birth rate range from -0.4 to -0.06, female wage elasticities of birth rate range from -0.6 to -0.17, male wage elasticities of birth rate range from -0.11 to $+0.23$.

Therefore, female education and wage rate reduce the birth rate in both high and low income countries. On the other hand, male education has a negative effect on the birth rate in high income countries but a positive effect in low income countries. Also male wage rates have a positive influence on the birth rate in low income countries, but both negative and positive influences on the birth rate in high income countries. Infant mortality rate in low income countries and family income in high income countries have a positive effect on the birth rate. Although the studies of the effect of economy on population growth are still far behind compared to the studies of the effect of population growth on the economy, many efforts have been made. However, this research is still not enough and further research is expected to be made in the future.

3. Interrelationships between Population and Economy

Here, we would like to shift our focus to the research on interrelationships between population and economic growth. First, perhaps surprisingly, we have to list the name of Malthus [1798]. Most people interpreted population growth in Malthusian theory as a dependent variable of output growth. In fact, Boserup [1965] was in opposition to such a Malthusian view and showed that population growth is instead an engine to change the economy as stated above. In other words, she reviewed the history of European agricultural development and criticized Malthusian theory because the theory had not considered the positive effect of population growth. Her theory extended that of Slicher van Bath [1963] and tried to clarify the positive effects of population growth. However, Malthus' theory also contained a consideration of interrelationships between population and economic growth.

The greatest contribution in this respect would be the studies of Ryozaburo Minami [1963a, b; 1971] in Japan as mentioned before (Chapter 1).

Judging from his work, Malthusian theory would be summarized as follows: People cannot survive without food. Therefore, population would be restricted by subsistence materials (first proposition). However, human's sex drive is so strong that it is easy for population to exceed the subsistence materials. In other words, population has a persistent tendency to exceed the level of nutrition (proliferate principal). The equilibrium between subsistence material and population is disturbed by the population's persistent tendency to exceed the level of nutrition. This decreases the living standard and several kinds of misery appear. Here, a reversing movement of population arises and it recovers equilibrium at a given subsistence level (regulation principal). However, the equilibrium would be recovered at a higher level, thus resisting the pressure of population growth which forces them into a lower level of living. In other words, people try to enlarge the level of subsistence material which is sufficient to support the increased numbers. Indeed, necessity is the mother of invention.

Therefore, subsistence materials would increase and this increase would cause population to increase further. As a result, population would increase in number. Therefore, population would increase whenever subsistence material increases if there is no powerful and conspicuous check (second proposition). That is, a forward movement of population occurs. However, this forward movement again prepares the next disturbance of equilibrium (proliferate principal). Minami showed that Malthus considered these to be repeated forward and backward movements, *i.e.*, cyclical up and down movements. From this explanation it is obvious that Malthus also has considered aspects of interrelationships between population and economic growth. In 1973, there was a conference in France which set out to consider the interrelationships between population and economic growth as mentioned before. The main discussion topics were as follows: (1) The concept of optimum population growth, (2) Fertility as an exercise in choice, (3) Economic factors in the decline of fertility in Europe, (4) Economic factors in the decline of fertility in the third world, (5) Population, resources and environment, (6) Population growth and employment, and (7) Migration and employment opportunities.

Gregory *et al.* [1972] made an econometric analysis of the interrelationship between population and economic growth. In their model, birth rate, per capita income, female labor force participation and infant mortality rate are four endogenous variables and education level, rate of unemployment, ratio of colored population, age composition, medical level and wage rate are six exogenous variables. They estimated the model in the USA by using a two-stage least square method which is shown in Table 6-2. We changed and applied their model to fit into the Japanese situation. We also expanded the analytical period from 1900 to 1970 and considered the problem of serial correlation which was not considered in their analysis. We also used a two-stage least square method for estimation and used the Cochrane and Orcutt method for serial correlation. Models 1 and 2 in Table 6-2 are a comparison table of these estimates. From this table, we can see that some variables do not have good t values in both countries. This might be a reflection of the statement that population and economy have a loose (not tight) relationship. However, the sign obtained in each variable is correct from the theoretical point of view.

Most of the variables obtained here have same signs in both countries. However, the effect of education level on birth rate and the effect of female labor force participation on per capita income, and the effect of birth rate and age composition on female labor force participation have a different sign between two countries. The effect of education level on birth rate and the effect of age composition on labor force participation have a large t value with different signs in these two countries. However, the minus sign of the effect of age composition (14–44 years old) on labor force participation in the USA is doubtful from the theoretical point of view. Therefore, the problem is the effect of education level on birth rate. The USA research has a minus sign which is widely observed by many studies. However, our Japanese research shows that the variable has a positive sign although it does not have a good t value.

It is not an unusual result to get a positive sign judging from the result of Hashimoto [1974] and T. Paul Schluz [1976]. Hashimoto showed in his estimate that the wife's education level had a positive effect in Japan. In our model, we took the share of people who finished the higher education as representing the education variable. However, it would be true that most of the highly educated people were male in the Meiji period. From these facts it would not be so unrealistic to obtain a positive sign for the variable of the husband's education in Japan. In most of the neoclassical models, birth rate is treated as a dependent variable of per capita income. Many

Table 6-2 A Summary Table of the Estimated Values of the Population Model in Japan and the United States

Dependent variables	Independent variables	Japan Model 1 Coefficient	t value	Japan Model 2 Coefficient	t value	U.S.A. Coefficient	t value
Birth rate	Per capita income	0.0016	0.3082	0.0079	0.6936	0.0205	1.2955
	Female labor force participation	−0.0208	−1.2462	−0.0217	−1.2983	−0.7407	−1.8476
	Infant mortality rate	0.0002	0.0856	−0.0001	−0.0049	−0.0378	−0.6483
	Education level	0.5940	1.4956	0.5572	1.5538	−3.4130	−2.1238
	Share of agriculture	0.0777	5.8850	0.0786	5.9319		
Per capita income	Female labor force participation	−0.1406	−1.3870	−0.0590	−0.6599	14.7900	2.5081
	Education level	19.6329	5.0182	3.9587	2.0278	92.6600	5.5221
	Real wage rate	15.1305	12.5152	6.6731	12.7344	8.5940	1.5273
Female labor force participation	Birth rate	0.2443	0.5764	Same as at left		−0.6399	−3.8047
	Real wage	0.1032	0.3332			0.5363	1.8192
	Age composition	1.4012	22.4431			−0.4224	−1.5249
	Share of agriculture	0.1347	3.4326				
Infant mortality rate	Per capita income	−0.3811	−1.5974	−0.7044	−1.3296	−0.0044	−0.4861
	Education level	2.5609	0.1547	−4.3018	−0.2811	−13.2400	−11.0610
	Medical level	−0.0239	−0.3472	−0.0524	−0.7910	−3.8630	−5.7734
	Share of agriculture	−0.4448	−0.6993	−0.5444	−0.8345		

In Model 2, we used the permanent income in Japan as a variable of per capita income.

famous Japanese econometric models such as those of Klein [1961], Ueno and Kinoshita [1965], and Klein and Shinkai [1963] use this type of analysis. On the other hand, the model of Denton and Spencer [1975] sets out to investigate the interrelationship between population and economic growth. They did not divide the whole economy into two sectors but had the intention to grasp population aspects in more detail. In their model, the total output is determined by the production function whose inputs are labor and capital.

Capital is accumulated through the investment function whose investment is equal to saving. The saving is obtained from multiplying saving rate by disposable income. Then, they applied the Easterlin's hypothesis [1966] which showed the swings between wage rate and fertility (*i.e.*, Decrease of Birth rate → Decrease of labor supply → Increase of wage rate → Increase of birth rate → Increase of labor supply → Decrease of wage rate → Decrease of birth rate). They concluded that we could not obtain any cyclical movement unless the birth rate elasticity of the wage rate is greater than two (*i.e.*, a one percentage increase of the wage rate would increase the birth rate by more than 2%). They further analyzed many results such as the effect of the fertility pattern on the economy, the effect of household and age composition on total consumption, the relationship between population growth and health cost, population growth and education cost, and population growth and the total government budget.

They obtained the following results: A rise of birth rate would increase the share of education cost in total government expenditure and decrease the share of health cost and other government expenditures. They further investigated the relationship between female labor force participation and fertility, especially how the differences in the timing of and interval between birth would affect female labor force participation. Then they obtained the following results: (1) A rise of birth rate gave the largest effect and the effect of interval of birth existed slightly in the short term but disappeared in the long term. (2) The effect of female wage rate on fertility was fairly large. Another characteristic of this model is that it is constructed to be able to include effects of migration from abroad explicitly. This came from the fact that they considered the Canadian situation. From these analyses, we can see that there are also many works which analyses an interrelationship between population and economic growth. However, further research is expected to be made in the future.

Conclusion

So far, we have seen the influence of population on the economy, the converse, and the interrelationships between the population and economy. These results were observed because of the fifth characteristic of population (*i.e.*, that it has interrelationships with the economy). Research in this chapter is closely related to the basic consideration of Chapter 1 and the positive effects of population discussed in Chapter 7. Here, we summarize our content into five points.

(1) To see the effects of population growth on the economy, the method of Coale and Hoover [1958] observes the effects of absolute population size, growth rate, and age distribution on the economy. However, it would be better to see how population is constructed (*e.g.*, classification of sex, age, occupation, religion, institution, and social class) and determine the effects of these classified items on the economy.

(2) There are many methods by which to see the effects of population on the economy, such as optimal population and optimistic versus pessimistic population. Malthus and Boserup are generally considered as two conflicting thinkers (a pessimistic populationist and an optimistic populationist, respectively). However, those two are rather complimentary of each other, as Simon also shows.

(3) It would be necessary to see both the positive and negative sides of population, as shown in Chapter 1. This is consistent with the thinking of Hicks, Kuznets, Sauvy, and Simon. The contribution of population in Chapter 1 is constructed systematically according to these people's ideas.

(4) There has not been as much research on the effects of economy on population as on those of population on the economy. However, the Malthus' first and second propositions, and the relationships between birth rate, marriage, and business cycle are classified into this category. One of the greatest contributions of this field is the theory of demographic transition. However, this theory has the same merits and demerits as Rostow's stage theory [1960]. The research of Leibenstein and Becker, who used the approach of consumption theory, are also classified into this category. Many econometric works, since the early stage's work of Weintraub, are also in this category. Judging from the survey of T. Paul

Shulz, there is a possibility that the elasticity of birth rate with respect to male education could have a positive sign, which we obtained in our research.

(5) Malthus was also one of the key researchers on the interrelationships between population and economic growth. Many econometric works have also used a simultaneous equation method, similar to those of Gregory, Campbell, and Cheng. We changed and applied their model to fit into the Japanese situation, as shown in Table 6-2.

Summaries (1)–(5) of the interrelationships between population and economy are clear. Econometric analysis, such as the simultaneous equation method of the interrelationships between population and economy, shows several important policy implications. Among them, there are two noteworthy points. First, the importance of education for economic development was reconfirmed again in the econometric method; this is consistent with the positive (but indirect) contribution of population (which has a relatively high educational level) in Chapter 7. Second, birth rate increases with the agricultural share, and their well-educated population created the technical change in Japan. Different from the ordinary case, the infant mortality rate did not increase alongside the increased agricultural share in Japan. This also contributed from the point of view of human resources. The contribution of agricultural technical change to the economy was largest in Japan and most stable among Asian countries (*e.g.*, China, Taiwan, and Thailand), as shown in Chapter 5. Here, econometric analysis leads us to reconfirm the importance of education in Japan. Further, we reconfirm the contribution of agricultural technical change to economic development in Japan.

Chapter 7

A Consideration of the Positive
Effects of Population*

Introduction

Rapid population growth in developing countries continues to be generally considered from a Malthusian point of view (Malthus [1798]) (*i.e.*, the economic effects of population are viewed negatively). The well-known basis for this point of view is that diminishing returns result as more labor is added to a fixed amount of land; further, population growth combined with a given amount of food carries the implication of less food for each individual. However, Simon [1977] has challenged this view, predicting that population growth will positively affect per capita income, at least long term.[1] Given its small land base relative to its population, the implication of the Malthusian argument for Japan, is clear: Population growth can only be expected to have a depressing effect on per capita income. The earlier research of Kelley *et al.* [1972a, b] showed population to have large negative effects,[2] but Minami and Ono [1972a, b] concluded that economic development

---

*The content of this chapter was developed and rewritten from Yamaguchi and Kennedy [1984b] to meet the purpose of the book. We appreciate *Developing Economies* and Dr. Kennedy for permitting the use of this paper for this book.

[1] Simon [1977] used a simulation model to predict the effect of population growth on per-worker income. For more-developed countries, he found that the effect of population growth on per-worker income, although initially negative, would become positive after 30–80 years. For less-developed countries, he found that moderate population growth would lead to higher per-worker income in the long run (after 75–150 years) than either zero or very fast population growth.

[2] Although the earlier research of Kelley and Williamson [1971] and Kelley *et al.* [1972b] showed the economic effects of population growth to be strongly negative, the results of their later research (Kelley and Williamson [1974]) showed population growth to have more positive effects, although they were less optimistic than was Simon [1977].

would have been retarded in Japan had population growth been significantly slower.

Japan has achieved dramatic increases in per capita income and agricultural and non-agricultural output since the Meiji Restoration of 1868. The purpose of this chapter is to estimate the direct and indirect contributions of population and labor growth to the growth of per capita income and sectoral output in Japan over the period 1880–1970. Other things being equal, considering per capita income growth, the direct contribution of population growth is negative, while that of labor growth is positive. Less obvious, however, are the positive indirect contributions that can result from both population and labor growth — "indirect" in the sense that they come by way of the influences of population and labor on the rate of technical change in either sector. In this chapter, we estimate the total contribution (*i.e.*, direct plus indirect contributions) of population and labor growth to agricultural and non-agricultural output growth in addition to per capita income growth, and we provide a sensitivity analysis and some policy implications of the results. In this chapter, we first consider the optimistic and pessimistic views of population growth. Second, we evaluate the direct contribution of population *cum* labor growth to the economy. Third, we assess the indirect contribution of population *cum* labor growth to the economy.

1. Optimistic and Pessimistic Views of Population Growth

Population growth can be viewed optimistically or pessimistically, depending on whether one sees its effects on the economy as positive or negative. Throughout most of history, the optimistic viewpoint has prevailed. The ancient Greeks and Romans and the more recent Mercantilists considered people to be a source of power. However, in the late 18th century, the Malthusian view gained prominence, and population growth came to be viewed negatively. The Malthusian view has been supported by much economic research, including that of Coale and Hoover [1958] and Meadows *et al.* [1972]. Wagner [1893] evaluated the positive effects of population on per capita income through labor and the negative effects of population through distribution. While Wagner considered only the positive effects of population derived from the labor supply, Keynes [1937] and Hansen [1941] conducted more complete evaluations of that positive effect by including consumption and demand factors.

Hicks [1960], Kuznets [1960], and Simon [1977] followed with evaluations of the positive effects of population growth. It is true that, other things being equal, population growth would decrease per capita income; this effect is strengthened by the resulting decrease in the labor participation rate. Further, an increase in the number of children leads to increases in consumption and reduced savings. However, various positive effects may result from population growth, and these should not be overlooked. The most obvious one is labor's contribution to output, which is strengthened by children's work and the extension of working hours by parents. A second positive effect derives from the scale of economy, division of labor, and increased competition. Third, the development of infrastructure and education are facilitated by high population density. Simon [1977] showed that high population growth had a positive effect on irrigation and agricultural investment in developing countries.

Fourth, insofar as necessity is the mother of invention, population pressure sometimes sparks economic progress. Fifth, an increased share of young people may increase sensitivity to new products, adaptability, and enthusiasm for new occupations. Further, young people have more opportunity for higher levels of education and labor mobility. Sixth, population growth facilitates the accumulation of knowledge and the discovery of natural resources. Further, the number of geniuses increases in absolute terms as population grows. These positive effects of population growth will depend on time and place; although they are difficult to measure directly, this study attempts to capture at least some of them by measuring the indirect effects of population growth via its influence on the rate of technical change.

2. Direct Contribution of Population *cum* Labor Growth to the Economy

As we showed in Chapter 2, the model is designed to estimate the influence of each exogenous variable on eight endogenous variables in a general equilibrium context. We referred to these influences of exogenous variables on endogenous variables as growth rate multipliers (or GRMs). The contribution of each exogenous variable to each endogenous variable is obtained by multiplying the value of the GRM by the historical growth rate of the exogenous variable, as shown in Chapter 2. This procedure is used in the following equations to estimate the direct contribution of population *cum* labor growth (*i.e.*, the sum of population's contribution and labor's contribution) to the growth of per capita income equation (7.1) and sectoral output equation (7.2)

$$CEPop_D = (EQ)\dot{Q} + (EL)\dot{L}, \qquad (7.1)$$

where $CEPop_D$ is the direct contribution of population *cum* labor growth to real per capita income growth, EQ (EL) is the influence of population (labor) growth on the growth of per capita income, $\dot{Q}(\dot{L})$ is the growth rate of population (labor),[3]

$$CY_i Pop_D = (Y_i Q)\dot{Q} + (Y_i L)\dot{L}, \qquad (7.2)$$

where $CYi Pop_D$ is the direct contribution of population *cum* labor growth to output growth in sector i ($i = 1, 2 =$ agricultural and non-agricultural sector, respectively), $Y_i Q$ ($Y_i L$) is the influence of population (labor) on output growth in sector i. Where $CY_2 Pop_D$ is the direct contribution of population *cum* labor growth to non-agricultural output growth, $\partial \dot{Y}_2/\partial \dot{Q}(\partial \dot{Y}_2/\partial \dot{L})$ is the influence of population (labor) growth on the growth of non-agricultural output.

Growth rate multipliers showing the separate influences of population and labor growth on the growth of per capita income and sectoral output are given for each five-year period, 1880–1965, in Table 7-1. The influence of population growth on per capita income growth (EQ) is negative. It is most strongly negative in 1905, when a 1% increase in population growth causes a 1.15% decrease in per capita income growth. Labor growth, on the other hand, has a positive influence on per capita income growth (EL), ranging from a low of 0.60 (1945) to a high of 0.83 (1885). The influence of population growth on agricultural output growth ($Y_1 Q$) is positive, whereas its influence on non-agricultural output growth ($Y_2 Q$) is negative. Labor growth affects both agricultural and non-agricultural output growth positively, the latter being more strongly affected. Growth rate multipliers embodying the influences of the rate of agricultural and non-agricultural technical changes on the growth of per capita income and sectoral output are also shown in Table 7-1.

---

[3]The direct contributions of population and labor growth to per capita income growth have been previously estimated in Yamaguchi and Binswanger [1975] using an earlier data set.

Table 7-1   Growth Rate Multipliers for the Effects of Population, Labor and Technical Change on Japanese Economy

Year	Per Capita Income				Agricultural Output				Non-agricultural Output				Agricultural Labor				Non-agricultural Labor			
	EQ	EL	ET_1	ET_2	Y_1Q γ_1'	Y_1L β_1'	Y_1T_1 α_1'	Y_1T_2 δ_1'	Y_2Q γ_2'	Y_2L β_2'	Y_2T_1 α_2'	Y_2T_2 δ_2'	L_1Q γ_1	L_1L β_1	L_1T_1 α_1	L_1T_2 δ_1	L_2Q γ_2	L_2L β_2	L_2T_1 α_2	L_2T_2 δ_2
1880	-1.09	0.79	0.50	0.59	0.10	0.49	1.00	-0.10	-0.28	1.08	0.00	1.28	0.12	0.90	0.00	-0.12	-0.30	1.26	0.00	0.30
1885	-1.12	0.83	0.42	0.70	0.08	0.51	0.95	-0.03	-0.23	0.99	0.14	1.09	0.10	0.93	-0.06	-0.04	-0.24	1.16	0.15	0.10
1890	-1.10	0.75	0.43	0.67	0.09	0.48	0.96	-0.05	-0.22	0.93	0.10	1.12	0.12	0.92	-0.05	-0.06	-0.25	1.17	0.11	0.14
1895	-1.10	0.74	0.40	0.70	0.08	0.49	0.94	-0.03	-0.20	0.86	0.13	1.06	0.12	0.93	-0.08	-0.04	-0.22	1.13	0.15	0.07
1900	-1.10	0.71	0.37	0.73	0.08	0.51	0.93	-0.01	-0.18	0.79	0.15	1.03	0.11	0.94	-0.09	-0.02	-0.21	1.12	0.17	0.03
1905	-1.15	0.71	0.36	0.78	0.13	0.48	0.90	-0.03	-0.24	0.79	0.18	1.06	0.17	0.90	-0.13	-0.04	-0.29	1.17	0.22	0.07
1910	-1.14	0.71	0.35	0.79	0.13	0.48	0.89	-0.03	-0.23	0.78	0.18	1.05	0.17	0.90	-0.14	-0.04	-0.28	1.16	0.22	0.06
1915	-1.11	0.64	0.32	0.80	0.14	0.47	0.88	-0.02	-0.19	0.68	0.16	1.03	0.19	0.90	-0.16	-0.03	-0.25	1.14	0.21	0.04
1920	-1.10	0.70	0.30	0.80	0.16	0.46	0.87	-0.03	-0.17	0.77	0.15	1.03	0.21	0.88	-0.18	-0.03	-0.22	1.13	0.19	0.04
1925	-1.09	0.70	0.29	0.79	0.17	0.49	0.86	-0.03	-0.16	0.77	0.13	1.03	0.22	0.87	-0.19	-0.04	-0.20	1.12	0.17	0.03
1930	-1.10	0.70	0.23	0.86	0.17	0.51	0.82	-0.01	-0.14	0.72	0.15	0.99	0.21	0.87	-0.22	0.01	-0.18	1.11	0.20	-0.01
1935	-1.08	0.66	0.23	0.86	0.17	0.46	0.83	-0.01	-0.12	0.69	0.13	1.00	0.22	0.88	-0.23	0.01	-0.17	1.10	0.18	-0.01
1940	-1.07	0.62	0.21	0.87	0.17	0.46	0.82	-0.01	-0.11	0.64	0.11	0.99	0.24	0.87	-0.25	0.01	-0.16	1.09	0.17	-0.01
1945	-1.05	0.60	0.22	0.84	0.11	0.49	0.85	0.05	-0.08	0.62	0.12	0.96	0.15	0.92	-0.22	0.07	-0.12	1.06	0.16	-0.05
1950	-1.08	0.62	0.22	0.86	0.16	0.46	0.83	-0.01	-0.12	0.64	0.12	1.00	0.22	0.88	-0.23	0.01	-0.18	1.10	0.18	-0.01
1955	-1.09	0.79	0.23	0.86	0.28	0.46	0.79	-0.06	-0.16	0.86	0.12	1.04	0.34	0.77	-0.26	-0.08	-0.20	1.13	0.15	0.04
1960	-1.08	0.74	0.16	0.92	0.26	0.42	0.77	-0.03	-0.12	0.77	0.11	1.01	0.36	0.79	-0.31	-0.04	-0.15	1.09	0.13	0.02
1965	-1.06	0.74	0.12	0.94	0.29	0.42	0.73	-0.02	-0.09	0.76	0.08	1.01	0.37	0.78	-0.34	-0.03	-0.11	1.07	0.10	0.01

These values will be used later, but it should be noted here that technical change in each sector affects per capita income growth and output positively in every case, except for the effect of non-agricultural technical change on agricultural output growth $(Y_1 T_2)$. Growth rate multipliers relevant to agricultural labor (L_1) and non-agricultural labor (L_2) are also given in Table 7-1 for later use. The direct contributions of population and labor growth to per capita income and sectoral output growth are reported for each decade, 1880–1970, in Table 7-2. The historical rates of growth for per capita income (E), agricultural output (Y_1) and non-agricultural output (Y_2) are also shown. The contribution of population growth [column (2)] to per capita income growth is negative in each decade while the contribution of labor growth [column (3)] is positive in each decade.

The former outweighs the latter (except the period of First Demographic Dividend, 1950–1960) yielding a total direct contribution of population *cum* labor growth. $CEPop_D$ [column (4)], which is negative, averaging -0.65 over the period 1880–1970.[4] The total direct contribution of population *cum* labor growth, $CY_1 Pop_D$ [column (8)] to agricultural output growth is positive in each decade given positive contributions from both population growth [column (6)] and labor growth [column (7)]. With respect to non-agricultural output growth, the total direct contribution of population *cum* labor growth, $CY_2 Pop_D$ [column (12)] is positive in each decade except 1940–1950, as the negative contribution of population growth [column (10)] is outweighed by the positive contribution of labor growth [column (11)].

3. Indirect Contribution of Population *cum* Labor Growth to the Economy

3.1. *Indirect Contribution of Population cum Labor Growth to the Growth of Per Capita Income and Sectoral Output*

In evaluating the contribution of population growth to economic development, Simon [1977] argued that population growth and technical change

---

[4]This result is consistent with Kelley and Williamson [1971] and Kelley *et al.* [1972b]. Note that if the labor participation rate had been less in Japan, as it might have been had population growth been greater, then the average value of $CEPop_D$ would likely be more negative.

Table 7-2 Direct Contribution of Population Growth and Labor Growth to the Growth of Real Per Capita Income and Sectoral Output (% per year)

Decade	(1) $\dot{E}$	(2) $(EQ)\dot{Q}$	(3) $(EL)\dot{L}$	(4) $CEPop_D$ (2)+(3)	(5) $\dot{Y}_1$	(6) $(Y_1Q)\dot{Q}$	(7) $(Y_1L)\dot{L}$	(8) $CYPop_D$ (6)+(7)	(9) $\dot{Y}_2$	(10) $(Y_2Q)\dot{Q}$	(11) $(Y_2L)\dot{L}$	(12) CY_2Pop_D (10)+(11)
1880–1890	2.7	−1.01	0.42	−0.59	3.4	0.07	0.26	0.33	3.7	−0.21	0.50	0.29
1890–1900	2.2	−1.10	0.44	−0.66	1.7	0.08	0.29	0.37	3.9	−0.20	0.52	0.32
1900–1910	1.3	−1.38	0.28	−1.10	2.2	0.16	0.19	0.35	2.6	−0.29	0.32	0.03
1910–1920	2.6	−1.33	0.38	−0.95	3.2	0.17	0.28	0.45	4.0	−0.23	0.41	0.18
1920–1930	0.5	−1.74	0.63	−1.11	1.1	0.27	0.44	0.71	2.4	−0.26	0.69	0.43
1930–1940	3.9	−1.19	0.99	−0.20	0.4	0.19	0.69	0.88	5.7	−0.13	1.04	0.91
1940–1950	—	−1.68	0.12	−1.56	−0.5	0.18	0.10	0.28	—	−0.13	0.12	−0.01
1950–1960	7.1	−1.31	1.74	0.43	3.6	0.34	1.01	1.35	9.2	−0.19	1.89	1.70
1960–1970	10.0	−1.17	0.96	−0.21	−1.0	0.32	0.55	0.87	11.9	−0.10	0.99	0.89

should not be seen as two independent forces in a race. Rather, technical change should be viewed as a function of population growth.[5] Population growth implies advances in knowledge and technology, economies of scale, and discoveries of resources. As population growth contributes to technical change it will indirectly contribute to per capita income and output growth. First, with respect to per capita income growth, the indirect contribution of population *cum* labor growth via agricultural and non-agricultural technical changes can be written as in Eq. (7.3):

$$CEPop_1 = ET_1 \frac{\partial \dot{T}_1}{\partial \dot{Q}} \dot{Q} + ET_1 \frac{\partial \dot{T}_1}{\partial \dot{L}} \dot{L} + ET_2 \frac{\partial \dot{T}_2}{\partial \dot{Q}} \dot{Q} + ET_2 \frac{\partial \dot{T}_2}{\partial \dot{Q}} \dot{L},$$

(7.3)

where $CEPop_1$ is the indirect contribution of population *cum* labor growth to real per capita income growth, $ET_1(ET_2)$ is the influence of the rate of agricultural (non-agricultural) technical change on per capita income growth, $\partial \dot{T}_1 / \partial \dot{Q} (\partial \dot{T}_2 / \partial \dot{Q})$ is the influence of population growth on the rate of agricultural (non-agricultural) technical change, and $\partial \dot{T}_1 / \partial \dot{L} (\partial \dot{T}_2 / \partial \dot{L})$ is the influence of labor growth on the rate of agricultural (non-agricultural) technical change.

The indirect contribution of population *cum* labor growth to sectoral output growth via agricultural and non-agricultural technical changes can be written as in Eq. (7.4):

$$CY_i Pop_1 = Y_i T_1 \frac{\partial \dot{T}_1}{\partial \dot{Q}} \dot{Q} + Y_i T_1 \frac{\partial \dot{T}_1}{\partial \dot{L}} \dot{L} + Y_i T_2 \frac{\partial \dot{T}_2}{\partial \dot{Q}} \dot{Q} + Y_i T_2 \frac{\partial \dot{T}_2}{\partial \dot{L}} \dot{L},$$

(7.4)

where $CY_i Pop_1$ is the indirect contribution of population *cum* labor growth to output growth in sector i, and $Y_i T_1 (Y_i T_2)$ is the influence of the rate of agricultural (non-agricultural) technical change on output growth in sector i. This section attempts to estimate the indirect contribution of population *cum* labor growth to the growth of per capita income and sectoral output. Three alternative approaches are used: the Residual and Verdoorn methods as

---

[5]Boserup [1965] and Clark [1967], among others have viewed technical change as a function of population growth.

employed by Simon [1977], and the "factor augmenting rate" method of ordinary growth theory as Table 7-3. of this chapter. Simon explains the Residual and Verdoorn methods as follows:

"The crucial feedback effect of population growth upon the level of productivity is embodied in two alternative ways. The first approach utilizes the notion of the "residual" found in empirical studies of productivity change; the residual is made a function of the labor force, because it seems reasonable to assume that the size of the labor force influences the amount of invention and innovation. The second approach takes advantage of 'Verdoorns Law', which asserts that the change in productivity is a function of total output (and total output obviously is a function of population size). It is reasonable to suppose that output in Verdoorn's Law is an empirical representation for the influence of the size of labor force upon productivity, and hence the two approaches describe the same phenomenon. And in fact they give similar results" (p. 10 of Simon [1977]). The factor augmenting rate method of ordinary growth theory is used by Kelley and Williamson [1974]. The efficiency of capital ($e^{\lambda K} K$) and efficiency of labor ($e^{\lambda L} L$) take into account two sets of factors, the first physical capital and labor (K and L) and the second technical progress variables which augment physical capital and labor (*i.e.*, $e^{\lambda K}$ and $e^{\lambda L}$). The direct and indirect contributions of population *cum* labor growth to per capita income and sectoral output growth are summed to obtain their total contribution.

The first approach used to estimate the indirect contribution of the growth of population *cum* labor to the growth of per capita income and sectoral output is the Residual method. It assumes, after Simon, that the size of the residual depends on the size of the labor force.[6] In our model, the residual is viewed as variation, in the level of technical change. From our model, the labor force of each sector can be explained by the model's exogenous variables. Therefore, we obtain the following four equations:

$$T_1 = a_1 L_1, \tag{7.5}$$

$$L_1 = B_1 T_1^{\alpha_1} L^{\beta_1} Q^{\gamma_1} T_2^{\delta_1}, \tag{7.6}$$

---

[6]In this chapter, we equate technical change in each sector to be proportional to the sector's labor force [Eqs. (7.5) and (7.7)]. This is the usual way for the Residual method.

Table 7-3   Three Methods of Measuring Indirect Effect of Population

Residual Method	$\begin{bmatrix} T_1 = a_1 L_1 \\ L_1 = B_1 T_1^{\alpha_1} L^{\beta_1} Q^{\gamma_1} T_2^{\delta_1} \\ T_2 = a_2 L_2 \\ L_2 = B_2 T_1^{\alpha_2} L^{\beta_2} Q^{\gamma_2} T_2^{\delta_2} \end{bmatrix}$

$$\rightarrow \begin{bmatrix} T_1 = A_1 L^{(\beta_1 + \delta_1 m)/(1-\alpha_1)} Q^{(\gamma_1 + \delta_1 n)/(1-\alpha_1)} \\ T_2 = A_2 L^m Q^n \end{bmatrix}$$

$$m = [\beta_2(1-\alpha_1) + \beta_1\alpha_2]/$$
$$[(1-\alpha_1)(1-\delta_2) - \alpha_2\delta_1]$$
$$n = [\gamma_2(1-\alpha_1) + \gamma_1\alpha_2]/$$
$$[(1-\alpha_1)(1-\delta_2) - \alpha_2\delta_1]$$

Verdoorn Method
$$\begin{bmatrix} T_1 = a_1' Y_1^{1/2} \\ Y_1 = B_1' T_1^{\alpha_{1'}} L^{\beta_{1'}} Q^{\gamma_{1'}} T_2^{\delta_{1'}} \\ T_2 = a_2' Y_2^{12} \\ Y_2 = B_2' T_1^{\alpha_{2'}} L^{\beta_{2'}} Q^{\gamma_{2'}} T_2^{\delta_{2'}} \end{bmatrix}$$

$$\rightarrow \begin{bmatrix} T_1 = A_1' L^{(\beta_{1'} + \delta_{1'} m')/(2-\alpha_{1'})} Q^{(\gamma^{1'} + \delta_{1'} n')/(2-\alpha_{1'})} \\ T_2 = A_2' L^{m'} Q^{n'} \end{bmatrix}$$

$$m' = (\alpha_2'\beta_1' + 2\beta_2' - \alpha_1'\beta_2')/$$
$$(4 - 2\alpha_1' - \alpha_2'\delta' - 2\delta_2' + \alpha_1'\delta_2')$$
$$n' = (\alpha_2'\gamma_1' + 2\gamma_2' - \alpha_1'\gamma_2')/$$
$$(4 - 2\alpha_1' - \alpha_2'\beta_1' - 2\delta_2' + \alpha_1'\delta_2')$$

Growth Theory Method
$$\begin{bmatrix} \dot{T}_1 = \lambda_K \beta + \lambda_L \alpha \\ \dot{T}_2 = \lambda_K \delta + \lambda_L \gamma \end{bmatrix}$$

$$\rightarrow \begin{bmatrix} CEPop_I = (ET_1 \times \lambda_L\alpha) + (ET_2 \times \lambda_L\gamma) \\ CY_iPop_I = (Y_iT_1 \times \lambda_L\alpha) + (Y_1T_2 \times \lambda_L\gamma) \end{bmatrix}$$

$$T_2 = a_2 L_2, \tag{7.7}$$

$$L_2 = B_2 T_1^{\alpha_2} L^{\beta_2} Q^{\gamma_2} T_2^{\delta_2}, \tag{7.8}$$

where T_1 (T_2) is agricultural (non-agricultural) technical change. L_1 (L_2) is the agricultural (non-agricultural) labor force, Q is population, L is total labor and B_1 (B_2) represents the other exogenous variables in the model.[7]

These four equations can be transformed into the following two equations :

$$T_1 = A_1 L^{(\beta_1 + \delta_1 m)/(1-\alpha_1)} Q^{(\gamma_1 + \delta_1 n)/(1-\alpha_1)}, \tag{7.9}$$

$$T_2 = A_2 L^m Q^n, \tag{7.10}$$

where

$$m = [\beta_2(1-\alpha_1) + \beta_1 \alpha_2]/[(1-\alpha_1)(1-\delta_2) - \alpha_2 \delta_1],$$

$$n = [\gamma_2(1-\alpha_1) + \gamma_1 \alpha_2]/[(1-\alpha_1)(1-\delta_2) - \alpha_2 \delta_1],$$

and where A_i includes the constant plus all other terms, with the exception of technical change in each sector, population and total labor.

The parameter values needed to solve Eqs. (7.9) and (7.10) are the growth rate multipliers given for agricultural and non-agricultural labors in Table 7-1. Solving these equations yield elasticity values of agricultural and non-agricultural technical changes with respect to population and labor growth. These elasticities are reported for each five-year period, 1880–1965, in Table 7-4. With respect to the rate of agricultural technical change ($\dot{T}_1$) both population growth ($\dot{Q}$) and labor growth ($\dot{L}$) influence it positively. A 1% increase in $\dot{Q}$ causes $\dot{T}_1$ to increase between 0.10 and 0.28%, while a 1% increase in $\dot{L}$ causes $\dot{T}_1$ to increase between 0.53 and 0.84%. With respect to the rate of non-agricultural technical change ($\dot{T}_2$), $\dot{Q}$ affects it negatively while L affects it positively. A 1% increase in $\dot{Q}$ causes $\dot{T}_2$ to decrease between 0.08 and 0.43%, while a 1% increase in $\dot{L}$ causes $\dot{T}_2$ to increase between 1.12 and 1.80%. If both population and labor growth increase by 1%, the percentage change in the rate of technical change in each sector equals the sum of the two relevant elasticities.

---

[7] B_1 and B_2 include total capital, land, agricultural demand shifter, and the relative wage rate.

Table 7-4   GRM of Population and Labor on Sectoral Technical Change

Year	$T_1 Q$	$T_1 L$	$T_2 Q$	$T_2 L$
1880	0.17 (0.14)	0.68 (0.34)	−0.43 (−0.39)	1.80 (1.50)
1885	0.10 (0.08)	0.82 (0.45)	−0.25 (−0.24)	1.43 (1.16)
1890	0.13 (0.10)	0.79 (0.41)	−0.27 (−0.24)	1.46 (1.10)
1895	0.12 (0.08)	0.81 (0.43)	−0.22 (−0.20)	1.35 (0.98)
1900	0.10 (0.08)	0.84 (0.47)	−0.20 (−0.17)	1.30 (0.89)
1905	0.16 (0.12)	0.75 (0.41)	−0.27 (−0.23)	1.43 (0.92)
1910	0.16 (0.12)	0.74 (0.41)	−0.26 (−0.22)	1.41 (0.90)
1915	0.17 (0.13)	0.74 (0.41)	−0.22 (−0.17)	1.35 (0.77)
1920	0.18 (0.15)	0.71 (0.38)	−0.19 (−0.15)	1.32 (0.85)
1925	0.19 (0.15)	0.69 (0.40)	−0.17 (−0.14)	1.28 (0.85)
1930	0.17 (0.15)	0.72 (0.43)	−0.14 (−0.12)	1.24 (0.78)
1935	0.18 (0.15)	0.73 (0.39)	−0.14 (−0.10)	1.22 (0.74)
1940	0.19 (0.14)	0.71 (0.38)	−0.13 (−0.09)	1.20 (0.68)
1945	0.13 (0.09)	0.69 (0.45)	−0.09 (−0.07)	1.12 (0.65)
1950	0.18 (0.14)	0.73 (0.39)	−0.15 (−0.10)	1.22 (0.69)
1955	0.28 (0.24)	0.53 (0.33)	−0.16 (−0.14)	1.26 (0.94)
1960	0.28 (0.21)	0.57 (0.32)	−0.12 (−0.10)	1.19 (0.81)
1965	0.28 (0.23)	0.56 (0.32)	−0.08 (−0.07)	1.14 (0.79)

Notes: 1. $TiQ = \partial \dot{T}_i / \partial \dot{Q}$, $TiL = \partial \dot{T}_i / \partial \dot{L}$.
2. Derived from Residual method (no parentheses) and Verdoorn method (Parentheses).

The elasticity values of Table 7-4 allow us to solve Eqs. (7.3) and (7.4) to obtain the Residual method's estimates of the indirect contribution of population *cum* labor growth to the growth of per capita income ($CEPop_1$), agricultural output ($CY_1 Pop_1$), and non-agricultural output ($CY_2 Pop_1$). These respective estimates are given in columns (2), (9), and (16) of Table 7-5. $CEPop_1$, for example, equals the sum of Q's contribution to $\dot{E}$ via $\dot{T}_1$, L's contribution to $\dot{E}$ via $\dot{T}_1$, Q's contribution to $\dot{E}$ via $\dot{T}_2$ and L's contribution to $\dot{E}$ via $\dot{T}_2$, as in Eq. (7.3). $CEPop_1$ is positive in each decade, ranging from a low of 0.15% per year (1940–1950) to a high of 2.56 (1950–1960). The indirect contribution of population *cum* labor growth to the growth of agricultural output ($CY_1 Pop_1$) and non-agricultural output ($CY_2 Pop_1$) is also positive in each decade. $CY_1 Pop_1$ ranges from 0.32 (1940–1950) to 1.06% per year (1930–1940) and $CY_2 Pop_1$ ranges from 0.12 (1940–1950) to 2.86 (1950–1960).

Table 7-5 Total Contribution of Population *Cum* Labor Growth to Per Capita Income and Sectoral Output Growth

(% per year)

Decade	Direct Contribution to Per Capita Income Growth ($CEPop_D$)	Indirect Contribution to Per Capita Income Growth ($CEPop_I$)			Total Contribution to Per Capita Income Growth ($COPop_T$)		
	(1)	Residual Method (2)	Verdoorn Method (3)	Factor Augmenting Rate Method (4)	Residual Method (5) $(1)+(2)$	Verdoorn Method (6) $(1)+(3)$	Factor Augmenting Rate Method (7) $(1)+(4)$
1880–1890	−0.59	0.55	0.38	0.99	−0.04	−0.21	0.40
1890–1900	−0.66	0.66	0.40	0.97	0.00	−0.26	0.31
1900–1910	−1.10	0.38	0.18	1.00	−0.72	−0.92	−0.10
1910–1920	−0.95	0.65	0.34	0.97	−0.30	−0.61	0.02
1920–1930	−1.11	0.97	0.59	0.93	−0.14	−0.52	−0.18
1930–1940	−0.20	1.74	1.01	0.93	1.54	0.81	0.73
1940–1950	−1.56	0.15	0.07	0.91	−1.41	−1.49	−0.65
1950–1960	0.43	2.56	1.88	0.93	2.99	2.31	1.36
1960–1970	−0.21	1.44	0.98	0.89	1.23	0.77	0.68
Average	−0.65	1.01	0.65	0.95	0.35	0.01	0.29

(*Continued*)

Table 7-5 *(Continued)*

Decade	Direct Contribution to Agric. Output Growth ($CY_1 Pop_D$)	Indirect Contribution to Agric. Output Growth ($CY_1 Pop_1$)			Total Contribution to Agric. Output Growth ($CY_1 Pop_T$)		
	(8)	Residual Method	Verdoorn Method	Factor Augmenting Rate Method	Residual Method	Verdoorn Method	Factor Augmenting Rate Method
		(9)	(10)	(11)	(12) $(8)+(9)$	(13) $(8)+(10)$	(14) $(8)+(11)$
1880–1890	0.33	0.47	0.28	0.93	0.80	0.61	1.26
1890–1900	0.37	0.56	0.31	0.92	0.93	0.68	1.29
1900–1910	0.35	0.43	0.28	0.88	0.78	0.63	1.23
1910–1920	0.45	0.56	0.35	0.86	1.01	0.80	1.31
1920–1930	0.71	0.77	0.51	0.84	1.48	1.22	1.55
1930–1940	0.88	1.06	0.62	0.82	1.94	1.50	1.70
1940–1950	0.28	0.32	0.20	0.81	0.60	0.48	1.09
1950–1960	1.35	1.03	0.69	0.74	2.38	2.04	2.09
1960–1970	0.87	0.72	0.46	0.71	1.59	1.33	1.58
Average	0.62	0.66	0.41	0.83	1.28	1.03	1.46

(Continued)

Table 7-5 (*Continued*)

Decade	Direct Contribution to Non-agric. Output Growth $(CY_2 Pop_D)$ (15)	Indirect Contribution to Non-agric. Output Growth $(CY_2 Pop_I)$			Total Contribution to Non-agric. Output Growth $(CY_2 Pop_T)$		
		Residual Method (16)	Verdoorn Method (17)	Factor Augmenting Rate Method (18)	Residual Method (19) (15) + (16)	Verdoorn Method (20) (15) + (17)	Factor Augmenting Rate Method (21) (15) + (18)
1880–1890	0.29	0.60	0.43	1.03	0.89	0.72	1.32
1890–1900	0.32	0.71	0.45	0.99	1.03	0.77	1.31
1900–1910	0.03	0.35	0.16	1.04	0.38	0.19	1.07
1910–1920	0.18	0.66	0.33	1.00	0.84	0.51	1.18
1920–1930	0.43	1.03	0.64	0.97	1.46	1.07	1.40
1930–1940	0.91	1.85	1.10	0.95	2.76	2.01	1.86
1940–1950	−0.01	0.12	0.04	0.90	0.11	0.03	0.89
1950–1960	1.70	2.86	2.10	0.97	4.56	3.80	2.67
1960–1970	0.89	1.49	1.01	0.90	2.38	1.90	1.79
Average	0.53	1.07	0.70	0.97	1.60	1.22	1.50

The second approach used to estimate the indirect contribution of the growth of population and labor to the growth of per capita income and sectoral output is the Verdoorn method. In each sector, we assume that technical change is a function of the square root of output, which in turn depends on population growth, as in the following four equations:

$$T_1 = a_1' Y_1^{1/2}, \tag{7.11}$$

$$Y_1 = B_1' T_1^{\alpha_1'} L^{\beta_1'} Q^{\gamma_1'} T_2^{\delta_1'}, \tag{7.12}$$

$$T_2 = a_2' Y_2^{1/2}, \tag{7.13}$$

$$Y_2 = B_2' T_1^{\alpha_2'} L^{\beta_2'} Q^{\gamma_2'} T_2^{\delta_2'}. \tag{7.14}$$

These four equations can be transformed into the following two equations:

$$T_1 = A_1' L^{(\beta_1' + \delta_1' m')/(2 - \alpha_1')} Q^{(\gamma_1' + \delta_1' n')/(2 - \alpha_1')}, \tag{7.15}$$

$$T_2 = A_2' L^{m'} Q^{n'}. \tag{7.16}$$

where

$$m' = (\alpha_2' \beta_1' + 2\beta_2' - \alpha_1' \beta_2')/(4 - 2\alpha_1' - \alpha_2' \delta_1' - 2\delta_2' + \alpha_1' \delta_2'),$$

$$n' = (\alpha_2' \gamma_1' + 2\gamma_2' - \alpha_1' \gamma_2')/(4 - 2\alpha_1' - \alpha_2' \delta_1' - 2\delta_2' + \alpha_1' \delta_2'),$$

and where A_i' includes the constant plus all other terms, with the exception of technical change in each sector, population and total labor.

The parameter values needed to solve Eqs. (7.15) and (7.16) are the growth rate multipliers given for agricultural and non-agricultural outputs in Table 7-1. Solving these equations yields elasticity values of agricultural and non-agricultural technical changes with respect to population and labor growth. These elasticities are also reported in Table 7-4 (in parentheses, for each five-year period, 1880–1965). As with the Residual method, the rate of agricultural technical change is positively influenced by both population and labor growth, while the rate of non-agricultural technical change is influenced negatively by population growth but positively by labor growth. The elasticity values of Table 7-4 allow us to solve Eqs. (7.3) and (7.4) to obtain the Verdoorn method's estimates of the indirect contribution of population *cum* labor growth to the growth of per capita income ($CEPop_1$), agricultural output ($CY_1 Pop_1$) and non-agricultural output ($CY_2 Pop_1$). These estimates are given in columns (3), (10) and (17) of Table 7-5 respectively. As with the Residual method, the indirect contribution of population *cum* labor growth to per capita income and sectoral output growth is positive in each decade. $CEPop_1$ ranges from a low of 0.07% per year to a high of 1.88%, CY_1Pop_1 from 0.20 to 0.69%, and CY_2Pop_1 from 0.04 to 2.10%. In each case the lows are in 1940–1950 and the highs in 1950–1960.

The final approach used to estimate the indirect contribution of the growth of population and labor to the growth of per capita income and sectoral output is the factor augmenting rate method. We used the following equations to calculate the contribution of capital and labor *cum* population growth to the rate of agricultural and non-agricultural technical changes:

$$\dot{T}_1 = \lambda_K \beta + \lambda_L \alpha, \tag{7.17}$$

$$\dot{T}_2 = \lambda_K \delta + \lambda_L \gamma. \tag{7.18}$$

where $\dot{T}_1$ ($\dot{T}_2$) equals the rate of technical change in the agricultural (non-agricultural) sector, λ_K (λ_L) is capital's (labor *cum* population's) rate of factor augmentation, β (α) is the factor share of capital (labor *cum* population) in the agricultural sector, and δ (γ) is the factor share of capital (labor *cum* population) in the non-agricultural sector.

Note that these equations assume identical factor augmenting rates (λ_K, λ_L) in both sectors. This implies either that technical change can be transferred between sectors or that the rates happen to coincide. In either case, this precluded varying rates of technical change between the two sectors, unlike with our own model where technical change is assumed to be sector specific. The contribution of the growth of labor *cum* population ($\dot{L}$) to the rate of agricultural technical change ($\dot{T}_1$) equals the elasticity of $\dot{T}_1$ with respect to $\dot{L}$ ($\partial \dot{T}_1/\partial \dot{L}$) multiplied by $\dot{L}$. In Eq. (7.17), labor *cum* population's contribution to the rate of agricultural technical change is represented by $\lambda_L \alpha$. Similarly, the contribution of $\dot{L}$ to the rate of non-agricultural technical change ($\dot{T}_2$) equals the elasticity of $\dot{T}_2$ with respect to $\dot{L}$ ($\partial \dot{T}_2/\partial \dot{L}$) multiplied by $\dot{L}$. This is represented in Eq. (7.18) by $\lambda_L \gamma$. Thus, the factor augmenting rate method allows us to rewrite Eqs. (7.3) and (7.4) as Eqs. (7.19) and (7.20) respectively.

$$CEPop_1 = (ET_1)\lambda_L \alpha + (ET_2)\lambda_L \gamma, \tag{7.19}$$

$$CY_iPop_1 = (Y_iT_1)\lambda_L \alpha + (Y_iT_2)\lambda_L \gamma. \tag{7.20}$$

Using Eqs. (7.17) and (7.18), given values for $\dot{T}_1$ and $\dot{T}_2$ (from Table 2-5) and values of factor shares (from Table 2-4),[8] we can solve for λ_L. Rather than determine values of λ_L for each decade, an average value over the period 1880–1970 is used. This is because L is most appropriately viewed as a long-term efficiency measure, in that increased efficiency of machinery and labor must usually be preceded by a lengthy period of research, education, or training. The calculation of λ_L depends on the values of $\dot{T}_1$ and $\dot{T}_2$ [Eqs. (7.17) and (7.18)]. But the values of $\dot{T}_1$ and $\dot{T}_2$ (particularly $\dot{T}_2$) fluctuate fairly widely in the short run more than can be reasonably expected to fluctuate. Hence, an average value is calculated for λ_L and equals 1.2.[9] Having calculated λ_L, we now solve Eqs. (7.19) and (7.20) to determine the indirect contribution of population *cum* labor growth on the growth of per capita income and sectoral output. This is done for each decade,[10] 1880–1970, and the results are reported in Table 7-5.

As with the Residual and Verdoorn methods, the indirect contribution of population *cum* labor growth to the growth of per capita income ($CEPop_1$), agricultural output (CY_1Pop_1), and non-agricultural output (CY_2Pop_1) is positive in each decade. $CEPop_1$ ranges from a low of 0.89% per year (1960–1970) to a high of 1% (1900–1910), CY_1Pop_1 from 0.71% (1960–1970) to 0.93% (1880–1990), and CY_2Pop_1 from 0.90% (1945–1950) and

---

[8]For each decade, the factor share of the median year is used. In the non-agricultural sector, the factor shares (γ and δ) are simply the values shown in Table 2-4. In the agricultural sector, it is necessary to account for the fact that land is included in the production function. The factor share of land is apportioned to labor and capital according to the proportion of labor and capital's individual factor shares to the sum of their factor shares. This portion of land's share is added to the values of α and β shown in Table 2-4. For example, the factor share for labor used in 1880–1890 is 0.83. This equals 0.57 (1885's value in Table 2-4) plus 0.26 which is labor's proportion (0.57/0.69) of land's factor share (0.31).

[9]This value of λ_L (=1.2) comes from substituting average values into Eqs. (7.17) and (7.18) and solving them: $1.6 = \lambda_K(0.16) + \lambda_L(0.84)$ and $2.0 = \lambda_K(0.32) + \lambda_L(0.68)$.

[10]Average values are used for λ_L (=1.2) and the factor shares (α, γ), while values for each decade are used for the growth rate multipliers (ET_1 and ET_2). GRM values used for each decade are the median years (from Table 7-1). The values of factor shares for each decade are also median years (from Table 2-4). Also, population *cum* labor may have an effect on the value of λ_K through new housing investment and equipment investment. However, it would be difficult to capture this effect in our model and would go beyond the scope of our study. Therefore, we follow the same approach as in ordinary growth theory: Kelley and Williamson [1971; 1974], Minami and Ono [1972a, b], and Ogawa and Suits [1982].

(1960–1970) to 1.04% (1900–1910).[11] Table 7-5 sums the direct and indirect contributions of population *cum* labor growth to the growth of per capita income and sectoral output to obtain their total contribution. This is done for each of the three methods used to estimate the indirect contribution. With respect to per capita income growth. In the early decades studied, 1880–1930, the negative direct contribution ($CEPop_D$) tends to dominate the positive indirect contribution ($CEPop_I$) under the Residual and Verdoorn methods, yielding a total contribution ($CEPop_T$) which tends to be negative.

Under the factor augmenting rate method, $CEPop_T$ during this period is positive in three decades (1880–1990, 1890–1900, and 1910–1920) and negative in two (1900–1910 and 1920–1930). However, in the later decades studied, 1930–1970, $CEpop_T$ is positive under each of the three methods in each decades, with the exception of the period of World War II (1940–1950), when it is strongly negative. Over the entire period, 1880–1970, the average of $CEPop_T$ is positive under the Residual method (0.35), the factor augmenting rate method (0.29) and the Verdoorn method (0.01). If the decade of World War II were excluded from the average, then the average of $CEPop_T$ would be more positive under the Verdoorn method (0.17). The total contribution of population *cum* labor growth to both agricultural output growth (CY_1Pop_T) and non-agricultural output growth (CY_2Pop_T) is positive in each decade, the contribution to the latter being the largest.[12] Under the Residual, Verdoorn, and factor augmenting rate methods, CY_1Pop_T averages 1.28, 1.03, and 1.46% per year, while CY_2Pop_T averages 1.60, 1.22, and 1.50%, respectively.

---

[11]The indirect contribution of population *cum* labor growth to per capita income and sectoral output growth will of course vary with varying economic and social conditions. In Japan, this indirect contribution would likely have been less were it not for the education, motivation, and adaptive capabilities of its population.

[12]Although the direct contribution of population *cum* labor growth tended to be less for non-agricultural than for agricultural output growth [given that population (Q) affected the former negatively but the latter positively], the indirect contribution, tended to be larger. The larger indirect contribution to output growth in the non-agricultural sector arose because Y_2T_2 exceeded Y_1T_1 and the cross effects of technical change in one sector on output growth in the other were asymmetric (*i.e.*, Y_1T_2 was negative while Y_2T_1 was positive). These asymmetric cross effects resulted from the push and pull of agricultural resources on the non-agricultural sector caused by sectoral technical change.

3.2. Sensitivity Analysis of Growth Rate Multipliers, and Some Policy Implications

This section examines sensitivity results to show how the influence of population *cum* labor on economic development (as measured by GRM values), is affected by the parameter values. The theoretical values of GRM can be calculated from A^{-1} matrix as follows:

$$ET_1 = [(\eta + 1 - \lambda)(\gamma\, l_1 + \delta k_1) - \eta\lambda]/|A|, \tag{7.21}$$

$$ET_2 = [(\eta + 1 - \lambda)(\alpha l_2 + \beta k_2) + \eta(\lambda - 1)]/|A|, \tag{7.22}$$

$$EQ = [(\eta + 1 - \lambda)\{(\gamma - \alpha)l_2 + (\delta - \beta)k_2\}$$
$$+ \lambda - 1]/|A|, \tag{7.23}$$

$$EL = [(\beta\gamma - \alpha\delta)(1 + \eta - \lambda)k_2$$
$$+ \{\alpha + \eta(\alpha - \gamma)\}(1 - \lambda)]/|A|, \tag{7.24}$$

$$Y_1 T_1 = [\{\varepsilon(1 - \lambda) + \eta\}(\gamma\, l_1 + \delta k_1) - \eta]/|A|, \tag{7.25}$$

$$Y_1 T_2 = [\varepsilon(1 - \lambda) + \eta](\alpha l_2 + \beta k_2)/|A|, \tag{7.26}$$

$$Y_1 Q = [(1 - \varepsilon)(\alpha l_2 + \beta k_2)]/|A|, \tag{7.27}$$

$$Y_1 L = [\{\varepsilon\beta\gamma\,(1 - \lambda) + \eta(\beta\gamma - \alpha\delta) + \alpha\varepsilon(1 - \lambda)(\gamma - 1)\}k_2$$
$$+ \alpha\varepsilon(1 - \lambda)]/|A|, \tag{7.28}$$

$$L_1 T_1 = [(\varepsilon\lambda - \eta - 1)l_2]/|A|, \tag{7.29}$$

$$L_1 T_2 = [\eta + \varepsilon(1 - \lambda)]l_2/|A|, \tag{7.30}$$

$$L_1 Q = [1 - \varepsilon]l_2/|A|, \tag{7.31}$$

$$L_1 L = [\{\delta\varepsilon(\lambda - 1) + \eta(\beta - \delta) + \beta(1 - \lambda\varepsilon)\}k_2$$
$$+ \varepsilon(1 - \lambda)]/|A|, \tag{7.32}$$

$$L_2 T_1 = [1 - \varepsilon\lambda + \eta]l_1/|A|, \tag{7.33}$$

$$L_2 T_2 = [\varepsilon(\lambda - 1) - \eta]l_1/|A|, \tag{7.34}$$

$$L_2 Q = [\varepsilon - 1]l_1/|A|, \tag{7.35}$$

$$L_2 L = [\{\delta\varepsilon(\lambda - 1) + \eta(\beta - \delta) + \beta(1 - \varepsilon\lambda)\}k_2$$
$$+ \delta\varepsilon(1 - \lambda) + \eta(\alpha - \gamma) + \alpha(1 - \varepsilon\lambda)]/\,|A|, \tag{7.36}$$

where

$$|A| = (\alpha + \beta)(1 + \eta - \lambda\varepsilon) - \eta$$
$$+ [-\alpha - \eta(\alpha - \gamma) + \varepsilon\{\gamma + (\alpha - \gamma)\lambda\}]l_1$$
$$+ [-\beta - \eta(\beta - \delta) + \varepsilon\{\delta + (\beta - \delta)\lambda\}k_1].$$

They allow us to determine how the direct and indirect influence of population *cum* labor on economic development is affected by changes in the parameter values. From these theoretical values of GRM, we can see that the negative direct effect of population *cum* labor on per capita income $(EQ + EL)$ becomes more negative as λ, l_1, k_1 and δ increase and less negative as ε, $|\eta|$, α, β and γ increase. The direct effect of population *cum* labor on agricultural output $(Y_1Q + Y_1L)$ would increase as α, β, γ and δ increase and would decrease as ε, $|\eta|$, λ, l_1 and k_1 increase. The direct effect of population *cum* labor on non-agricultural output $(Y_2Q + Y_2L)$ would increase as ε, $|\eta|$, λ, α, β, γ and δ increase and would decrease as l_1 and k_1 increase. Taking ε's effect on $EQ + EL$ as an example, we can show that ε is not included in the numerator of either EQ or EL, only in the denominator $|A|$.

Thus, we can determine ε's effect on $EQ + EL$ by determining its effect on $|A|$. Differentiating $|A|$ with respect to ε gives a positive result, judging from the ranges of the parameter values in Table 2-4, as in Eq. (7.37):

$$\partial|A|/\partial\varepsilon = (\alpha + \beta)(-\lambda) + [\gamma + (\alpha - \gamma)\lambda]l_1 + [\delta + (\beta - \delta)\lambda]k_1 > 0.$$
$$(7.37)$$

Increases in $|A|$ imply a value for $EQ + EL$ which is less negative. Thus, as ε increases, $EQ + EL$ becomes less negative. Similarly, we can show the effect of ε on $(Y_1Q + Y_1L)$ and on $(Y_2Q + Y_2L)$ as well as the effects of the other parameters. Table 7-6 reports the results of sensitivity runs for the year 1880 involving a single parameter, in turn, set equal to zero. The 1880 base values of the parameters are also shown. First the direct influences of population *cum* labor on per capita income $(EQ + EL)$, agricultural output $(Y_1Q + Y_1L)$, and non-agricultural output $(Y_2Q + Y_2L)$ are shown. For example, if α (labor's share in agricultural output) were reduced to zero (from 0.58) holding all other parameters at their base values, the value of $(EQ + EL)$ would change from -0.30 to -0.59.

Table 7-6   Sensitivity Analysis of the Direct and Indirect Effects of Population *cum* Labor on Per Capita Income and Sectoral Output

(% per year)

	Base[a]	$\alpha=0$	$\beta=0$	$\gamma=0$	$\delta=0$	$\eta=0$	$\varepsilon=0$	$l_1=0$	$k_1=0$	$\lambda=0$
$EQ+EL$	-0.30	-0.59	-0.31	-0.62	-0.29	-0.39	-0.48	-0.27	-0.30	-0.27
Y_1Q+Y_1L	0.60	0.01	0.59	0.31	0.51	0.69	0.79	0.62	0.60	0.62
Y_2Q+Y_2L	0.79	0.79	0.79	-0.02	0.63	0.53	0.25	0.84	0.80	0.73
T_1Q	0.17[b]	0.17	0.17	0.13	0.16	0.07	-20.03	0.34	0.16	0.05
	(0.14)[c]	(0.04)	(0.10)	(0.08)	(0.13)	(0.06)	(-26.41)	(0.23)	(0.16)	(0.04)
T_1L	0.68	0.68	0.68	0.70	0.65	0.93	35.77	0.37	0.69	0.93
	(0.34)	(-0.07)	(0.41)	(0.22)	(0.30)	(0.57)	(39.45)	(0.20)	(0.31)	(0.55)
T_2Q	-0.43	-0.43	-0.43	-0.32	-0.42	-0.16	49.03	0.00	-0.42	-0.13
	(-0.39)	(-0.39)	(-0.39)	(-0.02)	(-0.33)	(-0.16)	(74.24)	(-0.02)	(-0.33)	(-0.13)
T_2L	1.80	1.80	1.80	0.19	1.49	1.17	-84.12	1.00	0.18	1.17
	(1.50)	(1.50)	(1.50)	(0.00)	(1.17)	(0.86)	(-108.40)	(0.88)	(1.39)	(0.92)
$EPop_1$	1.23	1.28	1.25	0.35	1.03	1.11	-20.38	0.76	1.19	1.19
	(0.90)	(0.68)	(0.93)	(0.14)	(0.70)	(0.72)	(-21.68)	(0.56)	(0.84)	(0.86)
Y_1Pop_1	0.71	0.81	0.75	0.84	0.72	0.88	27.56	0.49	0.69	0.93
	(0.37)	(-0.06)	(0.43)	(0.31)	(0.35)	(0.57)	(25.30)	(0.24)	(0.34)	(0.57)
Y_2Pop_1	1.76	1.76	1.76	-0.14	1.33	1.33	-68.31	1.02	1.69	1.19
	(1.43)	(1.43)	(1.43)	(-0.02)	(1.05)	(0.86)	(-68.65)	(0.88)	(1.33)	(0.86)

Notes:

[a]The base values of the parameters for 1880 (from Table 2-4) are:

α (labor's share in agricultural output)   = 0.58
β (capital's share in agricultural output)   = 0.12
γ (labor's share in non-agricultural output)   = 0.80
δ (capital's share in non-agricultural output)   = 0.20
η (relative price elasticity of agricultural goods) = −0.60

ε (income elasticity of agricultural goods)   = 0.80
l_1 (proportion of labor in agriculture)   = 0.71
k_1 (proportion of capital in agriculture)   = 0.43
λ (share of income produced by agriculture) = 0.50

[b]Residual method.
[c]Verdoorn method in parentheses.

The indirect influence of population *cum* labor on per capita income ($EPop_1$) and sectoral output ($Y_i Pop_1$) can be written as in Eqs. (7.38) and (7.39):

$$EPop_1 = ET_1(T_1Q + T_1L) + ET_2(T_2Q + T_2L), \qquad (7.38)$$

$$Y_i Pop_1 = Y_i T_1(T_1Q + T_1L) + Y_i T_2(T_2Q + T_2L). \qquad (7.39)$$

The theoretical values of ET_1, ET_2, $Y_i T_1$ and $Y_i T_2$ can be obtained from the theoretical values of GRM. $T_i Q$ and $T_i L$ can be calculated from Eqs. (7.9), (7.10), (7.15), and (7.16) as follows: $T_1Q = (\gamma_1 + \delta_1 n)/(1 - \alpha)$, $T_1L = (\beta_1 + \delta_1 m)/(1 - \alpha_1)$, $T_2Q = n$, and $T_2L = m$ where m and n are defined as on Table 7-4 (Residual method), and $T_1Q = (\gamma_1' + \delta_1' n\prime)/(2 - \alpha_1')$, and $T_1L = (\beta_1' + \delta_1' m\prime)/(2 - \alpha_1')$, $T_2Q = n'$, and $T_2L = m'$ where m' and n' are defined as on Table 7-4 (Verdoorn method). Also α_i, β_i, γ_i and δ_i *etc.* are defined (as GRMs) as follows:

$$\alpha_i = L_i T_1, \quad \beta_i = L_i L, \quad \gamma_i = L_i Q, \quad \delta_i = L_i T_2, \quad \alpha_i' = Y_i T_1,$$

$$\beta_i' = Y_i L, \quad \gamma_i' = Y_i Q, \quad \delta_i' = Y_i T_2.$$

As shown earlier, the indirect effects of population *cum* labor depend on $T_i Q$ and $T_i L$, which include a number of parameters which are also GRM. However, sensitivity results of Q and L's influence on sectoral technical change (T_1Q, T_1L, T_2Q, T_2L), and the indirect influence of population *cum* labor on per capita income ($EPop_1$), agricultural output ($Y_1 Pop_1$), and non-agricultural output ($Y_2 Pop_1$) are also reported in Table 7-6 for both Residual method (no parentheses) and the Verdoorn method (in parentheses). For example, lowering α to zero while holding other parameters constant causes $EPop_1$ to increase from 1.23 to 1.28 under the Residual method and to decrease from 0.90 to 0.68 under the Verdoorn method. Therefore, we can summarize the effects of nine parameters on the indirect effects of population *cum* labor as follows: For the Residual method, the indirect effect of population *cum* labor on per capita income ($EPop_1$) would increase when all parameters except α and β increase. The indirect effect of population *cum* labor on agricultural output ($Y_1 Pop_1$) would increase when l_1 and k_1 increase and would decrease when ε, $|\eta|$, λ, α, β, γ and δ increase. The indirect effect of population *cum* labor on non-agricultural output ($Y_2 Pop_1$) would increase when ε, $|\eta|$, λ, γ, δ, l_1 and k_1 increase. α and β have no effect on Y_2.

For the Verdoorn method, the indirect effect of population *cum* labor on per capita income ($EPop_1$) would increase when all parameters except β increase. The indirect effect of population *cum* labor on agricultural output ($Y_1 Pop_1$) would increase when α, γ, δ, l_1 and k_1 increase and would decrease when β, ε, $|\eta|$, λ increase. The indirect effect of population *cum* labor on non-agricultural output ($Y_2 Pop_1$) would increase when ε, $|\eta|$, λ, γ, δ, l_1 and k_1 increase. α and β have no effect on Y_2. We can summarize the sensitivity results of Table 7-6 for the case of population *cum* labor's influence on per capita income as follows. Both the direct and indirect influence would decrease when ε, $|\eta|$, α and γ decrease (with the exception of the indirect influence of α under the Residual method). The direct influence would increase and the indirect influence would decrease when l_1, k_1, λ and δ decrease. The direct influence would decrease and the indirect influence would increase when β decreases.

A number of implications can be derived from the sensitivity results reported above, including the following: (1) The total influence (*i.e.*, direct plus indirect) of population *cum* labor on per capita income will be larger the higher the agricultural income elasticity (ε) and price elasticity ($|\eta|$). (2) In most cases, the total influence of population *cum* labor on per capita income will be larger the higher labor's share in both agriculture (α) and non-agriculture (γ). (3) As l_1, k_1 and λ increase, the direct influence of population *cum* labor on per capita income becomes more negative while the indirect influence becomes more positive. This implies that in the early stages of economic development (when l_1, k_1 and λ are relatively large) the total influence of population can be expected to be negative in economies lacking the capacity (*e.g.*, educational opportunities) for their population to increase the rate of technical change and thereby capture the positive indirect influence of population growth.

As well as considering how parameter values affect the influence of population *cum* labor on economic development, we need to consider how they affect the influence of technical change on development. For example, as ε increases, the influence of technical change in both sectors on per capita income (ET_1, ET_2) decreases.[13] Also, ET_1 decreases and ET_2 increases

---

[13]Increases in ε must increase the elasticities $T_1 Q$, $T_1 L$, $T_2 Q$ and/or $T_2 L$ enough to offset the decrease in ET_1 and ET_2 [in Eq. (7.38)]. Otherwise, increasing ε would not cause the indirect influence of population *cum* labor on per capita income ($EPop_T$) to become more positive.

with increases in $|\eta|$ and α and decreases in γ. Although increases in agricultural income and price elasticities increase the influence of population *cum* labor on per capita income, it is important to note that they reduce the influence of technical change on per capita income. This implies that in economies where the rates of technical change in both sectors exceed population growth, policies which reduce agricultural elasticities (perhaps by providing a demonstration effect for non-agricultural goods) may be recommended. But in economies with low rates of technical change, policies which reduce agricultural elasticities are to be avoided. This further implies that in the early stages of economic development, when the direct influence of population *cum* labor is highly negative and the rates of technical change tend to be low, policies which increase agricultural income and price elasticities should be seriously considered.

Conclusion

Throughout history the prevailing view of the economic effects of population growth has wavered from optimism to pessimism. Examples of the former include the ancient Greek and Roman views in which people were considered the source of power. The mercantilists and Adam Smith are also considered optimistic populationists. However, conventional wisdom today follows Malthus in viewing the economic effects of population growth negatively. But Simon has challenged the Malthusian view, predicting that population growth has a positive effect on per capita income, at least in the long run. This chapter measured the total contribution (including both positive and negative effects) of population *cum* labor growth on per capita income and sectoral output growth in Japan over the period 1880–1970. It used a two-sector growth accounting model. The model treated population and labor growth as separate variables so their contributions to per capita income and sectoral output growth could be estimated separately.

(1) The first step was to estimate the direct contribution of population *cum* labor growth to per capita income and sectoral output growth. The next step was to estimate the indirect contribution, via population and labor's influence on technical change in each sector. Three alternative methods were employed: the Residual method, the Verdoorn method, and the factor augmenting rate method. Each of the methods yielded consistent results.

(2) The next step was to obtain the total contribution of population *cum* labor growth to per capita income and sectoral output growth by combining their direct and indirect contributions. With respect to per capita income growth, the total contribution of population *cum* labor growth tended to be negative in the decades 1880–1930 and positive in the decades 1930–1970, with the exception of 1940–1950. However, over the period 1880–1970 population *cum* labor growth on average tended to make a positive contribution to per capita income growth under the Residual method (0.35% per year), the factor augmenting rate method (0.29% per year), and the Verdoorn method (0.01% per year).

(3) Population *cum* labor growth contributed positively to sectoral output growth. The average contribution to agricultural output growth ranged from 1.03 (Verdoorn) to 1.46% per year (factor augmenting rate), while the average contribution to non-agricultural output growth ranged from 1.22 (Verdoorn) to 1.60% per year (Residual). These results are of course dependent on our model and the particular data set used. Therefore, the results of a sensitivity analysis were reported to show how growth rate multiplier values are affected by changes in the parameters. Each of the three methods used to estimate the indirect contribution of population *cum* labor growth to per capita income and sectoral output growth was necessarily arbitrary and involved certain assumptions. However, the fact that each of three very different methods yielded consistent results provides fairly substantive evidence that population *cum* labor growth made a positive contribution to per capita income and sectoral output growth in Japan over the period 1880–1970.

(4) A number of implications can be derived from the sensitivity results reported above, including the following: (i) The total influence (*i.e.*, direct plus indirect) of population *cum* labor on per capita income will be positively associated with agricultural income elasticity (ε) and price elasticity ($|\eta|$). (ii) In most cases, the total influence of population *cum* labor on per capita income will be positively associated with both agricultural (α) and non-agricultural (γ) labor share. (iii) As l_1, k_1 and λ increase, the direct influence of population *cum* labor on per capita income becomes more negative, while its indirect influence becomes more positive. This implies that in the early stages of economic development (when l_1, k_1 and λ are relatively large) the total influence of

population is expected to be negative in economies that lack the capacity (*e.g.*, educational opportunities) for an increased rate of technical change across the population and thereby capture the positive, indirect influence of population growth.

(5) As well as considering how parameter values modulate the influence of population *cum* labor on economic development, we need to consider how they affect the influence of technical change on development. For example, as ε increases, the influence of technical change in both sectors on per capita income (ET_1, ET_2) decreases. Further, ET_1 decreases and ET_2 increases with increased $|\eta|$ and α and decreased γ. Although increases in agricultural income and price elasticity increase the influence of population *cum* labor on per capita income, it is important to note that they reduce the influence of technical change on per capita income. This implies that in economies where the rates of technical change in both sectors exceed population growth, policies that reduce agricultural elasticities (perhaps by providing a demonstration effect for non-agricultural goods) may be recommended. However, in economies with low rates of technical change, policies that reduce agricultural elasticities are to be avoided. This further implies that in the early stages of economic development, when the direct influence of population *cum* labor is highly negative, and the rates of technical change tend to be low, policies that increase agricultural income and price elasticities should be seriously considered. Finally, some policy implications suggested by the results were noted.

Summaries (1)–(5) are very clear. The following two points here are noteworthy. First, the negative contribution of population *cum* labor was largest (in terms of absolute value) earlier in economic development. However, the positive indirect contribution of population *cum* labor was larger in early economic development. This indirect contribution of population *cum* labor resulted from education, which created technical change. Therefore, in this chapter, we reconfirm that the education is critically important, especially early in economic development. Second, in the good economic conditions of the early stage of economic development, when the rate of technical change exceeds that of population growth, policies that demonstrate non-agricultural goods and increase the demand for non-agricultural goods are recommended. Similarly, in an economy that is not in such good condition, such as when the rate of population growth exceeds that of technical change, policies that promote increased consumption of agricultural goods are recommended. These policy implications would be very helpful to facilitate the economic development of developing countries.

Chapter 8

The Effects of Adult Longevity
on the National Saving Rate*

Introduction

In this chapter, we analyze steady state and out-of-steady-state effects of
the transition in adult longevity on the national saving rate using historical
data and international panel data. In the 20th century, many countries experienced mortality transition. During the first stage, mortality, especially infant
mortality, declines rapidly. Adult mortality declines after a while, and life
expectancy increases with gains in survival at older ages at the later stage of
mortality transition. As a result of demographic transition, many developed
countries experience population aging. Increases in the national saving rate
in the 20th century were also remarkable in many countries. With such
trends of life expectancy and the national saving rate in mind, the following questions are important to solve. First, how does higher life expectancy
influence the national saving rate? Second, how does a rapid increase in
life expectancy affect the national saving rate? Throughout this chapter, we
seek answers to these questions both theoretically and empirically. In the
beginning, we explain the effect of an increase in adult life expectancy on
the national saving rate in the steady state and out of steady state. Then, we
analyze the implications of the theory using historical data and world panel
data. To sum up, we find that rise in adult life expectancy has a large and
statistically significant effect on aggregate saving. The effects have been
especially pronounced in East Asia, given that mortality transition was very

*The content of this chapter was developed and rewritten from Kinugasa and Mason [2007]
to meet the purpose of the book. We appreciate *World Development* and Professor Mason
for permitting the use of this paper for this book.

rapid here. Further, gains in life expectancy are much more important than declines in child dependency. Population aging may not lead to lower saving rates in the future if life expectancy and the duration of retirement continue to increase.

1. Theoretical Background[1]

1.1. *Literature Reviews*

One of the most salient features of modern economic development is the increase in wealth and capital. In the US, for example, the gross non-residential capital stock grew at 4.1% per annum as compared with annual GDP growth of 3.6% between 1820 and 1992. The experience of the UK was quite similar, while in Japan over a shorter period, 1890 to 1992, the annual rate of growth of capital exceeded the annual rate of growth of GDP by 1.4%. The ratio of the gross non-residential capital stock to GDP increased more than four-fold, from 0.71 to 3.02 (Maddison [1995]). The extraordinary growth in wealth and capital was repeated, in a more condensed form, in the Newly Industrializing Economies. High rates of saving and investment in South Korea, Taiwan, Singapore, and several other Asian countries have led to rapid capital deepening. Why did this occur? The demand side undoubtedly played an important role. Technological innovation led to new and better equipment and machinery. Structural change led to industrialization and the growth of the manufacturing and service sectors with accompanying investment. The possibility explored in this study, however, is that the modern rise in wealth was driven in large part by an important supply side factor — the increase in adult life expectancy.

The proportion of adult life lived after age 60 began to increase steadily in the West in the late 19th century. In other parts of the world, increases began much later — in the middle of the 20th century. Retirement emerged as a significant feature of the lifecycle creating a powerful saving incentive. Institutional responses, the emergence of funded employment-based pension plans, the rise of the commercial financial service sector, the creation of tax incentives, and, in some countries, the establishment of funded

---

[1]Theoretical results are summarized here. More details are available in Kinugasa [2004].

public retirement systems reinforced the effects of increased longevity. Other responses, particularly the creation of transfer-based public pension programs in Latin America, Europe, and to a lesser extent in Japan and the US, undoubtedly undermined the incentive effects of a longer life span. That rising life expectancy leads to higher saving is not a new idea. Yaari's [1965] seminal work established the micro-level theoretical foundation. Since then, other scholars have explored the aggregate effects using steady-state models and simulation analysis (Lee *et al.* [2003]). Previous empirical work supports the existence of an important link between saving and life expectancy (Yaari [1965]; Davies [1981]; Zilcha and Friedman [1985]; Kuehlwein [1993]; Leung [1994]; Borsch-Supan [1996]; Schieber and Shoven [1996]; Bloom *et al.* [2003]; Kageyama [2003]).

The theoretical analysis described briefly in this section employs an overlapping generations (OLG) model which extends previous work to a dynamic context. A unique implication of the model is that the aggregate saving rate is influenced by both the level and the rate of change of adult life expectancy. Given the current level of mortality, countries experiencing rapid mortality transitions will have higher saving rates. The underlying logic behind this result is straight-forward. If a rapid mortality transition country is playing catch-up, the wealth required to support a longer retirement must be accumulated over a shorter period of time. Thus, saving rates must be elevated during the catch-up period.

The empirical analysis relies on two different approaches. Section 2 takes a historical perspective by looking at data for seven countries for which we can track saving and mortality trends over all or a substantial part of the entire demographic transition. In the sub-group of Western countries, adult life expectancy changed very slowly or not at all until the middle or end of the 19th century. Thereafter, life expectancy changed at a pace that was remarkably constant and varied little from one country to the next. The sub-group of Asian countries began their mortality transitions later, went through a catch-up period when adult longevity increased rapidly, followed by a period of steady increase at a rate similar to that found in the West. The difference in the demographic transitions between the West and East Asia offers a useful opportunity to compare the implications of our theoretical model with the experiences of these two groups of countries. Some of the idiosyncratic features of the saving trends are not explained by our model, but there is broad consistency. The increase in adult mortality was accompanied by a rise in aggregate saving rates in most countries. Rapid mortality transition was clearly accompanied by elevated saving rates.

In Sec. 3, we estimate the saving model using aggregate cross-national data. The evidence is consistent and robust in its support of the hypothesis that an increase in old-age survival leads to higher saving rates. In a sub-sample consisting of Western and East Asian countries, the rate of increase in old-age survival also has a positive effect on saving. In other parts of the developing world, however, we do not find evidence that the rate of change in old-age survival has an effect on saving. Why different patterns persist is an issue requiring further exploration and some possibilities are discussed below. Two additional features of the analysis are important. First, several recent studies conclude that changes in age structure, especially the decline in the youth dependency ratio, accounted for high saving rates especially in East Asia (Kelley and Schmidt [1996]; Higgins and Williamson [1997]). Simulation studies (Lee *et al.* [2000; 2001a; 2001b]) and empirical work based on household survey data (Deaton and Paxson [2000]) ascribe a substantially less important role for age structure. The empirical analysis presented here offers some reconciliation of these views. Once we control for adult life expectancy and its rate of change, the youth dependency ratio has a smaller effect than previously estimated. The decline in youth dependency accounts for about one-quarter of the increase in saving rates in East Asia, while changes in adult survival account for about three-quarters of the increase. Second, while some studies conclude that population aging will lead to substantial declines in aggregate saving rates, we do not find this to be the case. So long as adult survival continues to rise — as it has for many decades — population aging will not drive saving rates lower.

1.2. Overlapping Generations Model

Changes in adult survival influence aggregate saving in two ways in the lifecycle model employed here. First, there is a behavioral effect. The expected duration of retirement rises as the survival rate increases. Thus, individuals will consume less and save more during their working years in order to support more expected years of consumption and greater dis-saving during retirement. Second, there is a compositional effect as increases in the adult survival rate lead to an increase in the share of retirees in the adult population. Given that retirees are saving at a lower rate than workers, the compositional effect of an increase in adult survival is to reduce aggregate saving. The net effect on saving is considered in steady state and in dynamic settings. We summarize the dynamics in two ways: first, by considering the effect of a one-time increase in survival and, second, by considering the effect of continuing increases in survival. Considering these alternatives brings a clearer understanding of how the mortality transition — as it is actually evolving — will influence aggregate saving rates.

The behavioral and compositional effects of adult mortality are analyzed using a two-period OLG model. The advantage of this approach is its relative simplicity. A disadvantage is its neglect of another important demographic change — the changes in youth dependency driven by trends in fertility and child mortality. Previous theoretical work has already explored the effects of the number of children on saving in a continuous-age, steady-state framework (Mason [1987]) and in a dynamic OLG framework (Higgins [1994]). The empirical analysis presented below considers the effects of youth dependency relying on the Higgins OLG model. This allows a simpler and more focused theoretical analysis here on changes in adult mortality.

Consider a population consisting of two generations of adults. Each person lives for up to two periods — the first period as a working, prime-age adult and the second period as a retiree. All individuals survive their working period, and q_t survive to the end of their retirement period. The remaining members of the population $(1 - q_t)$ die at the end of the first period of life. In the OLG framework, q_t is the probability of reaching retirement age, the expected years lived during retirement, and the ratio of retirement years to working years for the average member of the population.[2] Individuals cannot foresee whether they will survive, but they know the value of q_t for the population. Costless annuities are available so that individuals protect themselves against longevity risk by purchasing an annuity. Individuals know the interest rate that the annuity will pay. The consumer's optimization problem is to maximize lifetime utility, assuming constant

---

[2]The interpretation of q becomes important in the empirical analysis.

relative risk aversion, $V_t = \frac{c_{\text{ALT},t}^{1-\theta}}{1-\theta} + \delta' q_t \frac{c_{\text{OLD},t+1}^{1-\theta}}{1-\theta}$, given the lifetime budget constraint: $w_t A_t = c_{\text{ALT},t} + \frac{q_t}{1+r_{t+1}} c_{\text{OLD},t+1}$; $c_{\text{ALT},t}$ is consumption while a prime-age adult and $c_{2,t+1}$ is consumption while elderly; δ is the discount factor, defined as $\delta' = 1/(1+\rho)$, where ρ is the discount rate; $1/\theta$ is the intertemporal elasticity of substitution; r_{t+1} is the interest rate; A_t is labor-augmenting technology; and w_t is the wage per unit of effective labor. Kinugasa [2004] shows that the per capita savings of prime-age adults and retirees are:

$$s_{\text{ALT},t} = \Psi_t A_t w_t = \frac{q_t \delta'^{\frac{1}{\theta}} A_t w_t}{q_t \delta'^{\frac{1}{\theta}} + (1+r_{t+1})^{\frac{\theta-1}{\theta}}},$$

$$s_{\text{OLD},t} = -s_{\text{ALT},t-1} = -\Psi_{t-1} A_{t-1} w_{t-1} = \frac{q_{t-1} \delta'^{\frac{1}{\theta}} A_{t-1} w_{t-1}}{q_{t-1} \delta'^{\frac{1}{\theta}} + (1+r_t)^{\frac{\theta-1}{\theta}}},$$

$$(8.1)$$

where Ψ_t is the share in wage income of saving by prime-age adults. An increase in the adult survival rate has an unambiguous positive effect on Ψ_t and, hence, on per capita saving by prime-age adults. An increase in the adult survival rate has an unambiguous negative effect on per capita saving by retirees. The response of the combined saving of workers and retirees to changes in survival depends on additional features of the macro-economy to which we now turn.

Gross domestic product (Y_t) is produced by a Cobb–Douglas production function with labor-augmenting technological growth, *i.e.*, $Y_t = K_t^\phi L_t^{1-\phi}$, where ϕ is the share of capital in GDP, $0 < \phi < 1$. $L_t = A_t N_{\text{ALT},t}$ is the aggregate labor supply measured in efficiency units. $N_{\text{ALT},t}$ is the population of prime-age adults and A_t is the technology index. The growth rate of the population of prime-age adults from time $t-1$ to time t is $n_t - 1$ and, hence, $N_{\text{ALT},t} = n_t N_{\text{ALT},t-1}$. The technological growth rate from time $t-1$ to time t is g_{t-1}. Hence, the relationship between the total lifetime labor income of prime-age adults and pensioners is given by $w_{t-1} A_{t-1} N_{\text{OLD},t} = w_t A_t N_{\text{ALT},t}/g_t n_t$. Using lower case letters to represent quantities per unit of effective worker, output per effective worker is $y_t = k_t^\phi$ and the capital-output ratio is $k_t^{\phi-1}$. The depreciation rate (ξ) is assumed to be constant; hence, depreciation as a share of GDP is $\xi k_t^{\phi-1}$. Total gross national saving is the sum of the saving of adults ($S_{\text{ALT},t}$), the saving of the elderly ($S_{\text{OLD},t}$) and depreciation (ξK_t). Dividing by Y_t yields the gross national saving rate at time t:

$$\frac{S_t}{Y_t} = (1 - \phi) \left(\Psi(q_t, k_t) - \Psi(q_{t-1}, k_{t-1}) \frac{1}{g_t n_t} \right) + \xi k_t^{1-\phi}. \tag{8.2}$$

The term $(1 - \phi)$ is the share of labor income in GNP, $\Psi_t(q_t, k_t)$ is saving by current workers as a share of current labor income, $-\Psi(q_{t-1}, k_{t-1}) \frac{1}{g_t n_t}$ is saving by current retirees as a share of current labor income, and $\xi k_t^{1-\phi}$ is depreciation as a share of current GNP.

(a) Steady-state rate of growth effects

The steady-state gross national saving rate is:

$$\left(\frac{S}{Y} \right)^* = (1 - \phi)\Psi(q^*, k^*) \left(\frac{gn - 1}{gn} \right) + \xi k^{*1-\phi}, \tag{8.3}$$

where the $*$ superscript denotes equilibrium values. Standard and well-known implications of the lifecycle model (Modigliani and Brumberg [1954]) follow directly from Eq. (8.3). First, the net saving rate is zero if the economy is not growing ($gn = 1$). If the economy is not growing, the lifetime earnings of retirees and workers are equal and, hence, the dis-saving by retirees will exactly balance the saving by workers. Second, the partial effect of an increase in the GDP growth rate is equal to the mean age of earning less the mean age of consumption, as in the variable rate-of-growth (VRG) model (Mason [1981; 1988] and Fry and Mason [1982]). As shown in Kinugasa, ψ is the difference between the mean ages of consumption and earning.[3] An important issue to clarify at this point is that the effect of the rate of growth of the population of children, not included in the theoretical model, will be very different than the rate of growth of the population of prime-age adults. If the child population is growing rapidly, workers will be supporting many children and, hence, saving will be depressed. The effects of child dependency are adequately addressed in the current literature (Mason [1988]; Higgins [1994]). The effects of child dependency are discussed more thoroughly and estimated below.

---

[3] In this model, the mean age of consumption is $(c_{1,t} + 2q_t c_{2,t+1})/(c_{1,t} + q_t c_{2,t+1})$ and the mean age of earning is 1.

(b) The effect of adult survival in steady state and in transition

The effect of changes in adult survival on saving depends on whether or not the capital–labor ratio and interest rates are endogenous. In a small open economy, the equilibrium capital–labor ratio and interest rates are determined by global economic conditions. A rise in domestic saving — and factors that influence the saving rate — will have no effect on domestic investment nor on domestic interest rates. In a closed economy, however, saving and investment are equal and the rate of interest is endogenously determined by the interplay of the supply of capital by households and the demand for capital by firms. The effect on saving of an increase in adult survival in each of these environments is considered in turn.

Saving in a small open economy

The effect of an increase in adult survival on the steady-state saving rate in a small open economy depends on the rate of growth of income. If the economy is growing, $gn > 1$, the steady-state saving rate rises with adult survival. In an economy with negative economic growth, the steady-state saving rate declines with an increase in adult survival. The steady-state saving rate given by Eq. (8.3) holds with k^* exogenously determined. An increase in adult survival leads to a rise in the share of labor income saved by prime-age adults, *i.e.*, $\partial \Psi^* / \partial q^* > 0$, but the dis-saving by retirees increases, as well. In a growing economy, the increase in saving by prime-age adults dominates the decline in saving by retirees and the aggregate saving rate rises with adult survival. In a declining economy, the decline in saving by retirees dominates and the aggregate saving rate declines as adult survival rises.

The response of saving rates in a dynamic context is more complex. The current saving rate is increasing in the rate of GDP growth during the previous period, g_t, because in an economy with rapid aggregate economic growth during the preceding period the size of current workers, measured in terms of total lifetime earnings, will be large relative to current retirees. The effect of the rate of economic growth will depend on adult survival or, to be more precise, on the expected duration of retirement of those who are currently working. In a dynamic context, however, adult survival is also changing. Consider a small open economy that is in equilibrium, but experiences an increase in the survival rate in period t. Prime-age adults respond by increasing their saving rates, while saving by retirees is unaffected. The aggregate saving rate must rise in period t. The transitory increase in saving is independent of the rate of economic growth gn. In period $t + 1$, dissaving by retirees rise and the aggregate saving rate declines. In the absence of further changes in survival, a new equilibrium saving rate is established in period $t + 1$. As shown above, the new equilibrium depends on the rate of economic growth. In a growing economy, it will be higher than the saving rate in period $t - 1$, but lower than the saving rate in period t.

Saving in a closed economy

In a closed economy, an increase in the saving rate leads to greater investment, capital deepening, more rapid growth in wages, and a decline in the interest rate. The supply of capital follows directly from the saving model presented above, because the capital stock in period $t + 1$ is equal to total saving by prime-age adults in period t. Expressed as capital per effective worker, the supply of capital in year $t + 1$ depends on the wage per effective worker in year t, the share of that wage that is saved by prime-age adults, and the rate of growth:

$$k_{t+1} = \frac{\psi(r_{t+1}, q_t) w_t(k_t)}{g_{t+1} n_{t+1}} = S_t(\underset{?}{r_{t+1}}, \underset{+}{w_t(k_t)}, \underset{+}{q_t}), \qquad (8.4)$$

where S_t is the supply function of capital. The effect of the interest rate on the supply of capital is ambiguous.[4] The wage is equal to the marginal product of an effective worker, $w_t = f(k_t) - k_t f'(k_t)$ and is increasing in capital per effective worker. An increase in the survival rate leads to an increase in the share of labor income saved by prime-age adults and, hence, capital per effective worker and the supply of capital.

The demand for capital, **D**, is governed by the marginal condition that the cost of capital equals the net return, *i.e.*, $r_{t+1} = f'(k_{t+1}) - \xi$. That $f'' < 0$ implies that the demand curve is downward sloping. The demand for capital

---

[4]In the simulation results presented further we assume that an increase in the interest rate leads to greater saving. Qualitative results hold unless an increase in interest rates have a large negative effect on saving — a possibility not supported by empirical evidence. For details see Kinugasa [2004].

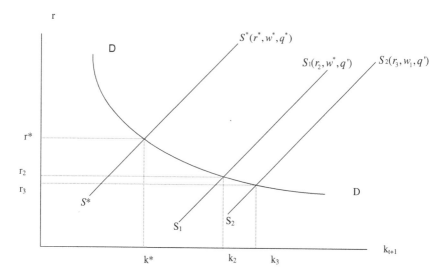

Figure 8-1   Demand and Supply of Capital in a Closed Economy

is independent of the survival rate. The effect of an increase in the survival rate from q^* to q' in period 1 is traced in Fig. 8-1. The demand curve, **DD**, is unaffected. Workers in period 1 increase their saving because in period 2 they expect to live longer and, perhaps, because they expect lower interest rates to depress the rate of return on annuities. Thus, the supply curve, **SS**, shifts to the right in period 2. This leads to a rise in capital per worker and wages for the new generation of workers. As a result, the saving function shifts further to the right, in part, because of the expected further decline in interest rates. The process continues until a new equilibrium is established.[5] Unless the decline in interest rates leads to a substantial reduction in saving by prime-age adults — a possibility not born out by empirical research — an increase in adult survival in period t leads to capital deepening.

The effect of survival on aggregate saving is readily inferred from its effect on capital per effective worker. In a closed economy, saving is equal to investment. Gross national saving is the sum of changes in asset holdings of prime-age adults and the elderly and depreciation, so that

---

[5]The economy converges in a non-oscillatory pattern to the steady state under plausible parameter values. See Kinugasa [2004] for details.

$S_t = S_{\text{ALT},t} + S_{\text{OLD},t} + \xi K_t = S_{\text{ALT},t} - S_{\text{ALT},t-1} + \xi K_t$. Gross investment is given by $I_t = K_{t+1} - (1 - \xi)K_t$. The national saving rate is:

$$\frac{S_t}{Y_t} = \left(g_{t+1}n_{t+1}\frac{k_{t+1}}{k_t} - 1 + \xi \right) k_t^{1-\phi}. \tag{8.5}$$

In steady state, the relationship simplifies to:

$$\left(\frac{S}{Y} \right)^* = (gn - 1 + \xi)k^{*1-\phi}. \tag{8.6}$$

From inspection of Eq. (8.6) an increase in the equilibrium capital–labor ratio and, hence, the capital–output ratio ($k^{1-\phi}$), leads to an increase in the equilibrium net saving rate (($gn - 1)k^{*1-\phi}$) in a growing economy. The gross saving rate increases if the depreciation rate plus the rate of growth is positive. During transition, as is clear from Eq. (8.5), the saving rate is elevated above the equilibrium level depending on the rate of capital deepening (k_{t+1}/k_t). As with the open economy case, a one-shot increase in the survival rate leads to a large increase in the saving rate for one generation followed by a decline in the saving rate to a steady-state level as a new equilibrium is established. In an economy with positive labor-augmenting growth, the net saving rate will be higher than the initial equilibrium, but lower than during the transition period.

Simulation results

Figure 8-2 compares the simulated saving rates in a small open economy and a closed economy produced by an increase in adult survival from 0.4 in year $t-1$ to 0.5 in year t.[6] The initial impact is large in both cases. The response is

---

[6]The parameters for the simulation model have been chosen with an eye for maintaining consistency with previous studies, *e.g.*, Barro and Sala-i-Martin [1995] and Higgins [1994]. Productivity growth and the rate of population growth are both set to 1.5% per year. The population growth rate for the world for 1820–1998 was somewhat slower at 1.0% per year (Maddison [1995]). For the 1950–2000, the population growth rate was somewhat faster at 1.75% per year (United Nations Population Division [2005]). We assume that the intertemporal elasticity of consumption is 1.3, following Higgins. This is an important parameter in the closed economy model because it implies that a higher interest rate will lead to a modest increase in saving rates. We have used a discount rate of 0.02 per annum as have Barro and Sala-i-Martin as compared with a discount rate of 0.025 in Higgins given our view that a low discount rate is more consistent with observed age-profiles of consumption

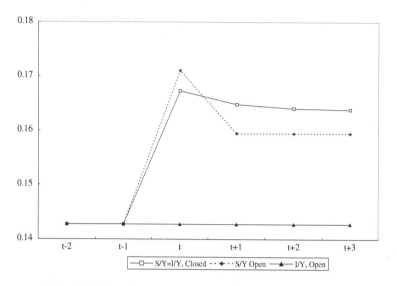

Figure 8-2   The Effect of an Increase in the Survival Rate at Time t

somewhat muted in the closed economy because the declines in interest rates lead to reduced saving rates among prime-age adults. A new equilibrium is established in period $t + 1$ in the open economy, but the adjustment is more gradual in the closed economy as described earlier. The equilibrium saving rate in the closed economy is greater than in the open economy, because of capital deepening in the closed economy. Higher net saving is required to sustain a higher capital–output ratio. Greater depreciation leads to an increase in gross saving beyond the increase in net saving. One would not be likely to observe the simulated saving paths shown in Fig. 8-2. Adult survival rates trend upward at a relatively constant rate in many countries — as we will show in upcoming sections. Figure 8-3 presents simulated saving rates assuming that adult survival increases by 0.1 per period starting from 0.4 in year $t - 1$. Otherwise, parameters are identical to those employed in the simulations presented in Fig. 8-2. The onset of adult mortality decline

---

that are relatively flat in most countries. We use standard values for the depreciation rate (5%) and the elasticity of output with respect to capital (1/3) — the same values used by Barro and Sala-i-Martin and Higgins. We part company with Higgins by assuming that a generation length is 30 years rather than 25. This assumption is based on recent estimates of the economic lifecycle showing that a generation length of 30 years is a more realistic representation (Lee *et al.* [2005]).

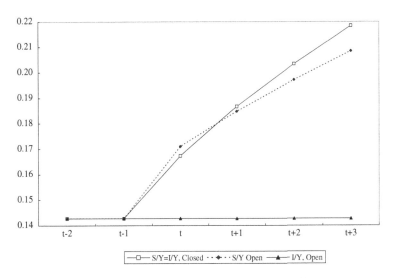

Figure 8-3   The Effect of a Continuing Increase in the Survival Rate

leads to a secular rise in saving rates that continues as long as adult survival rates continue to increase. Saving rates appear to be very nearly linear in adult survival after period $t - 1$ in the open economy case and after period t in the closed economy case.

2. Empirical Analysis with Historical Data

The modern mortality transition began in the West. Early gains were concentrated at young ages, but by 1900 old-age survival rates were rising steadily in Sweden, the United Kingdom, Italy, and the US — the four Western countries we examine below. The mortality transition began much later outside of the West. The three Asian populations for which we have relatively complete historical data — Japan, Taiwan, and India — did not experience significant gains in old-age survival until the middle of the 20th century. When the mortality transition began, however, it was very rapid as these Asian countries caught or, in the case of Japan, surpassed the West. Historical mortality transitions are of great interest here because of their implications for long-run trends in national saving rates. Previous empirical research — and the analysis presented in Sec. 3 — relies on data that cover a relatively small portion of the mortality transition. This is unfortunate given the long-term nature of the processes under consideration. The distinctive experiences of Asia and the West, however, provide an opportunity to assess long-term effects of mortality change on saving.

We begin with an examination of the mortality transitions of seven countries. The most widely available measures, life expectancy at birth and the crude death rate, are inappropriate because, early in the mortality transition, they are driven by changes in infant and child mortality. Whether the resultant increase in child dependency observed in many countries affected the accumulation of wealth is an issue considered below. The emphasis at this point, however, is on adult mortality. The measure of mortality used here and in the world panel analysis is the expected years lived during old-age relative to the expected years lived during the working years. This measures in very direct fashion how mortality decline influences the expected duration of retirement relative to the expected number of working years. It directly measures the influence of mortality on population age structure. It also reflects mortality change that occurs at any adult age. Ages 30 and 60 are used to delineate the working ages (30–59) and the old ages (60+). This choice may be puzzling to some, but it is based on recent empirical estimates of the economic lifecycle in a small group of developing and industrialized countries that find that individuals do not begin to produce as much as they consume until their late 20s and that by their late 50s or early 60s they are consuming more than they are producing (Lee *et al.* [2005]). Thus, individuals are only beginning to save toward retirement in their 30s and later and are beginning to rely on accumulated wealth beginning at about age 60.[7]

In six of the countries — all but India — we are able to construct an old-age survival index (q), also used in Sec. 4.[8] The old-age survival index

---

[7]Life tables used in the analysis here, and in other studies, are period tables based on current age-specific mortality rates. Thus, they describe the mortality experience of a synthetic cohort that lives its life subject to current mortality conditions. Using cohort-specific life tables would conform more closely to the theoretical model. Projected cohort life tables are not generally available, but they could be constructed using projected age-specific survival rates from the UN, for example. Given the simple methods used to project life expectancy, it seems doubtful that projected values contain additional information beyond that already captured by the two measures of survival included in our analysis.

[8]In India, we analyze life expectancy at age 30, which is highly correlated with the old-age survival index.

is the expected years lived after age 60 per expected year lived between the ages of 30 and 60 given the age-specific death rates during the year of observation. The value of q ranges from less than 0.2 expected years lived after age 60 per expected year lived between the ages of 30 and 60 in Taiwan *circa* 1900 to close to 0.8 in current day Japan. Historical data for Sweden allow us to trace the transition in old-age survival from the mid-18th century. The 250 years of data can be described remarkably well as consisting of a pre-transition period during which old-age survival was virtually stagnant and a transition period during which old-age survival increased steadily. In 1751, adults could expect to live about one-third of a year after age 60 for every year lived between the ages of 30 and 60. Between 1761 and 1876, the old-age survival index increased at an annual rate of only 0.0006. Between 1876 and 2001, the old-age survival index increased four times as rapidly — at an annual rate of 0.0026. Allowing for three short-run mortality crises — famine in 1772–1773, the Finnish War in 1808–1809, and the Spanish flu epidemic of 1918 — a piece-wise linear regression with one break-point at 1876 explains 93% of the variance in adult mortality (Table 8-1).[9]

The old-age survival transitions of the three other Western countries can be characterized in equally simple fashion. For the United Kingdom, old-age survival increased at an annual rate of 0.0009 between 1841 and 1900 and at a rate of 0.0024 between 1900 and 1998, with 96% of the variance explained by the piece-wise linear model with a single break point. The available data for Italy and the United States do not extend into the pre-transition period. Old-age survival in Italy from 1872–2000 and in the United States from 1900–2001 can be explained as consisting of a single transition period with old-age survival increasing by 0.0029 years per year in Italy and by 0.0033 years per year in the United States.

That the gains in these four countries have been remarkably constant during the 20th century has important — and unfortunate — implications for testing the dynamic saving model. In the absence of time series variation in the rate at which old-age survival is increasing, estimates of the

---

[9]The break points were assigned visually. A more precise iterative approach would improve the fit of the piece-wise linear approximations, but the analysis presented further would not be affected in any important way.

Table 8-1   Structural Changes of the Old-Age Survival Index

	Sweden	United Kingdom	Italy	United States	Japan	Taiwan	India
	1751–2002	1841–1998	1872–2000	1900–2001	1891–2001	1906–2002	1881–1997
t_1	1876	1900			1947	1940	1951
t_2					1989	1983	1989
t	0.0006***	0.0009***	0.0029***	0.0033***	0.0010***	0.0004	0.0392
	(0.0001)	(0.0001)	(0.0001)	(0.0002)	(0.0002)	(0.0010)	(0.0232)
$(t-t_1)d_1$	0.002***	0.0024***			0.0065***	0.0056***	0.3457***
	(0.0001)	(0.0001)			(0.0004)	(0.0011)	(0.0599)
$(t-t_2)d_2$					−0.0014***	−0.0024***	−0.3075*
					(0.0007)	(0.0003)	(0.1568)
Dm1773	−0.0231***	0.0004***	−0.1231***				
	(0.0027)		(0.0023)				
Dm1808	−0.1625***						
	(0.0063)						

(Continued)

Table 8-1 (*Continued*)

	Sweden	United Kingdom	Italy	United States	Japan	Taiwan	India
	1751–2002	1841–1998	1872–2000	1900–2001	1891–2001	1906–2002	1881–1997
Dm1918	−0.096*** (0.0040)						
Constant	0.2869*** (0.0080)	0.3205*** (0.0049)	0.2518*** (0.0053)	0.2245*** (0.0195)	0.3250*** (0.0104)	0.2860*** (0.0322)	22.7955*** (0.8454)
Adjusted R^2	0.9251	0.9587	0.9471	0.9585	0.9872	0.9944	0.9628
N	252	158	129	48	59	43	20
P-value	0.0000	0.0000	0.0000		0.0000	0.0000	0.0000
D.W.	0.5765	0.7026	0.397	0.0958	0.3897	0.3651	0.0338

Note: Dependent variables are adult survival index except for India. The dependent variable for India is life expectancy at age 30. The equation $q_t = \beta_0 + \beta_1 t + \beta_2 d_1(t - t_1) + \beta_3 d_2(t - t_2) + \varepsilon_t$ is estimated, where $d_1 = 1$ if $t \geq t_1$ and 0 otherwise, and $d_2 = 1$ if $t \geq t_2$ and 0 otherwise. Dm1773 is a dummy variable equal to 1 for year 1773. Dm1808 and Dm1918 are defined in similar fashion. N is number of observations. "P-value" is the p-value of F-test for the null hypothesis that β_1, β_2, and β_3 are all zero. D.W. is Durbin–Watson statistics. The low Durbin–Watson statistics imply serial correlation. The augmented Dickey–Fuller test indicates that some variables are not trend stationary.

effect of the rate of change in old-age survival will depend entirely on cross-country differences. Even though there are small year-to-year fluctuations and instances of more significant fluctuations, *e.g.*, the flu epidemic of 1918, short-term fluctuations may have little or no effect on long-term expectations. In our model, it is long-term expectations that matter. To add to the difficulties, the cross-national differences among the four Western countries are quite modest. The historical experience of the West is useful, however, to the extent that we explore the effect on saving of the shift from pre-transition to transition. We return to this issue below.

The mortality experience in East Asia is quite distinctive judging from the relatively complete data for Japan and Taiwan. Their pre-transition periods lasted until much later, but were followed by a significant catch-up period during which old-age survival increased quite rapidly. Having closed the mortality gap with the West, the gains in adult mortality have slowed. Recent mortality gains in Taiwan are similar to those found in the West while Japan continues to experience larger gains in old-age survival (Table 8-1). Indian life expectancy at age 30 also increased very gradually until 1951. For the next 40 years, substantial gains were achieved. The 1990s saw a marked slow-down. The pattern is similar to that found in Japan and Taiwan although direct comparison is not possible.

To what extent are the saving trends in these seven countries consistent with the predictions of our saving model? Three implications of the model can be examined. First, prior to the transition in old-age survival, saving rates would have been relatively low. Second, constant increases in old-age survival during the transition would have produced relatively constant increases in saving rates. Third, East Asian countries would have experienced relatively elevated saving rates during their period of rapid transition. Of course, these patterns would consistently emerge only if the trends in old-age survival dominated a myriad of other potentially important factors. First, were pre-transition saving rates low? Estimates for five pre-transition populations are available and presented in Table 8-2. In all cases, the pre-transition saving rates are low as compared with the saving rates that followed, but the UK saving rate during pre-transition is only slightly less than its transition saving rate and Taiwan's pre-transition saving rate is quite high as compared with the other countries. Second, are saving and old-age survival correlated? The observed saving rates are plotted against

Table 8-2   Mean National Saving Rates in Pre-Transition and Transition Periods

	Sweden	United Kingdom	Italy	United States	Japan	Taiwan	India[a]
Pre-transition	1751– 1875	1841– 1899	<1872	<1900	1891– 1947	1906– 1939	1900– 1950
Survival rate	0.31	0.34	na	na	0.35	0.24	24.0
Saving rate	7.3	11.6	na	na	15.7	22.1	6.9
Transition	1876– 2000	1900– 1998	1872– 2000	1900– 2001	1947– 2000	1940– 1999	1951– 1997
Survival rate	0.53	0.49	0.47	0.57	0.60	0.54	37.7
Saving rate	16.6	13	17.7	17.7	32.6	26.1	17.7

[a]Life expectancy at age 30 is presented instead of survival rate in India.

the observed survival values in Fig. 8-4 for each of the countries.[10] The US stands out as an exception with a negative simple correlation between saving rates and old-age survival. In the United Kingdom, the positive correlation is modest (0.37). In the other five countries, the correlation between the two variables ranges from 0.64 upward.

With the exception of Sweden, the correlation between q and saving disappears or turns negative at higher survival rates. The theoretical model offers two possible explanations for this phenomenon. One is that a slowdown in the rate of change in mortality, as occurred in Japan and in Taiwan, would cause saving rates to drop below the regression lines. A second is that a decline in the rate of economic growth would have a similar effect. Institutional change — especially the adoption of pay-as-you-go pension programs — looms large as a potential explanation. The third question is whether rapid changes in survival rates (observed mostly in the countries of East Asia) were associated with higher saving rates. As a simple analytic device we compare the countries at three benchmark old-age survival rates — 0.4, 0.5, and 0.6 — observed for the six countries for which we have

---

[10]In the regression analysis in Fig. 8-4, we checked the trend stationarity of the variables by Augmented Dickey–Fuller test and find that some variables are not trend stationary.

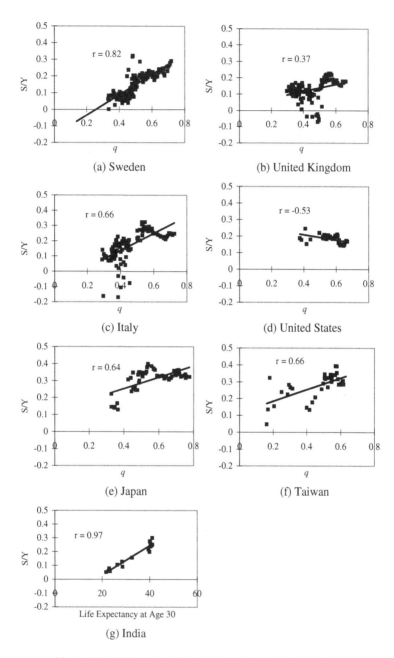

Figure 8-4   Adult Survival Index and the National Saving Rate

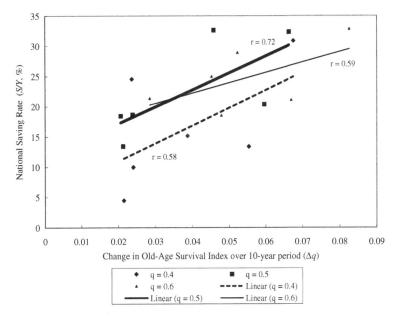

Figure 8-5   Changes in Old-Age Survival Index and the National Saving Rate

values (Fig. 8-5). There is a clear positive association between the national saving rate and the change in the old-age survival rates over the subsequent decade. The simple correlation between the variables ranges from 0.58 to 0.72. The effects are essentially identical for q equal to 0.4 and 0.5 and somewhat attenuated for 0.6. These results provide modest but consistent support for the dynamic model of adult survival and saving.

3.   Empirical Analysis with World Panel Data

3.1.   *Model Specification*

Estimates of national saving rates, life expectancy at birth, and other variables that may influence saving are available for 76 countries in 1965–1969 increasing to 94 countries in 1995–1999.[11] In this section, we present

---

[11]In our world panel data, all variables are averages for the subsequent five-year period. So, saving rate in 1965 is calculated as the mean of saving rates from 1965 to 1969 and a variable in 1995 is the mean of the variable from 1995 to 1999.

analysis of national saving rates employing these data. Using the world panel data offers advantages over the historical analysis. First, we can move to a multivariate framework that explicitly incorporates the role of other factors in determining national saving rates. Second, we can explore whether the Western/East Asian distinctions drawn in the historical analysis can be generalized to other countries of the world. There are also disadvantages that are discussed further. The empirical model incorporates the two effects of old-age survival derived from the OLG model presented in Sec. 2: the steady-state effect, which interacts with the rate of economic growth, and the transitory effect, which depends on the rate at which old-age survival is increasing. A linear approximation of the OLG model implies that both the steady-state effect (β_1) and the transitory effect (β_2) are positive in Eq. (8.7):

$$(S/Y)_t = \beta_0 + \beta_1 q_t \cdot Y_{\text{gr},t} + \beta_2 \Delta q_t + \beta_3 D1_t \cdot Y_{\text{gr},t}$$

$$+ \beta_4 Y_{\text{gr},t} + \beta_5 \text{PRI}_t + \varepsilon_t, \tag{8.7}$$

where S/Y is the national saving rate, q is the old-age survival index, Y_{gr} is the growth rate of GDP, Δq is the change in the old-age survival index during the previous five-year period, $D1$ is the youth dependency ratio, and PRI is the relative price of investment goods, and subscript t means year t.[12]

The basic empirical model incorporates three other saving determinants that have been explored in previous studies. The first is the effect of youth dependency. As youth dependency varies over the demographic transition, aggregate saving can be influenced in a variety of ways of which two seem particularly important. First, an increase in the number of children may have a direct effect on current household consumption because of the costs of additional children. The direction of the effect will depend, however, on whether or not a decline in the number of children is associated with a decline in total consumption by children. If the price of children relative to adults is rising and the demand for children is price inelastic, expenditures on children will increase as the number of children declines. In this instance, youth dependency would have a positive effect on saving. If the demand for children is price elastic or if the number of children is changing for reasons unrelated to changes in relative prices, youth dependency will have

---

[12]The effect of openness is explored in further sections.

a negative effect on saving (Mason [1987]). Changes in youth dependency may also influence saving because children provide old-age support either through familial support systems or through public pension and health care systems. To the extent that children are seen as a substitute for pension assets, youth dependency will have a negative effect on saving. The specification of the youth dependency effect follows the VRG model (Fry and Mason [1982]; Mason [1981; 1987]; Kelley and Schmidt [1996]).

The second effect included in the basic model is the rate-of-growth effect, that is a feature of the OLG model presented in Sec. 2 and lifecycle saving models in general (Modigliani and Brumberg [1954]). In an economy experiencing more rapid GDP growth, the lifetime earnings of young cohorts are greater relative to the lifetime earnings of older cohorts. To the extent that lifecycle saving is used to shift resources from younger to older ages, saving is concentrated among younger cohorts. Hence, the rate-of-growth effect is typically positive, but can in principle be negative.[13] The effect of GDP growth is variable, equal to $\beta_1 q_t + \beta_3 D1_t + \beta_4$, because the old-age survival rate and the youth dependency ratio influence the lifecycle profile of consumption. The coefficient β_4 has no economic interpretation in isolation and, hence, may be positive or negative depending on the effects of q and $D1$.

The third determinant included in the empirical model is the PRI following Taylor [1995] and Higgins and Williamson [1997]. The PRI captures the effect of changing interest rates. An increase in the interest rate will lead to an increase or decrease in saving by prime-age adults and by the elderly depending on the relative strengths of the substitution and wealth effects. Thus, the effect of the PRI on the national saving rate is an empirical issue. A potentially important extension of the model, considered below, allows for a transitory youth dependency effects following Higgins [1994] and Williamson and Higgins [2001]. A drop in youth dependency would induce prime-age adults to save more during their working years in anticipation that they would rely less on familial or public transfers during their retirement years. Current retirees would be unaffected as they are simply dis-saving

---

[13]The saving mechanism can be used to shift consumption to younger ages, by accumulating credit card debt, for example, but constraints on indebtedness limit the importance of these transactions.

the (small) assets they accumulated in the expectation that they would be supported by the many children they chose to bear. Hence, aggregate saving would rise steeply. In the next period, however, the higher saving by the new generation of prime-age adults would be offset by the higher dis-saving by the new generation of retirees. Hence, saving would decline from the transitory peak to a steady-state peak that would be higher than saving in period t, but lower than saving in period $t + 1$. Just as is the case for survival, the saving rate would depend on the current level of youth dependency and its rate of change.

3.2. *Variables, Definitions, the Sample, and Estimation Methods*

Except as noted below, all variables are taken directly from or constructed using data from the World Development Indicators (WDI) (World Bank [2003]). The saving rate (S/Y_t) is the average gross national saving rate for the five-year period t to $t + 4$. The rate of growth of income is measured by the growth rate of real GDP during the preceding five-year period. The PRI_t is taken directly from the Penn World Table (PWT) and is the average value for the period t to $t + 4$. The youth dependency ratio $(D1_t)$ is the ratio of the population 0–14 to the population 15–64. The old-age survival index (q) is the ratio of expected years lived after age 60 (T_{60}) to expected years lived between ages 30 and 60 $(T_{30} - T_{60})$ given contemporaneous age-specific death rates. T_x, total number of years lived after age x, is a standard life table value. Life tables are not available for many countries in many years. Hence, life expectancy at birth from the World Development Indicators (World Bank [2003]) were used in conjunction with Coale–Demeny model life tables (Coale and Demeny [1983]) to construct estimates of q.[14] The change in the old-age survival index is the average increase over the preceding five-year period, *i.e.*, $\Delta q_t = q_t - q_{t-5}$.

The full sample consists of 566 observations for 76 countries in 1965–1969 increasing to 94 countries in 1995–1999. Estimates for Western and East Asian countries and for Other Developing Countries are presented

---

[14]See Kinugasa [2004] for additional details. The Coale–Demeny Model Life Table is an approximation that does not fit certain countries very well, *e.g.*, countries with unusually high rates of mortality at prime-adult ages.

separately. Because the national saving rates may affect economic growth, previous empirical studies have relied on two-stage least squares (2SLS) method to deal with the endogeneity problem. We follow standard practice and present both ordinary least squares (OLS) and 2SLS estimates. OLS estimates are a useful complement to 2SLS estimates for two reasons. First, the rate of economic growth is for the five-year period preceding the saving rate rather than a contemporaneous measure. This may mitigate, although not eliminate, the endogeneity problem. Second, it is difficult to find strong instruments for economic growth and using weak instruments often does more harm than good (Bound *et al.* [1995]).

For the first-stage variables we follow Higgins and Williamson [1997] and use the lagged values of the national investment rate, the labor force growth rate, the PRI, the consumer price index, real GDP per worker, real GDP per capita, and a measure of openness. The rationale for including the investment rate and the labor force growth rate follows directly from the neo-classical growth model. The price variables are included to capture the effects of inflation on productivity growth. Per capita income measures are employed to incorporate the possible effects of convergence. Openness influences economic growth by creating a more competitive economic environment. All estimates include year and regional dummies, as well. Below we report the results of an over-identifying restriction test useful to judge the overall exogeneity of the instruments. We also use a Hausman test (Hausman [1978; 1983]) to assess whether the OLS and 2SLS estimates are statistically distinguishable.

3.3. Results

Estimates of the basic model, Eq. (8.7), are presented in Table 8-3. OLS and 2SLS estimates are both presented and they are generally similar. The instrument variables in the first-stage regression are jointly significant at the 1% level in all cases. The Hausman test implies that the GDP growth rate is potentially endogenous. For the non-Western/non-East Asia sample, the overidentifying restriction test indicates that we cannot reject the hypothesis that the instruments for economic growth are entirely exogenous. But the other samples do not pass the overidentifying restriction test, and thus parameter estimates are influenced to some extent by the endogeneity

Table 8-3   Estimated Saving Equation with Old-Age Survival Index and Youth Dependency

	(1) Whole World		(2) West and East Asia		(3) Non-West and Non-East Asia	
	OLS	2SLS	OLS	2SLS	OLS	2SLS
$q*Y_{gr}$	8.2055***	14.8399**	8.3714**	14.8129***	9.1327***	15.7251***
	(1.8606)	(2.6660)	(3.7148)	(3.5266)	(1.9979)	(2.9857)
dq	0.8615	0.5104	1.7954**	1.8115**	0.3284	−0.2538
	(0.5266)	(0.5752)	(0.8192)	(0.8519)	(0.5962)	(0.6823)
$D1*Y_{gr}$	0.7461	0.9319	−3.0912***	−1.7057	0.4379	1.0155
	(0.7639)	(0.9345)	(1.1164)	(1.1246)	(0.9871)	(1.2978)
Y_{gr}	−3.7274***	−6.5927***	−2.9073	−6.4693***	−3.6892**	−6.8710***
	(1.3526)	(1.9655)	(2.4628)	(2.3958)	(1.5577)	(2.4026)
PRI	−0.0053*	−0.0028	0.0422**	0.0350*	−0.0084**	−0.0064*
	(0.0032)	(0.0036)	(0.0207)	(0.0212)	(0.0035)	(0.0036)
y70	0.0100	0.0075	0.0093	0.0105	0.0069	0.0026
	(0.0181)	(0.0184)	(0.0161)	(0.0159)	(0.0251)	(0.0253)
y75	−0.0175	−0.0253	−0.0280*	−0.0250	−0.0261	−0.0373
	(0.0166)	(0.0176)	(0.0159)	(0.0159)	(0.0233)	(0.0241)
y80	−0.0253	−0.0290	−0.0280	−0.0167	−0.0433*	−0.0543
	(0.0165)	(0.0188)	(0.0198)	(0.0238)	(0.0222)	(0.0234)
y85	−0.0031	−0.0013	0.0001	0.0184	−0.0272	−0.0345
	(0.0163)	(0.0218)	(0.0173)	(0.0207)	(0.0226)	(0.0272)
y90	−0.0102	−0.0185	−0.0340*	−0.0255	−0.0258	−0.0398
	(0.0161)	(0.0197)	(0.0175)	(0.0191)	(0.0225)	(0.0257)

(Continued)

Table 8-3 (*Continued*)

	(1) Whole World		(2) West and East Asia		(3) Non-West and Non-East Asia	
	OLS	2SLS	OLS	2SLS	OLS	2SLS
y95	-0.0009	-0.0086	-0.0039	0.0196	-0.0339	-0.0598**
	(0.0168)	(0.0235)	(0.0197)	(0.0231)	(0.0235)	(0.0285)
East Asia	0.0312**	0.0189	0.1073***	0.0855***		
	(0.0137)	(0.0175)	(0.0165)	(0.0202)		
Other Countries	-0.1190***	-0.0915***				
	(0.0093)	(0.0125)				
Constant	0.1775***	0.1487***	0.1544***	0.1267***	0.0758***	0.0855***
	(0.0161)	(0.0245)	(0.0247)	(0.0306)	(0.0205)	(0.0305)
N	566	566	189	189	377	377
Adjusted R	0.4357	0.3945	0.4191	0.3848	0.1275	0.0852
P-values, Y_{gr}	0.0000	0.0000	0.0000	0.0000	0.0000	0.0000
P values, year dummies	0.2800	0.1160	0.0125	0.0006	0.2261	0.0954
Y_{gr} Effect	0.7203	1.1739	0.6967	1.4105	0.6177	0.7543
P-value, Hausman		0.0000		0.0037		0.0000

Note: The dependent variable is the national saving rate.
q: Adult survival index. Y_{gr}: GDP growth rate, $D1$: young dependency rate, Δq: change in the adult survival rate, PRI: price of investment goods, yXX dummy variables for year XX, N: number of observation. "*P*-value, Y_{gr}" is the *p*-value of *F*-test of the null hypothesis that the both coefficients of $q \cdot Y_{gr}$ and $D1 \cdot Y_{gr}$ are zero. "*P*-value, year dummies" is the *p*-value of *F*-test of the null hypothesis that all the year dummies are zero. "Y_{gr} Effect" is the partial effect of an increase in GDP growth. "*P*-value Hausman" is the *p*-value of Hausman test for the null hypothesis that economic growth rate is exogenous.
***denotes significant at 1% level, **denotes significant at 5% level, and *denotes significant at 10% level. Figures in parentheses are standard errors.

problem. The OLS and 2SLS parameter estimates differ substantially in magnitude as is evident in Table 8-3. The qualitative results are similar, however, and for the sake of brevity we will limit our discussion to the 2SLS results.

Old-age survival consistently has a large, statistically significant positive effect on national saving rates for the full sample and for the two sub-samples. The change in survival has a statistically significant positive effect on national saving in the West/East Asia (W/EA) sample, but not in the other sub-sample. The youth dependency effect is not statistically significant for the full sample or for the two sub-samples. The effect of PRI has a large positive effect in the W/EA and a smaller negative effect elsewhere, but the effects are only marginally significant. The rate of growth effect evaluated at the mean value of q and $D1$ is consistently positive with a value that ranges from 1.4 in W/EA to 0.75 in the non-W/EA sample. The regional dummy variables are statistically significant — positive for East Asia and negative for the non-West and non-East Asian countries. Thus, important regional differences in saving rates remain after controlling for demographic characteristics.

In analysis that is summarized only briefly here, we explored two other issues. First, we re-estimated the models presented in Table 8-3 to capture any transitory effects of youth dependency on saving by including the change in the youth dependency ratio. We did not find a significant transitory effect of youth dependency, nor did the inclusion of the change in youth dependency have any important effect on other aspects of the estimates. Old-age survival has a strong positive effect in all estimates; the change in old-age survival has a positive effect in W/EA but not elsewhere. The effects of other variables are similar to those reported in Table 8-3. Second, we investigated the possibility that the effect of demographic variables depended on whether the economy was open or closed. As shown in Figs. 8-2 and 8-3, openness influences the short-term and long-term effects of increased survival in a relatively complex fashion. Hence, the analysis was repeated (a) by sub-dividing the sample into countries that were relatively open and those that were relatively closed; or (b) by interacting the demographic variables with a measure of openness. Openness was measured using the Chinn and Ito [2005] *de jure* measure of financial openness. We found no statistically significant evidence that the effects of demographic variables were influenced by the degree of openness.

Two aspects of the results warrant emphasis: First, the results imply that the demographic transition has had an important effect on aggregate saving rates. Two different kinds of exercises show this to be the case. The first exercise is to calculate that share of the actual increase in saving rates in East Asia are explained by demographic variables. We find that demographic variables explain about half of the actual increase in saving rates in East Asia. Although substantial, the estimated effects are smaller than those found in recent aggregate analyses. In the studies by Higgins and Williamson and Kelley and Schmidt changes in age structure explain virtually all of the increase in saving rates in East Asia (Kelley and Schmidt [1996]; Higgins and Williamson [1997]). Here, the age structure effects are of similar magnitude to those found by Deaton and Paxson, while the effects of longevity would be part of the cohort effect in the Deaton and Paxson analysis (Deaton and Paxson [2000]). These results bridge the gap, to some extent, between the large effects found in aggregate level analyses and the much smaller effects found in micro-level analyses. The second exercise uses UN projections project saving rates. Projections for the West and East Asia allowing only the old-age survival ratio to change are presented in Fig. 8-6. Projections allowing both the old-age survival ratio and the youth dependency ratio to vary, while holding all other variables constant, are presented in Fig. 8-7.

The combined effect of the rise in adult mortality and the decline in youth dependency is to increase the aggregate saving rate between 1955–1960 and 2045 by 14.6 percentage points in East Asia, by 8.6 percentage points in the West, and by 11.4 percentage points in the remaining countries based on the 2SLS estimates. Improvements in adult mortality accounted for a little more than three-quarters of the increase in each region while the decline in the youth dependency ratio accounted for a little less than one-quarter of the increase. The second important feature of the results is the implication for population aging and aggregate saving. There is widespread concern, though limited empirical support, that population aging will lead to a decline in aggregate saving rates. The empirical results presented here do not support that conclusion. If old-age survival rates continue to increase, as is widely expected, our empirical results imply that saving rates will continue to rise. This empirical finding is consistent with the Lee *et al.* [2003] simulations and suggests that economic growth may not slow as much with population aging as is anticipated in some quarters.

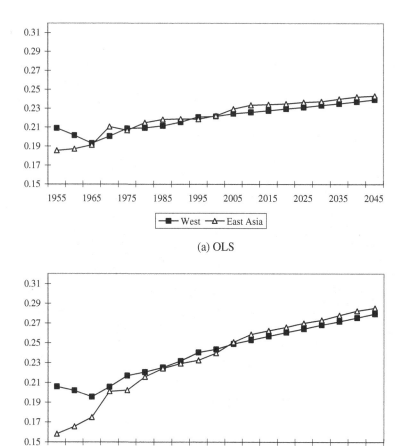

(a) OLS

(b) 2SLS

Figure 8-6   Projected Saving Rates of Western Countries and East Asia (Constant Youth Dependency, 1955–2050)

3.4. *Reservations*

An important unanswered question in this analysis is why no dynamic effect of old-age survival is found in the non-W/EA sample. One possibility is that drawbacks with the world panel data are responsible. The first limitation of the data is its relatively short time frame. For most economic analysis 30 years of data are more than adequate, but 30 years is only the length of a

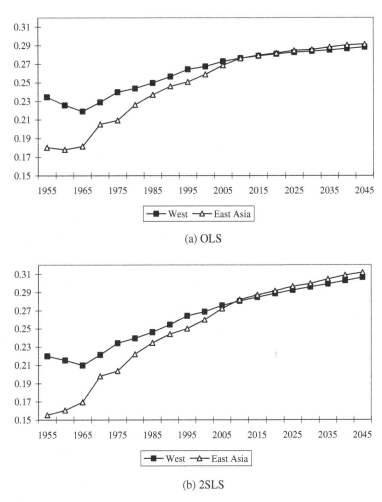

Figure 8-7 Projected Saving Rates of Western Countries and East Asia (Changing Youth Dependency, 1955–2050)

single generation. In a sense, we have a single observation of the OLG model presented in Sec. 2. The population of prime-age adults/workers of 1965 is the old-age population of 1995. A second difficulty, discussed in Sec. 3, is that the 1965–1999 period may not be well-suited for testing our theoretical saving model. The countries of the West enjoyed similar and relatively constant increases in old-age survival; hence, analyzing variation across countries or across time is unlikely to shed much light on the role of increases in old-age survival. The Asian experience may be more fertile ground to analyze as suggested in Sec. 3. What about the rest of the developing world? Until the mid-1980s, the gains in life expectancy were relatively constant across the world. That the simple correlation between life expectancy at birth for the first half of the 1960s and the second half of the 1960s was 0.997 for the 176 countries for which the UN reports estimates illustrate the point.

Two groups of countries experienced significant departures from their historical trends beginning in the mid-1980s primarily because of two important events — the break-up of the Soviet empire and the emergence of the HIV/AIDS epidemic in sub-Saharan Africa. Regional conflicts also played a role in the Middle East and Africa. If the saving model is applicable to these mortality crises, saving rates should have declined. Evidence on this point is limited, but Gregory *et al.* [1999] conclude that the rise of mortality rates among middle-aged Russian men depressed their saving rates.

A third and related issue is that the measures of mortality in the international panel data are not ideal. Although estimates of life expectancy at birth are reported by the World Bank, these values are often based on very incomplete information. We rely on model life tables to transform life expectancy at birth into the old-age survival ratio described in the previous section. Whether this is appropriate in all circumstances and, in particular, is reliable under severe mortality crises is a question to which we do not have a satisfactory answer. Moreover, the measure of the speed of mortality decline is for five-year periods. It may be that expectations about increases in old-age survival evolve much more slowly. Perhaps even generation length changes in old-age survival — a measure more consistent with our theoretical model — would be more appropriate. It is not our intention to suggest that absence of a dynamic effect in the non-W/EA sample must surely be the fault of the data rather than the model. More fundamental explanations are possible. Higher saving rates are not the only possible response to an increase in the number of years lived at old age. One possibility is that consumption at old age may decline. Another is that the elderly may choose to increase their labor force participation, although the opposite is the case as an empirical matter with the recent exception of the US and a few other countries. Still another response is that transfer systems, either public or familial, may expand to meet the needs of a growing elderly population. Further work on these topics is clearly needed.[15]

Conclusion

The main conclusions can briefly be summarized as follows.

(1) According to the OLG model, the national saving rate increases (decreases) in the steady state if GDP is growing (decreasing) because saving of prime-age adults is more (less) than dis-saving of the elderly in the economy.

(2) Our OLG model indicates that transitory effect of an increase in life expectancy on the national saving rate is positive because it only increases saving of prime-age adults. As a result, more rapid increase in life expectancy usually causes a higher national saving rate.

(3) Using historical data, several implications of theoretical models are confirmed, specifically the fact that rapid transition in adult mortality has led to higher saving rates. In Asian countries, a period of rapid change in adult survival was accompanied by an accelerated increase in the saving rate.

(4) The analysis of world panel data shows that the level of adult survival has a positive effect on the national saving rate if GDP is growing.

(5) A significant effect of the rate of change of adult survival is not found in the analysis based on the world data or in that based on the developing countries' data. The rate of change in adult survival has a significant positive effect on the national saving rate within a sub-sample of advanced economies.

This is not the first chapter to conclude that the increased duration of life could lead to higher saving rates. At the individual or household level, it is obvious that higher saving rates are a likely response to an increased duration of retirement. The effect on aggregate saving is more complex, however, because there are both behavioral responses and age composition effects at

---

[15]Our theoretical model and empirical analysis assume that demand side of capital is implicit. Therefore, the framework is more appropriate for capacity-constrained economies than demand-constrained economies.

play. An important contribution of this chapter is to show that the aggregate saving rate depends on both the level and the rate at which adult survival is increasing. The empirical results provide strong and consistent evidence that an increase in the portion of adult life lived at old ages leads to an increase in saving rates. This finding holds for all samples and specifications. The historical evidence suggests and the international panel data confirms that the increase in adult survival was a major impetus to the rise in the wealth of many nations.

The evidence for the dynamic effect, that is, the effect of the rate of change in old-age survival, is more fragile. When analysis is confined to the W/EA sample, we find a statistically significant effect. Moreover, the long-run historical patterns available for countries from East Asia and the West are consistent with the dynamic effect. In other parts of the contemporary developing world, however, we do not find any support for a dynamic effect. There are two additional important implications of the empirical analysis. The first is that the demographic transition had a strong positive effect on aggregate saving rates, but most of the effects were a response to improvements in old-age survival rather than to changes in youth dependency. This result may help to reconcile the divergent findings of studies based on the analysis of aggregate data and household survey data. The second important implication is that population aging will not lead to a decline in saving rates. Any compositional effects associated with population aging are outweighed by the behavioral effects of continued increases in longevity.

Appendix Details of the OLG Model

Individuals live at most for two periods. With probability $1 - q_t$ they die at the end of period 1 and with probability q_t at the end of period 2. The probabilities are known but individuals have no information about their own survival. The consumer's optimization problem is to maximize lifetime utility, assuming constant relative risk aversion, $V_t = \frac{c_{ALT,t}^{1-\theta}}{1-\theta} + \delta q_t \frac{c_{OLD,t+1}^{1-\theta}}{1-\theta}$, given the lifetime budget constraint. Consumption at prime age in period t is $c_{ALT,t}$ and $c_{OLD,t+1}$ is consumption at old age during period $t + 1$; δ is the discount factor, defined as $\delta = 1/(1 + \rho)$, where ρ is the discount rate; and $1/\theta$ is the intertemporal elasticity of substitution. Prime-age adults earn $A_t w_t$. A_t is labor-augmenting technology and w_t is wage per unit of effective labor. They divide their earnings into current consumption and saving for old age, so that:

$$c_{\text{ALT},t} + s_{\text{ALT},t} = A_t w_t, \tag{A.1}$$

where $s_{\text{ALT},t}$ is the saving of prime-age adults. Elderly adults are retired and consume what they saved while young. Insurance against longevity risk is available. An annuity is purchased at the beginning of prime age. If insurance companies are risk neutral and annuity markets are perfect, the rate of return to survivors is $[(1 + r_{t+1})/q_t]$, where r_{t+1} is the riskless interest rate on saving. The return to annuities is $[(1 + r_{t+1})/q_t]$. In this situation, returns to insurance are greater than a regular note. Thus, individuals save only in the form of insurance and consume:

$$c_{\text{OLD},t+1} = \frac{1 + r_{t+1}}{q_t} s_{\text{ALT},t}. \tag{A.2}$$

From (A.1) and (A.2), the lifetime budget constraint of the individuals at prime age is:

$$w_t A_t = c_{\text{ALT},t} + \frac{q_t}{1 + r_{t+1}} c_{\text{OLD},t+1}. \tag{A.3}$$

The corresponding Lagrangian is:

$$L = \frac{c_{\text{ALT},t}{}^{1-\theta}}{1 - \theta} + \delta q_t \frac{c_{\text{OLD},t+1}{}^{1-\theta}}{1 - \theta} - \lambda \left(c_{\text{ALT},t} + \frac{q_t}{1 + r_{t+1}} c_{\text{OLD},t+1} - A_t w_t \right),$$

where λ is a Lagrangian multiplier. First-order conditions are:

$$\frac{\partial L}{\partial c_{\text{OLD},t}} = c_{\text{ALT},t}{}^{-\theta} - \lambda = 0, \tag{A.4}$$

$$\frac{\partial L}{\partial c_{\text{OLD},t+1}} = \delta q_t c_{\text{OLD},t+1}{}^{-\theta} - \frac{q_t}{1 + r_{t+1}} \lambda = 0, \tag{A.5}$$

$$\frac{\partial L}{\partial \lambda} = -c_{\text{ALT},t} - \frac{q_t}{1 + r_{t+1}} c_{\text{OLD},t+1} + A_t w_t = 0. \tag{A.6}$$

Substituting (A.4) and (A.5) into equation yields:

$$\lambda = \frac{\left[1 + q_t \delta^{\frac{1}{\theta}} (1 + r_{t+1})^{\frac{1-\theta}{\theta}} \right]^{\theta}}{A_t^{\theta} w_t^{\theta}}. \tag{A.7}$$

Substituting back for λ yields:

$$c_{\text{ALT},t} = \frac{(1 + r_{t+1})^{\frac{1-\theta}{\theta}} A_t w_t}{q_t \delta^{\frac{1}{\theta}} + (1 + r_{t+1})^{\frac{1-\theta}{\theta}}}, \tag{A.8}$$

$$c_{\text{OLD},t+1} = \frac{\delta^{\frac{1}{\theta}} (1 + r_{t+1}) A_t w_t}{q_t \delta^{\frac{1}{\theta}} + (1 + r_{t+1})^{\frac{1-\theta}{\theta}}}. \tag{A.9}$$

From the budget constraints in Eqs. (A.1) and (A.2) and Eqs. (A.8) and (A.9), we can calculate saving by prime-age adults ($s_{\text{ALT},t}$) and the elderly ($s_{\text{OLD},t}$). Saving of prime-age adult is:

$$s_{\text{ALT},t} = \Psi_t A_t w_t = \frac{q_t \delta^{\frac{1}{\theta}} A_t w_t}{q_t \delta^{\frac{1}{\theta}} + (1 + r_{t+1})^{\frac{\theta-1}{\theta}}}, \tag{A.10}$$

where Ψ_t is the share in wage income saved by prime-age adults. The elderly consume assets accumulated while working plus interest income from the annuity. But the return on the annuity is part of their income, so: $s_{\text{OLD},t} = \left(\frac{1+r_t}{q_t} - 1\right) s_{\text{ALT},t-1} - c_{\text{OLD},t} = -s_{\text{ALT},t-1}$. Saving of the elderly is:

$$s_{\text{OLD},t} = -s_{\text{ALT},t-1} = -\Psi_{t-1} A_{t-1} w_{t-1} = \frac{q_{t-1} \delta^{\frac{1}{\theta}} A_{t-1} w_{t-1}}{q_{t-1} \delta^{\frac{1}{\theta}} + (1 + r_t)^{\frac{\theta-1}{\theta}}}. \tag{A.11}$$

Equations (A.10) and (A.11) correspond to set of equations (8.1) in the text. From Eq. (A.11), the effect of an increase in the survival rate at time t on the share of wage income saved by prime-age adults is:

$$\frac{\partial \Psi_t}{\partial q_t} = \frac{\delta^{\frac{1}{\theta}} \left[q_t \delta^{\frac{1}{\theta}} + (1 + r_{t+1})^{\frac{\theta-1}{\theta}} \right] - q_t \delta^{\frac{2}{\theta}}}{\left[q_t \delta^{\frac{1}{\theta}} + (1 + r_{t+1})^{\frac{\theta-1}{\theta}} \right]^2}$$

$$= \frac{\delta^{\frac{1}{\theta}} (1 + r_{t+1})^{\frac{\theta-1}{\theta}}}{\left[q_t \delta^{\frac{1}{\theta}} + (1 + r_{t+1})^{\frac{\theta-1}{\theta}} \right]^2} > 0.$$

Thus, an increase in survival rate increases the share of saving by prime-age adults.

Gross domestic product (Y_t) is produced by a Cobb–Douglas production function with labor-augmenting technological growth, *i.e.*, $Y_t = K_t^{\phi} L_t^{1-\phi}$, where ϕ is the share of capital in GDP, $0 < \phi < 1$. $L_t = A_t N_{\text{ALT},t}$ is the aggregate labor supply measured in efficiency units. $N_{\text{ALT},t}$ is the population of prime-age adults and A_t is the technology index. The population growth rate per generation is $n - 1$ and, hence, $N_{\text{OLD},t} = N_{\text{ALT},t}/n$. The technological growth rate per generation is $g - 1$. Hence, the relationship between the total lifetime labor income of prime-age adults and pensioners is given by $w_{t-1} A_{t-1} N_{\text{OLD},t} = w_t A_t N_{\text{ALT},t}/gn$. Using lower case letters to represent quantities per unit of effective worker, output per effective worker is $y_t = k_t^\phi$ and the capital–output ratio is $k_t^{\phi-1}$. The depreciation rate (ξ) is assumed to be constant; hence, depreciation as a share of GDP is $\xi k_t^{\phi-1}$.

Total gross national saving is the sum of the saving of adults $(S_{1,t})$, the saving of the elderly $(S_{2,t})$ and depreciation (ξK_t). Dividing by Y_t yields the gross national saving rate at time t:

$$\frac{S_t}{Y_t} = (1 - \phi)\left(\Psi(q_t, k_t) - \Psi(q_{t-1}, k_{t-1})\frac{1}{gn}\right) + \xi k_t^{1-\phi}. \qquad \text{(A.12)}$$

This equation corresponds to Eq. (8.2) in the text. The term $(1 - \phi)$ is the share of labor income in GNP, $\Psi_t(q_t, k_t)$ is saving by current workers as a share of current labor income, $-\Psi(q_{t-1}, k_{t-1})\frac{1}{gn}$ is saving by current retirees as a share of current labor income, and $\xi k_t^{1-\phi}$ is depreciation as a share of current GNP.

The steady-state gross national saving rate is:

$$\left(\frac{S}{Y}\right)^* = (1 - \phi)\Psi(q^*, k^*)\left(\frac{gn - 1}{gn}\right) + \xi k^{*1-\phi}, \qquad \text{(A.13)}$$

where the * superscript denotes equilibrium values. This equation corresponds to Eq. (8.3) in the text.

In a small open economy, capital is perfectly mobile. Residents can borrow and lend in the international capital market at the world interest rate. The assumption of a small open economy implies that the country is sufficiently small not to influence the world interest rate. According to the arbitrage condition, the marginal product of domestic capital is equal to the world interest rate; thus, $\phi k_t^{\phi-1} - \xi = r_{w,t}$. The capital stock per effective worker is:

$$k_t = \left(\frac{\phi}{r_{w,t} + \xi} \right)^{\frac{1}{1-\phi}}. \tag{A.14}$$

The aggregate capital stock is given by $K_t = A_t N_{1,t} k_t$. Equation (A.14) implies that capital per effective worker is determined solely by the world interest rate and the parameters of the production process. The rate of growth of the labor force does not affect k_t, nor does the survival rate affect k_t.

In the absence of international capital flows, domestic saving equals investment. Gross national saving is the sum of changes in asset holdings of prime-age adults and the elderly and depreciation, so that $S_t = S_{\text{ALT},t} + S_{\text{OLD},t} + \xi K_t = S_{\text{ALT},t} - S_{\text{ALT},t-1} + \xi K_t$. Gross investment is given by $I_t = K_{t+1} - (1 - \xi) K_t$. Because saving is equal to investment, $S_{\text{ALT},t} = K_{t+1}$. The saving of the young is equal to the capital stock in the next period. Thus, the supply of capital is:

$$K_{t+1} = S_{\text{ALT},t} = s_{\text{ALT},t} N_{\text{ALT},t}. \tag{A.15}$$

Noting that $K_{t+1} = A_{t+1} N_{1,t+1} k_{t+1}$, Eq. (A.15) can be rewritten as:

$$k_{t+1} = \frac{\Psi(r_{t+1}, q_t) w_t(k_t)}{gn} = S_t(r_{t+1}, w_t(k_t), q_t), \tag{A.16}$$

where S_t denotes the supply of capital per unit of effective labor. Equation (A.16) corresponds to Eq. (8.4) in the text.

Here, as a matter of convenience we set Ω_t and X_t as: $\Omega_t = 1 + q_t \delta^{\frac{1}{\theta}} (1 + r_{t+1})^{\frac{1-\theta}{\theta}}$, and $X_t = q_t \delta^{\frac{1}{\theta}} (1 + r_{t+1})^{\frac{1-\theta}{\theta}}$, where Ω^{-1} is the share of labor income consumed in prime age and $X\Omega^{-1}$ is the share saved by prime-age adults, so that $\Psi = X\Omega^{-1}$. From Eq. (A.16), the following equation is obtained:

$$(1 - \phi) X_t(q_t, r(k_{t+1})) k_t^{\phi} = k_{t+1} gn \Omega_t(q_t, r(k_{t+1})). \tag{A.17}$$

If the survival rate is constant, capital per effective worker will approach the steady state:

$$k^* = \left[\frac{(1 - \phi) X(q^*, r(k^*))}{gn \Omega(q^*, r(k^*))} \right]^{\frac{1}{1-\phi}}, \tag{A.18}$$

where k^* and q^* denote capital per unit of effective labor and the survival rate in steady state, respectively. Assuming variables other than capital per effective worker at times t and $t + 1$ are constant in Eq. (A.17), the relationship between k_t and k_{t+1} is described as:

$$\frac{dk_{t+1}}{dk_t} = \frac{(1 - \phi)f'(k_t)X_t\Omega_t^{-1}}{gn + [gnk_{t+1} - (1 - \phi)f(k_t)](\frac{1-\theta}{\theta})X_t\Omega_t^{-1}[1 + f'(k_{t+1}) - \xi]^{-1}f''(k_{t+1})}.$$

$$\text{(A.19)}$$

In Eq. (A.19), gnk_{t+1} is saving and $(1-\phi)f(k_t)$ is earning per prime-age adult at time t. Because saving is less than earning, $gnk_{t+1} < (1 - \phi)f(k_t)$. Note that $f'' < 0$ and that $0 < X\Omega^{-1} < 1$ hold.

Substituting Eq. (A.18) into Eq. (A.19), the numerator of the right-hand side of Eq. (A.19) reduces to ϕgn in steady state. Thus, $0 < \frac{dk_{t+1}}{dk_t} < 1$ is satisfied at least around the steady state unless the intertemporal elasticity of substitution $(1/\theta)$ is much less than 1. If $0 < \frac{dk_{t+1}}{dk_t} < 1$ holds in Eq. (A.19), the steady state is stable. Also, if the intertemporal elasticity of substitution is much less than 1, it is possible that the denominator of Eq. (A.19) is negative. For simplicity, we assume that $0 < \frac{dk_{t+1}}{dk_t} < 1$ holds; in other words, the economy converges in a non-oscillatory pattern.

Suppose the survival rate is constant in steady state. Then, in steady state, the equilibrium of the capital market in Eq. (A.17) is given by:

$$(1 - \phi)X(q^*, r(k^*))k^{*\phi} = k^*gn\Omega(q^*, r(k^*)). \quad \text{(A.20)}$$

Calculating total differentials of both sides of Eq. (A.20) and simplifying the results yields the following expression of the relationship between capital per effective worker and the survival rate:

$$\frac{dk^*}{dq^*} = \frac{\Omega^{*-1}\delta^{\frac{1}{\theta}}[1 + f'(k^*) - \xi]^{\frac{1-\theta}{\theta}}[(1 - \phi)k^{*\phi} - k^*gn]}{gn + [gnk^* - (1 - \phi)f(k^*)](\frac{1-\theta}{\theta})X^*\Omega^{*-1}}$$
$$\times [1 + f'(k^*) - \xi]^{-1}f''(k^*) - X^*\Omega^{*-1}(1 - \phi)f'(k^*)$$

$$\text{(A.21)}$$

Equation (A.18) and $0 < \frac{dk_{t+1}}{dk_t} < 1$ imply that the denominator of Eq. (A.21) is positive. Because saving of prime-age adults is less than wage income, $(1-\phi)k^{*\phi} - k^*gn > 0$ holds, so that the numerator is also positive. Therefore, $\frac{\partial k^*}{\partial q^*} > 0$ holds.

Consider the effect of an anticipated one-time increase in life expectancy at time t and assume that q stays at q^* in subsequent periods. In Eq. (A.17), assuming that all variables other than k_{t+1} and q_t are constant, we can characterize the relationship between the changes of q_t and k_{t+1} as:

$$\frac{dk_{t+1}}{dq_t} = \frac{\Omega_t^{-1}\delta^{\frac{1}{\theta}}[1 + f'(k_{t+1}) - \xi]^{\frac{1-\theta}{\theta}}[(1-\phi)k^{*\phi} - k_{t+1}gn]}{gn + [gnk_{t+1} - (1-\phi)f(k_t)](\frac{1-\theta}{\theta})X_t\Omega_t^{-1}[1 + f'(k_{t+1}) - \xi]^{-1}f''(k_{t+1})}.$$

$$(A.22)$$

The denominator of the right-hand side of Eq. (A.22) is equal to that of Eq. (A.19). We assume that $0 < \frac{dk_{t+1}}{dk_t} < 1$ holds, so that the denominator of Eq. (A.22) is positive. As we discussed above, $(1-\phi)k^{*\phi}$ is wage earning at time t, and $k_{t+1}gn$ is the saving per prime-age adult. Because saving of the young does not exceed earning, $(1-\phi)k^{*\phi} - k_{t+1}gn > 0$, the numerator is positive and $\frac{dk_{t+1}}{dq_t} > 0$ holds.

A greater survival rate brings capital deepening ($\partial k^*/\partial q^* > 0$). If the GDP growth rate is greater than the depreciation rate, the saving rate increases. If GDP is growing at a rate less than the rate of depreciation, an increase in q^* has a negative effect on the saving rate.

The effect of the national saving rate of a one-time, anticipated increase of the survival rate is $\frac{\partial (S_t/Y_t)}{\partial q_t} = \frac{gn}{k^{*\phi}}\frac{dk_{t+1}}{dq_t} > 0$. An anticipated increase in the survival rate at time t leads to a higher national saving rate. At time t, saving by prime-age adults increases, which causes an increase in k_{t+1}. The supply of capital increases and the saving rate increases. The effect of an increase in the survival rate at time t on the national saving rate at time $t + 1$ is:

$$\frac{\partial (S_{t+1}/Y_{t+1})}{\partial q_t} = k_{t+1}^{-\phi}\left[gn\left(\frac{\partial k_{t+2}}{\partial k_{t+1}} - \frac{k_{t+2}}{k_{t+1}}\phi\right) - (1-\phi)(1-\xi)\right]\frac{\partial k_{t+1}}{\partial q_t},$$

where $0 < \partial k_{t+2}/\partial k_{t+1} < 1$ and $\partial k_{t+1}/\partial q_t > 0$ hold. For plausible parameter values, this expression is negative. The saving at time $t + 1$ is the difference between the wealth at time $t + 2$ and $t + 1$. An increase in q_t induces capital deepening at time $t+1$, but the wealth of the previous period and depreciation are also higher than at time t. The net increase in wealth at time $t + 1$ is less than that at time t. In a closed economy, the survival rate at time t also influences the saving rate at time $t + 2$. This stands in contrast to the case of small open economy. The survival rate at time t has a negative effect on the saving rate after time $t + 2$.[16]

16

$$\frac{\partial(S_{t+2}/Y_{t+2})}{\partial q_t} = k_{t+2}{}^{-\phi}\left[gn\left(\frac{\partial k_{t+3}}{\partial k_{t+2}} - \frac{k_{t+3}}{k_{t+2}}\phi\right) - (1-\phi)(1-\xi)\right]\frac{\partial k_{t+2}}{\partial k_{t+1}}\frac{\partial k_{t+1}}{\partial q_t},$$

$0 < \partial k_{t+3}/\partial k_{t+2} < 1, 0 < \partial k_{t+2}/\partial k_{t+1} < 1$, and $\partial k_{t+1}/\partial q_t > 0$ hold, therefore, in the right-hand side of this equation, the value inside the bracket is negative for plausible parameters, so that the saving rate at time t has a negative effect on the saving rate at time $t + 2$. In the same way, the effects of the survival rate at time t on the saving rate after time $t + 2$ can be derived. q_t has a negative effect on the saving rate after time $t + 2$.

Chapter 9

Two Demographic Dividends, Saving, and Economic Growth

Introduction

In this chapter, we analyze the effects of first and second demographic dividends on saving and economic growth. The first demographic dividend (first dividend, hereafter) refers to an advantageous stage in that the share of the working-age population in the total population increases during the process of demographic transition. The second demographic dividend (second dividend, hereafter) is derived from an increase in adult longevity. As adult longevity increases, individuals tend to save more in order to prepare for old age, which can induce capital accumulation and economic growth. Using the data on the first and second dividends in Mason's [2005] study, we estimate the effects of the two demographic dividends on the national saving rate and per capita growth in GDP using cross-country data. Our results show that these effects are different in different regions. We find that the first dividend seems to be less important and the second demographic dividend more important for saving and growth in Western and high-performing East Asian countries than in others. Chapter 9 is organized as follows. In Sec. 2, we review the literature and present the theoretical background of demographic dividends. We then explain the model and data used in the analysis. Section 2 describes the empirical results on the effects of demographic dividends on saving. In Sec. 3, we discuss the empirical results on the effects of demographic dividends on economic growth. Lastly, we present the conclusions of this study.

1. Measurement of Demographic Dividends and Data

1.1. *Literature Review*

As Mason [2005; 2007], Mason and Kinugasa [2008] insist, most countries experience demographic dividends, and demographic dividends are quite important for economic growth. According to these authors, there are two kinds of demographic dividends. The first dividend derives from the fact that the share of the working-age population in the total population increases during the process of demographic transition. People of a working age tend to produce and save more than children and the elderly, and first dividend can contribute to economic growth greatly. However, the first dividend does not last forever. Lower fertility causes shortages in the working-age population over the long run. The second demographic dividend is related to an increase in adult longevity. As adult longevity increases, individuals tend to save more, in order to prepare for old age. Higher saving induces an accumulation of wealth, which causes economic growth. The second dividend has slowly gained modest attention; however, recent studies have stressed its increasing importance.

Demographic effects on economic growth through the labor force have been analyzed empirically in various studies. Kelley and Schmidt [2001; 2005]; Bloom and Williamson [1998]; Bloom *et al.* [2000] found that age distribution has a great influence on the growth of per capita income. These studies stress first dividend. They also found that a long life expectancy at birth significantly promotes economic growth, however, they do not describe the contribution of life expectancy as second demographic dividend. Several studies have stressed the importance of demographic change in terms of saving. Modigliani and Brumberg [1954] and Tobin [1967] suggest a lifecycle model of saving. The lifecycle model suggests that individuals save in order to prepare for their old age while they are working, and spend their saving after they retire. According to the lifecycle model, higher population growth leads to a higher national saving rate because the younger generations are larger than the older ones. The effects of longevity, especially the longevity of adults has drawn attention of economists recently. Mason's [1987] variable rate-of-growth (VRG) model developed lifecycle model considering age earning and consumption profiles. Mason [1981; 1987], Higgins and Williamson [1997], and Lee *et al.* [2003] analyzed the effect of age distribution on national saving rate and found that the first dividend contributes to increased national saving.

Recently, the second dividend has attracted demographers' attention. The effect of adult longevity on saving has been analyzed theoretically and empirically by many researchers such as Kinugasa and Mason [2007] and Mason and Kinugasa [2008]. The degree of the second demographic dividend is calculated and its importance stressed by Mason [2005; 2007], Mason and Lee [2006], and Ogawa [2007]. However, the effects of second dividend on growth and saving have not been analyzed empirically in previous studies. There is much debate on how to calculate the two demographic dividends. While the first demographic dividend is related to the labor force and support ratio, the second dividend is related to saving behavior. We used the data of the first and second demographic dividends calculated by Mason [2005], and analyzed the effects of the two dividends on national saving rates and economic growth using cross-country data.

1.2. *Measurement of Demographic Dividends*

The effects of the first dividend on economic growth are shown in Mason [2005]. Details regarding the first and second dividends are described in Mason and Lee [2006] and Mason [2005]. These first define the effective number of consumers (N) and the effective number of producers (L) where "a" is the age and "t" is the time period.

$$N(t) = \sum_a \alpha(a) P(a, t), \qquad (9.1)$$

$$L(t) = \sum_a \gamma(a) P(a, t), \qquad (9.2)$$

$P(a, t)$ is the population of those with age a. $\alpha(a)$ is an age-specific weight for variation by age in consumption, and it can be related to physiological needs, culture, preferences, etc. $\gamma(a)$ is an age-specific weight for productivity related to age. Output per effective consumer (Y/N) can be expressed in the following equation:

$$\frac{Y(t)}{N(t)} = \frac{L(t)}{N(t)} \cdot \frac{Y(t)}{L(t)}. \qquad (9.3)$$

In Eq. (9.3), taking the natural log of both sides and differentiating with respect to time, the following equation can be obtained.

$$\dot{y}(t) = \dot{L}(t) - \dot{N}(t) + \dot{y}^l(t). \tag{9.4}$$

The dot above the variable indicates the growth rate. The rate of growth in output per effective consumer ($\dot{y}$) is the sum of the rate of growth of the support ratio ($\dot{L}(t) - \dot{N}(t)$) and the rate of growth of productivity ($\dot{y}^l$). The first dividend is defined as the rate of growth of the support ratio.

In order to calculate the second dividend, Mason [2005] used wealth held by those aged 50 and older. Many young working-age adults are responsible for childrearing, and it is likely that they cannot save for retirement; however, they concentrate on wealth accumulation after the age of 50. Here, we will briefly explain the determinants of wealth accumulation as they appear in Mason [2005]. Let $N(\leq b, t + x)$ be the effective number of consumers born in year b by year t who are alive in year $t + x$. Let $b = t - a$, $N(\leq b, t + x)$ be the effective number of consumers "a" years older in year t who are alive in year $t + x$. The relative per capita cross-sectional age profile of consumption is assumed to be fixed and shifting upward at rate g_c and total consumption of the cohort born before age b in year $t + x$ is given by $\bar{c}(t)e^{g_c x}N(\leq b, t + x)$, where $\bar{c}(t)$ is consumption per effective consumer in year t. The present value of the future lifetime consumption of the cohort born in year $t - a$ or earlier is given by

$$\bar{c}(t)PVN(\leq b, t) = \bar{c}(t) \sum_{x=0}^{\omega-a} e^{(g_c-r)x} N(\leq b, t + x), \tag{9.5}$$

where ω is the maximum age achieved. If the shape of the per capita cross-sectional age profile of production is fixed and shifting upward at rate g_y, the total production of the cohort born before age b in year t is $\bar{y}^l(t)e^{g_y x}L(\leq b, t + x)$, where $\bar{y}^l(t)$ is production or labor income per effective producer and $L(\leq b, t + x)$ is the effective number of producers born in year b or earlier. The present value of future lifetime production of the cohort born in year $b = t - a$ or earlier is

$$\bar{y}^l(t)PVL(\leq b, t) = \bar{y}^l \sum_{x=0}^{\omega-a} e^{(g_y-r)x} L(\leq b, t + x). \tag{9.6}$$

Without bequests, the lifetime budget constraint is expressed as

$$W(\leq b, t) = \bar{c}(t)PVC(\leq b, t) - \bar{y}^l(t)PVL(\leq b, t). \qquad (9.7)$$

From Eq. (9.7), the ratio of wealth to total labor income is given as

$$w(\leq b, t) = [\bar{c}(t)/\bar{y}^l(t)]PVC(\leq b, t)/N(t) - PVL(\leq b, t)/L(t), \qquad (9.8)$$

where $w(\leq b, t) = W(\leq b, t)/Y^l(t)$. Equation (9.8) can be rewritten as

$$w(\leq b, t) = [C(t)/Y^l(t)]PVC(\leq b, t)/L(t) - PVL(\leq b, t)/L(t). \qquad (9.9)$$

$PVC(\leq b, t)/L(t)$ is the present value of the future lifetime production of all persons who were born in year b or earlier per effective producer in year t. The second dividend is calculated based on Eq. (9.9). The second dividend is the growth rate of wealth of those 50 and older, and therefore, g_y and g_c are assumed to be constant at 0.015 and the ratio of consumption to labor income to equal 1.0. The ratio of wealth of those 50 and older is used to represent the demographic dividend. Age earning and consumption profiles are based on those of the United States in 2000 in Mason [2005]. In the model, it is assumed that there is no bequest motive, change in retirement, social security, and familial transfer for simplicity.

1.3. *Saving Equations*

The effects of the demographic dividends on saving and economic growth are estimated using world panel data. In the case of saving, the following equation can be introduced:

$$S/Y = \beta_0 + \beta_1 \text{Dvd1} + \beta_2 \text{Dvd2} + \beta_3 Y_{gr} + \beta_4 \text{PRI}$$
$$+ \sum_t \beta_t \text{Year} + \sum_i \beta_i \text{Region} + \varepsilon, \qquad (9.10)$$

S/Y is the national saving rate; Dvd1 is the first dividend; Dvd2 is the second dividend; Y_{gr} is the GDP growth rate; PRI is the price level of investment goods; and Year is year dummy. Both the first and second dividends are expected to have a positive effect on the national saving rate. The first and second dividends reflect the transitory effects of demographic change on saving. The saving equation is estimated by ordinary least squares (OLS).

Because it is possible that the national saving rate and economic growth rate influence each other, we also estimate the saving equation by two-staged least squares (2SLS). For the 2SLS estimates, logged GDP per capita, price level and openness are used as instrument variables.[1]

1.4. *Economic Growth Equations*

The determinants of growth in GDP per capita are estimated by using three kinds of econometric models. The growth equation is based on the conditional convergence hypothesis.[2] According to this hypothesis, poor economies grow faster than rich economies and catch up with them in the long run. Conditional convergence means that the convergence hypothesis holds true after controlling some variables related to economic growth.

Model 1:

$$Y/N_{\mathrm{gr}} = \beta_0 + \beta_1 \mathrm{Dvd1} + \beta_2 \mathrm{Dvd2} + \beta_3 \ln(Y/N) + \beta_4(I/Y)$$
$$+ \beta_5 \mathrm{Price} + \beta_6 \mathrm{Open} + \sum_t \beta_t \mathrm{Year} + \sum_i \beta_i \mathrm{Region} + \varepsilon.$$
$$(9.11)$$

Model 1 estimates the effects of two demographic dividends on productivity growth. It is expected that demographic dividends have positive effects on economic growth. This model also estimates the effects of the investment rate on economic growth. It should be positive because higher investment rates can induce higher capital accumulation. GDP per capita is included in order to verify whether the convergence hypothesis holds. The convergence hypothesis holds if the coefficient of GDP per capita is negative. "Open" is the ratio of the sum of imports and exports to GDP and reflects the openness of the economy. Openness affects economic growth by creating a more competitive environment. "Price" is the price level. It is included

---

[1]These instrumental variables are used in economic growth equations. See the explanations of economic growth equations for the details about the instruments.

[2]The conditional convergence hypothesis was introduced in Barro and Sala-i-Martin [1992; 1995].

to capture the effect of inflation on economic growth. Model 1 is estimated by OLS.

Models 2 and 3:

Here, it is possible that demographic dividends significantly affect the rate of investment. Demographic dividends influence the saving behavior of individuals. This affects economic growth when the wealth is invested.[3] Model 2 estimates the determinants of growth in GDP per capita excluding the investment rate in Model 1. Model 3 assumes that demographic dividends have an effect only through investment. Model 3 is estimated by OLS and 2SLS. In the 2SLS estimation, the first and second demographic dividends and price of investment goods are used for the instrument variables.

1.5. Data Descriptions

We used world panel data from 1965 to 1999. All variables except demographic dividends were calculated as the average of five years. For example, variables for 1965 are averages from the years 1965 to 1969. The demographic dividends for every five years were obtained from Mason [2005]. A summary of the data is presented in Appendix Table 9-1. We first derived the equation using data from all over the world. In addition, estimates for Western and East Asian countries and for other developing countries were presented separately.[4] The data of the first and second demographic dividends came from Mason [2005]. The data for all the other variables were obtained from the *Penn World Table*.

The first and second dividends of the whole world and two subsamples are shown in Fig. 9-1. In 1965, the mean of the first dividend in the world, the subsamples of West and East Asian countries, and the remainder of the countries was negative. In 1970, the mean of the first dividend in Western and East Asian countries became positive; however, the mean for the whole

---

[3] The effect can be different depending on whether or not the investment is held domestically.

[4] As Kinugasa and Mason [2007] found, empirical results within the subsample of Western and East Asian countries are quite different from those with whole world and the remaining countries.

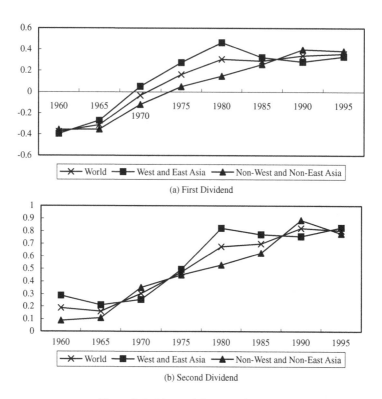

Figure 9-1   First and Second Dividends

world was still negative. The second dividend was positive throughout the sample period. From 1965 to 1980, both first and second dividends increased rapidly in the whole world and in all subsamples. In Western and East Asian countries, the first dividend decreased in 1985 and in 1990, and increased slightly in 1995. In non-Western and non-East Asian countries, the first dividend continued to increase from 1965 to 1990 and decreased somewhat in 1995. In 1990, the first dividend in non-Western and non-East Asian countries rose higher than in Western and East Asian countries. The second dividend remained high in Western and East Asian countries from 1980 to 1995. In non-Western and non-East Asian countries, the second dividend increased from 1970 to 1990, but decreased by a small amount in 1995. In developed countries, the first dividend will probably become quite small or negative and the second dividend will continue to be high, although it may not increase rapidly in the future.

2. The Effects of Demographic Dividends on Saving

Table 9-1 presents the empirical results of the saving equation of Model 1. When we estimate the equation with data from all over the world, the first demographic dividend has a positive and significant effect on the national saving rate for both the OLS and 2SLS estimates. The coefficient of the second dividend is positive but not significant. Within the subsample of Western and East Asian countries, the first dividend is not significant; however, the second dividend is significantly positive for both estimates. Within the subsample of non-Western and non-East Asian countries, the first dividend is significantly positive for the OLS estimate. The second dividend is not significant in the OLS estimate, but significant in the 2SLS estimate. GDP growth rate is significantly positive in four out of six estimates in Table 9-1. The Hausman test indicates that the 2SLS estimates are significantly different from the OLS estimates for the whole world and non-Western/East Asian countries.

3. The Effects of Demographic Dividends on Growth

Table 9-2 presents the estimated results of the growth equation in Models 1 and 2. In the regression with the whole world data and the subsample of non-Western and non-East Asian countries, the first dividend has a positive and significant effect, but the second dividend does not have a significant effect on economic growth. Within the subsample of Western and East Asian countries, the effect of the second dividend seems to be greater than that of the first dividend, but it is not statistically significant. The national investment rate has a positive effect on economic growth in all the estimates in Table 9-2. When we estimate the growth equation without the national investment rate (Model 2), first, the demographic dividend has a significant effect on growth with the whole world sample and subsample of non-Western and non-East Asian countries. The effect of the second dividend is significant at the 10% level in Western and East Asian countries but not significant in the whole sample and for the remaining countries. It is possible that the second dividend is important through investment. The results of Model 6 show that the investment rate has positive and significant effects on economic growth.

Table 9-3 presents the empirical results when we estimate the growth equation without the two demographic dividends. The national investment

Table 9-1 Estimated Saving Equations with Demographic Dividends (Model 1)

	(1) Whole World		(2) West and East Asia		(3) Non-West Non-East Asia	
	OLS	2SLS	OLS	2SLS	OLS	2SLS
Dvd1	0.05*** (0.013)	0.035*** (0.018)	−0.003 (0.017)	−0.005 (0.018)	0.064*** (0.015)	1.689 (1.034)
Dvd2	0.009 (0.008)	0.01 (0.009)	0.031** (0.013)	0.028** (0.014)	0.003 (0.009)	0.049*** (0.020)
Y_{gr}	0.441*** (0.140)	1.756 (0.801)	0.686*** (0.217)	0.95* (0.508)	0.361** (0.166)	0.006 (0.010)
PRI	−0.003 (0.003)	−0.001 (0.004)	0.056** (0.023)	0.053*** (0.021)	−0.009** (0.004)	−0.005 (0.006)
y70	−0.001 (0.018)	0.006 (0.018)	0.007 (0.020)	0.01 (0.020)	−0.003 (0.025)	0.003 (0.025)
y75	−0.034** (0.017)	−0.023 (0.017)	−0.022 (0.020)	−0.017 (0.021)	−0.046** (0.022)	−0.036 (0.022)
y80	−0.054*** (0.017)	−0.031 (0.021)	−0.011 (0.027)	−0.002 (0.028)	−0.068*** (0.022)	−0.053** (0.023)
y85	−0.038** (0.017)	0.006 (0.030)	0.027 (0.022)	0.039 (0.028)	−0.064*** (0.023)	−0.025 (0.033)
y90	−0.037** (0.017)	−0.001 (0.025)	0.005 (0.023)	0.013 (0.026)	−0.056** (0.023)	−0.021 (0.030)

(Continued)

Table 9-1 *(Continued)*

	(1) Whole World		(2) West and East Asia		(3) Non-West Non-East Asia	
	OLS	2SLS	OLS	2SLS	OLS	2SLS
y95	−0.04**	0.015	0.014	0.032	−0.064***	−0.024
	(0.018)	(0.034)	(0.025)	(0.037)	(0.023)	(0.035)
East Asia	0.025	−0.022	0.028*	0.021		
	(0.018)	(0.035)	(0.017)	(0.020)		
Non-West, Non-East Asia	−0.142***	−0.154***				
	(0.007)	(0.010)				
Constant	0.22	0.152***	0.125***	0.113***	0.102***	0.024
	(0.015)	(0.041)	(0.025)	(0.037)	(0.020)	(0.057)
N	605	605	195	195	410	410
Adjusted R^2	0.416	0.306	0.262	0.255	0.11	0.159
P-value, year dummies	0.017	0.145	0.027	0.093	0.008	0.053
P-value, Hausman		0.075		0.613		

Note: The dependent variable is the national saving rate. Dvd1 is the first dividend, Dvd2 is the second dividend; Y_{gr} is the growth rate of GDP. PRI is the price of investment goods, yXX is the dummy variables of year 19XX. "East Asia" is the dummy variable for East Asian countries. "Non-West, Non-East Asia" is the dummy variable for Non-Western and Non-East Asian countries. "*P*-value, region dummies" is the *p*-value of the *F*-test for the null hypothesis that all the region dummies are zero. *N* is number of observation. "*P*-value, Hausman" is the *p*-value of the Hausman test for the null hypothesis that Y_{gr} is exogenous. Adjusted R^2 in 2SLS estimate is dropped when STATA did not calculate the statistics.

Table 9-2 Estimated Growth Equations (Models 1 and 2)

	Model 1			Model 2		
	(1) Whole World	(2) West and East Asia	(3) Non-West, Non-East Asia	(1) Whole World	(2) West and East Asia	(3) Non-West, Non-East Asia
Dvd1	0.012***	0.008	0.011***	0.012***	0.005	0.011***
	(0.003)	(0.009)	(0.004)	(0.004)	(0.011)	(0.004)
Dvd2	0.000	0.006	−0.001	0.001	0.011*	0.000
	(0.002)	(0.005)	(0.003)	(0.003)	(0.006)	(0.003)
I/Y	0.131***	0.118	0.132***			
	(0.028)	(0.081)	(0.024)			
ln y	−0.003	−0.008	−0.002	0.001	−0.007	0.003
	(0.002)	(0.006)	(0.002)	(0.002)	(0.006)	(0.002)
Price	−0.009*	0.000	−0.011	−0.005	0.005	−0.008
	(0.005)	(0.005)	(0.009)	(0.005)	(0.006)	(0.010)
Open	0.000	0.000	0.000	0.000**	0.000	0.000
	(0.000)	(0.000)	(0.000)	(0.000)	(0.000)	(0.000)
y70	−0.015***	−0.016***	−0.014***	−0.014***	−0.015***	−0.013**
	(0.004)	(0.005)	(0.005)	(0.004)	(0.006)	(0.005)
y75	−0.015***	−0.024***	−0.011**	−0.015***	−0.026***	−0.01*
	(0.004)	(0.009)	(0.006)	(0.005)	(0.007)	(0.006)
y80	−0.027***	−0.024*	−0.029***	−0.029***	−0.028***	−0.029***
	(0.005)	(0.013)	(0.006)	(0.005)	(0.012)	(0.006)
y85	−0.022***	−0.019*	−0.023***	−0.026***	−0.023***	−0.026***
	(0.004)	(0.010)	(0.005)	(0.004)	(0.009)	(0.005)
y90	−0.027***	−0.034	−0.024***	−0.032***	−0.038***	−0.028***
	(0.005)	(0.009)	(0.006)	(0.005)	(0.008)	(0.006)
y95	−0.017***	−0.023	−0.015***	−0.022***	−0.03***	−0.018***
	(0.004)	(0.008)	(0.005)	(0.004)	(0.008)	(0.005)
East Asia	0.006	0.001		0.016***	0.006	
	(0.006)	(0.01)		(0.006)	(0.007)	
Non-West, Non-East Asia	−0.008			−0.014***		
	(0.004)			(0.005)		
Constant	0.045**	0.081	0.029*	0.033***	0.087*	0.007
	(0.019)	(0.041)	(0.017)	(0.018)	(0.046)	(0.017)
N	605	195	410	605	195	410
Adjusted R^2	0.24	0.266	0.157	0.18	0.219	0.092
P-value, year dummies	0.000	0.001	0.000	0.000	0.000	0.000

Note: The dependent variable is the growth rate of GDP. See the note for Table 9-1.

Table 9-3   Estimated Growth Equations (Model 3)

	(1) Whole World		(2) West and East Asia		(3) Non-West Non-East Asia	
	OLS	2SLS	OLS	2SLS	OLS	2SLS
I/Y	0.135***	0.08	0.128	0.209***	0.134***	0.044
	(0.028)	(0.063)	(0.080)	(0.081)	(0.024)	(0.052)
ln$y$	0.000	0.002	−0.008	−0.01*	0.001	0.004*
	(0.002)	(0.002)	(0.006)	(0.006)	(0.002)	(0.002)
Price	−0.011	−0.009	−0.001	−0.004	−0.012	−0.01
	(0.005)	(0.006)	(0.004)	(0.004)	(0.009)	(0.010)
Open	0.000	0.000	0.000	0.000	0.000	0.000
	(0.000)	(0.000)	(0.000)	(0.000)	(0.000)	(0.000)
y70	−0.012***	−0.012***	−0.014***	−0.014***	−0.012**	−0.011
	(0.004)	(0.004)	(0.005)	(0.005)	(0.005)	(0.005)
y75	−0.01**	−0.01**	−0.018**	−0.017**	−0.007	−0.006**
	(0.004)	(0.004)	(0.007)	(0.008)	(0.005)	(0.006)
y80	−0.021***	−0.021***	−0.016*	−0.013	−0.023***	−0.023***
	(0.005)	(0.004)	(0.009)	(0.009)	(0.005)	(0.005)
y85	−0.015***	−0.017***	−0.012*	−0.009	−0.017***	−0.019***
	(0.004)	(0.004)	(0.007)	(0.007)	(0.005)	(0.005)
y90	−0.02***	−0.021***	−0.027***	−0.024***	−0.017***	−0.019***
	(0.004)	(0.005)	(0.007)	(0.007)	(0.005)	(0.006)
y95	−0.01***	−0.012***	−0.016**	−0.012*	−0.008*	−0.01**
	(0.004)	(0.004)	(0.007)	(0.007)	(0.005)	(0.005)
East Asia	0.012*	0.017**	0.009	0.003		
	(0.006)	(0.008)	(0.011)	(0.011)		
Non-West, Non-East Asia	−0.004	−0.007				
	(0.004)	(0.005)				
Constant	0.015	0.009	0.08*	0.075*	0.002	−0.014
	(0.018)	(0.017)	(0.042)	(0.043)	(0.015)	(0.016)
N	605	605	195	195	410	410
Adjusted R^2	0.220	0.209	0.251	0.226	0.142	0.111
P-value, year dummies	0.000	0.000	0.003	0.010	0.000	0.000
P-value, Hausman		0.000		0.000		0.000

Note: The dependent variable is the growth rate of GDP. See the notes for Tables 9-1 and 9-2.

rate is significantly positive for all estimates. In the 2SLS estimates, the national investment rate is significantly positive for only Western and East Asian countries. The Hausman test implies that the 2SLS estimates are significantly different from the OLS estimates for all estimates. Therefore, investment could be quite important for economic growth, and demographic dividends would greatly influence the investment rate.

Conclusion

The main conclusions can briefly be summarized as follows.

(1) This study uses the data of the two demographic dividends calculated by Mason [2005], and estimates their effects on saving and economic growth. We find that the effects of the two demographic dividends on saving and growth are different in different regions.

(2) The first dividend has been important for saving and economic growth in the whole world and in non-Western and non-East Asian countries.

(3) The first dividend seems to be less important in Western and East Asian countries, in particular.

(4) The second dividend is important for saving in Western and East Asian countries.

(5) The second dividend is important for economic growth, mainly through investment in Western and East Asian countries.

The demographic dividends are important for economic development because development can increase productivity, the size of the labor force, and capital accumulation. The first dividend has attracted the attention of several population economists; however, the importance of the second dividend has been noticed only recently. With reference to conclusions (1), (2), and (3), the first dividend could be important especially in the early stages of economic development. We should note that the cost of raising a child in developed countries is increasing due to higher education costs, even though the number of children is generally decreasing in these countries. Regarding conclusion (4), as Kinugasa and Mason [2007] insist, it is possible that Western and East Asian countries are more self-reliant than other countries, and the lifecycle model of our theory could be more applicable to these countries. In developing countries, familial transfer may be more common, and such transfers need to be considered. In addition, banking and credit systems could be different in different regions, which might affect the two demographic dividends on saving and growth. Finally, as is mentioned in conclusion (5), higher saving stimulated by the second dividend could be invested effectively, which would induce economic growth.

Appendix Table 9-1   Summary of Variables

Variable	N	(1) Whole World Mean	Standard Deviation	N	(2) West and East Asia Mean	Standard Deviation	N	(3) Non-West, Non-East Asia Mean	Standard Deviation
Dvd1	605	0.1746	0.4896	195	0.2688	0.3870	410	0.1298	0.5260
Dvd2	605	0.6285	0.7004	195	0.7740	0.5148	410	0.5592	0.7641
S/Y	605	0.1228	0.1223	195	0.2268	0.0742	410	0.0734	0.1090
Y/N_{gr}	605	0.0164	0.0304	195	0.0281	0.0271	410	0.0108	0.0304
Y_{gr}	605	0.0383	0.0343	195	0.0367	0.0344	410	0.0391	0.0343
PRI	605	0.8574	0.7542	195	0.8128	0.3978	410	0.8786	0.8739
$\ln(Y/N)$	605	8.2899	1.0537	195	9.3461	0.6183	410	7.7875	0.8206
K/Y	605	0.1583	0.0859	195	0.2372	0.0601	410	0.1208	0.0692
Price	605	0.5911	0.3703	195	0.8296	0.4295	410	0.4776	0.2738
Open	605	55.3268	31.5533	195	53.7635	32.7668	410	56.0703	30.9727

Note: N is number of observations. For descriptions of variables, see the notes of Tables 9-1 and 9-2.

Chapter 10

The Effect of Demographic Change
on Industrial Structure*

Introduction

This research analyzed the effects of demographic change on industrial structure in terms of capital accumulation, revealing that demographic change considerably affects capital accumulation, which plays an important role in transforming the industrial structure. We combined the overlapping generations model formulated by Kinugasa and Mason [2007] and the general equilibrium growth accounting model of Yamaguchi [1982b; 2001] for simulating the effects of demographic change on agricultural and non-agricultural outputs, labor, and capital. The effect of demographic change, particularly changes in the number of children, adult longevity, and child survival rate, on capital growth was analyzed using the overlapping generations model. Further, we investigated the effect of capital growth on agricultural and non-agricultural outputs and inputs using the general equilibrium growth accounting model.

The present study's simulation analysis conducted using Japanese data revealed that a rapid decline in the number of children and a rapid increase in adult longevity stimulated capital accumulation and increased the importance of non-agricultural constituents from the 1960s to the 1990s. Simulated capital growth not only increased non-agricultural output and capital to a greater extent than it did to the corresponding agricultural constituents, and increased non-agricultural labor and decreased non-agricultural labor.

*The content of this chapter was developed and rewritten from Kinugasa and Yamaguchi [2008] to meet the purpose of the book. We appreciate *Journal of Population Studies* for permitting the use of this paper for this book.

In recent years, there has been a decrease in the working-age population, which comprises of people whose savings are normally higher than those of the other generations though the adult longevity in Japan had moderately increased; hence, we cannot expect a rapid increase in aggregate capital in the future. Therefore, the advantages of the non-agricultural sector in Japan could disappear, and agriculture could become increasingly important in the near future.

1. Capital in the General Equilibrium Growth Accounting Model

1.1. *Literature Reviews*

Demographic transition is one of the most important stylized facts with regard to economic development. In the early stages of development, both fertility and mortality are high and stagnant; the latter is high because of poor nutrition and medical technology, while the former is high in order to replace the lives that are lost due to high infant mortality. During the first stage of demographic transition, mortality — particularly infant mortality — declines rapidly. However, there is no immediate decline in fertility; consequently, the population dramatically increases with the decline in mortality. Fertility begins to decline much later than mortality. In many developed countries, both fertility and mortality are low, and population aging is developing into a serious problem. A considerable number of researches have attempted to examine the economic implications of demographic transition. During a demographic transition, the young dependency rate decreases while the share of working-age population increases. Bloom and Williamson [1998], Bloom *et al.* [2000], and Kelley and Schmidt [2001; 2005] have found that changes in age structure accordingly change the labor force, thus greatly contributing to economic growth. Demographic transition also influences saving behavior. According to the lifecycle hypothesis, individuals save when they are young and employed and spend their savings after retirement (Modigliani and Brumberg [1954]; Tobin [1967]). Further, changes in young dependency alter the age-earning and consumption profiles. In particular, a higher young dependency can result in an increased consumption at a younger age (Mason [1981; 1987]; Higgins and Williamson [1997]). Moreover, increased adult longevity can increase the saving of prime-age adults, resulting in capital accumulation (Kinugasa and Mason [2007]; Lee *et al.* [2001])

Industrialization is another important stylized fact pertaining to economic development. As Engel's and Petty–Clark's laws suggest, agricultural dependency is high in the initial period of economic development but declines with the continued development of the economy. Hence, economic development and agricultural dependency are closely related. It is necessary to have an agricultural technical change at the onset of economic development in order to push labor or capital into the non-agricultural sector. Many studies have attempted to explain economic development in conjunction with an agricultural technical change through a consideration of a "dual economy" (Lewis [1954]; Ranis and Fei [1961]; Jorgenson [1961]; Kelley *et al.* [1972b]). According to the concept of a dual economy, an economy can be separated into two categories — the agricultural sector and the non-agricultural sector. The agricultural sector is traditional, self-sufficient, and characterized by low productivity. The non-agricultural sector is modern, profitable, and highly productive. Yamaguchi [1982b; 2001] and his colleagues have established the general equilibrium growth accounting model in their previous studies on dual economy. The authors have examined the effects of eight exogenous variables on a corresponding number of endogenous ones, revealing important findings.[1]

Thus far, previous studies have not conducted detailed research on the relationship between industrial structure and components of demographic transition such as changes in fertility, child and adult mortality, and labor force. This chapter attempts to explore the link between demographic transition and industrialization. For this, we have combined an overlapping generations model and the general equilibrium growth accounting model and examined the manner in which demographic transition influences capital accumulation and industrial structure, with particular reference to agricultural dependency. Figure 10-1 presents the outline of this research. Our findings suggest that demographic transition — particularly declining fertility and increasing longevity — leads to capital accumulation, which facilitates industrialization.

---

[1]The variables and findings are further explained in Sec. 2.

The Effects of Demographic Change on Industrialization
Demographic change (decline in fertility, increase in adult survival)
    ↓ (Overlapping generations model) Increase in saving,
Capital accumulation
    ↓   (General Equilibrium Growth Accounting Model)
Industrialization

Figure 10-1   Outline of this Research

1.2. Growth Rate Multipliers and Capital

Yamaguchi and Binswanger [1975], Yamaguchi [1982b; 2001], and
Yamaguchi and Kennedy [1984a; 1984b] developed the model of the dual
economy. The authors considered a two-sector economy consisting of the
agricultural and non-agricultural sectors and established a general equilibrium growth accounting model.[2] Further, they calculated the effects of eight
exogenous variables on eight endogenous ones.[3] Each effect is referred to as
a "growth rate multiplier" (GRM), which reflects the percentage of increase
in an endogenous variable due to a 1% increase in a certain exogenous one.
GRMs are expressed by aligning endogenous and exogenous variables; for
example, $Y_1 K$ is the effect of a 1% increase in aggregate capital on agricultural output. Yamaguchi and colleagues also calculated the contributions of
exogenous variables to endogenous ones by multiplying the GRMs and the
growth rates of the exogenous variables.

Table 10-1 presents the GRMs with respect to capital. According to
the above-mentioned researchers' findings, aggregate capital (K) has the
following effects on the endogenous variables.[4] An increase in aggregate
capital increases both agricultural and non-agricultural outputs. An increase

---

[2]This model is further explained in Chapter 2.

[3]The exogenous variables are agricultural technical growth (T_1), non-agricultural technical
growth (T_2), population (Q), total labor force (L), aggregate capital (K), land (B), demand
shifter of agricultural products (a), and wage gap between agricultural and non-agricultural
sectors. The endogenous variables are agricultural output (Y_1), non-agricultural output
(Y_2), agricultural labor (L_1), non-agricultural labor (L_2), agricultural capital (K_1), non-
agricultural capital (K_2), relative price of agricultural goods with respect to non-agricultural
products (P), and income (E).

[4]These findings are valid for the entire period in the analysis except 1945. Japan was involved
in a war around 1945; hence, this year can be considered as an exceptional situation.

Table 10-1　Growth Rate Multipliers with Respect to Capital in Japan 1890–2000

	$Y_1 K$	$Y_2 K$	$K_1 K$	$K_2 K$	$L_1 K$	$L_2 K$
1890	0.10	0.30	0.96	1.03	−0.02	0.05
1895	0.10	0.33	0.96	1.02	−0.02	0.04
1900	0.09	0.37	0.97	1.01	−0.02	0.03
1905	0.09	0.41	0.95	1.02	−0.03	0.05
1910	0.09	0.42	0.94	1.02	−0.03	0.05
1915	0.09	0.51	0.94	1.02	−0.03	0.04
1920	0.09	0.41	0.94	1.01	−0.03	0.04
1925	0.08	0.40	0.94	1.01	−0.03	0.03
1930	0.10	0.46	0.97	1.01	−0.02	0.02
1935	0.11	0.51	0.96	1.01	−0.03	0.02
1940	0.09	0.55	0.97	1.00	−0.02	0.01
1945	0.11	0.53	1.02	1.00	0.01	−0.01
1950	0.09	0.55	0.97	1.00	−0.02	0.01
1955	0.08	0.30	0.92	1.01	−0.05	0.03
1960	0.09	0.37	0.93	1.01	−0.06	0.02
1965	0.11	0.32	0.92	1.01	−0.06	0.02
1970	0.10	0.32	0.93	1.01	−0.06	0.02
1975	0.11	0.37	0.92	1.00	−0.05	0.03
1980	0.10	0.32	0.94	1.00	−0.06	0.01
1985	0.11	0.40	0.92	1.01	−0.05	0.02
1990	0.10	0.32	0.91	1.00	−0.07	0.01
1995	0.09	0.35	0.93	1.01	−0.06	0.02
2000	0.11	0.32	0.92	1.01	−0.06	0.02

Note: The data are adopted from Yamaguchi [1982b], and the values are newly estimated.

in aggregate capital has a greater effect on non-agricultural output than on agricultural output, $(Y_2 K > Y_1 K > 0)$. An increase in aggregate capital has a positive effect on both agricultural and non-agricultural capitals, and its effect on non-agricultural capital is greater than that on agricultural capital $(K_2 K > K_1 K > 0)$. An increase in aggregate capital decreases agricultural labor but increases non-agricultural labor $(L_1 K < 0, L_2 K > 0)$. These findings imply that capital accumulation induces growth in both agricultural and non-agricultural sectors; however, it has a greater positive effect on non-agricultural growth. Therefore, capital accumulation is likely to accelerate industrialization. The research using GRMs assumes the possibility of exogenous aggregate capital. Although this assumption is necessary for this study, the actual factors that influence aggregate capital are somewhat controversial. Demographic change can alter the saving behaviors of consumers, which can consequently influence capital accumulation.

2. Capital Accumulation in the Overlapping Generations Model

2.1. *Consumer's Optimization*

An overlapping generations model is established in this section in order to gauge the effects of demographic change on capital accumulation. Based on Higgins [1994] and Kinugasa and Mason [2007], the overlapping generations model takes into account the existence of different generations at the same time. According to Higgins' assumption, there are three generations comprising children, prime-age adults, and the elderly. Child age, prime age, and old age are set at age zero, one, and two, respectively. Children are considered as dependent and not employed. Prime-age adults take care of children, work, and save for their old age. The elderly are retired and spend the savings accumulated by them in their prime age.[5] We have assumed that not all children can survive to prime age and not all prime-age adults can survive after retirement.

The preferences of the prime-age adults at time t are given by the following additively separable utility function:

$$V_t = \lambda_{\text{ALT}} \frac{c_{\text{ALT},t}^{1-\theta}}{1-\theta} + \frac{\lambda_{\text{OLD}} q_t}{1+\rho} \frac{c_{\text{OLD},t+1}^{1-\theta}}{1-\theta} + \kappa n_t^{1-\varepsilon} \lambda_{\text{CLD}} \frac{c_{\text{CLD},t}^{1-\theta}}{1-\theta},$$

$$(10.1)$$

where $c_{\text{ALT},t}$, $c_{\text{OLD},t+1}$, and $c_{\text{CLD},t}$ represent the consumption of the prime-age adults, the elderly, and the dependent children, respectively. q_t is the survival rate of prime-age adults till old age and is used as a measure of adult longevity. Prime-age adults decide their own consumption at present as well as after retirement; they also decide their children's consumption. The parameter κ implies the rate at which parents discount the utility of children, and it is assumed that $\kappa < 0$. It is also assumed that $\varepsilon > 0$, so that the marginal utility with respect to the number of children declines

---

[5]For simplicity, this model assumes that there are neither bequests nor transfers from children to parents.

according to the number of children. λ_{CLD}, λ_{ALT}, and λ_{OLD} represent the relative importance of consumption in a consumer's children, prime age, and post-retirement, respectively. ρ is the discount rate, that is, the rate of time preference. The intertemporal elasticity of substitution[6] is given by $(1/\theta)$. If $(1/\theta) > 1$, an increase in the interest rate will increase the saving of prime-age adults; however, if $(1/\theta) < 1$, the increase in the interest rate will have the opposite effect on saving.

Prime-age adults work and obtain the wage income $A_t w_t$ per unit of labor, in which A_t is the level of technology and w_t is the wage per effective worker. Prime-age adults are endowed with one unit of time. Raising one child takes up v units of time, and prime-age adults with n children work for $(1 - vn)$ units of time. Prime-age adults allocate their earnings to their own consumption, that of their children, and for saving. The budget constraint of prime-age adults is given as follows:

$$c_{ALT,t} + n_t c_{CLD,t} + s_{AKT,t} = A_t w_t (1 - vn_t), \qquad (10.2)$$

where $s_{ALT,t}$ represents the saving of prime-age adults. We assume the availability of insurance against longevity risk.[7] An annuity is purchased at the onset of prime age if insurance companies are risk neutral and annuity markets are perfect. The rate of return for the surviving elderly is $((1 + r_{t+1})/q_t)$, where r_{t+1} represents the riskless interest rate on saving. The return with regard to annuities is $((1 + r_{t+1})/q_t)$. Returns for insurance are higher than the regular norm; therefore, individuals restrict their saving to insurance. After their retirement, the elderly consume the proceeds of their savings. Thus, the budget constraint of the elderly is given as follows:

$$c_{OLD,t+1} = (1 + r_{t+1}) s_{ALT,t} / q_t. \qquad (10.3)$$

---

[6]Intertemporal elasticity of substitution is elasticity of substitution between consumption at different point and expressed as

$$\frac{\partial \ln(c_{t+1}/c_t)}{\partial \ln[u'(c_t)/u'(c_{t+1})]}\bigg|_{u=\bar{u}},$$

where $u'(c_t)$ is marginal utility of consumption and $\bar{u}$ is constant utility level. High intertemporal elasticity of substitution means that the consumer's desire to smooth consumption is low.

[7]Yaari [1965] and Blanchard [1985] provide a detailed discussion on this issue.

According to the budget constraints of the prime-age adults and the elderly, the lifetime budget constraint faced by prime-age adults is derived as follows:

$$w_t A_t (1 - \nu n_t) = c_{\text{ALT},t} + n_t c_{\text{CLD},t} + \frac{q_t}{1 + r_{t+1}} c_{\text{OLD},t+1}. \quad (10.4)$$

Consumers determine their children's consumption and their own consumption in prime age and after retirement, thus maximizing life utility as given in Eq. (10.1) under the lifetime budget constraint in Eq. (10.3). The saving of prime-age adults is also calculated according to these results, as follows:

$$s_{\text{ALT},t} = \frac{q_t \left(\frac{\lambda_{\text{OLD}}}{\lambda_{\text{ALT}}(1+\rho)} \right)^{\frac{1}{\theta}} (1 + r_{t+1})^{\frac{1-\theta}{\theta}} (1 - \nu n_t) A_t w_t}{1 + \left(\frac{\kappa \lambda_{\text{CLD}}}{\lambda_{\text{ALT}}} \right)^{\frac{1}{\theta}} n_t^{\frac{\theta-\varepsilon}{\theta}} + q_t \left(\frac{\lambda_{\text{OLD}}}{\lambda_{\text{ALT}}(1+\rho)} \right)^{\frac{1}{\theta}} (1 + r_{t+1})^{\frac{1-\theta}{\theta}}}. \quad (10.5)$$

In Eq. (10.5), $\partial s_{\text{ALT},t} / \partial q_t > 0$; hence, the saving of prime-age adults increases along with an increase in the adult survival rate. Evidently, if consumers are aware of the fact that they will live longer, they are more likely to have higher saving in preparation for old age. Equation (10.5) also implies $\partial s_{\text{ALT},t} / \partial n_t < 0$ if $\theta > \varepsilon$. The saving of prime-age adults decreases with an increase in the number of children as long as $\theta > \varepsilon$. Moreover, the expenditure on children correspondingly increases with an increase in the number of children, while the wage income of prime-age adults decreases because raising children requires the expenditure of time. Therefore, higher fertility decreases the saving of prime-age adults.

2.2. Determinants of Aggregate Capital

We assume a small open economy in order to keep the interest rate constant with the world interest rate.[8] Gross national saving at time $t(S_t)$ is given by the change in aggregate asset plus depreciation, that is, $S_t = (D_{t+1} + F_{t+1}) - (K_t + F_t) + \xi K_t$, where D is domestic assets, F is foreign assets,

---

[8]Perfect capital mobility is assumed to exist in a small open economy, in which the domestic economy is able to borrow and lend in the international capital market at a given interest rate. Whether the economy is lending or borrowing capital is an important issue; however, we are merely concerned with the aggregate capital holdings of a country for the sake of simplicity.

and ξ is the depreciation rate. Net national saving $(S_t - \xi K_t)$ is equal to the aggregate national income minus total consumption; therefore,

$$(K_{t+1} + F_{t+1}) - (K_t + F_t)$$
$$= w_t(1 - vn_t)A_tN_{1,t} + r_t(K_t + F_t)$$
$$- (n_tc_{\text{CLD},t}N_{\text{CLD},t} + c_{\text{ALT},t}N_{\text{ALT},t} + c_{\text{OLD},t}N_{\text{OLD},t}), \quad (10.6)$$

where $N_{0,t}$ is the number of children; $N_{1,t}$, the number of prime-age adults; and $N_{2,t}$, the number of the elderly. Substituting $n_tc_{\text{CLD},t}N_{\text{CLD},t} + c_{\text{ALT},t}N_{\text{ALT},t}$ and $c_{\text{OLD},t}$ from Eqs. (10.2) and (10.3) in Eq. (10.6), we get the following equation:

$$K_{t+1} = D_{t+1} + F_{t+1} = s_{\text{ALT},t}N_{\text{ALT},t}. \quad (10.7)$$

From Eq. (10.7), the total saving of prime-age adults at time t formulates the aggregate capital in the next period.[9] Higher saving of prime-age adults results in higher capital accumulation. In this context, the number of prime-age adults at t is expressed as $N_{\text{ALT},t} = p_tN_{0,t-1} = p_tn_{t-1}N_{\text{ALT},t-1}$, where p_t is the survival rate of children. Therefore, Eq. (10.7) can be rewritten as follows:

$$K_{t+1} = s_{\text{ALT},t}p_tn_{t-1}N_{\text{ALT},t-1}. \quad (10.8)$$

From the simulation analysis, we would like to ascertain the effects of demographic change on the growth rate in aggregate capital. The growth rate of capital $\dot{K}_t$ is defined as follows:

$$\dot{K}_t = \frac{K_t - K_{t-1}}{K_{t-1}}. \quad (10.9)$$

According to Eqs. (10.8) and (10.9), an increase in adult longevity at t does not influence the growth rate of capital. In addition, the effect of an increase in adult longevity at time t on the growth rate of capital at time $t + 1$ is

---

[9]In this scenario, the economy's aggregate capital *stock* at t is equal to the *flow* of saving at $t - 1$. This occurs because the model has only one period of working life and wealth is not accumulated across generations.

given by the following equation:

$$\frac{\partial \dot{K}_{t+1}}{\partial q_t} = \frac{(\partial s_{1,t}/\partial q_t)p_t n_{t-1} N_{\text{ALT},t-1}}{K_t} > 0. \tag{10.10}$$

Equation (10.10) indicates that an increase in adult longevity at t increases the growth rate of aggregate capital at time $t+1$ due to an increase in the saving of prime-age adults at t.[10]

The number of children at time t does not influence the growth rate of capital at time t. The effect of an increase in the number of children at t on the growth rate of capital at $t+1$ is as follows:

$$\frac{\partial \dot{K}_{t+1}}{\partial n_t} = \frac{\partial s_{\text{ALT},t}/\partial n_t}{K_t} < 0. \tag{10.11}$$

The number of children at time t decreases the capital stock at $t+1$. If the number of children increases at t, prime-age adults save less in the same period; thus, less capital is accumulated at time $t+1$. The effect of the number of children at t on the growth of capital at $t+2$ is given by the following equation:

$$\frac{\partial \dot{K}_{t+2}}{\partial n_t} = \frac{s_{1,t}p_t N_{\text{ALT},t} - (\partial s_{\text{ALT},t}/\partial n_t)p_t n_{t-1} N_{\text{ALT},t-1}}{K_{t+1}^2} > 0. \tag{10.12}$$

The number of children at time t increases the number of prime-age adults who can accumulate capital at $t+1$, which results in higher capital accumulation at $t+2$. Also, less capital is accumulated at $t+1$, which gives rise to a higher growth rate of capital at time $t+2$. Therefore, the growth rate of aggregate capital increases at $t+2$ if fertility increases at t. Evidently, an increase in fertility prevents capital accumulation in the short run. However, once children become older, the increase in prime-age population stimulates capital accumulation. Our theory implies that stylized demographic changes such as declining fertility and mortality either increase or decrease

---

[10]The effects of adult longevity at t on growth in capital at time $t+1$ are given as $\frac{\partial \dot{K}_{t+2}}{\partial q_t} = \frac{-(\partial s_{\text{ALT},t}/\partial q_t)p_t n_{t-1} K_{t+2}}{K_{t+1}^2} < 0$. An increase in the adult longevity at t decreases the growth in capital at $t+2$ because of the increase in the denominator. This circumstance and Eq. (10.10) indicate that a continuing rapid increase in adult longevity increases the speed of capital accumulation.

the growth in aggregate capital stock; therefore, a detailed simulation analysis would be beneficial. In the next section, we have set the values for the parameters in order to simulate the influence of demographic change on capital accumulation in Japan.

3. Simulation Analysis of Demographic Change and Industrialization

In this section, we have applied the findings from the GRM in Sec. 1 in combination with the theory mentioned in Sec. 2 for analyzing the effect of demographic change on capital accumulation. The analysis estimates the manner in which changes in young dependency and adult survival affect the change in aggregate capital in Japan and how the influence of demographic change on aggregate capital affects agricultural and non-agricultural outputs and inputs. In this, we have assumed the consumer's optimization to be identical in both agricultural and non-agricultural sectors. Growth in aggregate capital is determined according to the theory described in Sec. 2.[11] According to Eq. (10.8), simulated aggregate capital is calculated. Also, we simulate the growth of aggregate capital based on Eq. (10.9). The contributions of the eight above-mentioned exogenous variables to the eight endogenous variables[12] are determined in Sec. 1.[13]

Figure 10-2 presents historical changes in adult longevity, the number of children per prime-age adult, and child survival rate. Initially, the number of children was high; there was no significant change in this figure until

---

[11]The results used for aggregate capital include foreign and domestic capital. The data regarding domestic capital may be more appropriate for calculating the contributions of the exogenous variables to the endogenous variables because the capital kept by domestic persons in foreign countries is likely to have a significantly weaker effect on industrialization in the domestic economy. In a small open economy, the saving behaviors of consumers do not influence the domestic capital. It would be beneficial to consider a model of a closed or an open economy in which capital is not perfectly mobile. However, in this study, we have assumed a small open economy and used the results for aggregate capital inclusive of both foreign and domestic capitals for simplicity. At least, there were some empirical evidences that demographic change influenced domestic investment to a great extent (Higgins [1994]; Higgins and Williamson [1997]).

[12]Please see footnote 3 for the explanation of endogenous variables.

[13]The parameters and data sources are described in Appendix.

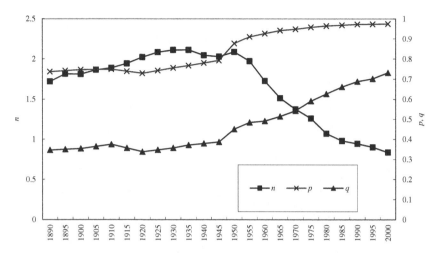

Figure 10-2   Historical Changes in the Number of Children and Adult and Child Survival in Japan, 1890–2000

Note: n represents the number of children per prime-age adult, p represents the child survival rate, and q is the adult survival rate. Appendix describes the method by which these values are calculated.

around 1955.[14] However, this number declined very rapidly from the 1960s to the 1990s, and it is quite low in recent times. The child survival rate was almost constant until 1945; this figure increased rapidly within the 10 years after World War II and has been almost one since the 1980s. The adult survival rate was also low and stagnant before World War II, after which it rapidly increased until around 1990. Since then, the adult survival rate has also constantly increased. As presented in Fig. 10-1, Japan experienced considerably rapid demographic transitions in the latter half of the 20th century.

In this study, we have simulated the extent to which the level and growth of aggregate capital have been influenced by the changes in the number of children and child and adult survival in Japan. Figure 10-3 presents the simulated level and growth of aggregate capital and the contribution of this capital to industrial change. As depicted in Fig. 10-3(a), the simulated

---

[14]It is necessary to note that the number of children includes the information regarding conception and still births. In this study, we have not discussed these issues in detail for the sake of simplicity; however, these issues require further discussion.

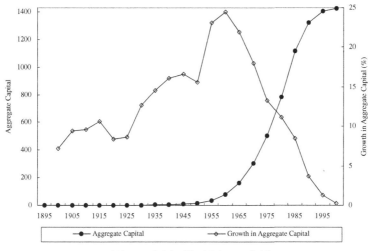

(a) Aggregate Capital and Growth in Aggregate Capital

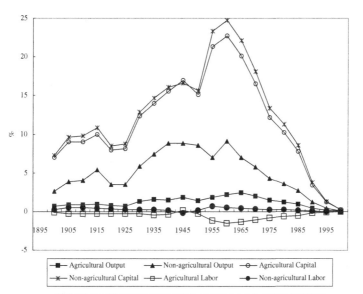

(b) Contribution of Aggregate Capital to Agricultural and Non-agricultural Inputs and Outputs

Figure 10-3   Simulated Capital and Its Contribution to agriculture and Non-agriculture Under Demographic Change in Japan

Note: Level of aggregate capital is a relative value of aggregate capital when the technological level in 1980 is set to be 1.

aggregate capital was low and stagnant until 1955 but increased rapidly from the 1960s. Although aggregate capital achieved a high level in 1990, the levels of simulated aggregate capital did not change greatly from 1995 to 2000. The simulated growth rate of aggregate capital slightly declined in the 1920s with an increase in the number of children; however, it again increased from 1925 to 1945. The simulated growth in capital was quite high between 1960 and 1970 due to a rapid increase in adult and child survival and a rapid decline in the burden of youth dependency. Since the 1970s, the simulated growth rate of capital rapidly declined due to a rapid decrease in the growth in prime-age adults; moreover, the simulated capital growth rate was nearly zero in 2000.

Figure 10-3(b) presents the simulated contributions of aggregate capital to non-agricultural outputs and inputs. An increase in capital due to demographic change has increased both agricultural and non-agricultural outputs. The contribution of capital to non-agricultural output is much higher than that to agricultural output. Aggregate capital positively contributes to agricultural and non-agricultural capital to a great extent; however, it contributes more to non-agricultural capital than it does to agricultural capital. An increase in aggregate capital decreases agricultural labor, while increasing non-agricultural labor. The contributions of aggregate capital to labor in the two sectors are relatively low; however, Fig. 10-3(b) indicates that the simulated aggregate capital decreased agricultural labor to a comparatively greater extent from the 1960s to the 1970s. The results confirm that demographic change in Japan stimulated capital accumulation from 1900 to 2000. Accumulated capital contributed to a growth in output in both agricultural and non-agricultural sectors; moreover, aggregate capital affected the non-agricultural sector more favorably than it did the agricultural sector because (1) the non-agricultural sector experienced a greater increase in capital than did the agricultural sector, and (2) agricultural labor decreased while non-agricultural labor increased, thus absorbing the agricultural labor. Therefore, demographic change increases the importance of the non-agricultural sector.

Figure 10-4 represents simulated capital and its contribution to industrialization, while assuming the adult survival rate to remain constant throughout the period. In Fig. 10-4(a), the level and growth of aggregate capital track similar paths to those in Fig. 10-3(a). The simulated level of aggregate

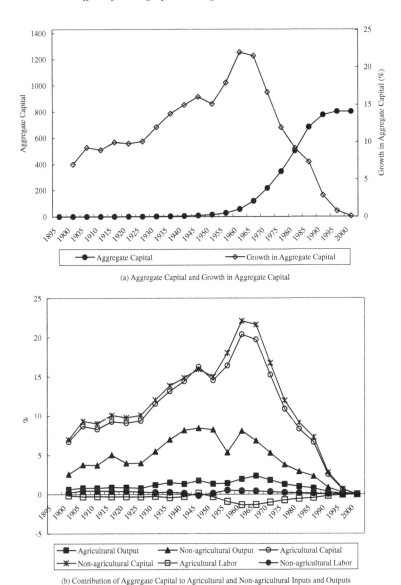

(a) Aggregate Capital and Growth in Aggregate Capital

(b) Contribution of Aggregate Capital to Agricultural and Non-agricultural Inputs and Outputs

Figure 10-4 Simulated Capital and Its Contribution to Agriculture and Non-agriculture Under Constant Adult Survival

Note: Adult and child survival rates and other parameters are the same as in Fig. 10-2. We assume that throughout the period, the adult survival rate is constant at its 1900 level. See also the note of Fig. 10-3.

capital for the period after the 1980s is much lower than that in Fig. 10-3(a), while the simulated growth rate of aggregate capital is found to be similar. In most cases, the growth rate of capital is lower in Fig. 10-4 as compared to Fig. 10-3. Moreover, the simulated growth rate of capital became negative in 2000. Assuming that the number of children was constant throughout the simulated period in Fig. 10-4, we also simulated capital and its contribution to the agricultural and non-agricultural outputs and inputs. The simulated level and growth in aggregate capital in Fig. 10-5(a) significantly differs from the corresponding levels in Figs. 10-2 and 10-3. The simulated aggregate capital was low and stagnant until 1975. From 1980 onward, the simulated level of capital rapidly increased. Similarly, the simulated growth in aggregate capital was low until 1955, which significantly increased in 1960 due to a rapid increase in the adult and child survival rates. The growth rate of capital remained at a high level from 1965 to 2000 as a result of the increasing adult survival rate. Figure 10-5(b) indicates that the changes in the adult and child survival rates increased both agricultural and non-agricultural outputs. In addition, the contribution of capital to non-agricultural output was much larger than that to agricultural output. The simulated contributions of capital to agricultural and non-agricultural capital are much higher than those to output and labor in each sector. With the exception of 1945, the simulated aggregate capital consistently increased the non-agricultural capital to a greater extent than it did agricultural capital, and the gap between the contributions of capital to agricultural and non-agricultural capitals widened after 1960. An increase in the simulated aggregate capital decreased agricultural labor and increased non-agricultural labor. Moreover, it is found that after 1960, a higher growth in the simulated aggregate capital caused a more serious decrease in agricultural labor than before.

To summarize, our simulation analysis has demonstrated that demographic change — particularly pertaining to a decrease in the number of children and an increase in adult longevity — has increased the saving of prime-age adults, thus greatly contributing to capital accumulation after World War II. Capital accumulation has increased both agricultural and non-agricultural outputs and increased the relative importance of the non-agricultural sector as compared to the agricultural one. Growth in capital has resulted in a greater increase in non-agricultural output and capital than in the

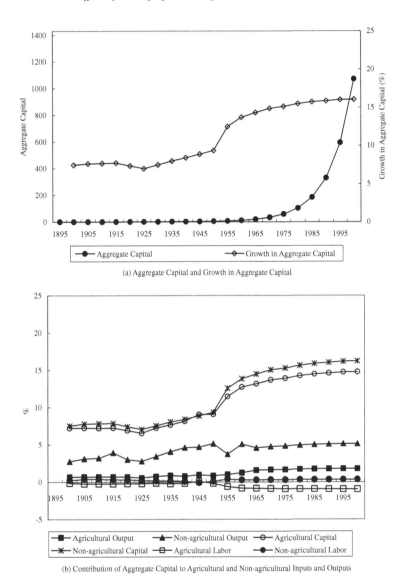

(a) Aggregate Capital and Growth in Aggregate Capital

(b) Contribution of Aggregate Capital to Agricultural and Non-agricultural Inputs and Outputs

Figure 10-5 Simulated Capital and Its Contribution to Agriculture and Non-agriculture Under Constant Number of Children

Note: Number of children, child survival rate, and other parameters are the same as in Fig. 10-2. We assume that throughout the period, the number of children is constant at its 1900 level. See also the note of Fig. 10-3.

corresponding agricultural constituents. Due to accumulated capital, non-agricultural labor has increased, whereas agricultural labor has decreased. In this context, would it be possible to predict the future scenario? Japanese fertility in recent times is at an extremely low level, which is likely to increase the saving of prime-age adults due to the reduced burden of youth dependency. However, the continuing low fertility has also decreased the number of prime-age adults who can accumulate wealth. An increased adult longevity could contribute to capital accumulation, but in the future, it would be difficult to offset the negative effect of decreasing labor force on capital accumulation. The simulated growth in capital for the year 2000 was almost zero with respect to Japanese demographic change, and it was negative when we assumed adult longevity to remain unchanged. Considering Japan's demographic characteristics, capital growth may continue to decrease in the future, while a decline in aggregate capital may shortly decrease the importance of non-agriculture and increase that of agriculture.

Conclusion

The main conclusions can briefly be summarized as follows:

(1) Previous researches have not analyzed the effect of demographic change on industrial structure from the aspect of capital accumulation.

(2) The GRMs in the general equilibrium growth accounting model indicate that a higher growth of aggregate capital increases the relative importance of the non-agricultural sector as compared to agriculture; it also increases non-agricultural output and capital to a greater extent than it does the agricultural counterparts. Moreover, aggregate capital decreases agricultural labor, while increasing non-agricultural labor.

(3) Our overlapping generations model demonstrates that an increase in the number of children decreases the saving of prime-age adults, while an increase in adult longevity increases them. An increase in adult longevity also promotes capital accumulation. An increase in the number of children represses capital accumulation in the short run, but it stimulates future capital accumulation because in time, the children enter the labor market and begin to save.

(4) The simulation analysis shows that the rapid decline in the number of children and the rapid increase in adult and child longevity from

the 1950s to the 1990s greatly contributed to capital accumulation and industrialization.

(5) According to the results of simulation analysis, the growth in labor force has declined since the 1990s, which could lead to slower capital accumulation. The growth in aggregate capital in Japan may become negative in the future; this implies that the relative importance of non-agriculture as compared to agriculture is not likely to persist.

Our research indicates that demographic change influences industrial structure through capital accumulation. The remarkable industrialization in the latter half of the twentieth century can be explained in relation to the rapid demographic change, to some extent. In the near future, the importance of agriculture may increase according to the demographic and capital conditions in Japan. However, in recent times, the share of agricultural income (or labor) in total income (or labor) is shrinking, in conjunction with a decline in the food self-sufficiency ratio in Japan. It is suggested that Japanese society as a whole should reevaluate the importance of agriculture as an employment opportunity. There is extensive scope for further research in this area. First, it is imperative to establish a theory that separately considers the respective consumption of agricultural and non-agricultural households, even though such a theory may increase the endogenous variables and further complicate the model. Second, it is necessary to take into account the phenomenon of intergenerational transfer. Social security and familial transfer can influence saving behavior; moreover, these systems have dramatically changed in the twentieth century and will continue to change in the future.

Appendix: Simulation Method and Descriptions of Parameters

The level and the growth of aggregate capital are simulated according to the theory described in Sec. 2. Using the GRM in Table 10-1 and the simulated growth rate of aggregate capital, we calculate the contribution of the simulated aggregate capital to agricultural and non-agricultural outputs and inputs, with respect to the demographic change. Contribution of the simulated aggregate capital to agricultural and non-agricultural outputs and inputs are calculated by multiplying simulated growth in aggregate capital by GRM in Table 10-1. We simulate the aggregate capital in Eq. (10.1) and growth in aggregate capital in Eq. (10.9) under the following assumptions.

Each age consists of 30 years. Children are from 0 to 29 years old, prime-age adults are from 30 to 59 years old, and the elderly are from 60 to 89 years old. Therefore, each period should also consist of 30 years. However, in Eq. (10.8), the capital in the next period is determined based on the saving behavior as seen 30 years ago, which is not a realistic assumption. Therefore, we assume one period to consist of 5 years; that is, aggregate capital is determined by the saving behavior of prime-age adults 5 years before. $\dot{K}$, growth rate of aggregate capital per one year, is calculated every 5 years.

According to Higgins [1994], the values of the following parameters are assumed. The utility weights are assigned as follows: $\lambda_{CLD} = 0.5$, $\lambda_{ALT} = 1$, and $\lambda_{OLD} = 0.9$, which implies that the consumption of the children is 50%, while that of the elderly is 90% of the prime-age consumption. θ is determined to be such that the intertemporal elasticity of substitution $(1/\theta)$ is 1.3. Under this value of θ, an increase in interest rate moderately increases the saving of prime-age adults. κ is set at 0.53, so that the utility of children discounted and is equivalent to 53% of prime-age adult's utility. ν is set at 0.1 so that 10% of working time is devoted to raise one children. It is assumed that ε is 0.1; hence, the marginal utility in the number of children declines to a very small extent with a decline in the number of children. Wage (w) is set constant at 1. The technological level is assumed to be 1 in 1890 and its annual growth is set at 0.15%. The interest rate (r) is set at 0.05% for a year; therefore, $1 + r = 4.322$ for 30 years. In this study, we have used the GRMs calculated in Table 10-1. Yamaguchi [1982b; 2001] calculates these from 1880 to 1965, whereas we have recalculated them from 1970 to 2000.

For the number of children, we have divided the population aged 0–29 by that aged 30–59. The data were obtained from the *Historical Statistics of Japan* from the Statistics Bureau and the Statistical Research and Training Institute in Japan. The adult and child survival rates were calculated using the life table from the Health and Welfare Statistics Association in Japan. The adult survival rate is defined as $\sum_{x=60}^{89} L_x / \sum_{x=30}^{59} L_x$, where L_x is number of years lived between the exact age x and the exact age $x + 1$.[15] The child survival rate is defined as $\sum_{x=30}^{59} L_x / \sum_{x=0}^{29} L_x$.

---

[15]Where data for the total population were unavailable, we used the mean of the adult (child) survival rates for males and females.

Appendix

Appendix Table 1   Average Growth Rates of Endogenous and Exogenous Variables

En. Variable	No	1880~ 1890	1890~ 1900	1900~ 1910	1910~ 1920	1920~ 1930	1930~ 1940	1940~ 1950	1950~ 1960	1960~ 1970
Y_1	1	2.4	1.4	2.2	3.1	1.3	0.5	−0.3	4.7	2.3
	2	3.4	1.7	2.2	3.2	1.1	0.4	−0.5	3.6	2.1
P_1Y_1	3	5.0	7.8	4.5	16.3	−4.4	15.2	37.5	6.5	—
	4	2.5	6.4	3.9	16.0	−4.6	11.2	—	10.0	9.8
	5	12.0	7.5	4.4	16.8	−4.5	12.6	—	—	—
	6	—	—	—	—	—	15.2	37.3	8.4	9.0
	7	3.4	6.9	4.2	16.1	−4.5	12.0	—	7.9	10.7
Y_2	8	4.3	4.5	2.9	4.2	2.5	6.3	—	8.9	11.9
L_1	9	0.0	0.1	0.0	−1.2	0.0	−0.3	1.7	−1.7	−3.6
	10	−0.3	0.0	−0.1	−0.1	0.0	−0.3	1.7	−1.7	−3.5
L_{1M}	11	−0.2	0.0	−0.1	0.0	0.0	−1.7	2.2	−2.1	−3.9
L_{1F}	12	−0.3	−0.1	−0.2	−0.1	0.0	1.2	1.5	−1.4	−1.7
L_2	13	1.7	1.4	1.3	3.2	1.7	2.8	—	4.7	2.9
K_1	14	0.7	1.0	1.7	0.9	1.0	0.7	−1.4	4.6	8.9
	15	0.1	0.4	0.8	0.5	0.7	0.3	−0.3	3.0	7.4
	16	0.1	0.5	1.3	0.5	0.7	0.4	−0.2	3.6	8.3
K_2	17	3.3	3.5	4.5	6.7	4.8	4.7	—	6.3	11.5
P	18	6.3	−1.9	−0.8	0.7	−3.3	7.2	—	−1.5	2.1
P'	19	−0.9	4.0	1.8	10.5	−3.1	7.2	148.1	2.6	6.2
	20	2.2	5.6	2.6	11.5	−2.7	4.6	—	3.6	4.8
P_1	21	−0.5	4.1	1.7	12.3	−5.6	10.1	12.9	5.3	8.3
	22	−0.1	4.3	1.8	13.2	−5.6	10.1	—	5.2	12.3
	23	−0.3	4.5	2.1	12.9	−5.4	10.5	—	2.9	7.0
P_2	24	−0.3	7.2	3.0	11.5	−1.8	3.4	—	3.9	4.8
	25	−1.3	5.1	2.1	10.6	−6.4	6.3	15.3	−0.9	−0.9
PY	26	—	—	—	—	—	—	—	9.4	10.8
	27	5.9	7.4	3.0	15.8	−0.9	10.7	49.9	13.7	17.4

(*Continued*)

Appendix Table 1   (*Continued*)

En. Variable	No	1880~1890	1890~1900	1900~1910	1910~1920	1920~1930	1930~1940	1940~1950	1950~1960	1960~1970
	28	7.0	8.5	5.0	15.3	−0.3	10.9	—	—	—
	29	5.6	8.8	5.1	16.0	−0.7	10.0	50.1	15.0	16.5
	30	—	—	—	—	—	11.5	49.1	15.1	16.4
	31	—	—	—	—	—	10.6	74.0	14.5	16.2
	32	—	—	—	—	—	—	—	12.7	16.1
PE	33	4.7	7.7	3.9	14.6	−2.1	8.8	—	13.6	15.3
	34	4.9	7.7	3.9	14.3	−1.9	8.7	—	—	—
	35	—	—	—	—	—	10.4	47.8	101.8	15.3
	36	—	—	—	—	—	9.5	45.9	13.2	14.9
	37	4.7	7.7	3.9	14.6	−2.2	8.8	—	13.6	15.3
E	38	2.7	2.2	1.3	2.6	0.5	3.9	—	7.1	10.0
	39	—	—	—	—	—	−2.8	6.6	8.0	8.3
	40	2.7	2.1	1.2	2.7	0.7	4.0	—	—	—
	41	5.2	2.2	1.1	2.5	0.5	4.1	—	—	—
	42	—	—	—	—	—	3.5	3.5	7.0	10.0
Y	43	3.6	3.2	2.5	3.8	2.1	5.1	—	8.2	11.1
	44	4.3	2.8	2.3	4.1	2.4	6.0	—	—	—
Y_2	45	3.7	3.9	2.6	4.0	2.4	5.7	—	9.2	11.9

Ex. Variable

En. Variable	No	1880~1890	1890~1900	1900~1910	1910~1920	1920~1930	1930~1940	1940~1950	1950~1960	1960~1970
T_1	46	3.2	1.3	1.8	3.5	1.0	0.4	−1.2	4.1	3.0
T_2	47	1.7	1.9	0.1	−0.9	−0.5	2.0	—	4.1	6.3
B	48	0.4	0.6	0.7	0.7	−0.1	0.3	−0.4	0.4	−0.5
K	49	2.3	2.6	3.6	5.3	4.2	4.2	—	—	—
	50	1.5	2.6	3.3	5.0	3.8	4.0	—	—	—
	51	—	—	—	—	—	—	—	6.1	11.3
	52	1.6	3.0	3.5	5.5	3.2	4.5	—	—	—
	53	—	—	3.9	4.5	3.6	3.9	—	5.8	—
	54	2.8	2.1	2.4	4.1	2.6	3.7	—	—	—
	55	2.2	1.7	2.1	3.6	2.9	3.3	—	—	—
	56	4.2	1.7	2.3	3.7	3.2	3.5	—	—	—
	57	—	—	—	—	—	—	—	5.6	9.1
L	58	0.5	0.6	0.4	0.6	0.9	1.5	0.2	2.2	1.3
	59	1.5	0.9	0.6	0.4	0.8	0.9	0.2	2.3	1.3
Q	60	0.9	1.0	1.2	1.2	1.6	1.1	1.6	1.2	1.1
F	61	0.8	2.8	5.3	4.5	3.7	2.1	8.1	10.2	9.2
	62	0.1	3.4	6.0	5.1	3.9	2.0	—	10.7	9.9
a	63	4.2	−2.2	−0.4	0.6	−2.8	0.9	—	−4.7	−4.1
m_w	64	−2.0	0.9	−2.8	1.8	−3.4	4.6	—	−3.1	8.7

(*Continued*)

Appendix Table 1 *(Continued)*

←

The Source of Data of Appendix Table 1
Appendix Table 1 shows the growth rates of endogenous and exogenous variables in each 10 year from 1880 to 1970.
Endogenous variables are necessary for the vector x and exdogenous variables are necessary for the vector b in matrix form $Ax = b$ of our model (see Chapter 2). Here, we show the source of these Data.

(1) Endogenous variables: Line 1 to Line 45

1. $O - S$, p. 288, Total Output of Agriculture in 1934–1936 Constant Prices at the Farm Gate.
2. *LTES*, 9, p. 182, Value Added in Agriculture (1934–1936 Prices: Net Depreciation).
3. *LTES*, 9, p. 182, Value Added in Agriculture (Current Prices: Net Depreciation).
4. *LTES*, 9, p. 146, Farm Value of Agriculturral Production: Current Prices.
5. *LTES*, 1, p. 204, Net Domestic Product of Primary Industry: Current Prices, 1885–1940.
6. *LTES*, 1, p. 203, Net Domestic Product of Primary Industry at Factor Cost: Current Prices 1930–1971.
7. $Y - H$, Appendix, p. 30, Gross Value Added of Agriculture, Current Prices at Farm Gate.
8. [(Line 29/Line 20) $\times$ 100] $-$ Line 1.
9. $O - S$, p. 293, Agricultural Labor.
10. *LTES*, 9, Number of Agricultural Gainful Workers.
11. *LTES*, 9, Number of Agricultural Gainful Workers: Male.
12. *LTES*, 9, Number of Agricultural Gainful Workers: Female.
13. Line 55 $-$ Line 10.
14. $Y - H$, Appendix, p. 34, Agricultural Fixed Capital.
15. *LTES*, 9, p. 210, Gross Capital Stock in Agriculture: 1934–1936 prices.
16. *LTES*, 9, p. 212, Net Capital Stock in Agriculture: 1934–1936 prices.
17. Line 46 $-$ Line 14.
18. $Y_2 = $ [(Line 29/Line 20) $\times$ 100] $-$ Line 1. $P_2 = $ [Line 29 $-$ (B) in Line 23]/Y_2. From this P_2, $P = $ (Line 23/P_2) $\times$ 100.
19. *LTES*, 8, p. 135, Consumer's Price Indexes (1934–1936 $=$ 100, General: All Items).
20. $O - S$, p. 387, GNE deflater (1934–1936 $=$ 100).
21. *LTES*, 9, p. 164, Indexes of Prices received by Farmers: All Commodities (1934–1936 $=$ 100).
22. *LTES*, 9, p. 164, Indexes of Prices received by Farmers: All Commodities (Linked Index).
23. (A) $O - S$, p. 288, Agricultural Output in 1934–1936 Prices at the Farm Gate. (B) $O - S$, p. 284, Agricultural Output in Current Prices at the Farm Gate. Line 23 $=$ $(B/A) \times$ 100.

Appendix Table 1   (*Continued*)

24. P_2 of Line 18.
25. *LTES*, 8, p. 192–193, Price Indexes of Manufacturing and Mining Products.
26. $O-S$, p. 282, GDP of Agriculture, Forestry and Fishery in 1965 Prices, 1953–1970.
27. *H S J E*, p. 28, Net National Income.
28. *LTES*, 1, p. 202, Net Domestic Product by Industry at Market Prices: Current Prices, 1885–1940.
29. *LTES*, 1, p. 178, Gross National Expenditure: Current Prices, 1885–1940.
30. *LTES*, 1, p. 179, Gross National Expenditure: Current Prices, 1930–1971.
31. *LTES*, 1, p. 203, Net Domestic Product by Industry at Factor Cost: Current Prices, 1930–1971.
32. $O - S$, p. 281, GDP of Agriculture, Forestry and Fishery in Current Prices, 1953–1970.
33. *LTES*, 1, p. 237, Gross National Product, Disposable Income etc. per Capita: Current Prices, 1885–1940.
34. *LTES*, 1, p. 237, Net National Product, Disposable Income etc. per Capita: Current Prices, 1885–1940.
35. *LTES*, 1, p. 237, Gross National Product, Disposable Income etc. per Capita: Current Prices, 1930–1971.
36. *LTES*, 1, p. 237, Net National Product, Disposable Income etc. per Capita: Current Prices, 1930–1971.
37. (Line 29)/(Line 57).
38. (Line 37)/(Line 20).
39. *J SY*, Various issues.
40. *LTES*, 1, p. 237, Gross National Product, Disposable Income etc. per Capita: 1934–1936 Prices, 1885–1940.
41. *LTES*, 1, p. 237, Net National Product, Disposable Income etc. per Capita: 1934–1936 Prices, 1885–1940.
42. *LTES*, 1, p. 237, Gross National Expenditure, per Capita: 1934–1936 Prices, 1930–1971.
43. (Line 29)/(Line 20) × 100.
44. $O - S$, p. 278, Gross Domestic Product at Market Prices in 1934–1936 Prices, 1885–1930.
45. Non-agricultural output: Obtain the real output by calculating (Line 29/ Line 20) × 100.
    Deduct Line 2 from the obtained value.

(2) Exogenous variables: Line 46 to Line 64

46. Calculate $\dot{T}_1$ by using the equation $\dot{T}_1 = Y_1 - \alpha \dot{L}_1 - \beta \dot{K}_1 - (1 - \alpha - \beta)\dot{B}$.
47. Calculate $\dot{T}_2$ by using the equation $\dot{T}_2 = \dot{Y}_2 - \gamma \dot{L}_2 - \delta \dot{K}_2$.
48. $O - S$, p. 293, Arable Land.

Appendix Table 1 (*Continued*)

←

49. $O - S$, p. 366, Total Gross Capital Stock in 1934–1936 Prices (Non-residential Building).
50. *LTES*, 3, p. 148, Aggregate Capital Stock (Residence excluded): 1934–1936 Prices (Gross).
51. $O - S$, p. 369, Total Gross Capital Stock in 1965 Prices (Non-residential Total), from 1954.
52. *LTES*, 3, p. 149, Aggregate Capital Stock (Residence excluded): 1934–1936 Prices (Net).
53. *LTES*, 3, p. 262, Gross Capital Stock: Private: 1960 Prices, 1905–1960.
54. *LTES*, 3, p. 149, Aggregate Capital Stock (Residence included): 1934–1936 Prices (Net), 1880–1940.
55. *LTES*, 3, p. 149, Aggregate Capital Stock (Residence included): 1934–1936 Prices (Gross), 1880–1940.
56. $O - S$, p. 366, Total Gross Capital Stock in 1934–1936 Prices (Non-residential Building).
57. $O - S$, p. 369, Total Gross Capital Stock in 1965 Prices (Include Residential Building), from 1954.
58. $O - S$, p. 392, Gainful Workers.
59. *HSJE*, p. 56, Total Labor Force.
60. $O - S$, p. 392, Population.
61. *LTES*, 9, p. 186, Farm Value of Current Inputs: 1934–1936 Prices.
62. *LTES*, 9, p. 185, Farm Value of Current Inputs: Deflated by Indexes of Prices Paid by Farmers.
63. $\dot{a} = \dot{Y}_1 - \dot{Q} - \eta\dot{P} - \epsilon\dot{E}$
64. We can obtain these values from Table 4-1.

Here, *LTES*: Ohkawa and Umemura [Various years],

$O - S$: Ohkawa and Shinohara [1979], *HSJE*: Bank of Japan [1966], and

$Y - H$: Yamada and Hayami [1972].

Appendix Table 2   Growth Rates of Endogenous and Exogenous Variables

	Endogenous Variable								Exogenous Variable				
	Y_1	Y_2	K_1	K_2	L_1	L_2	P	E	Q	B	F	L	K
1880~1881	−4.3	—	1.2	—	0.0	1.0	—	—	0.8	0.1	4.7	0.3	—
~1882	3.1	—	0.2	—	−0.0	0.4	—	—	0.8	0.2	1.1	0.1	—
~1883	−0.4	—	0.6	—	0.0	1.7	—	—	0.8	0.5	0.0	0.5	—
~1884	−3.8	—	−1.1	—	0.0	2.1	—	—	1.1	0.1	4.4	0.6	—
~1885	11.2	—	1.3	—	−0.0	1.7	—	—	0.9	0.2	−5.3	0.4	—
~1886	7.0	6.1	1.1	5.7	−0.0	0.9	−0.5	5.7	0.6	0.3	1.1	0.2	3.8
~1887	4.8	6.8	0.1	1.8	0.0	1.0	−4.9	5.6	0.4	0.5	0.0	0.3	1.1
~1888	−3.1	6.8	0.1	5.5	0.0	2.3	−10.0	2.1	0.8	0.5	1.1	0.7	3.3
~1889	−11.2	14.2	1.2	2.1	0.0	2.8	19.5	4.0	1.1	0.2	0.0	0.9	1.7
~1890	20.3	−12.7	1.5	1.4	0.1	2.2	27.8	−4.0	1.1	0.4	1.0	0.8	1.5
Average	2.4	4.3	0.7	3.3	0.0	1.7	6.3	2.7	0.9	0.4	0.8	0.5	2.3
1890~1891	−6.1	19.7	1.1	0.9	0.1	1.6	17.2	9.3	0.8	0.4	5.4	0.6	1.0
~1892	4.8	−4.6	1.7	2.6	0.0	1.8	3.2	−2.3	0.6	0.3	3.0	0.6	2.3
~1893	−5.9	11.8	0.9	1.4	−0.0	1.9	5.2	4.9	0.9	0.2	3.0	0.5	1.2
~1894	11.5	1.3	0.2	4.0	0.0	1.5	9.5	3.6	0.7	0.5	1.9	0.5	2.5
~1895	−1.3	9.8	1.9	3.4	0.1	1.3	−11.3	5.2	1.0	0.6	−0.9	0.5	2.8
~1896	−8.6	3.2	1.8	5.4	0.3	0.7	−1.5	−1.2	1.0	0.4	2.8	0.5	4.1
~1897	−4.3	−1.4	1.0	6.3	−0.0	1.9	−1.5	−3.1	1.0	0.6	2.8	0.6	4.3
~1898	29.1	−3.9	1.2	3.5	0.2	1.0	18.1	3.5	1.1	0.6	0.9	0.5	2.7
~1899	−10.7	14.1	−0.2	3.3	0.3	0.7	−22.7	4.7	1.2	1.0	3.6	0.4	2.1
~1900	5.9	−4.8	0.0	3.9	0.1	1.3	−0.7	−2.9	1.0	0.4	5.2	0.5	2.6
Average	1.4	4.5	1.0	3.5	0.1	1.4	−1.9	2.2	1.0	0.6	2.8	0.6	2.6
1900~1901	8.7	1.6	1.0	3.1	−0.0	1.5	−8.2	2.4	1.2	0.4	6.6	0.4	2.4
~1902	−16.5	5.6	1.1	3.1	0.2	1.0	9.3	−2.5	1.3	0.3	3.8	0.5	2.4
~1903	18.2	−5.2	1.5	2.9	−0.1	1.8	11.0	−0.3	1.3	0.0	5.9	0.5	2.5
~1904	8.5	10.9	−0.0	3.4	0.0	1.4	−11.0	8.7	1.3	0.7	−5.6	0.5	2.3
~1905	−18.1	−0.6	2.0	4.4	−0.1	1.1	−6.3	−6.9	1.0	0.3	2.9	0.3	3.7
~1906	16.2	−3.9	3.4	4.5	1.5	−1.8	3.9	0.4	0.8	0.3	3.6	0.3	4.2
~1907	6.9	4.6	2.9	5.5	−0.3	2.0	5.1	4.4	0.8	1.5	13.9	0.5	4.7
~1908	3.4	1.0	0.8	6.1	−0.3	1.9	−7.0	0.6	1.1	0.7	7.9	0.5	4.6
~1909	0.6	4.6	2.2	5.5	−0.8	2.3	−12.3	2.1	1.1	1.7	13.0	0.3	4.5
~1910	−6.2	10.6	1.9	5.5	−0.3	1.4	7.5	4.1	1.2	0.8	0.5	0.3	4.4
Average	2.2	2.9	1.7	4.5	−0.0	1.3	−0.8	1.3	1.2	0.7	5.3	0.4	3.6
1910~1911	9.5	0.1	1.0	6.7	0.7	0.1	17.2	1.3	1.3	0.9	12.5	0.4	5.1
~1912	−0.3	−4.4	1.0	6.6	−0.0	1.7	6.4	−4.6	1.3	0.9	−0.8	0.6	5.1
~1913	1.8	2.9	1.0	5.8	−0.1	2.1	−4.5	1.1	1.4	0.4	13.0	0.7	4.6

(Continued)

Appendix Table 2 (*Continued*)

	Endogenous Variable								Exogenous Variable				
	Y_1	Y_2	K_1	K_2	L_1	L_2	P	E	Q	B	F	L	K
~1914	8.6	−1.8	0.6	4.9	−0.1	1.9	−31.2	−0.2	1.4	0.4	−3.9	0.6	3.8
~1915	0.1	9.3	1.0	3.7	−4.9	9.3	−5.7	4.9	1.3	0.7	−3.3	0.6	3.0
~1916	5.6	8.1	1.3	4.8	−1.3	3.6	1.9	5.9	1.3	0.8	2.9	0.8	4.0
~1917	−4.0	12.5	1.0	7.3	0.4	1.4	13.3	6.3	1.2	0.8	8.7	0.8	5.9
~1918	−0.9	11.0	0.7	8.6	−6.0	8.8	26.0	6.7	1.1	1.0	7.6	0.5	6.9
~1919	9.0	3.9	0.7	8.9	0.4	0.1	17.5	4.4	0.6	0.5	18.0	0.2	7.2
~1920	1.6	−0.1	0.4	9.0	−1.2	2.4	−33.6	−0.3	0.5	0.4	−9.3	0.5	7.4
Average	3.1	4.2	0.9	6.7	−1.2	3.2	0.7	2.6	1.2	0.7	4.5	0.6	5.3
1920~1921	−8.4	6.1	0.8	6.6	0.7	1.3	12.5	−0.4	2.9	0.0	0.0	1.0	5.5
~1922	5.4	0.2	0.4	5.6	−0.6	2.3	−20.3	0.1	1.2	0.1	1.6	0.8	4.7
~1923	−6.2	−3.0	1.2	4.2	−3.4	5.2	16.8	−5.0	1.2	−0.7	12.0	0.8	3.7
~1924	2.8	2.8	0.6	4.0	1.5	−1.3	9.4	1.5	1.3	−0.6	2.3	0.0	3.4
~1925	8.0	5.1	1.1	4.4	−0.9	2.5	1.9	4.2	1.4	−0.2	2.8	0.8	3.9
~1926	−5.0	2.5	0.8	5.3	−0.3	2.5	−9.4	−0.8	1.6	−0.0	12.9	1.1	4.6
~1927	8.3	4.5	1.3	5.2	0.5	−0.1	−13.6	3.8	1.5	0.1	1.2	0.1	4.6
~1928	−1.4	5.5	1.3	4.8	1.0	1.3	1.9	2.4	1.5	0.2	3.3	1.2	4.3
~1929	0.9	0.3	1.1	4.2	1.4	0.9	2.3	−0.8	1.3	0.1	7.2	1.1	3.8
~1930	8.4	0.0	1.4	3.3	0.3	2.6	−34.4	0.2	1.5	0.3	−6.3	1.5	3.1
Average	1.3	2.5	1.0	4.8	0.0	1.7	−3.3	0.5	1.6	−0.1	3.7	0.9	4.2
1930~1931	−12.1	3.8	1.1	3.1	0.7	1.3	8.2	−1.3	1.5	0.6	9.3	1.0	2.9
~1932	5.7	2.9	0.7	3.3	1.6	0.3	19.8	1.9	1.4	0.6	−8.9	0.9	3.0
~1933	13.9	7.4	0.5	4.1	−1.1	3.0	1.4	7.1	1.5	0.6	−2.1	1.0	3.7
~1934	−17.7	15.7	0.2	4.4	−1.2	2.7	10.9	7.2	1.3	0.2	10.9	0.9	3.9
~1935	6.1	5.9	0.5	4.6	−1.8	3.8	9.7	4.5	1.3	0.2	2.3	1.2	4.2
~1936	10.8	1.0	0.8	5.3	0.1	2.1	1.5	1.3	1.2	0.4	14.7	1.2	4.8
~1937	1.2	4.4	−0.2	5.3	−1.6	1.7	−3.8	3.1	0.7	0.1	−3.6	0.2	4.7
~1938	−3.1	7.5	0.5	4.6	−1.3	1.8	−1.5	5.1	0.5	−0.2	9.5	0.5	4.1
~1939	7.3	7.4	1.6	6.1	−0.8	2.4	28.9	6.8	0.5	−0.0	0.0	1.0	5.7
~1940	−7.3	6.1	1.1	5.5	2.7	8.4	−3.4	3.2	0.7	−0.0	−10.9	6.1	5.1
Average	0.5	6.3	0.7	4.7	−0.3	2.8	7.2	3.9	1.1	0.3	2.1	1.5	4.2
1940~1941	−11.9	—	−2.4	—	0.5	—	—	—	—	−0.3	−5.4	—	—
~1942	8.2	—	−2.0	—	−2.4	—	—	—	—	−0.3	−5.7	—	—
~1943	−5.5	—	−3.8	—	−0.8	—	—	—	—	−0.5	−19.2	—	—
~1944	−7.5	—	−5.7	—	1.1	—	—	—	—	−1.2	−23.0	—	—
~1945	−7.7	—	−6.0	—	3.3	—	—	—	—	−3.7	−53.8	—	—
~1946	3.9	—	−3.1	—	4.4	—	—	—	—	0.4	13.7	—	—

(*Continued*)

Appendix Table 2 (*Continued*)

	Endogenous Variable								Exogenous Variable				
	Y_1	Y_2	K_1	K_2	L_1	L_2	P	E	Q	B	F	L	K
~1947	−2.6	—	1.5	—	4.3	—	—	—	—	0.4	97.3	—	—
~1948	13.8	—	2.6	—	5.5	—	—	—	—	0.3	26.5	—	—
~1949	−7.2	—	3.5	—	5.8	—	—	—	—	0.3	38.7	—	—
~1950	13.7	—	1.7	—	−4.6	—	—	—	—	0.3	12.0	—	—
Average	−0.3	—	−1.4	—	1.7	—	—	—	—	−0.4	8.1	—	—
1950~1951	−2.1	−2.1	3.8	—	−4.7	5.9	—	—	1.6	0.3	6.2	1.2	—
~1952	13.9	—	1.5	—	2.1	3.8	—	—	1.4	0.2	−2.6	3.1	—
~1953	−12.9	8.9	4.5	—	−0.7	0.1	13.4	4.1	1.3	0.1	43.1	5.6	—
~1954	8.3	5.8	3.6	—	−1.0	3.3	−4.6	4.6	1.4	0.5	7.7	1.6	—
~1955	27.1	6.4	5.1	—	0.8	4.9	−6.7	7.8	1.1	0.7	7.9	3.4	4.1
~1956	−4.9	10.3	−4.1	—	−2.5	4.2	−7.0	7.0	1.0	0.5	6.6	1.7	4.7
~1957	4.8	8.3	13.1	—	−2.0	4.5	−3.2	7.0	0.8	0.5	4.5	2.2	6.1
~1958	2.5	5.8	4.9	—	−4.5	3.1	0.3	4.4	0.9	0.3	1.6	0.5	6.5
~1959	6.1	9.6	5.4	—	−1.7	2.3	−2.8	8.1	0.9	0.1	12.6	1.0	6.8
~1960	3.7	15.5	7.5	—	−2.9	3.8	−1.2	13.1	0.8	0.0	4.0	1.7	8.2
Average	4.7	8.9	4.6	6.3	−1.7	4.7	−1.5	7.1	1.2	0.4	10.2	2.2	6.1
1960~1961	0.8	17.4	7.8	—	−2.6	2.7	2.2	14.5	0.9	0.2	4.6	1.1	10.0
~1962	5.1	6.5	9.2	—	−2.3	2.5	6.8	5.3	0.9	−0.0	10.8	1.1	11.5
~1963	−1.7	11.8	16.1	—	−5.3	3.1	1.9	9.4	1.0	−0.3	7.8	0.8	10.9
~1964	5.0	14.4	12.9	—	−3.6	2.9	2.1	12.4	1.0	−0.3	13.1	1.2	11.7
~1965	1.3	5.2	1.4	—	−3.7	3.4	3.1	3.8	1.1	−0.6	5.6	1.6	10.3
~1966	3.7	10.3	5.4	—	−3.2	3.8	5.1	9.0	0.7	−0.1	15.0	2.1	10.0
~1967	9.0	13.8	16.3	—	−2.5	3.1	2.2	12.1	1.1	−0.9	8.9	1.8	10.7
~1968	3.1	15.2	11.6	—	−2.4	2.6	−1.1	13.1	1.1	−0.7	0.9	1.5	11.8
~1969	−1.4	12.7	2.8	—	−3.3	1.7	3.7	10.5	1.1	−0.7	19.4	0.7	12.2
~1970	−2.2	11.1	5.4	—	−6.1	2.8	−4.8	9.1	1.1	−0.9	5.3	1.0	13.3
Average	2.3	11.9	8.9	11.5	−3.6	2.9	2.1	10.0	1.1	−0.5	9.2	1.3	11.3

Appendix Table 3 Theoretically Calculated Value of Growth Rate Multiplier

$$|A| = (\alpha+\beta)(1+\eta-\lambda\varepsilon)-\eta+[-\alpha-\eta(\alpha-\gamma)+\varepsilon\{\gamma+(\alpha-\gamma)\lambda\}]l_1+[-\beta-\eta(\beta-\delta)+\varepsilon\{\delta+(\beta-\delta)\lambda\}]k_1 > 0$$

$c_{11} = A|Y_1 a = \alpha l_2 + \beta k_2 > 0$

$c_{12} = \eta(\alpha+\beta-\gamma-\delta)+l_1[\eta(\gamma-\alpha)+\gamma(1-\lambda)\varepsilon]$
$\quad + k_1[\eta(\delta-\beta)+\delta(1-\lambda)\varepsilon] > 0$

$c_{13} = \varepsilon(1-\lambda)(\alpha l_2 + \beta k_2) > 0$

$c_{14} = |A|Y_1 L = [\varepsilon\beta\gamma(1-\lambda)+\eta(\beta\gamma-\alpha\delta)$
$\quad + \alpha\varepsilon(1-\lambda)(\gamma-1)]k_2 + \alpha\varepsilon(1-\lambda) > 0$

$c_{15} = |A|Y_1 K = \varepsilon\beta(1-\lambda)l_1 + [\eta(\alpha\delta-\beta\gamma)$
$\quad + (1-\lambda)\delta\varepsilon(\alpha+\beta)l_2 > 0$

$c_{16} = l_2 k_2[\beta\{(\alpha-\gamma)\eta+\gamma\varepsilon(\lambda-1)\}$
$\quad + \alpha\{(\delta-\beta)\eta+(1-\lambda)\delta\varepsilon\}]+\alpha\delta\varepsilon(\lambda-1)l_2$
$\quad + \beta\gamma\varepsilon(1-\lambda)k_2 \gtreqless 0$

$c_{17} = \eta(\beta k_2 + \alpha l_2) < 0$

$c_{18} = -\varepsilon(\alpha l_2 + \beta k_2) < 0$

$|A|Y_1 Q = c_{11} + c_{18} = (1-\varepsilon)(\alpha l_2 + \beta k_2) > 0$

$|A|Y_1 T_1 = c_{12} - c_{17} = [\varepsilon(1-\lambda)+\eta](\gamma l_1 + \delta k_1)$
$\quad - \eta > 0$

$|A|Y_1 T_2 = c_{13} + c_{17} = [\varepsilon(1-\lambda)+\eta||\alpha l_2 + \beta k_2| < 0$

$c_{21} = |A|Y_2 a = -(\delta k_1 + \gamma l_1) < 0$

$c_{22} = (1-\varepsilon\lambda)(\delta k_1 + \gamma l_1) > 0$

$c_{23} = [(\alpha-\gamma)\eta+\alpha(1-\varepsilon\lambda)]l_2 + [(\beta-\delta)\eta$
$\quad + \beta(1-\varepsilon\lambda)]k_2 > 0$

$c_{24} = |A|Y_2 L = \gamma[\beta(1-\varepsilon\lambda)+\eta(\beta-\delta)]k_2$
$\quad + (\delta k_1 + \gamma)[\eta(\alpha-\gamma)+\alpha(1-\varepsilon\lambda)] > 0$

$c_{25} = |A|Y_2 K = [(\beta-\delta)\eta+\beta(1-\varepsilon\lambda)](\delta+\gamma l_1)$
$\quad + \delta[(\alpha-\gamma)\eta+\alpha(1-\varepsilon\lambda)]l_2 > 0$

$c_{26} = \delta k_2[\{(\delta-\beta)\eta+\beta(\lambda\varepsilon-1)]l_1$
$\quad + [\eta(\alpha-\gamma)+\alpha(1-\lambda\varepsilon)]l_2]-\delta l_2[\eta(\alpha-\gamma)$
$\quad + \alpha(1-\lambda\varepsilon)]+k_2 l_1[(\beta-\delta)\eta+\beta(1-\lambda\varepsilon)] > 0$

$c_{27} = -\eta(\delta k_1 + \gamma l_1) > 0$

$c_{28} = \varepsilon(\delta k_1 + \gamma l_1) > 0$

$|A|Y_2 Q = c_{21} + c_{28} = (\varepsilon-1)(\delta k_1 + \gamma l_1) < 0$

$|A|Y_2 T_1 = c_{22} - c_{27} = (1-\varepsilon\lambda+\eta)(\delta k_1 + \gamma l_1) > 0$

$|A|Y_2 T_2 = c_{23} + c_{27} = (\eta+1-\varepsilon\lambda)(\alpha l_2 + \beta k_2) - \eta > 0$

(Continued)

Appendix Table 3   *(Continued)*

$$|A| = (\alpha + \beta)(1 + \eta - \lambda\varepsilon) - \eta + [-a - \eta(\alpha - \gamma) + \varepsilon\{\gamma + (\alpha - \gamma)\lambda\}]l_1 + [-\beta - \eta(\beta - \delta) + \varepsilon\{\delta + (\beta - \delta)\lambda\}]k_1 > 0$$

$c_{31} = |A|K_1 a = k_2 > 0$

$c_{32} = (\varepsilon\lambda - 1)k_2 < 0$

$c_{33} = \varepsilon(1 - \lambda)k_2 > 0$

$c_{34} = |A|K_1 L = [\eta(\gamma - a) + a(\lambda\varepsilon - 1) + \gamma(1 - \lambda)\varepsilon]k_2 < 0$

$c_{35} = |A|K_1 K = [(\lambda - 1)\varepsilon\gamma + (a - \gamma)\eta + a(1 - \varepsilon\lambda)]l_2$
$\qquad\quad + \varepsilon(1 - \lambda) > 0$

$c_{36} = k_2[l_2\{\gamma(\lambda - 1)\varepsilon + (a - \gamma)\eta + a(1 - \lambda\varepsilon)\}$
$\qquad\quad + (1 - \lambda)\varepsilon\gamma] > 0$

$c_{37} = \eta k_2 < 0$

$c_{38} = -\varepsilon k_2 < 0$

$|A|K_1 Q = c_{31} + c_{38} = (1 - \varepsilon)k_2 > 0$

$|A|K_1 T_1 = c_{32} - c_{37} = (-\eta + \varepsilon\lambda - 1)k_2 < 0$

$|A|K_1 T_2 = c_{33} + c_{37} = [\varepsilon(1 - \lambda) + \eta]k_2 < 0$

$c_{41} = A|K_2 a = k_1 < 0$

$c_{42} = (1 - \varepsilon\lambda)k_1 > 0$

$c_{43} = (\lambda - 1)\varepsilon k_1 < 0$

$c_{44} = |A|K_2 L = [a - \varepsilon\gamma + (\varepsilon\lambda - \eta)(\gamma - a)]k_1 > 0$

$c_{45} = |A|K_2 K = l_2[\eta(a - \gamma) + a(1 - \lambda\varepsilon) + (\lambda - 1)\varepsilon\gamma] + \eta(\beta - \delta)$
$\qquad\quad + \beta(1 - \lambda\varepsilon) + (1 - \lambda)\varepsilon\gamma > 0$

$c_{46} = k_1[l_2\{\gamma\varepsilon(1 - \lambda) + \eta(\gamma - a) + a(\lambda\varepsilon - 1)\}$
$\qquad\quad + \gamma(\lambda - 1)\varepsilon] < 0$

$c_{47} = -\eta k_1 > 0$

$c_{48} = \varepsilon k_1 > 0$

$|A|K_2 Q = c_{41} + c_{48} = (\varepsilon - 1)k_1 < 0$

$|A|K_2 T_1 = c_{42} - c_{47} = (1 - \varepsilon\lambda + \eta)k_1 > 0$

$|A|K_2 T_2 = c_{43} + c_{47} = [\varepsilon(\lambda - 1) - \eta]k_1 > 0$

(Continued)

Appendix Table 3 *(Continued)*

$$|A| = (\alpha + \beta)(1 + \eta - \lambda\varepsilon) - \eta + [-\alpha - \eta(\alpha - \gamma) + \varepsilon\{\gamma + (\alpha - \gamma)\lambda\}]l_1 + [-\beta - \eta(\beta - \delta) + \varepsilon\{\delta + (\beta - \delta)\lambda\}]k_1 > 0$$

$c_{51} = |A|L_1a = l_2 > 0$

$c_{52} = (\varepsilon\lambda - 1)l_2 < 0$

$c_{53} = \varepsilon(1 - \lambda)l_2 > 0$

$c_{54} = |A|L_1L = [\delta\varepsilon(\lambda - 1) + \eta(\beta - \delta) + \beta(1 - \lambda\varepsilon)]k_2 + \varepsilon(1 - \lambda) > 0$

$c_{55} = |A|L_1K = [\delta\varepsilon(1 - \lambda) + \beta(\varepsilon\lambda - 1) + \eta(\delta - \beta)]l_2 < 0$

$c_{56} = l_2[\delta(\lambda - 1)\varepsilon + \{\delta(1 - \lambda)\varepsilon + (\delta - \beta)\eta + \beta(\lambda\varepsilon - 1)\}k_2] < 0$

$c_{57} = \eta l_2 < 0$

$c_{58} = -\varepsilon l_2 < 0$

$|A|L_1Q = c_{51} + c_{58} = (1 - \varepsilon)l_2 > 0$

$|A|L_1T_1 = c_{52} - c_{57} = (\varepsilon\lambda - \eta - 1)l_2 < 0$

$|A|L_1T_2 = c_{53} + c_{57} = [\eta + \varepsilon(1 - \lambda)]l_2 < 0$

$c_{61} = |A|L_2a = l_1 < 0$

$c_{62} = (1 - \varepsilon\lambda)l_1 > 0$

$c_{63} = \varepsilon(\lambda - 1)l_1 < 0$

$c_{64} = |A|L_2L = [\delta\varepsilon(\lambda - 1) + \eta(\beta - \delta) + \beta(1 - \varepsilon\lambda)]k_2 + \delta\varepsilon(1 - \lambda) + \eta(\alpha - \gamma) + \alpha(1 - \varepsilon\lambda) > 0$

$c_{65} = |A|L_2K = [(\beta - \delta)(\eta - \varepsilon\lambda) + \beta - \varepsilon\delta]l_1 > 0$

$c_{66} = l_1[k_2\{\delta\varepsilon(\lambda - 1) + \eta(\beta - \delta) + \beta(1 - \lambda\varepsilon)\} + \delta\varepsilon(1 - \lambda)] > 0$

$c_{67} = -\eta l_1 > 0$

$c_{68} = \varepsilon l_1 > 0$

$|A|L_2Q = c_{61} + c_{68} = (\varepsilon - 1)l_1 < 0$

$|A|L_2T_1 = c_{62} - c_{67} = (1 - \varepsilon\lambda + \eta)l_1 > 0$

$|A|L_2T_2 = c_{63} + c_{67} = [\varepsilon(\lambda - 1) - \eta]l_1 > 0$

(Continued)

Appendix Table 3   (Continued)

$$|A| = (\alpha + \beta)(1 + \eta - \lambda\varepsilon) - \eta + [-\alpha - \eta(\alpha - \gamma) + \varepsilon\{\gamma + (\alpha - \gamma)\lambda\}]l_1 + [-\beta - \eta(\beta - \delta) + \varepsilon\{\delta + (\beta - \delta)\lambda\}]k_1 > 0$$

$c_{71} = |A|Pa = (\gamma - \alpha)l_2 + (\delta - \beta)k_2 > 0$

$c_{72} = (\varepsilon\gamma - 1)[(\gamma - \alpha)l_2 + (\delta - \beta)k_2] < 0$

$c_{73} = \varepsilon(1 - \lambda)[(\gamma - \alpha)l_2 + (\delta - \beta)k_2] < 0$

$c_{74} = |A|PL = [(1 - \varepsilon\lambda)(\alpha\delta - \gamma\beta) + \varepsilon\gamma(1 - \lambda)$
$\quad (\alpha + \delta - \gamma - \beta)]k_2 + \varepsilon(1 - \lambda)(\gamma - \alpha)k_1 > 0$

$c_{75} = |A|PK = [\{\beta(\lambda\varepsilon - 1) + \delta(1 - \lambda)\varepsilon\}(\alpha - \gamma) + \{\alpha(\lambda\varepsilon - 1)$
$\quad + \gamma(1 - \lambda)\varepsilon\}(\delta - \beta)]l_1$
$\quad + (\alpha + \beta)(\lambda\varepsilon - 1)(\beta - \delta) + [\beta(\lambda\varepsilon - 1)$
$\quad + \delta(1 - \lambda)\varepsilon](\alpha + \beta - 1) \gtrless 0$

$c_{76} = [[\alpha(\lambda\varepsilon - 1)(\beta - \delta) + (\gamma - \alpha)\{\beta(\lambda\varepsilon - 1)$
$\quad + \delta\varepsilon(1 - \lambda)\}]l_2 + \gamma\varepsilon(1 - \lambda)(\delta\beta)l_1k_2$
$\quad + \delta\varepsilon(1 - \lambda)(\alpha - \gamma)l_2 > 0$

$c_{77} = \delta\varepsilon(1 - \lambda)k_1 + \beta(1 - \varepsilon\lambda)k_2 + \gamma\varepsilon(1 - \lambda)l_1$
$\quad + \alpha(1 - \varepsilon\lambda)l_2 > 0$

$c_{78} = \varepsilon[(\alpha - \gamma)l_2 + (\beta - \delta)k_2 < 0$

$|A|PQ = c_{71} + c_{78} = (1 - \varepsilon)[(\gamma - \alpha)l_2 + (\delta - \beta)k_2 > 0$

$|A|PT_1 = c_{72} - c_{77} = (\varepsilon - 1)[(\gamma l_2 + \delta k_2) + (\lambda - 1)\varepsilon < 0$

$|A|PT_2 = c_{73} + c_{77} = (1 - \varepsilon)(\alpha l_2 + \beta k_2)$
$\quad + (1 - \lambda)\varepsilon > 0$

$c_{81} = |A|Ea = -[\delta(1 - \lambda) + \beta\lambda]k_1 - [\gamma(1 - \lambda) + \alpha\lambda]l_1$
$\quad + (\alpha + \beta)\lambda < 0$

$c_{82} = l_2[\lambda\eta(\alpha - \gamma) + \gamma(\lambda - 1)] + k_2[\lambda\eta(\beta - \delta)$
$\quad + \delta(\lambda - 1)] + (1 - \lambda) > 0$

$c_{83} = (1 - \lambda)[\{(\alpha - \gamma)\eta + \alpha\}l_2 + \{(\beta - \delta)\eta + \beta\}k_2] > 0$

$c_{84} = |A|EL = (\beta\gamma - \alpha\delta)(1 + \eta)k_2$
$\quad + [\alpha + \eta(\alpha - \gamma)](1 - \lambda) > 0$

$c_{85} = |A|EK = (1 - \lambda)[\beta + \eta(\beta - \delta)]$
$\quad + (1 + \eta - \lambda)(\alpha\delta - \beta\gamma)l_2 > 0$

$c_{86} = [\lambda\eta\beta(\alpha - \gamma)l_2 + \eta\gamma(1 - \lambda)(\beta - \delta)]l_1$
$\quad + \beta\gamma(1 - \lambda)l_1 + \lambda\eta\alpha(\delta - \beta)l_2k_2 + [\alpha\delta(\lambda - 1)$
$\quad + \eta\rho\delta(\lambda - 1)(\alpha - \gamma)]l_2k_1 > 0$

$c_{87} = \eta[\{-\alpha\lambda + (\lambda - 1)\gamma\}l_1 + \{-\lambda\beta + (\lambda - 1)\delta\}k_1$
$\quad + (\alpha + \beta)\lambda] > 0$

$c_{88} = -[\{\beta + (\beta - \delta)\eta\}k_2 + \{\alpha + (\alpha - \gamma)\eta\}l_2] < 0$

$|A|EQ = c_{81} + c_{88} = (\delta - \beta)(1 - \lambda + \eta)k_2$
$\quad + (\gamma - \alpha)(1 - \lambda + \eta)l_2 + \lambda - 1 < 0$

$|A|ET_1 = c_{82} - c_{87} = [\eta + (1 - \lambda)(\gamma l_1 + \delta k_1) - \eta\lambda > 0$

$|A|ET_2 = c_{83} + c_{87} = (\eta + 1 - \lambda)(\alpha l_2 + \beta k_2) + \eta(\lambda - 1) > 0$

*The Sign shown has some exception cases. Therefore, the sign shown is an ordinary case.

Appendix Table 4　Calculated Value of Growth Rate Multiplier

	Ag. Output Y_1T_1	Y_1T_2	Y_1K	Y_1L	Y_1Q	Non-ag. Output Y_2T_1	Y_2T_2	Y_2K	Y_2L	Y_2Q
1880	1.00	-0.10	0.10	0.50	0.10	0.00	1.28	0.26	1.02	-0.3
1885	0.95	-0.03	0.11	0.51	0.08	0.14	1.09	0.23	0.95	-0.2
1890	0.96	-0.05	0.10	0.48	0.09	0.10	1.12	0.30	0.88	-0.2
1895	0.94	-0.03	0.10	0.49	0.08	0.13	1.06	0.33	0.81	-0.2
1900	0.93	-0.01	0.09	0.51	0.08	0.14	1.03	0.37	0.75	-0.2
1905	0.90	-0.03	0.09	0.48	0.13	0.18	1.06	0.41	0.76	-0.2
1910	0.89	-0.03	0.09	0.48	0.13	0.18	1.05	0.42	0.75	-0.2
1915	0.88	-0.02	0.09	0.47	0.14	0.15	1.03	0.51	0.62	-0.2
1920	0.87	-0.03	0.09	0.46	0.16	0.14	1.03	0.41	0.71	-0.2
1925	0.86	-0.03	0.09	0.49	0.17	0.13	1.02	0.40	0.71	-0.2
1930	0.82	0.01	0.10	0.51	0.17	0.13	0.99	0.46	0.63	-0.1
1935	0.83	0.01	0.11	0.46	0.17	0.11	1.00	0.51	0.56	-0.1
1940	0.82	0.01	0.09	0.46	0.17	0.10	0.99	0.55	0.51	-0.1
1945	0.84	0.05	0.11	0.49	0.11	0.10	0.97	0.53	0.50	-0.07
1950	0.83	0.01	0.09	0.46	0.16	0.10	1.00	0.55	0.52	-0.10
1955	0.79	-0.06	0.08	0.47	0.28	0.12	1.03	0.30	0.82	-0.16
1960	0.77	-0.03	0.09	0.42	0.26	0.10	1.01	0.37	0.72	-0.11
1965	0.73	-0.02	0.11	0.42	0.29	0.08	1.01	0.32	0.74	-0.09

(*Continued*)

Appendix Table 4 (*Continued*)

	Ag. Capital	K_1T_1	K_1T_2	K_1K	K_1L	K_1Q	Non-ag. Capital	K_2T_1	K_2T_2	K_2K	K_2L	K_2Q
1880		0.00	−0.24	0.95	−0.19	0.24		0.00	0.18	1.04	0.15	−0.18
1885		−0.12	−0.08	0.97	−0.13	0.20		0.09	0.06	1.02	0.10	−0.15
1890		−0.10	−0.12	0.96	−0.14	0.22		0.06	0.08	1.03	0.09	−0.14
1895		−0.14	−0.07	0.96	−0.12	0.21		0.08	0.04	1.02	0.07	−0.12
1900		−0.18	−0.03	0.97	−0.12	0.21		0.09	0.02	1.01	0.06	−0.11
1905		−0.24	−0.07	0.95	−0.18	0.32		0.11	0.03	1.02	0.08	−0.14
1910		−0.26	−0.07	0.94	−0.19	0.33		0.10	0.03	1.02	0.07	−0.12
1915		−0.28	−0.05	0.94	−0.18	0.34		0.08	0.02	1.02	0.06	−0.10
1920		−0.30	−0.06	0.94	−0.20	0.35		0.07	0.01	1.01	0.04	−0.08
1925		−0.30	−0.06	0.94	−0.22	0.36		0.05	0.01	1.01	0.04	−0.06
1930		−0.36	0.02	0.97	−0.21	0.34		0.05	0.00	1.01	0.03	−0.05
1935		−0.37	0.01	0.96	−0.20	0.35		0.05	0.00	1.01	0.02	−0.04
1940		−0.38	0.02	0.97	−0.20	0.36		0.04	0.00	1.00	0.02	−0.04
1945		−0.35	0.11	1.02	−0.14	0.24		0.04	−0.01	1.00	0.02	−0.03
1950		−0.38	0.01	0.97	−0.20	0.37		0.04	0.00	1.00	0.02	−0.04
1955		−0.38	−0.11	0.92	−0.32	0.49		0.04	0.01	1.01	0.03	−0.05
1960		−0.41	−0.05	0.93	−0.27	0.47		0.04	0.00	1.01	0.02	−0.04
1965		−0.41	−0.03	0.92	−0.27	0.44		0.03	0.00	1.01	0.02	−0.03

(*Continued*)

Appendix Table 4 (*Continued*)

| | Ag. Labor | | | | | Non-ag. Labor | | | | |
	L_1T_1	L_1T_2	L_1K	L_1L	L_1Q	L_2T_1	L_2T_2	L_2K	L_2L	L_2Q
1880	0.00	0.12	−0.02	0.90	0.12	0.00	0.30	0.06	1.24	−0.30
1885	−0.06	−0.04	−0.02	0.93	0.10	0.15	0.10	0.04	1.16	−0.24
1890	−0.05	−0.06	−0.02	0.92	0.12	0.11	0.14	0.05	1.16	−0.25
1895	−0.08	−0.04	−0.02	0.93	0.11	0.15	0.07	0.04	1.13	−0.22
1900	−0.09	−0.02	−0.02	0.94	0.11	0.17	0.03	0.03	1.12	−0.21
1905	−0.13	−0.04	−0.03	0.90	0.17	0.22	0.07	0.05	1.17	−0.29
1910	−0.14	−0.04	−0.03	0.90	0.17	0.22	0.06	0.05	1.16	−0.28
1915	−0.16	−0.03	−0.03	0.90	0.19	0.21	0.04	0.04	1.14	−0.25
1920	−0.18	−0.03	−0.03	0.88	0.21	0.19	0.04	0.04	1.12	−0.22
1925	−0.19	−0.04	−0.03	0.87	0.22	0.17	0.03	0.03	1.12	−0.20
1930	−0.22	0.01	−0.02	0.87	0.21	0.20	−0.01	0.02	1.11	−0.18
1935	−0.23	0.01	−0.03	0.88	0.22	0.18	−0.01	0.02	1.10	−0.17
1940	−0.25	0.01	−0.02	0.87	0.24	0.17	−0.01	0.01	1.09	−0.16
1945	−0.22	0.07	0.01	0.91	0.15	0.17	−0.05	−0.01	1.07	−0.12
1950	−0.23	0.01	−0.02	0.88	0.22	0.18	−0.01	0.01	1.10	−0.18
1955	−0.26	−0.08	−0.05	0.78	0.34	0.15	0.04	0.03	1.13	−0.20
1960	−0.31	−0.04	−0.06	0.79	0.36	0.13	0.02	0.02	1.09	−0.15
1965	−0.34	−0.03	−0.06	0.78	0.37	0.10	0.01	0.02	1.07	−0.11

(*Continued*)

Appendix Table 4 (*Continued*)

Relative Price	PT_1	PT_2	PK	PL	PQ	Per Capita Income	ET_1	ET_2	EK	EL	EQ
1880	-1.00	0.95	0.07	0.18	0.05		0.50	0.59	0.18	0.76	-1.09
1885	-1.02	0.98	0.07	0.20	0.04		0.42	0.70	0.19	0.80	-1.12
1890	-1.02	0.97	0.13	0.16	0.05		0.43	0.67	0.22	0.73	-1.10
1895	-1.04	0.98	0.18	0.13	0.06		0.40	0.70	0.25	0.71	-1.10
1900	-1.05	0.99	0.24	0.05	0.06		0.37	0.73	0.29	0.68	-1.10
1905	-1.07	0.98	0.24	0.03	0.10		0.36	0.78	0.33	0.69	-1.15
1910	-1.08	0.98	0.25	0.00	0.10		0.35	0.79	0.34	0.68	-1.14
1915	-1.10	0.98	0.34	-0.09	0.12		0.31	0.80	0.42	0.59	-1.11
1920	-1.09	0.98	0.24	0.01	0.11		0.30	0.80	0.34	0.66	-1.09
1925	-1.09	0.98	0.25	-0.03	0.10		0.29	0.79	0.33	0.66	-1.08
1930	-1.11	1.01	0.32	-0.12	0.10		0.22	0.86	0.42	0.61	-1.09
1935	-1.12	1.00	0.36	-0.12	0.12		0.21	0.86	0.46	0.55	-1.07
1940	-1.15	1.01	0.43	-0.17	0.14		0.19	0.87	0.49	0.50	-1.06
1945	-1.14	1.04	0.45	-0.15	0.09		0.20	0.84	0.47	0.50	-1.04
1950	-1.15	1.01	0.43	-0.17	0.14		0.21	0.86	0.48	0.51	-1.06
1955	-1.08	0.98	0.14	0.00	0.10		0.23	0.86	0.27	0.77	-1.09
1960	-1.12	0.98	0.20	0.00	0.13		0.16	0.92	0.34	0.69	-1.08
1965	-1.09	0.99	0.13	0.03	0.10		0.12	0.94	0.31	0.72	-1.06

Appendix Table 5   Growth Rate Multiplier of Imperfect Competition

	$Y_1 N_w$	$Y_2 N_w$	$K_1 N_w$	$K_2 N_w$	$L_1 N_w$	$L_2 N_w$	PN_w	EN_w
1880	−0.14	0.73	−0.13	0.10	−0.36	0.88	0.63	0.29
1885	−0.11	0.60	−0.03	0.02	−0.32	0.74	0.65	0.35
1890	−0.13	0.55	−0.05	0.03	−0.35	0.73	0.60	0.29
1895	−0.13	0.47	−0.01	0.01	−0.35	0.87	0.58	0.27
1900	−0.13	0.41	0.01	−0.00	−0.34	0.86	0.56	0.26
1905	−0.15	0.39	0.01	−0.00	−0.37	0.84	0.55	0.26
1910	−0.15	0.37	0.01	−0.01	−0.37	0.82	0.54	0.25
1915	−0.17	0.28	0.04	−0.01	−0.41	0.79	0.50	0.18
1920	−0.20	0.29	0.05	−0.01	−0.46	0.66	0.55	0.18
1925	−0.22	0.27	0.06	−0.01	−0.48	0.61	0.57	0.16
1930	−0.22	0.22	0.11	−0.02	−0.47	0.59	0.57	0.16
1935	−0.25	0.18	0.12	−0.01	−0.49	0.38	0.57	0.12
1940	−0.27	0.15	0.13	−0.01	−0.51	0.34	0.56	0.09
1945	−0.25	0.17	0.13	−0.01	−0.48	0.38	0.56	0.11
1950	−0.26	0.17	0.12	−0.01	−0.48	0.38	0.56	0.11
1955	−0.34	0.23	0.13	−0.05	−0.54	0.32	0.70	0.14
1960	−0.31	0.16	0.15	−0.01	−0.58	0.25	0.64	0.12
1965	−0.34	0.12	0.19	−0.01	−0.62	0.18	0.66	0.11

	$Y_1 N_r$	$Y_2 N_r$	$K_1 N_r$	$K_2 N_r$	$L_1 N_r$	$L_2 N_r$	PN_r	EN_r
1880	−0.15	0.11	−0.59	0.45	0.01	0.03	0.22	−0.02
1885	−0.13	0.07	−0.57	0.41	0.00	−0.01	0.22	0.00
1890	−0.11	0.04	−0.54	0.35	0.03	−0.07	0.15	−0.02
1895	−0.12	0.10	−0.62	0.36	0.01	−0.01	0.24	0.03
1900	−0.13	0.12	−0.68	0.33	0.00	0.01	0.28	0.05
1905	−0.11	0.10	−0.67	0.30	0.01	−0.02	0.24	0.05
1910	−0.11	0.09	−0.71	0.26	0.01	−0.02	0.29	0.04
1915	−0.10	0.10	−0.74	0.22	0.02	−0.02	0.24	0.05
1920	−0.16	0.12	−0.94	0.21	−0.07	0.07	0.34	0.06
1925	−0.16	0.11	−0.97	0.17	−0.07	0.06	0.33	0.05
1930	−0.09	0.04	−0.83	0.12	−0.02	−0.02	0.18	0.03
1935	−0.10	0.04	−0.85	0.10	0.03	−0.02	0.19	0.02
1940	−0.07	0.04	−0.82	0.09	0.02	−0.02	0.15	0.02
1945	−0.07	0.04	−0.86	0.10	0.02	−0.02	0.16	0.03
1950	−0.08	0.04	−0.87	0.09	0.02	−0.02	0.15	0.02

(Continued)

Appendix Table 5   (*Continued*)

	$Y_1 N_r$	$Y_2 N_r$	$K_1 N_r$	$K_2 N_r$	$L_1 N_r$	$L_2 N_r$	PN_r	EN_r
1955	−0.09	0.01	−0.88	0.09	0.02	−0.02	0.14	0.00
1960	−0.09	0.02	−0.87	0.08	0.04	−0.02	0.16	0.01
1965	−0.11	0.01	−0.87	0.07	0.05	−0.02	0.18	0.00

(注) $N_w = m_w m_2 / m_1$, $N_r = m_r m_4 / m_3$. Also, if we define each element of A^{-1} as c_{ij}, and γ (δ) as output elasticity non-agricultural Labor(capital), then we can obtain the growth rate multiplier as follows:

$$Y_1 N_w = c_{16} + \gamma c_{17} \quad L_1 N_w = c_{56} + \gamma c_{57} \quad Y_1 N_r = -c_{16} + \delta c_{17} \quad L_1 N_r = -c_{56} + \delta c_{57}$$
$$Y_2 N_w = c_{26} + \gamma c_{27} \quad L_2 N_w = c_{66} + \gamma c_{67} \quad Y_2 N_r = -c_{26} + \delta c_{27} \quad L_2 N_r = -c_{66} + \delta c_{67}$$
$$K_1 N_w = c_{36} + \gamma c_{37} \quad P N_w = c_{76} + \gamma c_{77} \quad K_1 N_r = -c_{36} + \delta c_{37} \quad P N_r = -c_{76} + \delta c_{77}$$
$$K_2 N_w = c_{46} + \gamma c_{47} \quad E N_w = c_{86} + \gamma c_{87} \quad K_2 N_r = -c_{46} + \delta c_{47} \quad E N_r = -c_{86} + \delta c_{87}$$

Appendix Table 6 Contributions of Eight Endogenous Variables to Eight Exogenous Variables

(1) Agricultural Output (Y_1)

	Y_1	CY_1T_1	CY_1T_2	CY_1K	CY_1L	CY_1Q	CY_1B	CY_1a	CY_1N
1880–1890	3.4 (100)	2.9 (85)	−0.1 (−3)	0.5 (15)	0.1 (3)	0.1 (3)	0.1 (3)	1.7 (50)	−1.9 (−56)
1890–1900	1.7 (100)	1.1 (65)	−0.1 (−6)	0.5 (29)	0.2 (12)	0.1 (6)	0.2 (12)	−0.9 (−53)	0.6 (35)
1900–1910	2.2 (100)	1.5 (68)	−0.00 (0)	0.5 (23)	0.1 (5)	0.1 (5)	0.2 (9)	−0.2 (−9)	0 (0)
1910–1920	3.2 (100)	2.9 (91)	0.0 (0)	0.6 (19)	0.2 (6)	0.2 (6)	0.2 (6)	0.3 (9)	−1.2 (−38)
1920–1930	1.1 (100)	0.8 (73)	0.0 (0)	0.4 (36)	0.4 (36)	0.3 (27)	−0.0 (0)	−1.5 (−136)	0.7 (64)
1930–1940	0.4 (100)	0.2 (50)	0.0 (0)	0.4 (100)	0.6 (150)	0.2 (50)	0.1 (25)	0.5 (125)	−1.6 (−400)
1940–1950	−0.5	−1.0	—	—	0.1	0.2	−0.1	—	—
1950–1960	3.6 (100)	3.2 (89)	−0.2 (−6)	0.5 (14)	1.0 (28)	0.3 (8)	0.1 (3)	−3.3 (−92)	2.0 (56)
1960–1970	2.1 (100)	2.2 (105)	−0.1 (−5)	1.2 (57)	0.5 (24)	0.3 (14)	−0.1 (−5)	−3.1 (−148)	1.2 (57)

(2) Non-agricultural Output (Y_2)

	Y_2	CY_2T_1	CY_2T_2	CY_2K	CY_2L	CY_2Q	CY_2B	CY_2a	CY_2N
1880–1890	3.7 (100)	0.4 (11)	1.9 (51)	0.5 (14)	0.5 (14)	−0.2 (−5)	0.0 (0)	−4.7 (−127)	5.3 (143)
1890–1900	3.9 (100)	0.2 (5)	2.0 (51)	2.0 (23)	0.5 (13)	−0.2 (−5)	0.0 (0)	2.1 (54)	−1.6 (41)
1900–1910	2.6 (100)	0.3 (12)	0.1 (4)	1.5 (58)	0.3 (12)	−0.3 (−12)	0.0 (0)	0.3 (12)	0.4 (15)
1910–1920	4.0 (100)	0.5 (13)	−0.9 (−2)	2.7 (68)	0.4 (10)	−0.2 (−5)	0.0 (0)	−0.4 (−10)	1.9 (48)
1920–1930	2.4 (100)	0.1 (4)	−0.5 (−21)	1.7 (71)	0.6 (25)	−0.3 (−13)	0.0 (0)	1.5 (63)	−0.7 (−29)
1930–1940	5.7 (100)	0.1 (2)	2.0 (35)	2.1 (37)	0.8 (14)	−0.1 (−2)	0.0 (0)	−0.3 (−5)	1.1 (19)
1940–1950	—	−0.1	—	—	0.1	—	—	—	—
1950–1960	9.2 (100)	0.5 (5)	4.2 (46)	1.8 (20)	1.8 (20)	−0.2 (−2)	0.0 (0)	1.9 (21)	−0.8 (−9)
1960–1970	11.9 (100)	0.2 (2)	6.3 (53)	1.6 (30)	1.0 (8)	−0.1 (−1)	0.0 (0)	0.9 (8)	0.2 (2)

(Continued)

Appendix Table 6   (*Continued*)

(3) Agricultural Capital (K_1)

	K_1	CK_1T_1	CK_1T_2	CK_1K	CK_1L	CK_1Q	CK_1B	CK_1a	CK_1N
1880–1890	0.7 (100)	−0.4 (−57)	−0.1 (−14)	2.2 (314)	−0.1 (−14)	0.2 (29)	0.0 (0)	4.2 (600)	−5.3 (−757)
1890–1900	1.0 (100)	−0.2 (−20)	−0.1 (−10)	2.5 (250)	−0.1 (−10)	0.2 (20)	0.0 (0)	−2.3 (−230)	1.0 (100)
1900–1910	1.7 (100)	−0.4 (−24)	−0.0 (0)	3.4 (200)	−0.1 (−6)	0.4 (24)	0.0 (0)	−0.4 (−24)	−1.2 (−71)
1910–1920	0.9 (100)	−1.0 (−111)	0.0 (0)	5.0 (555)	−0.1 (−11)	0.4 (44)	0.0 (0)	0.7 (78)	−4.1 (−456)
1920–1930	1.0 (100)	−0.3 (−30)	0.0 (0)	4.0 (400)	−0.2 (−20)	0.6 (60)	0.0 (0)	−3.5 (−350)	0.4 (40)
1930–1940	0.7 (100)	−0.1 (−14)	0.0 (0)	4.0 (571)	−0.3 (−43)	0.4 (57)	0.0 (0)	1.1 (157)	−4.4 (−629)
1940–1950	−1.4 (100)	0.4 (−29)	– (–)	– (–)	−0.0 (0)	0.4 (−29)	0.0 (0)	– (–)	– (–)
1950–1960	4.6 (100)	−1.6 (−35)	−0.5 (−11)	5.6 (122)	−0.7 (−15)	0.6 (13)	0.0 (0)	−5.8 (−126)	7.0 (152)
1960–1970	8.9 (100)	−1.2 (−14)	−0.2 (−2)	10.4 (117)	−0.4 (−4)	0.5 (6)	0.0 (0)	−4.7 (−53)	3.3 (37)

(4) Non-agricultural Capital (K_2)

	K_2	CK_2T_1	CK_2T_2	CK_2K	CK_2L	CK_2Q	CK_2B	CK_2a	CK_2N
1880–1890	3.3 (100)	0.3 (9)	0.1 (3)	2.4 (73)	0.1 (3)	−0.1 (−3)	0.0 (0)	−3.1 (−94)	3.6 (109)
1890–1900	3.5 (100)	0.1 (3)	0.1 (3)	2.7 (77)	0.0 (0)	−0.1 (−3)	0.0 (0)	1.4 (40)	−0.7 (−20)
1900–1910	4.5 (100)	0.2 (4)	0.0 (0)	3.7 (82)	0.0 (0)	−0.2 (−4)	0.0 (0)	0.2 (4)	0.6 (13)
1910–1920	6.7 (100)	0.3 (4)	−0.0 (0)	5.4 (81)	0.0 (0)	−0.1 (−1)	0.0 (0)	−0.2 (−3)	1.3 (19)
1920–1930	4.8 (100)	0.0 (0)	−0.0 (0)	4.2 (88)	0.0 (0)	−0.1 (−2)	0.0 (0)	0.6 (13)	0.1 (2)
1930–1940	4.7 (100)	0.0 (0)	0.0 (0)	4.2 (89)	0.0 (0)	−0.0 (0)	0.0 (0)	−0.1 (−2)	0.6 (13)
1940–1950	– (–)	−0.0 (–)	– (–)	– (–)	0.0 (–)	−0.1 (–)	0.0 (–)	– (–)	– (–)
1950–1960	6.3 (100)	0.2 (3)	0.0 (0)	6.2 (98)	0.1 (2)	−0.1 (−2)	0.0 (0)	0.6 (10)	−0.7 (−11)
1960–1970	11.5 (100)	0.1 (1)	0.0 (0)	11.4 (99)	0.0 (0)	−0.0 (0)	0.0 (0)	0.4 (3)	−0.3 (−3)

(*Continued*)

Appendix Table 6 (*Continued*)

(5) Agricultural Labor (L_1)

	L_1	CL_1T_1	CL_1T_2	CL_1K	CL_1L	CL_1Q	CL_1B	CL_1a	CL_1N
1880–1890	0.0 (–)	−0.2 (–)	−0.1 (–)	−0.1 (–)	0.5 (–)	0.1 (–)	0.0 (–)	2.2 (–)	−2.4 (–)
1890–1900	0.1 (100)	−0.1 (−100)	−0.1 (100)	−0.1 (−100)	0.6 (600)	0.1 (100)	0.0 (0)	−1.3 (−130)	1.0 (100)
1900–1910	0.0 (–)	−0.2 (–)	−0.0 (–)	0.1 (–)	0.4 (–)	0.2 (–)	0.0 (–)	−0.2 (–)	−0.3 (–)
1910–1920	−1.2 (100)	−0.6 (50)	0.0 (0)	−0.2 (17)	0.5 (−42)	0.2 (−17)	0.0 (0)	0.4 (−33)	−1.5 (125)
1920–1930	0.0 (0)	−0.2 (–)	0.0 (–)	−0.1 (–)	0.8 (–)	0.4 (–)	0.0 (–)	−2.1 (–)	1.2 (–)
1930–1940	−0.3 (100)	−0.1 (33)	0.0 (0)	−0.1 (33)	1.3 (−433)	0.2 (−67)	0.0 (0)	0.7 (−233)	−2.3 (767)
1940–1950	1.7 (100)	0.3 (18)	– (–)	– (–)	0.2 (12)	0.2 (12)	0.0 (0)	– (–)	– (–)
1950–1960	−1.7 (100)	−1.1 (65)	−0.3 (18)	−0.3 (18)	1.7 (−100)	0.4 (−24)	0.0 (0)	−4.0 (235)	−1.9 (112)
1960–1970	−3.6 (100)	−1.0 (28)	−0.2 (6)	−0.7 (19)	1.0 (−28)	0.4 (−11)	0.0 (0)	−3.9 (108)	−0.2 (6)

(6) Non-agricultural Labor (L_2)

	L_2	CL_2T_1	CL_2T_2	CL_2K	CL_2L	CL_2Q	CL_2B	CL_2a	CL_2N
1880–1890	1.7 (100)	0.5 (29)	0.2 (12)	0.1 (6)	0.6 (35)	−0.2 (−12)	0.0 (0)	−5.1 (−300)	5.6 (329)
1890–1900	1.4 (100)	0.2 (14)	0.1 (7)	0.1 (7)	0.7 (50)	−0.2 (−14)	0.0 (0)	2.4 (171)	−1.9 (−136)
1900–1910	1.3 (100)	0.4 (31)	0.0 (0)	0.2 (15)	0.5 (38)	−0.3 (−23)	0.0 (0)	0.4 (31)	0.1 (8)
1910–1920	3.2 (100)	0.7 (22)	−0.0 (0)	0.2 (6)	0.7 (22)	−0.3 (−9)	0.0 (0)	−0.5 (−16)	2.4 (75)
1920–1930	1.7 (100)	0.2 (12)	−0.0 (0)	0.1 (6)	1.0 (59)	−0.3 (−18)	0.0 (0)	2.0 (118)	−1.3 (−76)
1930–1940	2.8 (100)	0.1 (4)	−0.0 (0)	0.1 (4)	1.7 (61)	−0.2 (−7)	0.0 (0)	−0.5 (−18)	1.6 (57)
1940–1950	−1.0 (100)	−0.2 (20)	– (–)	– (–)	0.2 (−200)	−0.2 (200)	0.0 (0)	– (–)	– (–)
1950–1960	4.7 (100)	0.6 (13)	0.2 (4)	0.2 (4)	2.5 (53)	−0.2 (−4)	0.0 (0)	2.4 (51)	1.0 (21)
1960–1970	2.9 (100)	0.3 (10)	0.1 (3)	0.2 (7)	1.4 (48)	−0.1 (−3)	0.0 (0)	1.2 (41)	0.1 (3)

(*Continued*)

Appendix Table 6   (*Continued*)

(7) Relative price (Ag./Non-ag.) (P)

	P	CPT_1	CPT_2	CPK	CPL	CPQ	CPB	CPa	CPN
1880–1890	6.3 (100)	−3.2 (51)	1.7 (27)	0.2 (3)	0.1 (2)	0.0 (0)	−0.2 (−3)	0.8 (12)	6.9 (110)
1890–1900	−1.9 (100)	−1.4 (74)	1.9 (−100)	0.5 (−26)	0.1 (−5)	0.1 (−5)	−0.2 (11)	−0.6 (32)	−2.3 (121)
1900–1910	−0.8 (100)	−1.9 (238)	0.1 (−13)	0.9 (−113)	0.0 (0)	0.1 (−13)	−0.5 (63)	−0.1 (13)	0.6 (−75)
1910–1920	0.7 (100)	−3.9 (−557)	−0.9 (−129)	1.8 (257)	−0.1 (−14)	0.1 (14)	−0.3 (−43)	0.2 (29)	3.0 (543)
1920–1930	−3.3 (100)	−1.1 (33)	−0.5 (15)	1.1 (−3.3)	−0.0 (0)	0.2 (−6)	0.0 (0)	−1.0 (30)	−2.0 (61)
1930–1940	7.2 (100)	−0.4 (−6)	2.0 (28)	1.5 (21)	−0.2 (−3)	0.1 (1)	−0.1 (−1)	0.4 (6)	3.9 (54)
1940–1950	– (–)	1.4 (–)	– (–)	– (–)	−0.0 (–)	0.1 (–)	0.2 (–)	– (–)	– (–)
1950–1960	−1.5 (100)	−4.4 (239)	4.0 (−267)	0.9 (−60)	0.0 (0)	0.1 (−7)	−0.2 (13)	−1.2 (80)	−0.7 (47)
1960–1970	2.1 (100)	−0.4 (17)	6.2 (295)	1.5 (71)	0.0 (0)	0.1 (5)	0.2 (10)	−1.1 (−52)	−4.7 (−224)

(8) Per Capita Income (E)

	E	CET_1	CET_2	CEK	CEL	CEQ	CEB	CEa	CEN
1880–1890	2.7 (100)	1.3 (48)	1.2 (44)	0.4 (15)	0.4 (15)	−1.0 (−37)	0.1 (4)	−2.4 (−89)	2.7 (100)
1890–1900	2.2 (100)	0.5 (23)	1.3 (59)	0.7 (32)	0.4 (18)	−1.1 (−50)	0.1 (5)	1.1 (50)	−0.8 (−36)
1900–1910	1.3 (100)	0.6 (46)	0.1 (8)	1.2 (92)	0.3 (23)	−1.4 (−108)	0.1 (8)	0.2 (15)	0.2 (15)
1910–1920	2.6 (100)	1.1 (42)	−0.7 (−27)	2.2 (85)	0.4 (15)	−1.3 (−50)	0.1 (4)	−0.2 (−8)	1.0 (38)
1920–1930	0.5 (100)	0.3 (60)	−0.4 (−80)	1.4 (280)	0.6 (120)	−1.7 (−340)	−0.0 (0)	0.8 (160)	−0.5 (−100)
1930–1940	3.9 (100)	0.1 (3)	1.7 (44)	1.9 (49)	0.8 (21)	−1.2 (−31)	0.0 (0)	−0.2 (−5)	0.8 (21)
1940–1950	– (–)	−0.2 (–)	– (–)	– (–)	0.1 (–)	−0.0 (–)	0.0 (–)	– (–)	– (–)
1950–1960	7.1 (100)	0.9 (13)	3.5 (49)	1.6 (23)	1.7 (24)	−1.3 (18)	0.0 (0)	1.0 (14)	−0.3 (−4)
1960–1970	10.0 (100)	0.4 (4)	5.9 (59)	3.5 (35)	0.9 (9)	−1.2 (120)	−0.0 (0)	0.7 (7)	0.2 (2)

References

Adelman, I. (1963). An Economic Analysis of Population Growth, *American Economic Review* 53, pp. 314–339.

Adelman, I. and Morris, C.T. (1966). A Quantitative Study of Social and Political Determinants of Fertility, *Economic Development and Cultural Change* 14, pp. 129–157.

Akino, M. and Hayami, A. (1973). *Nougyo Seicho no Gensen* 1880–1965 (*Sources of Agricultural Growth* 1880–1965), eds. Ohkawa, K. and Hayami, Y., Chapter 1 *"Nihon Keizai no Chouki Bunseki"* (*Long-term Analysis of Japanese Economy*), (Nihon Keizai Shinbunsha, Tokyo), pp. 23–51.

Akino, M. and Hayami, Y. (1974). Sources of Agricultural Growth in Japan. 1880–1965, *Quarterly Journal of Economics* 88, pp. 454–479.

Arrow, K.J. (1962). The Economic Implications of Learning by Doing, *Review of Economic Studies* 29, pp. 155–173.

Bank of Japan (1966). *Hundred Year Statistics of the Japanese Economy* (*HSJE*), (Statistics Department, Tokyo).

Barro, R. and Sala-i-Martin, X. (1992). Convergence, *Journal of Political Economy* 100, pp. 223–251.

Barro, R. and Sala-i-Martin, X. (1995). *Economic Growth*, (MIT Press, Cambridge, MA).

Becker, G.S. (1960). An Economic Analysis of Fertility, *Proceedings of Demographic and Economic Change in Developed Countries*, University National Bureau Conference Series 11, pp. 240–230.

Becker, G.S. (1965). A Theory of the Allocation of Time, *Economic Journal* 75, pp. 493–517.

Ben-Porath, Y. (1973). Economic Analysis of Fertility in Israel: Point and Counter Point, *Journal of Political Economy* 81, Supp., pp. 202–233.

Beveridge, W.H. (1923). Population and Unemployment, *Economic Journal* 33, pp. 447–475.

Blacker, C.P. (1968). Stages in Population Growth, *Eugenic Review* 39, pp. 88–102.

Blake, J. (1968). Are Babies Consumer Durables? A Critique of the Economic Theory of Reproductive Motivation, *Population Studies* 22, pp. 5–25.

Blanchard, O. (1985). Debt, Deficits, and Finite Horizons, *Journal of Political Economy* 93, pp. 223–247.

Bloom, D., Canning, D. and Malaney, P. (2000). Demographic Change and Economic Growth in Asia, eds. Chu, C. and Lee, R. *"Population and Economic Change in East Asia"*, *Population and Development Review* (Supplement) 26, pp. 257–290.

Bloom, D.E., Canning, D. and Graham, B. (2003). Longevity and Life-cycle Savings, *Scandinavian Journal of Economics* 105, pp. 319–338.

Bloom, D. and Williamson, J. (1998). Demographic Transitions and Economic Miracles in Emerging Asia, *World Bank Economic Review* 12, pp. 419–455.

Boeke, J.H. (1953). *Economics and Economic Policy of Dual Societies*, (Institute of Pacific Relations, New York).

Borsch-Supan, A. (1996). *Future Global Capital Shortages: Real Threat or Pure Fiction?*, Organization for Economic Co-operation and Development, *"The Impact of Population Ageing on Savings, Investment and Growth in the OECD Area,"* (Organization for Economic Co-operation and Development, Paris), pp. 103–141.

Boserup, E. (1965). *The Conditions of Agricultural Growth: The Economics of Agrarian Change under Population Pressure*, (Aldine Publishing Co, Chicago).

Bound, J., Jaeger, D.A. and BakFer, R.M. (1995). Problems with Instrumental Variables Estimation when the Correlation between the Instruments and the Endogenous Explanatory Variable is Weak, *Journal of the American Statistical Association* 90, pp. 443–450.

Bureau of Statistics (various years). *Japan Statistics Yearbook (JAY)*, (Office of the Prime Minister, Tokyo).

Butz, W.P. and Ward, M.P. (1979). The Emergence of Countercyclical U.S. Fertility, *American Economic Review* 69, pp. 318–328.

Cannan, E. (1888). *Elementary Political Economy*, (H. Milford, London).

Chinn, M. and Ito, H. (2005). What Matters for Financial Development? Capital Controls, Institutions, and Interactions, *National Bureau of Economic Research Working Paper*, No. 11370.

Christensen, L.R. and Jorgenson, D.W. (1970). U.S. Real Product and Real Factor Input, 1929–1967, *Review of Income and Wealth* 16, pp. 39–47.

Clark, C. (1940). *The Conditions of Economic Progress*, (Macmillan Press, London).

Clark, C. (1967). *Population Growth and Land Use*, (Macmillan Press, London).

Coale, A.J. (1967). Factors Associated with the Development of Low Fertility: A Historic Summary, *Proceedings of the World Population Conference*, 1965, held in Belgrade, Vol. II, United Nations, pp. 205–209.

Coale, A.J. (ed.) (1976). *Economic Factors in Population Growth*, (Macmillan Press, London and Basingstoke).

Coale, A.J. and Demeny, P. (1983). *Regional Model Life Tables and Stable Populations*, 2nd edn. (Academic Press, New York).

Coale, A.J. and Hoover, E.M. (1958). Population Growth and Economic Development in Low-Income Countries: A Case Study of India's Prospects, (Princeton University Press, Princeton).

Cobb, C.W. and Douglas, P.H. (1928). A Theory of Production, *American Economic Review* 18, pp. 139–165.

Davis, K. and Blake, J. (1956). Social Structure and Fertility: An Analytic Framework, *Economic Development and Cultural Change* 4, pp. 211–235.

Dalrymple, D.G. (1969). Technological Change in Agriculture: Effects and Implications for the Developing Nations, Foreign Agricultural Service, U.S. Department of Agriculture, Agency for International Development.

Davies, J.B. (1981). Uncertain Lifetime, Consumption, and Dissaving in Retirement, *Journal of Political Economy* 89, pp. 561–577.

Deaton, A. and Paxson, C.H. (2000). Growth, Demographic Structure, and National Saving in Taiwan, *Population and Economic Change in East Asia, A Supplement to Population and Development Review* 26, pp. 141–173.

Denison, E.F. (1962). *The Source of Economic Growth in the United States and the Alternatives before Us*, (Committee for Economic Development, New York).

Denton, F.T. and Spencer, B.G. (1975). *Population and the Economy*, (Saxon House, England).

De Tray, D.N. (1973). Child Quality and the Demand for Children, *Journal of Political Economy* 81, Part II, pp. S70–S95.

Diewert, W.D. (1973). Functional Forms for Profit and Transformation Functions, *Journal of Economic Theory* 6, pp. 284–316.

Dixit, A. (1970). Growth patterns in a Dual Economy, *Oxford Economic Paper* 22, pp. 229–234.

Domar, E.D. (1946). Capital Expansion Rate of Growth and Employment, *Econometrica* 14, pp. 137–250.

Duesenberry, J.S. (1960). Comment, *Demographic and Economic Change in Developed Countries*, University National Bureau Conference Series 11, (Princeton University Press, Princeton), pp. 231–234.

Easterlin, R.A. (1961). American Baby Boom in Historical Perspective, *American Economic Review* 51, pp. 869–911.

Easterlin, R.A. (1966). Economic-Demographic Interactions and Long Swings in Economic Growth, *American Economic Review* 56, pp. 1063–1104.

Easterlin, R.A. (1969). Towards a Socioeconomic Theory of Fertility: Survey of Recent Research on Economic Factors in American Fertility, eds. Behrman, S.J. *et al.*, *"Fertility and Family Planning: A World View,"* (Ann Arbor, Michigan).

Easterlin, R.A. (1973). *Relative Economic Status and the American Fertility Swing*, ed. Sheldon, E.B., Chapter 5 *"Family Economic Behavior: Problems and Prospects,"* (J.B. Lippincott Company, Philadelphia), pp. 170–223.

Easterlin, R.A. (1976). The Conflict between Aspirations and Resources, *Population and Development Review* 2, pp. 417–425.

Easterlin, R.A. (1978). *The Economics and Sociology of Fertility: A Synthesis*, ed. Tilly, C., Chapter 2, *"Historical Studies of Changing Fertility,"* (Princeton University Press, Princeton), pp. 57–133.

Easterlin, R.A., Pollak, R.A. and Wachter, M.L. (1980). Toward a More General Economic Model of Fertility Determination: Endogenous Preferences and Natural Fertility, ed. Easterlin, R.A., Chapter 2, *"Population and Economic Change in Developing Countries,"* (University of Chicago, Chicago), pp. 81–150.

Easterlin, R.A. and Crimmins, E. (1985). *The Fertility Revolution: A Supply-Demand Analysis*, (University of Chicago Press, Chicago).

Ezaki, M. (1977). *Nihonkeizai no Model Bunseki (Model Analysis of Japanese Economy)*, (Soubunsha, Tokyo).

Ezaki, M. (1984). Book Review: Yamaguchi, M. Nihon Keizai no Seicho-Kaikei-Bunseki — Jinko, Nougyo, Keizai-Hatten (Growth Accounting for the Japanese Economy — Population, Agriculture and Economic Development), *Kokumin-Keizai Zasshi* 149, pp. 116–120.

Fei, J. and Ranis, G. (1964). *Development of the Labor Surplus Economy: Theory and Policy*, (Irwin, Homewood. Ill).

Fisher, A. (1945). *Economic Progress and Social Security*, (Macmillan, London).

Friedlander, S. and Silver, M. (1967). A Quantitative Study of the Determinants of Fertility Behavior, *Demography* 4, pp. 30–70.

Fry, M. and Mason, A. (1982). The Variable Rate of Growth Effect in the Life Cycle Model, *Economic Inquiry* 20, pp. 426–442.

Fujino, S. (1965). *Nihon no Keikijunkan — Junkanteki Hatten Katei no Rironteki, Toukeiteki, Rekisiteki Bunseki (Business Cycle of Japan — Theoretical, Statistical and Historical Analysis of the Process of Cyclical Development*, (Keiso Shobo, Tokyo).

Gerschenkron, A. (1962). *Economic Backwardness in Historical Perspective, a Book of Essays*, (Belknap Press of Harvard University Press, Cambridge, Massachusetts).

Gerschenkron, A. (1968). *Continuity in History, and Other Essays*, (Belknap Press of Harvard University Press, Cambridge, Massachusetts).

Gollin, D., Parente, S. and Rogerson, R. (2002). The Role of Agriculture in Development, *American Economic Review* 92, pp. 160–164.

Goodwin, W. (1796). *Political Justice*, 2nd edn. (London, England).

Gregory, P.R. Campbell, J.M. and Cheng, B.S. (1972). A Simultaneous Equation Model of Birth Rates in the United States, *Review of Economics and Statistics* 54, pp. 374–380.

Gregory, P.R., Mokhtari, M. and Schrettl, W. (1999). Do the Russians Really Save that Much? Alternate Estimates from the Russian Longitudinal Monitoring Survey, *Review of Economics and Statistics* 54, pp. 374–380.

Grigg, D. (1980). *Population Growth and Agrarian Change: An Historical Perspective*, (Cambridge University Press, Cambridge).

Grillches, Z. (1964). Research Expenditures, Education, and the Aggregate Agricultural Production Function, *American Economic Review* 54, pp. 961–974.

Guillaumont, P. (1976). The Optimal Rate of Population Growth, ed. Coale, A.J., Chapter 2, *"Economic Factors in Population Growth,"* (Macmillan Press, London and Basingstoke), pp. 29–62.

Hansen, A.H. (1941). *Fiscal Policy and Business Cycles*, (Norton, New York).

Hara, Y. (1976). Book Review of Hayami, Y. and others (A Century of Agricultural Growth in Japan. Its Relevance to Asian Development), *Asian Studies* 22, pp. 59–77.

Harris, J. and Todaro, M.P. (1970). Migration, Unemployment and Development: A Two Sector Analysis, *American Economic Review* 60, pp. 126–142.

Harrod, R.F. (1939). An Essay in Dynamic Theory, *Economic Journal* 49, pp. 14–33.

Hashimoto, M. (1974). Economics of Postwar Fertility in Japan: Differentials and Trends, *Journal of Political Economy* 82, pp. 170–194.

Hatai, Y. (1963). Noka-Jinko-Ido to Keiki-Hendo — Minami, Ono, Namiki Ronso ni-tuite (Migration of Rural Population and Business Cycles: On the Controversy between Minami-Ono and Namiki), *Economic Studies Quarterly* 14, pp. 28–32.

Hausman, J.A. (1978). Specification Tests in Econometrics, *Econometrica* 46, pp. 1251–1271.

Hausman, J.A. (1983). Specification and Estimation of Simultaneous Equations Models, eds. Griliches, Z. and Intriligator, M.D. Chapter 7, *"Handbook of Econometrics"*, Volume 1, (North Holland, Amsterdam, Holland), pp. 391–448.

Hayami, Y. (1973). *Nihonnogyo no Seicho Katei (The Process of Agricultural Development in Japan)*, (Sobunsha, Tokyo).

Hayami, Y. and Ruttan, V.W. (1970). Korean Rice, Taiwan Rice, and Japanese Agricultural Stagnation: An Economic Consequence of Colonialism, *Quarterly Journal of Economics* 84, pp. 562–589.

Hayami, Y. and Ruttan, V.W. (1971, 1985 (Revised edition)). *Agricultural Development — An International Perspective.* (Johns Hopkins Press, Baltimore).

Hayashi, F. and Prescott, E.C. (2008). The Pressing effect of Agricultural Institutions on the Prewar Japanese Economy, *Journal of Political Economy* 116, pp. 573–632.

Hazledine T. and Moreland, R.S. (1977). Population and Economic Growth: A World Cross-Section Study, *Review of Economics and Statistics* 59, pp. 253–263.

Hicks, J. (1960). *The Social Framework*, 3rd edn. (Oxford University Press, Oxford).

Hicks, J. (1966). *The Theory of Wages*, 2nd edn. (Macmillan and St. Martin's Press, London and New York).

Hicks, J. (1976). Discussion, ed. Coale, A.J., Chapter 3, *"Economic Factors in Population Growth,"* (Macmillan Press, London and Basingstoke), pp. 74–77.

Higgins, B. (1956). The Dualistic Theory of Underdeveloped Areas, *Economic Development and Cultural Change* 4, pp. 99–108.

Higgins, M. (1994). *The Demographic Determinants of Savings, Investment and International Capital Flows*, Ph.D. Dissertation, Department of Economics, Harvard University Cambridge, MA.

Higgins, M. and Williamson, J. G. (1997). Age Structure Dynamics in Asia and Dependence on Foreign Capital, *Population and Development Review* 23, pp. 261–293.

Houthaker, H. (1957). An International Comparison of Household Expenditure Patterns, Commemorating the Century of Engel's Law, *Econometrica* 25, pp. 532–551.

Ichimura, S. (1973). Comment to Minami and Ono Paper, eds. Ohkawa, K. and Hayami, Y., Chapter 5 *"Nihon Keizai no Chouki Bunseki"* (*Long-term Analysis of Japanese Economy*), (Nihon Keizai Shinbunsha, Tokyo), pp. 224–226.

Inada, M. and Yamamoto, H. (2010). Analysis of Migration Decisions of Chinese Japonica Rice Farmers, *Discussion Paper* 145, Institute of Economic Research, Chuo University.

Ishikawa, S. (1966). Kaihatsu-Katei no Noukou-Kan Shikin-Ido (Net Resource Flow between Agriculture and Industry), *The Economic Review* 17, pp. 202–208.

Ishikawa, S. (1967). *Economic Development in Asian Perspective*, (Kinokuniya, Tokyo).

Ito, M. (1978). Senzenki Nihon no Roudou Shijyou: Lewisian approach ni tsuite (Labor Market of Pre-war Japan: Some Considerations for Lewisian approach), Paper presented at the *conference of Western part of Japan Association of Economics and Econometrics.*

Japan. Statistic Bureau and Statistic Research and Training Institute (2006). *"Historical Statistics of Japan"* http://www.stat.go.jp/data/chouki/02.htm, (November 25, 2006).

Japan. Health and Welfare Statistics Association (various years), *Seimeihyo (Life Table)*.

Johnson, H.G. (1966). Factor Market Distortions and the Share of the Transformation Curve, *Econometrica* 34, pp. 686–698.

Johnston, B.F. (1951). Agricultural Productivity and Economic Development in Japan, *Journal of Political Economy* 59, pp. 498–513.

Jorgenson, D.W. (1961). The Development of a Dual Economy, *Economic Journal* 71, pp. 309–334.

Jorgenson, D.W. (1973). Comment to Minami and Ono Paper, eds. Ohkawa, K. and Hayami, Y., Chapter 5 *"Nihon Keizai no Chouki Bunseki"* (*Long-term Analysis of Japanese Economy*), (Nihon Keizai Shinbunsha, Tokyo), pp. 219–223.

Jureen, L. (1956). Long-Term Trends in Food Consumption: A Multi-Country Study, *Econometrica* 25, pp. 532–551.

Kageyama, J. (2003). The Effects of a Continuous Increase in Lifetime on Saving, *Review of Income and Wealth* 49, pp. 163–183.

Kamiya, K. (1941). Nogyo-Roudo no Seisan-sei ni tsuite (On the Productivity of Labor in Agriculture), *Journal of Rural Economics* 17, pp. 23–48.

Kaneda, H. (1968). Long-Term Changes in Food Consumption Patterns in Japan, 1878–1964, *Food Research Institute Studies* 8, pp. 3–32.

Kao, C.H.C. Anschel, K.R. and Eicher, C.K. (1964). Disguised Unemployment in Agriculture: A Survey, eds. Eicher, C. and Witt, L., Chapter 7, *"Agriculture in Economic Development,"* (McGraw-Hill, New York), pp. 129–144.

Kashiwa, S. (1960). *Nihon Nougyo Gairon (Outline of Japanese Agriculture)*, (Youkendo, Tokyo).

Kashiwa, S. (1962). *Nougaku Genron (The Principles of Agriculture)*, (Yokendo, Tokyo).

Kato, Y. (1963). Bumon-Kan Shikin-Ido to Nouka no Chochiku, Toushi (Money Flow between Sectors, and Saving and Investment of Farm), eds. Ohkawa, K., Chapter 3 in Part 3 *"Nihon-Nougyo no Seicho Bunseki" (Growth Analysis of Japanese Agriculture)*, (Daimeido, Tokyo), pp. 117–131.

Kato, Y. (1970). Choki Nougyo niokeru Seihu no Yakuwari (The Role of Government in Long Term Agricultural Money), eds. Kawano, J. and Kato, Y., Chapter 11 *"Nihon Nougyo to Keizai Seicho" (Japanese Agriculture and Economic Growth)*, (Tokyo University Press, Tokyo), pp. 241–262.

Kelley, A.C. and Schmidt, R.M. (1996). Saving, Dependency and Development, *Journal of Population Economics* 9, pp. 365–386.

Kelley, A.C. and Schmidt, R.M. (2001). Economic and Demographic Change: A Synthesis of Models, Findings, and Perspectives, eds. Nancy, B., Kelley, A.C. and Sinding, S., Chapter 4 *"Population Matters: Demographic Change, Economic Growth, and Poverty in the Developing World,"* (Oxford University Press, New York), pp. 67–105.

Kelley, A.C. and Schmidt, R.M. (2005). Evolution of Recent Economic-Demographic Modeling: A Synthesis, *Journal of Population Economics* 18, pp. 275–300.

Kelley, A.C. and Williamson, J.G. (1971). Writing History Backwards: Meiji Japan Revised, *Journal of Economic History* 31, pp. 729–776.

Kelley, A.C. and Williamson, J.G. (1973). Modeling Economic Development and General Equilibrium Histories, *American Economic Review* 63, pp. 450–458.

Kelley, A.C. and Williamson, J.G. (1974). *Lessons from Japanese Development*, (University of Chicago Press, Chicago).

Kelley, A.C., Williamson, J.G. and Cheetham, R.J. (1972a). Biased Technological Progress and Labor Force Growth in a Dualistic Economy, *Quarterly Journal of Economics* 86, pp. 426–447.

Kelley, A.C., Williamson J.G. and Cheetham, R.J. (1972b). *Dualistic Economic Development: Theory and History*, (University of Chicago Press, Chicago).

Kendrick, J.W. (1961). *Productivity Trends in the United States*, National Bureau of Economic Research, (Princeton University Press, New York).

Keynes, J. (1919). The Economic Consequences of the Peace, 1971 (1st edn., 1919) in *The Collected Writings of John Maynard Keynes*, Vol. II (Macmillan Press Ltd, London).

Keynes, J. (1937). Some Economic Consequences of a Declining Population, *Eugenics Review* 29, pp. 13–17.

Kinugasa, T. (2004). *Life Expectancy, Labor Force, and Saving*, Ph.D. Dissertation, Department of Economics, (Honolulu, HI, University of Hawaii at Manoa).

Kinugasa, T. and Mason, A. (2007). Why Countries Become Wealthy: The Effects of Adult Longevity on Saving, *World Development* 35, pp. 1–23.

Kinugasa, T. and Yamaguchi, Y. (2008). The Effect of Demographic Change on Industrial Structure: A Study Using the Overlapping Generations and General Equilibrium Growth Accounting Models, *Journal of Population Studies* 42, pp. 21–40.

Kirk, D. (1960). The Influence of Business Cycles on Marriage and Birth Rates, *Proceedings of Demographic and Economic Change in Developed Countries*, University National Bureau Conference Series 11, pp. 241–260.

Klein, L.R. (1961). A Model of Japanese Economic Growth, 1878–1937, *Econometrica* 29, pp. 277–292.

Klein, L.R. and Shinkai, Y. (1963). An Econometric Model of Japan, 1930–59, *International Economic Review* 4, pp. 1–28.

Kuznets, S. (1960). Population Change and Aggregate Output, *Proceedings of Demographic and Economic Change in Developed Countries*, University National Bureau Conference Series 11, pp. 324–351.

Kuznets, S. (1974). An Interpretation of the Economic Theory of Fertility: Promising Path or Blind Alley? *Journal of Economic Literature* 12, pp. 457–479.

Kuznets, S. (1975). The Economic Theory of Fertility Decline, *Quarterly Journal of Economics* 89, pp. 1–31.

Kuehlwein, M. (1993). Life-Cycle and Altruistic Theories of Saving with Lifetime Uncertainty, *Review of Economics and Statistics* 75, pp. 38–47.

Laitner, J. (2000). Structural Change and Economic Growth, *Review of Economic Studies* 67, pp. 545–561.

Lee, R. D., Lee, S.-H. and Mason, A. (2005). *Charting the Economic Lifecycle*, Mimeo.

Lee, R., Mason, A. and Miller, T. (2000). Life Cycle Saving and the Demographic Transition in East Asia, *Population and Development Review* 26 (Supplement), pp. 194–219.

Lee, R., Mason, A. and Miller, T. (2001a). Saving, Wealth, and Population, eds. Birdsall, N., Kelley, A.C. and Sinding, S.-W., Chapter 6 *"Population Matters: Demography, Poverty, and Economic Growth,"* (Oxford University Press, Oxford), pp. 137–164.

Lee, R., Mason, A. and Miller, T. (2001b). Saving, Wealth, and the Demographic Transition in East Asia, ed. Mason, A., *"Population Change and Economic Development in East Asia: Challenges Met, Opportunities Seized,"* (Stanford University Press, Stanford), pp. 155–184.

Lee, R., Mason, A. and Miller, T. (2003). From Transfers to Individual Responsibility: Implications for Savings and Capital Accumulation in Taiwan and the United States, *Scandinavian Journal of Economics* 105, pp. 339–357.

Lee, T.H. (1968). *Intersectoral Capital Flows in the Economic Development of Taiwan, 1895–1960*, Ph.D. dissertation, Cornell University, University Microfilms, Ann Arbor.

Leibenstein, H. (1957). *Economic Backwardness and Economic Growth*, (Wiley, New York).

Leibenstein, H. (1974). An Interpretation of the Economic Theory of Fertility: Promising Path or Blind Alley?, *Journal of Economic Literature* 12, pp. 457–479.

Leibenstein, H. (1975). The Economic Theory of Fertility Decline, *Quarterly Journal of Economics* 89, pp. 1–31.

Leung, S.F. (1994). Uncertain Lifetime, the Theory of the Consumer, and the Life Cycle Hypothesis, *Econometrica* 62, pp. 1233–1239.

Lewis, A.W. (1954). Economic Development with Unlimited Supplies of Labor, *Manchester School of Economics and Social Studies* 22, pp. 139–191.

List, F. (1841). *Das Nationale System der Politischen Okonomie*, (Cotta, Stuttgart, Arthur Sommer).

Maddison, A. (1995). *Monitoring the World Economy 1820–1992*, (OECD, Paris, France).

Malthus, R. (1798). *An Essay on the Principle of Population, as it Affects the Future Improvement of Society, with Remarks on the Speculations of Mr. Godwin, M. Condorcet, and Other Writers*, (J. Johnson, St. Paul's Church Yard, London).

Mason, A. (1981). An Extension of the Life-Cycle Model and its Application to Population Growth and Aggregate Saving, *East-West Population Institute Working Paper No. 4*, Honolulu.

Mason, A. (1987). National Saving Rates and Population Growth: A New Model and New Evidence, eds. Johnson, D.G. and Lee R.D., *"Population Growth and Economic Development: Issues and Evidence, Social Demography series"* (University of Wisconsin Press, Madison, WI), pp. 523–560.

Mason, A. (1988). Saving, Economic Growth, and Demographic Change, *Population and Development Review* 14, pp. 113–144.

Mason, A. (2005). Demographic Transition and Demographic Dividends in Developed and Developing Countries, Paper presented at the *United Nations Expert Group Meeting on Social and Economic Implications of Changing Population Age Structure*, New York.

Mason, A. (2007). Demographic Dividends: The Past, the Present, and the Future, eds. Mason, A. and Yamaguchi, M., Chapter 4, *"Population Change, Labor Markets and Sustainable Growth: Towards a New Economic Paradigm,"* (Elsevier Press, Amsterdam).

Mason, A. and Kinugasa, T. (2008). East Asian Development: Two Demographic Dividends, *Journal of Asian Economics* 19, pp. 389–400.

Mason, A. and Lee, R. (2006). Reform and Support Systems for the Elderly in Developing Countries: Capturing the Second Demographic Dividend, *GENUS* 57, pp. 11–35.

Mansfield, E. (1968). *The Economics of Technological Change*, (W.W. Norton & Company Inc., New York).

Matsuyama, K. (1992). Agricultural Productivity, Comparative Advantage, and Economic Growth, *Journal of Economic Theory* 58, pp. 317–334.

Meade, J.E. (1955). *Trade and Welfare*, (Oxford Univ. Press, New York).

Meadows, D.H., Meadows, D.L., Randers, J. and Behrens III, W.W. (1972). *The Limit to Growth*, (Universe Books, New York).

Meier, G.M. (ed.) (1976). *Leading Issues in Economic Development*, 3rd edn. (Oxford University Press, New York).

Michael, R.T. (1973). Education and the Derived Demand for Children, *Journal of Political Economy* 81, Part II, pp. S279–S288.

Mill, J.S. (1848). *Principles of Political Economy*, (Longman, Green and Co., London).

Minami, R. (1970). *Nihon Keizai no Tenkanten (Turning Point of Japanese Economy)*, (Sobun-sha, Tokyo).

Minami, R. (1981a). *Nihon no Keizaihatten (Economic Development of Japan)*, (Touyo Keizai Shimpo-sha, Tokyo).

Minami, R. (1981b). Nougyo Roudo no Seisan Danryokusei no Chouki-teki Henka — Keisoku to Bunseki (Long-Term Change of Agricultural Labor Elasticity of Output — Measurement and Analysis), *Economic Review* 32, pp. 358–366.

Minami, R. and Ono, A. (1962). Nouka-Jinko-Ido to Keiki-Hendo to no Kankei ni tuiteno Oboegaki (Note on the Relationship between Business Cycle and Agricultural Population Movement), *Economic Studies Quarterly* 12, pp. 64–66.

Minami, R. and Ono, A. (1963). Nouka Jinko-Ido to Keiki Hendo — Namiki Shi no Han-hihan ni tuite (Agricultural Labor Movement and Business Cycle — A Further Comment on M. Namiki's Rejoinder), *Economic Studies Quarterly* 14, pp. 64–66.

Minami, R. and Ono, A. (1971). Nijyu Kouzou-Ka no Bukka Hendou (Price Movement under Dual Structure), *Economic Studies Quarterly* 22, pp. 42–50.

Minami, R. and Ono, A. (1972a). Economic Growth with Dual Structure: An Econometric Model of the Prewar Japanese Economy, *mimeographed*, Japan Economic Research Center, 1972.

Minami, R. and Ono, A. (1972b). Keizai Seicho to Nijuu Kouzo (Economic Growth and Dual Structure), *Economic Review* 23, pp. 309–322.

Minami, R. and Ono, A. (1975a). Nijuu Kouzouka no Koyou to Chingin (Employment and Wage under Dual Structure), eds. Ohkawa, K. and Minami, R., Chapter 4 in Part 2 *"Kindai Nihon no Keizai Hatten" (Economic Development of Modern Japan)*, (Touyo Keizai Shimpousha, Tokyo), pp. 466–496.

Minami, R. and Ono, A. (1975b). Youso Syotoku, Bunpairitsu oyobi Yousokakaku (Factor Income Distribution Share and Factor Price), eds. Ohkawa, K. and Minami, R., Chapter 7 in part 1 *"Kindai Nihon no Keizai Hatten"* (*Economic Development of Modern Japan*), (Touyo Keizai Shimpousha, Tokyo), pp. 150–177.

Minami, R. and Ono, A. (1975c). Hiichiji Sangyo no Yoso Syotoku to Bunpairitu (Factor Income and Distribution Share in Nonprimary Industry), eds. Ohkawa, K. and Minami, R., Chapter 6 in Part 3 *"Kindai Nihon no Keizai Hatten" (Economic Development of Modern Japan)*, (Touyo Keizai Shimpousha, Tokyo), pp. 553–568.

Minami, R. and Ono, A. (1978). Youso syotoku to Bunpairitu no Suikei — Minkan Hi-Ichiji Sangyo (Estimation of Factor Incomes and Factor Shares — Non-Primary Industries), *Economic Review* 29, pp. 143–169.

Minami, Ryozaburo (1963a). *Jinko Riron (Theory of Population)*, (Chikura Syobo Press, Tokyo).

Minami, Ryozaburo (1963b). *Zinko-shisoshi (History of Population Thought)*, (Chikura-syobo, Tokyo).

Minami, Ryozaburo (1971). *Jinkogaku Soron (General Theory of Population)*, (Chikura Syobo Press, Tokyo).

Ministry of Internal Affairs and Communications Statistics Bureau. (1958–1973). Labor Force Survey. (Ministry of Internal Affairs and Communications Statistics Bureau, Tokyo).

Modigliani, F. and Brumberg, R. (1954). Utility Analysis and the Consumption Function: An Interpretation of Cross-Section Data, ed. Kurihara, K.K., Chapter 15, *"Post-Keynesian Economics"* (Rutgers University Press, New Brunswick), pp. 388–436.

Mosk, C.A. (1983). *Patriarchy and Fertility: Japan and Sweden, 1880–1960*, (Academic Press, New York).

Nakamura, J. (1966). Agricultural Production and the Economic Development of Japan, 1987–1922, (Princeton University Press, Princeton).

Nakayama, I. and Minami, R. (1959). *Tekido Jinko (Optimum Population)*, (Keiso Syobo, Tokyo).

Namboodri, N.K. (1972). Some Observations on the Economic Framework for Fertility Analysis, *Population Studies* 26, pp. 182–206.

Namiki, M. (1956). Noka jinko no idokeitai to syugyo-kouzo (Movement Form of Farm Labor and Labor Structure), eds. Tohata, S., *"Nougyo ni okeru Senzai Sitsugyo" (Latent Unemployment in Agriculture)*, (Nihon hyouron Shimposha, Tokyo), pp. 195–294.

Namiki, M. (1962). Minami-Ono shi no Hihan ni Kotaeru (Answer to the Minami-Ono's Critics), *Economic Studies Quarterly* 12, pp. 67–69.

Nelson, R.R. (1956). A Theory of the Low-level Equilibrium Trap in Underdeveloped Economies, *American Economic Review* 46, pp. 894–908.

Notestein, F.W. (1950). The Population of the World in the year 2000, *Journal of the American Statistical Association* 45, pp. 335–349.

Ogawa, N. (1982). Population and Development: Lessons From the Japanese Meiji Experience Revisited, *Jinkougaku Kenkyu (Journal of Population Studies)* 5, pp. 35–42.

Ogawa, N. (2007). Population Aging and Economic Growth: The Role of two Demographic Dividends in Japan, eds. Coulmas, F., Conrad, H., Schad-Seifert, A. and Vogt, G., Chapter 45, *"The Demographic Challenge: A Handbook About Japan,"* (Brill Academic Pub, Leiden), pp. 821–840.

Ogawa, N. and Mason, A. (1986). An Economic Analysis of Recent Fertility in Japan: An Application of the Butz-Ward Model, *Jinkougaku Kenkyu (Journal of Population Studies)* 9, pp. 5–15.

Ogawa, N. and Suits, D. (1982). Lessons on Population and Economic Change from the Japanese Meiji Experience, *Developing Economies* 20, pp. 196–219.

Ohbuchi, H. (1988). *Shussyouryoku no Keizaigaku (Economics of Fertility)*, (Chuo Daigaku Shuppanbu, Tokyo).

Ohkawa, K. (1945). *Shokuryou Keizai no Riron to Keisoku (Theory and Measurement of Food Economy)*, (Nihon Hyouronsha, Tokyo).

Ohkawa, K. (1955). *Nougyo no Keizai Bunseki (Economic Analysis of Agriculture)*, (Daimeido, Tokyo).

Ohkawa, K. (1968). Nihon Keizai no Seisan-Bunpai, 1905–1963 — Zanyo no Bunseki (Production and Distribution of Japanese Economy, 1905–1963 — Residual Analysis), *Economic Review* 19, pp. 133–151.

Ohkawa, K. (1972). *Differential Structure and Agriculture: Essays on Dualistic Growth*, (Kinokuniya, Tokyo).
Ohkawa, K. (1975). Kajou Shuugyo: Sairon (Surplus Labor: Second Discussion), eds. Ohkawa, K. and Minami, R., Chapter 9 in Part 1 *"Kindai Nihon no Keizai Hatten"* (*Economic Development of Modern Japan*), (Touyo Keizai Shimposha, Tokyo), pp. 210–227.
Ohkawa, K. and Rosovsky, H. (1960). The Role of Agriculture in Modern Japanese Economic Development, *Economic Development and Cultural Change* 9, Part 2, pp. 43–68.
Ohkawa, K. and Umemura, M. (ed.) (1966 and following years). *Long-Term Economic Statistics* (*Estimates of Long-Term Economic Statistics of Japan Since 1868*), (Toyo Keizai Shimposha, Tokyo).
Ohkawa, K. and Rosovsky, H. (1973). *Japanese Economic Growth: Trend Acceleration in the Twentieth Century*, (Stanford University Press, California).
Ohkawa, K. and Shinohara, M. (ed.) (1979). *Patterns of Japanese Economic Development: A Quantitative Appraisal* (Yale University Press, New Haven and London).
Ohlin, G. (1976). Economic Theory Confronts Population Growth, ed. Coale, A.J., Chapter 1, *"Economic Factors in Population Growth,"* (Macmillan Press, London and Basingstoke), pp. 3–16.
Ohyabu, K. (1969). Wagakuni ni okeru Seisan-Kansu-Bunseki no Tenbo (A Review of Production Function Analyses in Japan), eds. Yamada, L., Emi, K. and Mizoguchi, T., Chapter 4 in Number 1, *"Nihon-keizai no Kouzo-Hendo to Yosoku"* (*The Structural Change and Future of the Japanese Economy*), (Syunjun-sha, Tokyo), pp. 105–137.
Okun, B. (1958). *Trend in Birth Rates in the United States Since 1870*, (Johns Hopkins University Press, Baltimore).
Overbeek, J. (1974). *History of Population Theories*, (Rotterdam University Press, Netherlands).
Perlman, M. (1975). Some Economic Growth Problems and the Part Population Plays, *Quarterly Journal of Economics* 89, pp. 247–256.
Petersen, W. (1969). *Population*, 2nd edn. (Macmillan, London).
Ranis, G. (1959). The Financing of Japanese Economic Development, *Economic History Review* 113, pp. 440–454.
Ranis, G. and Fei, J. (1961). A Theory of Economic Development, *American Economic Review* 51, pp. 533–565.
Ricard, D. (1817). On the Principles of Political Economy and Taxation, (John Murray, London).
Rostow, W. (1960). *The Stages of Economic Growth: A Non-Communist Manifesto*, (Cambridge University Press, Cambridge).
Ruttan, V.W. (1965). Growth Stage Theories and Agricultural Development Policy, *Australian Journal of Agricultural Economics* 9, pp. 17–32.
Ruttan, V.W. (1966). Considerations in the Design of a Strategy for Increasing Rice Production in South East Asia, Paper Prepared for Presentation at the *Pacific Science Congress Session on Modernization of Rural Areas*, Tokyo.
Ruttan, V.W. (1968). *Growth Stage Theories, Dual Economy Models and Agricultural Development Policy*, Department of Agricultural Economics, University of Guelph, Pub. No. AE.

Ruttan, V.W. (1969). Comment: Two Sector Models and Development policy, ed. Wharton, Chapter 11 *"Subsistence Agriculture and Economic Development,"* (Aldine Publishing Company, Chicago), pp. 353–360.

Sanderson, W.C. (1976). On Two Schools of the Economics of Fertility, *Population and Development Review* 2, pp. 469–477.

Sato, K. (1971). Nihon no Hi-ichiji Keizai no Seicho to Gijutsu Shinpo 1930–1967 (Economic Growth and Technical Change of Non-primary Sector of Japan 1930–1967), *Economic Studies Quarterly* 22, pp. 38–54.

Sato, R. (1968a). Technical Progress and the Aggregate Production Function in Japan (1930–1960), *Economic Studies Quarterly* 19, pp. 15–24.

Sato, R. (1968b). *Keizai Seicho no Riron (The Theory of Economic Growth),* (Keiso Syobo, Tokyo).

Sauvy, A. (1976). The Optimal Change of a Population, ed. Coale, A.J., Chapter 3, *"Economic Factors in Population Growth,"* (Macmillan Press, London and Basingstoke), pp. 63–73.

Schieber, S.J. and Shoven, J.B. (1996). *Population Aging and Saving for Retirement,* eds. Landau, R., Taylor, T. and Wright, G., *"The Mosaic of Economic Growth,"* (Stanford University Press, Stanford, CA), pp. 150–172.

Schmookler, J. (1952). The Changing Efficiency of the American Economy: 1869–1938, *Review of Economics and Statistics* 34, pp. 214–231.

Schulz, P.T. (1976). A Micro-economic Model of Choice, ed. Coale, A.J., Chapter 4, *"Economic Factors in Population Growth,"* (Macmillan Press, London and Basingstoke), pp. 89–124.

Schulz, T.W. (1953). *The Economic Organization of Agriculture,* (McGraw-Hill, New York).

Sen, A.K. (1966). Peasants and Dualism with or without Surplus Labor, *Journal of Political Economy* 74, pp. 425–450.

Shinohara, M. (1973). Koudoseicho no shoyouin (Some Factors of High Economic Growth), eds. Emi, K. and Shionoya, Y., Chapter 2, Section 2 *"Nihon Keizairon"* (*Study of Japanese Economy*), (Yuhikaku, Tokyo), pp. 65–89.

Shintani, M. (1993). *Tai no Keizaihatten ni kansuru Suuryoteki Kenkyu: 1950–1990 (Quantitative Research on the Economic Development of Thailand: 1950–1990),* (Seinangakuin Kenkyusho, Fukuoka).

Shintani, M. (1983). *Nihon-nougyou no Seisankansuu Bunseki (Production Function Analysis of Japanese Agriculture),* (Daimeido, Tokyo).

Simon, J.L. (1977). *The Economics of Population Growth,* (Princeton University Press, Princeton).

Simmons, G.B. (1985). *Theories of Fertility,* eds. Farooq, G.M. and Simmons, G.B., Chapter 2 *"Fertility in Developing Countries: An Economic Perspective on Research and Policy Issues,"* (Macmillan Press, London), pp. 20–66.

Silver, M. (1965). Birth, Marriages, and Business Cycles in the United States, *Journal of Political Economy* 73, pp. 237–255.

Slicher van Bath, B.H. (1963). *The Agrarian History of Western Europe, A.D. 500–1850,* (Uitgeverij Het Spectrum N.V, Netherlands).

Smith, A. (1776). An Inquiry into the Nature and Causes of the Wealth of Nations, (Modern Library Edition 1967).

Solow, R.M. (1956). A Contribution to the Theory of Economic Growth, *Quarterly Journal of Economics* 70, pp. 65–94.

Solow, R.M. (1957). Technical Change and the Aggregate Production Function, *Review of Economics and Statistics* 39, pp. 312–320.

Solow, R.M. (1960). Investment and Technical Progress, eds. Arrow, K.J., Karlin, S. and Suppes, P., Chapter 7 *"Mathematical Methods in the Social Science,"* (Stanford University Press, Stanford), pp. 89–104.

Srikantan, K.S. (1982). The Threshold Hypothesis, ed. Ross, J.A., *"International Encyclopedia of Population 1"* (Collier-Macmillan, London), pp. 266–267.

Statistical Data Bank and Information Dissemination Division, National Statistical Office, Thailand (Various Issues). *Statistical Yearbook,* (National Statistical Office, Thailand).

Taira, K. (1970). *Economic Development and the Labor Market in Japan,* (Columbia University Press, New York & London).

Tang, A.M. (1963). Research and Education in Japanese Agricultural Development, 1880–1938, *Economic Studies Quarterly* 13, pp. 27–41, 91 –99.

Takayama, A. (1963). On a Two Sector Model of Economic Growth: A Comparative Statics Analysis, *Review of Economic Studies* 30, pp. 95–104.

Taylor, A. (1995). Debt, Dependence and the Demographic Transition: Latin America in to the Next Century, *World Development* 23, pp. 869–879.

Temple, J. (2005). Dual Economy Models: A Primer For Growth Economists, *Manchester School,* 73, pp. 435–478.

Teranishi, J. (1972). Nihon Keizai no Tenbo (Senzen no bu sono 1) (Perspective of Japanese Economy (No. 1 of Pre-World War II)), *Economic Review* 23, pp. 12–26.

Teranishi, J. (1976). Nokokan Shikin Ido Saiko (Jo), (The Role and Pattern of Flow of Funds between Agriculture and Non-agriculture in Japanese Economic Development (Part I)), *Keizai Kenkyu* 27, pp. 323–335.

Teranishi, J. (1977). Nokokan Shikin Ido Saiko (Ge), (The Role and Pattern of Flow of Funds between Agriculture and Non-agriculture in Japanese Economic Development (Part II)), *Keizai Kenkyu* 28, pp. 43–61.

Thaer, A. (1798). *Einleitung zur Kenntniß der Englischen Landwirthschaft und Ihrer Neueren Practischen und Theoretischen Fortschritte in Rücksicht auf Vervollkommnung Deutscher Landwirthschaft für Denkende Landwirthe und Cameralisten (Introduction to Knowledge of English Agriculture and its New Practical and Theoretical Progress in Consideration of Completed German Agriculture for Considerate Farmer and Financier),* (Bey den Gebrüdern Hahn, Hannover).

Thompson, W.S. (1929). Population, *American Journal of Sociology* 34, pp. 959–975.

Tobin, J. (1967). Life Cycle Savings and Balanced Growth, ed. Fellner, W., Chapter 32, *"Ten Economic Studies in the Tradition of Irving Fisher,"* (Wiley, New York), pp. 127–153.

Todaro, M.P. (1969). A Model of Labor Migration and Urban Unemployment in Less Developed Countries, *American Economic Review* 59, pp. 138–148.

Tolley, G.S. and Smidt, S. (1964). Agriculture and the Secular Position of the U.S. Economy, *Econometrica* 32, pp. 554–575.

Tsujimura, K. and Watanabe, T. (1966). Seisankansu to Gijutsu Shinpo: Tenbou (Production Function and Technical Progress: Perspective), *Economic Studies Quarterly* 16, pp. 12–26.

Ueno, Y. and Kinoshita, S. (1965). *Nihon Keizai no Seicho Moderu (Growth Model of Japanese Economy),* (Touyo-Keizai Shimposha, Tokyo).

Umemura, M. (1968). Yugyoshasu no Shin-Suikei: 1871–1920 Nen (New Estimate of Gainful Worker: 1871–1920), *Keizai Kenkyu* 19, (October 1968).

Umemura, M. (1969). Meijiki no Jinko Seicho (Population Growth in Meiji Period), eds. Syakai Keizai Gakkai (Social and Economic History Association), Chapter 3, in Number 2, Part 1 *"Keizaishi ni Okeru Jinko"* (*Population in Economic History*), (Keio Tsuushin, Tokyo), pp. 118–141.

United Nations Population Division (2005). *World Population Prospects: The 2004 Revision*, (United Nations, New York).

United Nation (various years). *Demographic Yearbook*, (United Nations, New York).

Uzawa, H. (1961). On a Two Sector Model of Economic Growth: I, *Review of Economic Studies* 29, pp. 40–47.

Uzawa, H. (1963). On a Two Sector Model of Economic Growth: II, *Review of Economic Studies* 30, pp. 105–118.

Wagner, A. (1893). *Grundlegung der Politischen Okonomie*, 3. Leipzig. (Aful).

Watanabe, T. (1965). Economic Aspects of Dualism in the Industrial Development of Japan, *Economic Development and Cultural Change* 13, pp. 293–312.

Watanabe, T. (1970). *Suuryo Keizai Bunseki* (*Analysis of Quantitative Economy*), (Soubunsha, Tokyo).

Watanabe, T. and Egaitsu, F. (1968). Roudoryoku no Shitsu to Keizai Seicho (Quality of Labor force and Economic Growth), *Economic Studies Quarterly* 19, pp. 38–52.

Weintraub, R. (1962). The Birth Rate and Economic Development, An Empirical Study, *Econometrica* 30, pp. 812–817.

Williamson, J. and Higgins, M. (2001). The Accumulation and Demography Connection in East Asia, ed. Mason, A., Chapter 5 *"Population Change and Economic Development in East Asia: Challenges Met, Opportunities Seized,"* (Stanford University Press, Stanford), pp. 123–154.

Willis, R.J. (1973). A New Approach to the Economic Theory of Fertility Behavior, *Journal of Political Economy* 81, pp. S14–S64.

Woodland, A.D. (1976). Modeling the Production Sector of an Economy: A Selective Survey and Analysis, *Discussion Paper, No. 76-21*. Department of Economics, University of British Columbia, Vancouver, B. C.

Yaari, M.E. (1965). Uncertain Lifetime, Life Insurance, and the Theory of the Consumer, *The Review of Economics Studies* 32, pp. 137–150.

Yamada, S. and Hayami, Y. (1972). Growth Rates of Japanese Agriculture, 1880–1965, Paper presented to *Conference on Agricultural Growth in Japan, Korea, Taiwan and the Philippines*.

Yamaguchi, M. (1969). *Keizai seicho to Shotoku Junkan* (*Economic Growth and Income Distribution*), M.S. Thesis, Kyoto University.

Yamaguchi, M. (1972). Technical Change and Population Growth in the Economic Development of Japan and the United States, *Economic Development Center Annual Report*, University of Minnesota.

Yamaguchi, M. (1973). *Technical Change and Population Growth in the Economic Development of Japan*, Ph.D. Dissertation, University of Minnesota, (University Microfilms, Ann Arbor, Michigan).

Yamaguchi, M. (1975). Book Review of Hayami, Y. Nihon-Nougyo no Seicho-Katei (Growth Process of Japanese Agriculture), *Economic Studies Quarterly* 26, pp. 75–76.

Yamaguchi, M. (1977). An Econometric Analysis of Japanese Population Growth, *Kobe University Economic Review* 23, pp. 57–72.

Yamaguchi, M. (1982a). *Nihon Keizai no Seicho Kaikei Bunseki (Growth Accounting for the Japanese Economy)*, (Yuhikaku, Tokyo).

Yamaguchi, M. (1982b). The Sources of Japanese Economic Development: 1880–1970, *Economic Studies Quarterly* 33, pp. 126–146.

Yamaguchi, M. (1985). Interrelationships between Population and Economic Growth, *Kobe University Economic Review* 31, pp. 15–32.

Yamaguchi, M. (1986). Some Critical Analysis of Japanese Economic Development, *Kobe University Economic Review* 32, pp. 41–68.

Yamaguchi, M. (1987). Kajyo-Syuugyo to Nihon no Keizai Hatten (Surplus Labor and Japanese Economic Development), *Kokumin Keizai Zasshi* 155, pp. 37–56.

Yamaguchi, M. (1997). Growth Accounting for the Thai Economy — Surplus Labor and Economic Development, *Kobe University Economic Review* 43, pp. 23–38.

Yamaguchi, M. (2001). *Jinko Seicho to Keizai Hatten: Shoshi Koureika to Jinko Bakuhatsu to no Kyouzon (Population Growth and Economic Development: Coexistence of Aging Population and Population Explosion)*, (Yuhikaku, Tokyo).

Yamaguchi, M. and Binswanger, H. (1975). The Role of Sectoral Technical Change in Development: Japan, 1880–1965, *American Journal of Agricultural Economics* 57, pp. 269–278.

Yamaguchi, M. and Kennedy, G. (1983). General Equilibrium Growth Accounting: The Case of Japanese Agriculture, 1880–1970, *Discussion paper no. 83-01*. Department of Agricultural Economics, University of British Columbia, Vancouver, B.C., July.

Yamaguchi, M. and Kennedy, G. (1984a). A Graphic Model of the Effects of Sectoral Technical Change: The Case of Japan, 1880–1970, *Canadian Journal of Agricultural Economics* 32, pp. 71–92.

Yamaguchi, M. and Kennedy, G. (1984b). Contribution of Population Growth to Per Capita Income and Sectoral Output Growth in Japan 1880–1970, *Developing Economies* 22, pp. 237–263.

Yamaguchi, M. and Tanaka, K. (2006). Change in Agricultural Surplus Labor and the Economic Development of Japan: Some Comparisons with the Cases of Thailand, China and Taiwan, *Kobe University Economic Review* 52, pp. 9–26.

Yasuba, Y. (1969). Jinko Kenkyu no Igi to Houho — Keizai Hattenron no Tachiba Kara (Significance and Method of Population Study — A View from the Theory of Economic Development), eds. Syakai Keizaishi Gakkai (Social and Economic History Association), Chapter 3 in Number 1, Part 1 *"Keizaishi ni Okeru Jinko" (Population in Economic History)*, (Keio Tsuushin, Tokyo), pp. 31–49.

Yasuba, Y. (1980). *Keizai Seichou-ron (Treatise of Economic Growth)*, (Chikuma Syobo, Tokyo).

World Bank (2003). *World Development Indicators 2003*, Washington, D. C.

Zarembka, P. (1972). *Toward a Theory of Economic Development*, (Holden-Day, San Francisco).

Zilcha, I. and Friedman, J. (1985). Saving Behavior in Retirement when Life Horizon in Uncertain, *Economic Letters* 17, pp. 63–66.

Author Index

Subject Index

Printed in the United States
By Bookmasters